Human and Divine Being

VERITAS
Series Introduction

"... the truth will set you free" (John 8:32)

In much contemporary discourse, Pilate's question has been taken to mark the absolute boundary of human thought. Beyond this boundary, it is often suggested, is an intellectual hinterland into which we must not venture. This terrain is an agnosticism of thought: because truth cannot be possessed, it must not be spoken. Thus, it is argued that the defenders of "truth" in our day are often traffickers in ideology, merchants of counterfeits, or anti-liberal. They are, because it is somewhat taken for granted that Nietzsche's word is final: truth is the domain of tyranny.

Is this indeed the case, or might another vision of truth offer itself? The ancient Greeks named the love of wisdom as *philia*, or friendship. The one who would become wise, they argued, would be a "friend of truth." For both philosophy and theology might be conceived as schools in the friendship of truth, as a kind of relation. For like friendship, truth is as much discovered as it is made. If truth is then so elusive, if its domain is *terra incognita*, perhaps this is because it arrives to us—unannounced—as gift, as a person, and not some thing.

The aim of the Veritas book series is to publish incisive and original current scholarly work that inhabits "the between" and "the beyond" of theology and philosophy. These volumes will all share a common aspiration to transcend the institutional divorce in which these two disciplines often find themselves, and to engage questions of pressing concern to both philosophers and theologians in such a way as to reinvigorate both disciplines with a kind of interdisciplinary desire, often so absent in contemporary academe. In a word, these volumes represent collective efforts in the befriending of truth, doing so beyond the simulacra of pretend tolerance, the violent, yet insipid reasoning of liberalism that asks with Pilate, "What is truth?"—expecting a consensus of non-commitment; one that encourages the commodification of the mind, now sedated by the civil service of career, ministered by the frightened patrons of position.

The series will therefore consist of two "wings": (1) original monographs; and (2) essay collections on a range of topics in theology and philosophy. The latter will principally be the products of the annual conferences of the Centre of Theology and Philosophy (www.theologyphilosophycentre.co.uk).

Conor Cunningham and Eric Austin Lee, *Series Editors*

Human and Divine Being

A Study on the Theological Anthropology of Edith Stein

DONALD WALLENFANG

FOREWORD BY
JOHN C. CAVADINI

CASCADE Books • Eugene, Oregon

HUMAN AND DIVINE BEING
A Study on the Theological Anthropology of Edith Stein

Veritas 23

Copyright © 2017 Donald Wallenfang. All rights reserved. Except for brief quotations in critical publications or reviews, no part of this book may be reproduced in any manner without prior written permission from the publisher. Write: Permissions, Wipf and Stock Publishers, 199 W. 8th Ave., Suite 3, Eugene, OR 97401.

Cascade Books
An Imprint of Wipf and Stock Publishers
199 W. 8th Ave., Suite 3
Eugene, OR 97401

www.wipfandstock.com

PAPERBACK ISBN: 978-1-4982-9336-5
HARDCOVER ISBN: 978-1-4982-9338-9
EBOOK ISBN: 978-1-4982-9337-2

Cataloguing-in-Publication data:

Names: Wallenfang, Donald. | Cavadini, John C., foreword.

Title: Human and divine being : a study on the theological anthropology of Edith Stein / Donald Wallenfang ; foreword by John C. Cavadini.

Description: Eugene, OR : Cascade Books, 2017 | Series: Veritas 23 | Includes bibliographical references and index.

Identifiers: ISBN 978-1-4982-9336-5 (paperback) | ISBN 978-1-4982-9338-9 (hardcover) | ISBN 978-1-4982-9337-2 (ebook)

Subjects: LCSH: Stein, Edith, Saint, 1891–1942. | Theological anthropology—Christianity. | Philosophical theology.

Classification: BT701.3 .W35 2017 (print) | BT701.3 .W35 (ebook)

Manufactured in the U.S.A.   04/10/17

To my father, John Michael Wallenfang (1947–2003),
and my mother, Linda Jo Wallenfang (1948–2013)

"At the father's death, he will seem not dead, for he leaves after him one like himself, whom he looked upon through life with joy, and in death, without regret."

Sirach 30:4–5 (NABRE)

"Indeed, we had accepted within ourselves the sentence of death, that we might trust not in ourselves but in God who raises the dead."

2 Corinthians 1:9 (NAB)

And to the Sundarams, especially Sathish Andrew,
witness to hope and determined determination

Ricorda questa sera, perché sarà l'inizio dell'eternità.
Dante Alighieri

The hand of the Lord came upon me, and he led me out in the spirit of the Lord and set me in the center of the broad valley. It was filled with bones. He made me walk among them in every direction. So many lay on the surface of the valley! How dry they were! He asked me: Son of man, can these bones come back to life? "Lord God," I answered, "you alone know that." Then he said to me: Prophesy over these bones, and say to them: Dry bones, hear the word of the Lord! Thus says the Lord God to these bones: Listen! I will make breath enter you so you may come to life. I will put sinews on you, make flesh grow over you, cover you with skin, and put breath into you so you may come to life. Then you shall know that I am the Lord. I prophesied as I had been commanded.

—Ezekiel 37:1–7 (NABRE)

Contents

Foreword by John C. Cavadini | xi

Acknowledgments | xvii

Introduction | xxi

Chapter 1: On Human Vocation | 1
    I. The Revelatory Dialectic of Potency–Act   3
    II. Creaturely Existence as Intersubjective Becoming   9
    III. Universal Human Vocation: Awakening to Eternal Being   14

Chapter 2: Spiritual Being | 21
    I. Contemporary Polemics in Pneumatology   22
    II. *Kreuzeswissenschaft*: The Science of the Cross   26
    III. The Pneumatological Matrix of Edith Stein   34
    IV. Conclusion   50

Chapter 3: The Soul as the Form of the Body | 54
    I. The Possibility of the Human Soul   54
    II. Aristotle's Four Kinds of Causality   57
        a. Material Causality   58
        b. Efficient Causality   59
        c. Formal Causality   63

viii   Contents

           d. Final Causality   71

           e. Summary of the Four Kinds of Causality   74

    III. Actuality, Potentiality, and *Logos*   77

    IV. Toward an Ontology of Spirit   82

     V. The Rational Soul and Its Redemption   86

    VI. Conclusion   92

Chapter 4: The Soul as Inner Life and as Substantial Image of God the Father | 94

      I. Conscious Spiritual Being   95

     II. Getting at the Heart of the Matter   99

    III. The Substance of Spiritual Being   102

    IV. The Analogy of Material Being   107

     V. The Analogy of Divine Being   110

    VI. Conclusion   115

Chapter 5: The Soul as Spiritual Vessel | 117

      I. *Entrée* into Divine Love   118

     II. The Meaning of Self-Surrender   123

    III. Afterlife of the Soul and Union with God   131

           a. Death   132

           b. The Hypostatic Union of Christ   136

           c. The Hypostatic Union of the Soul with God   142

    IV. Conclusion   146

Chapter 6: The Antinomy of Material Being | 149

      I. Clarification of Terms   152

     II. Ontology of Matter   158

    III. The Human Body and the Possibility of Its Regeneration   163

Chapter 7: Empathy and the Other | 174

    I. The Paradox of Alterity: An Ode to Otherness   175

    II. The Essence of Empathy   180

        1. "Acts in which foreign experience is comprehended"   183

        2. "An act which is primordial as present experience though non-primordial in content"   183

        3. "An experience of our own announcing another one"   184

        4. "The basis of intersubjective experience [that] becomes the condition of possible knowledge of the existing outer world"   187

    III. The Individual Soul and the Other   189

        a. The Soul in Relation to the Other (*l'Autre*) in General   190

        b. The Soul in Relation to the Personal Other (*l'Autrui*)   191

        c. The Soul in Relation to the Voice of the Other within the Self: Conscience   193

    IV. Conclusion   194

Chapter 8: The Logic of the Cross | 196

    I. Edith and the Cross   198

    II. The Dark Night of Solitude   202

    III. The Cruciform Pattern of the Cross   207

        a. Alterity   210

        b. Humility   212

        c. Love   215

    IV. Conclusion   218

Epilogue: An Addendum to Suffering | 220

Bibliography | 225

Index | 237

Foreword

I AM PLEASED AND HONORED to be asked to write a foreword for this magnificent book by a young scholar. Donald Wallenfang warns us at the outset that "Stein's masterpieces in philosophical theology are rigorous and dense," and that "it is a great feat just to read through one of them in its entirety," and I would add, in English, let alone in German, because some of Stein's most important works have not yet been translated into English. A true introduction to the thought of Edith Stein could not do it honor unless it was to some degree in its own right "rigorous and dense." Indeed, Wallenfang has "sifted carefully" through Stein's works, all of them, to produce a synthesis that, let the reader be forewarned then, is surely properly described as "rigorous and dense"! But the careful reader will find herself amply repaid for her efforts in sustained attention. And the book is designed, at any rate, to be read in manageable chunks of short chapters in order to encourage the reader and to assist her in mastering its contents. For all of its difficulty, it also manages to mirror faithfully one of the other salient features of Edith Stein's work no matter how abstruse—the way in which it is nevertheless suffused with a warmth that glows from every page.

The rigor of this book, and of Edith Stein's philosophical/theological anthropology, which is the subject of this book, gives it the feeling of alterity, of "otherness," to adopt one of Stein's favorite expressions from her earliest work on empathy. In turn, its alterity is itself a function—at least, I believe I have learned this from the book—of the banality with which most of us, steeped in a reductionist culture, greet the central question of *Human and Divine Being*, "What does it mean to be human?" with a complacency of the obvious. Whatever it does mean, we know from the outset of cultural presupposition that it is culturally constructed without remainder, because, whatever it means, there is, before and behind and under these cultural constructions, nothing but matter and energy and natural law. For even those of us who are believers have a hard time, for example, imagining spirit as actually *something*. And, as Stein in Wallenfang's re-voicing shows, we *therefore* have a hard time imagining even matter as *something*. For being *something* implies form, and if there is truly form, and not the *simulacrum* of form that a purely natural-law description of reality provides, then there is *something* higher than matter that allows matter to also be *something* instead of a random association of entities that have no name but what we arbitrarily attach to it and which therefore can generate nothing with a name except that which we arbitrarily attach to it ("construct").

The seemingly irreducible alterity of this book, and of Edith Stein's peculiar combination, or mitigation, of phenomenology with metaphysics, as Wallenfang displays it to us, makes it something like a great work of fantasy. If you read J. R. R. Tolkien's *The Lord of the Rings* (which I hasten to add is not mentioned in Wallenfang's book), for example, you find yourself in a fictional world with its own unique geography and logic, its own languages and peoples, mythic creatures, and history. Because it is a work of fantasy, and because that is agreed upon between reader and author from the beginning, the reader accepts its alterity as something postulated if not believed. But in accepting these terms, literally in accepting the new language(s) and logic of the fictional world, one finds, after one has thoroughly lived in the new world, that one has actually accepted an enhanced way of speaking and thinking about one's own world, which in turn becomes re-enchanted, the locus of a kind of fantasy-come-true.

In the case of Edith Stein, and of Wallenfang's book as a distillation of her thought, it is as though we have a work of fantasy to approach. It is cast as "fantasy" by those of us, all of us, who, even if believers, almost unconsciously accept a reductionist worldview, we who live in the Twilight of the Idols where we know that the philosophers are the greatest web-spinners of all, who have by abstraction "arrive[d] at their stupendous concept, 'God.'" And thus "that which is last, thinnest, and emptiest," the "last smoke of evaporating reality," is placed "first, as *the* cause, as *ens realissimum*,"[1] that which is absolutely most real. To enter the world where spirit is real, where spirit is *something*, and *therefore* where matter is real, is *something*, is to enter a world that has been constructed as fantasy for us by Nietzsche and all the prophets of suspicion who have, as his heirs, deconstructed metaphysical language describing it as a fictional language—who have, like Nietzsche,

---

1. *Twilight of the Idols*, as translated by Walter Kaufmann.

asked with incredulity, "Why did mankind have to take seriously the brain afflictions of sick web-spinners?" But Donald Wallenfang beguiles us, by his carefully disciplined step-by-step process, into accepting terms of agreement analogous to those between the fantasy author and her reader, and we are led, little by little, into learning (what seems) a fantasy language, feeling our way to using it, and discovering, in so doing, that we have actually taken it into our own world and that our own world is re-enchanted as a fantasy-too-good-to-be-true-come-true. We learn that we had lost a knack for precise language in describing various grades of reality because we did not believe these distinctions were true. Wallenfang helps us recover this language for ourselves and makes us realize how impoverished we are without it.

We learn that "spiritual being is not just a negative verbal placeholder for the so-called opposite of material being"—something vague and fictional—but that "the term signifies the fullness, plentitude, and perfection of being as that which gives itself to the point of fecund abandonment" (159). We are given language to have confidence that this is so. We learn here that self-giving does not exist in the penumbra of a placeholder in the universe, a placeholder for that which is really real, matter, but that self-giving *is* what is really real. But, surprisingly, we learn that this in turn means that "the term 'matter'" is not used by Stein "as a meaningless conceptual placeholder" either, but instead, that what physicists call matter, that is, atomic matter, is always already "formed matter." "The hydrogen atom, for example, is an instance of formed matter." We discover that there would *be* no matter, as we commonly understand the term, if "form" had not preceded it and brought it into being, as *something*. In a brilliant *tour de force* of reversal, Wallenfang enables us to see how Stein gives us the language for seeing how the theory of evolution, far from displaying evidence of random change, shows us the impossibility of reductionism, if you have the language to analyze and describe it properly: "The theory of evolution presupposes a formal impetus toward life, organization and order. Whether that uncreated impetus is called 'nature' or 'god(s)' is a matter of semantics." "However," he continues, "philosophically and theologically speaking, if one wishes to use 'nature' as a substitute for 'god(s)' within a postmodern metanarrative of material reductionism, let's at least come clean about the matter. Nature as such did not 'give birth' to itself. Even its own etymology suggests otherwise, for *nascor* means 'to be born' and that which is born is born of something other than itself." By this route we arrive back at "pure spiritual being, itself immutable and the logical condition for the possibility of material being and its diversification" (168).

At this point, the theologian may be wondering if in this fantasy world that we are learning to recognize as our own world, the philosophical vocabulary has rendered the theological otiose and has voided revelation of its unique contribution. Such a worry is unfounded, we learn, because as Stein elaborates the case, the origin of matter in an act of creation is something that philosophy is incapable of grasping: "For Stein, natural reason is not able to comprehend the very act of creation" (159). This is because the act of creation is an act of free self-giving that reveals what is "really real" in the first place. In fact, it is an act of grace that is only revealed in its fullest dimensions in the sacrifice of Christ on the cross, a pure gift, a gift so purely gift that it could never be anticipated, deserved, merited, or controlled: "Christ's vicarious offering of himself unto death on a cross of wood expresses divine grace to a degree that even surpasses the divine act of creation from nothing" (197). Wallenfang masterfully entices us, step by step, into the fantasy world, or so it will seem to the "wise" of 1 Corinthians 1:18–19, which is all of us, of the cross, and to be more precise, the world rendered intelligible by the "science of the cross." "By taking . . . careful and convicting steps, we have brought the paradigm of the cross into the light of comprehension, if only by attempting to peer momentarily into its dark luminosity and to heed its saturating meaning and power." (218) We must, in passing, note the beauty of expression here!

Having beguiled us this far, Wallenfang may be allowed to continue: "It must be said that one cannot help trembling in approaching the topic of the cross. Yet it is the cross that reveals both what it is to be fully human and what it is to be less than human" (218). Wallenfang brilliantly shows how Edith Stein's "science of the cross" is the key to her whole enterprise, and, not as a *principle* of self-giving, or a *concept* of the fullness of meaning, but as an act, a concrete deed, not that which is the "last, the thinnest, and the emptiest" because the highest conceptual abstraction, but this *one concrete act* that "reached its climax in the hour of Jesus's passion when he handed himself over, 'becoming obedient to death, even death on a cross' (Phil 2:8)." In another beautiful sentence, Wallenfang notes, "In other words, God has nothing left to give to his Bride, the Church. All has been given her without remainder. This is the definitive meaning of the cross" (210). Far from an abstraction, the cross remains open as an irreducible invitation to faith. If faith is granted, then understanding can come. It can come with all of the philosophical language intended to guarantee that this act of divine self-giving can be glorified, can be seen as that which really reveals the most really real, that which enables us to understand even matter as real, as God-touched, because it, too, is ultimately a function of unmerited gift; it is itself a dim reflection of the primal self-giving life of God and a reminder, in its own small way, that the suffering which life calls us to is the way in which we make room for the other in our lives, even as God "made room" for matter and everything that is "formed" through it or in relation to it in His. And so we may confidently take our place in the universe of empathetic, loving communion that God intended all along.

The book ends with an original poem about the death of a Carmelite nun and the suffering it entailed. We know from the book, recapitulated in this poem, that this suffering was not meaningless. We know from the poem that the book it recapitulates was all along more poetry than prose. We were enticed all along into reading an extended prose poem as the intelligible structure of a momentary peering, a saturating meaning and power, that will always surpass, and thereby guarantee, intelligibility everywhere and always to those who will be enticed, and believe.

It is with profound appreciation that I pass this book on, offering it to the attention of the careful reader, who will, I guarantee, find herself in capable, empathetic hands.

John C. Cavadini
Director of the McGrath Institute for Church Life
Professor of Theology
The University of Notre Dame
December 23, 2016

Acknowledgments

DIFFICULT AS IT IS to acknowledge certain people who have had a direct influence on the making of this book, with the risk of failing to mention some, I nevertheless would like to thank those who come to mind most immediately. First, I reference the acknowledgments section of my book *Dialectical Anatomy of the Eucharist: An Étude in Phenomenology* (2017), as it is fitting to recognize all of those mentioned there once again. More to the point of the present book, however, I will focus my gratitude on those circles of scholars related in a particular way to the contents herein.

To my fellow Stein scholars in the Edith Stein Circle, thank you for your encouragement and solidarity in approaching Stein's work with zeal, rigor, and innovation. May we continue to substantiate the cause for Edith Stein to be named a "Doctor of the Church." The following colleagues deserve special mention, especially as related to the 2013 Edith Stein Circle conference at King's University College in London, Ontario, and to the 2015 International Stein Conference at the University of Vienna and the Pontifical Institute of Benedict XVI, Heiligenkreuz: Mette Lebech, Hanna-Barbara Gerl-Falkovitz, Francesco Alfieri, Christof Betschart, Roberto Maria Perastu, Rathan Almeida, Michele Kueter Petersen, Robert McNamara, René Raschke, Rosalia Caruso, Claudia Mariéle Wulf, Haddy Bello, Bernardo Álvarez Gutiérrez, Feliciana Merino Escalera, Haydn Gurmin, Antonio Calcagno, John Sullivan, Jacob Torbeck, Walter Redmond, Anna Maria Pezzella, Angela Ales Bello, Marian Maskulak, Pamela Fitzpatrick, Thomas Gricoski, Michael Andrews, Leonard and Joyce Avrech Berkman, Ken Casey, Eduardo González Di Pierro, Joachim Feldes, Kathleen Haney, Harm Klueting,

Jennie Latta, Judith Parsons, Juan Francisco Pinilla Aguilera, Marianne Sawicki, Sarah Borden Sharkey, Gloria Zúñiga y Postigo, Laura Beer, Paulina Monjaraz Fuentes, Patricia Morrison, and Suzanne Batzdorff. Again, I thank all of my colleagues from St. Norbert College, Loyola University Chicago, and Walsh University. Your friendship and inspiration are life-giving.

To my new publishing family at Wipf and Stock, especially Charlie Collier, Conor Cunningham, Eric Austin Lee, and Matt Wimer, thank you for welcoming my book for publication with Cascade Books in the Veritas series, and for all of your expertise lent throughout the editing process. Thank you, also, for letting me be myself as an author and for affording a venue through which to pursue the truth without ideological obstruction. To Jacob Martin, Calvin Jaffarian, and Chris Graham, thank you for your expertise, insight, and assiduity throughout the editing and design process. To the five anonymous readers of this book, thank you for your frankness, your attention to detail, and your honest feedback, which has worked to sharpen the manuscript to its present form. All remaining deficiencies and shortcomings are, of course, my own. Thank you to the Secular Discalced Carmelites of the Akron/Cleveland Community of the Holy Family. May this book be an ongoing conversation partner for our spiritual itinerary toward the summit of Mount Carmel: *Zelo zelatus sum pro Domino Deo exercituum.*

Thank you to the following publishers for granting permission to reprint portions of the following texts:

> Some material from chapter 1 appeared previously as "Awaken, O Spirit: The Vocation of Becoming in the Work of Edith Stein," *Logos: A Journal of Catholic Thought and Culture* 15 (2012) 57–74.

> Some material from chapter 2 appeared previously as "*Geisteswissenschaft*: Edith Stein's Phenomenological Sketch of the Essence of Spirit," in *Intersubjectivity, Humanity, Being: Edith Stein's Phenomenology and Christian Philosophy*, edited by Mette Lebech and John Haydn Gurmin (Oxford: P. Lang, 2015) 499–524.

> Some material from chapter 4 appeared previously as "The Heart of the Matter: Edith Stein on the Substance of the Soul," *Logos: A Journal of Catholic Thought and Culture* 17 (2014) 118–42.

> Some material from chapters 3–5 appeared previously as "Soul Power: Edith Stein's Meta-Phenomenological Construction of the Human Soul," in *Edith Stein: Women, Social-Political Philosophy, Metaphysics and Public History; New Approaches and*

Applications, edited by Antonio Calcagno (Cham: Springer, 2015) 167–80.

Finally, to my wife, Megan Joanna, and our awesome children, Ellen Agnes, Aubin Augustine, Tobias Xavier, Callum Ignatius, Simeon Irenaeus, and Oliver Isidore, you inspire me with every breath, thought and heartbeat. You have taught me the art of love and the meaning of being human in relation to eternal being. I love you!

Introduction

WHAT IS IT TO be human? How are human beings different from other types of being in the universe? What are the integral parts that make up the human being? How can we approach the makeup of human being in a responsible and interdisciplinary way? Such questions are vitally important for all times, and today is no exception. How we answer these questions determines how we treat each other and how we live our lives. This book is a careful study on the theological anthropology of twentieth-century saint Edith Stein (1891–1942), as relevant for today's context of twenty-first-century postmodern skepticism and disenchantment.[1] Theological anthropology refers to a branch of study that concentrates on understanding what it is to be human in relation to God. To omit the adjective "theological" would reduce the assessment of the human being from the start and would curtail the scientific possibilities of being in general. Theological anthropology at the very least puts forth the question of God while asking the question of the human. This approach is intellectually responsible and open to possibility because the question of God is the question of the infinite, that is, the question of infinite mystery. Without the question of God, we risk interpreting the human being as unrelated to infinite mystery. This is a very dangerous interpretation indeed. In her February 20, 1917, letter to Roman Ingarden, at the tender age of twenty-five, five years prior to her conversion to the Catholic faith, Stein writes: "I find that many people will

---

1. Though Stein eventually would take the religious name, Teresa Benedicta of the Cross, upon entering the Carmelite monastery in Cologne in 1933, she will be referred to as Edith Stein for the sake of consistency throughout this book.

cut corners (to totally avoid the religious experience) though it is impossible to conclude a teaching on person without going into the God question, and it is impossible to understand history . . . It is *the* question that interests me."[2] Emerging from her atheistic slumber, Stein refused to close herself off to the fullness of human experience and reflection. She confessed that personhood is bound to the question of God: the enigma of human personhood is rooted in the mystery of the personal God. History's meaningfulness prevails as long as it is interpreted according to its golden thread, the unifying *logos*, in which remembrance and parousia are joined as one. Future hope depends on the past redeemed. Today, more than ever, we must conduct a renewed project in theological anthropology in order to ascertain the truth and meaning of what it is to be human. This task takes place at the intersection of philosophy and theology, for it is these disciplines that are able to marshal the most fundamental levels of questioning in a holistic way. If a young person's education, for instance, is deprived of the disciplines of philosophy and theology, s/he will develop a distorted understanding of human personhood and will attempt to find meaning in life with the most fertile sources of meaning vacant to the mind. Therefore it is necessary to continue to recapitulate the sources of theological anthropology by using the most up-to-date methods and structures of thought.[3]

This book seeks to present a holistic theological anthropology for today by elucidating the work of Edith Stein. She thought through the layers of what it is to be human in an exhaustive way, and her written works are an ample testament to the intellectual heights to which she soared. Her two great works, *Potency and Act* (completed in 1931 but first published in German in 1998) and *Finite and Eternal Being* (completed in 1937 but first published in German in 1950), especially probe the wonder and mystery of human being in relation to divine being. Stein combines two methods in particular within her work: phenomenology and metaphysics.[4] These two

---

2. Stein, *Letters to Roman Ingarden*, 49–50 (letter of February 20, 1917).

3. Even a project in philosophical anthropology, in the end, misses the mark without the inclusion of theology. See Beckmann-Zöller, "Edith Stein's Theory of the Person," 61: "Philosophical anthropology is incomplete because it can only claim ontologically and theologically that the finite refers to the infinite." This is to say that, without recourse to the idea of God—the Infinite—and divine revelation as a source for insight and knowledge, our various anthropologies remain only in effigy.

4. In Stein's day, as Husserl's new method of phenomenology was gaining a following rather rapidly, debates arose (in which Stein was embroiled at the time) around the question of whether phenomenology tended toward realism or idealism. Since such categories can be limiting by their reductionist and polemic character, suffice it to say that Stein's brand of phenomenology moved toward the realist side of the debate. See, for example, Beckmann-Zöller, "Edith Stein's Theory of the Person," 55: "In order to

methods remain the most essential for a study in theological anthropology. They open the vistas of truth-seeking in response to the question, what is it to be human? In radical dialectical tension, phenomenology and metaphysics work together to throw further light on the meaning of being, on the givenness of experience, and on the vocation to authentic ethical action.

Phenomenology intends to be a purely descriptive method of investigation. The main question it asks is, what gives? Yes, it's as simple as that. It concentrates on the phenomenon that gives itself to human consciousness. Without determining the parameters of the phenomenon's giving ahead of time, phenomenological perception awaits the arrival of whatever gives itself by bracketing out any presuppositions or inclinations that would set limits on what may give itself and how it may give itself. It intentionally brackets and sets aside the so-called "natural attitude" that "is indeed simultaneous with the practical person."[5] A solely pragmatic approach to life rules out mystery as a hindrance to practical goals (unless, of course, mystery sells). For phenomenology, however, it is the natural attitude that must be leveraged in order to behold the intrinsic mystery of life and the unexpected givenness of all that gives. Angela Ales Bello writes that "a phenomenological analysis can never be considered complete once and for all. We are pushed to start anew over and over again [*immer wieder*] in the attempt to find a definitive structure, even though the quest produces imperfect results. This entails approaches that come close to the phenomenon of the interiority of the human being, make evident valid aspects and structures—but never exhaust consciousness itself."[6] The nature of phenomenology is always open-ended and embarks on an infinite hermeneutic of that which gives itself to conscious perception.[7] Phenomenology is never

---

gain knowledge about the individuality of the human being—even about the difference between the sexes—Stein uses the realist phenomenological method." Also, see Gerl-Falkovitz's introduction to Stein, *Letters to Roman Ingarden*, especially 13.

5. Stein, *Letters to Roman Ingarden*, 111 (letter of June 24, 1918).

6. Ales Bello, "Edmund Husserl and Edith Stein," 148.

7. For the notion of an infinite hermeneutic, especially that associated with "saturated phenomena," see Marion, *Being Given*, 211, 229: "Generalizing, I will say that it is fitting to admit phenomena of $n + 1$ horizons, as it was necessary to admit spaces of $n + 1$ dimensions—whose properties saturate the imagination. Here bedazzlement paves the way for an infinite hermeneutic . . . The plurality of horizons practically forbids constituting the historical event into *one* object and demands substituting an endless hermeneutic in time; the narration is doubled by a narration of the narrations. More: in this hermeneutic labor, the proliferation of horizons implies also the proliferation of the sciences used, as well as of the literary genres"; and Marion, *In Excess*, 126–27: "The face of the other person requires in this way an infinite hermeneutic, equivalent to the 'progress toward the infinite' of morality in Kant . . . The face of the other person compels me to believe in my own eternity, like a need of reason or, what comes back to

done describing. Phenomenology generates layers of interpretation encircling each and every experienced phenomenon. Neither phenomena nor consciousness ever is exhausted in phenomenology's description of their interplay. Phenomenology, much further than psychology, is that discipline that is able to conduct a scientific investigation of the inner life of the person as it accesses and analyzes the abundance of meanings that go before and behind every experience.

Into the twenty-first century, Jean-Luc Marion (1946–), in his phenomenology of givenness, has extended—in the most precise way—the scope of phenomenology from the trajectory set by Edmund Husserl (1859–1938) (with whom Stein studied) and Martin Heidegger (1889–1976). Emmanuel Levinas (1906–95), who greatly influenced the work of Marion, is a key phenomenologist to understand also. He makes a compelling case to set ethics as first philosophy rather than privileging ontology or even givenness. Both Marion and Levinas are helpful figures to comprehend while studying the work of Stein in order to sort out retrospectively her use of the term *givenness* and her penchant for otherness, empathy and ethics. However, more directly influential for Stein were her teacher, Edmund Husserl, the father of phenomenology, and Thomas Aquinas (1225–74), the angelic metaphysician. Husserl and Aquinas leave the most significant impression on Stein and her original dialectical method of blending phenomenology and metaphysics.[8]

Metaphysics, for its part, examines that which is inherently necessary for all that is. It delves into the question of being by ordering the first principles for thought and the causal matrix of existence. For example, the first principle of theoretical reason is the principle of non-contradiction. Without this a priori gauge for reasoning, one thing could not be distinguished from another. Another first principle deals with causality: every effect has a prior cause. Without the coherence of causality there would be no science worthy of the name. In addition to establishing first principles for knowledge, metaphysics offers an arsenal of vocabulary to decipher accurately the meaning of being.[9] Some examples of these terms are being, substance,

---

the same thing, as the condition of its infinite hermeneutic."

8. For a helpful work on understanding the similarities and differences between Husserl and Aquinas, see Stein's creative imaginary dialogue between them, "Husserl and Aquinas: A Comparison," in Stein, *Knowledge and Faith*, 1–63.

9. Regarding the pointed difference between phenomenology and metaphysics as methods, see Stein's remark to Roman Ingarden in her letter of August 1, 1923 <1922>, in Stein, *Letters to Roman Ingarden*, 201: "I am in reasonable agreement with you regarding what you write about the shortcomings of the phenomenological method. I notice something similar when I am occasionally with people who have training in Scholasticism. It has the precise, thoroughly formed set of concepts that we

accidents, essence/nature, genus, species, cause, matter, form, potency and act. The last two terms, potency and act, play a key role in the work of Stein. They serve as the foundational hermeneutic for inquiring into the meaning of being and into the truth and meaning of what it is to be human. Such terms will be unpacked substantially throughout the course of this book.

It should be stated at the outset that Stein's masterpieces in philosophical theology are rigorous and dense. It is a great feat just to read through one of them in its entirety. That is why I found it necessary to attempt to sift carefully through the works of Stein and put forth a summative analysis of her anatomical conception of the human being—body, soul, and spirit. Much rumination on her texts, as well as on the secondary literature surrounding her texts, was required in order to synthesize the primary elements of her lifelong project in theological anthropology. In a 1928 letter to her Benedictine friend, Callista Kopf, Stein writes, "That it is possible to worship God by doing scholarly research is something I learned, actually, only when I was busy with [the translation of] St. Thomas [Aquinas's *Quaestiones de Veritate* from Latin into German]."[10] And this, too, I have experienced in doing scholarly research on the work of Edith Stein. It often happens that scholarship becomes a form of prayer and worship of God. It is impossible to study a scholar's work without simultaneously becoming acquainted with the person behind the work. As many Stein scholars note, it is impossible to study Stein's philosophical and theological works without becoming acquainted with the soul of the woman behind the words.[11] With

---

[phenomenologists] are missing. What we are missing, of course, is immediate contact with things, the breath of life for us, because our conceptual apparatus so easily closes us off to the acceptance of something new."

10. Stein, *Self-Portrait in Letters*, 54.

11. See Ales Bello, *Edith Stein*, 5: "Every time I go to write about Edith Stein I feel torn between two opposing needs: to disseminate her thoughts and to have restraint to do so as not to violate the secret of her soul. In fact, in telling the 'story' of this character it is not possible to separate the intellectual contribution from the existential and spiritual vicissitudes which accompany it" ("Ogni volta che mi accingo a scrivere su Edith Stein mi sento combattuta fra due opposte esigenze, quella di divulgare il suo pensiero e quella di avere ritegno a farlo per non violare il 'segreto' della sua anima. Infatti nel 'raccontare' questo personaggio non è possibile separare il contributo intellettuale dalla vicenda esistenziale e spirituale che l'accompagna"; translation my own); Baseheart, *Person in the World*, x, 30: speaking of the title of her own book, Baseheart writes, "The title, *Person in the World*, refers to Stein's person and to her philosophy. Neither can be considered in isolation ... [Stein's] reading and philosophizing proceed beyond the natural attitude and the 'givenness' of primordial experience to phenomenological analyses of person and community. Her investigations are scientific and holistic, embracing a study of human being in all its interconnections. They are directed toward revealing the person's essential qualities of head and heart and the activities of thinking, feeling, and loving in the context of the universal and of the individual. In so doing, her

Potency and Act published as recently as 2009 in English, for instance, the time has come to apply the depth of Stein's work urgently to twenty-first-century problems. Lately there has been a burgeoning of scholarship on the work of Stein, including several international societies devoted to studying her work, such as The International Association for the Study of the Philosophy of Edith Stein, founded in 2009. Through such organizations and the efforts to translate Stein's work, her intellectual insights are becoming more and more accessible for scholars on an international scope. The aim of this project is to advance not only the intellectual genius of Stein, but to advance the cause of the dignity of the human person throughout the world for years to come.[12]

Among Stein's notable works on theological anthropology, two books have yet to appear in English translation: *Der Aufbau der menschlichen Person: Vorlesungen zur philosophischen Anthropologie* (The structure of the human person: Lectures on philosophical anthropology) and *Was ist der Mensch? Theologische Anthropologie* (What is the human? Theological anthropology). Written in 1932–33 during the time she worked as a lecturer at the German Institute for Scientific Pedagogy in Münster, these two works focus their lens on understanding the essence of the human person for the sake of authentic human education. The former text is, as its title indicates, an exclusively philosophical analysis of the human person, especially through the grammar of metaphysics.[13] This work represents a

---

own experience of persons and personhood and her own personality emerge in a way that gives access to abstract conclusions in a context of concrete human experience—an important aim of phenomenology"; MacIntyre, *Edith Stein*, 1: "What is important about philosophy is the way in which a life informed by the activities of philosophical enquiry and guided by its conclusions will be significantly different from the life of someone in other respects like the philosopher, but untouched by philosophy"; and in Stein's own words: "At the moment, I face the decision of converting to Catholicism. I have not written to you about what led me to this. Actually, it is very difficult to say and I certainly cannot write about it. In any case, in recent years, I have lived very much more than I have philosophized. My works are all expressions of what has occupied me in life because the way I am now, I just have to reflect over it all" (*Letters to Roman Ingarden*, 192, letter of October 15, 1921).

12. As will be demonstrated through the course of this book, human dignity rests ultimately upon the fact that human beings are created in the *imago Dei*. Tracing this foundational doctrine through the whole of Stein's work will reinforce the etiology of value that itself is based on the fundamental value of human dignity emerging from a holistic theological anthropology. See Lebech, *On the Problem of Human Dignity*, 164: "That human dignity is a *fundamental* value founded on the real human being, hence means that the human being is valued not because of something else (e.g. some higher value), but because of itself, and in turn is the reason why many other things are valued."

13. See Betschart, *Unwiederholbares Gottessiegel*, 200–201: "The Christian concept of the human in *Aufbau der menschlichen Person* is placed within a

project in philosophical anthropology primarily, and so is not informed by Church doctrines as is Stein's culminating work, *Finite and Eternal Being*. Only eight pages that make up the final chapter, entitled "Pipeline from the Philosophical to the Theological Contemplation of the Human," enter into explicit discussion with theology, minus the few pages that speak of eternal spiritual being as divine.

The latter text, *Was ist der Mensch?*, turns its attention to Catholic doctrine on the human person in order to illuminate more extensively the meaning of being human. It is an unfinished work and contains no less than 792 references, almost all taken from magisterial doctrinal formulations spanning the history of the Catholic Church. The text is comprised of Stein's careful elucidation of ecclesial doctrine as it has accumulated and developed over the centuries. Much of the text consists of direct citations of papal and conciliar documents, as well as material from Plato, Augustine, Thomas, Bonaventure, and Duns Scotus. The work is Stein's fervent attempt to piece together the meaning, nature and vocation of the human person as revealed through the incarnate Person of Christ and the truth about his identity as disclosed through Church teaching.[14] In the foreword to *Was ist der Mensch?*, Stein writes that "this book aims to highlight *the image of the human*, as contained in our [Catholic] *doctrine of faith*. According to the scientific parlance of our day, one would tend to name it a *dogmatic anthropology*. The task has imposed itself upon me in my efforts to arrive at the foundation of *education*. That each educational science and educational work is guided by an *idea of the human* and decisively determined by it, no one will deny."[15] Stein found it essential to discover the nature of

---

phenomenological-metaphysical perspective and goes as far as possible with natural cognitive abilities so that the mysteries of faith are considered only at the edge within the investigation" ("Das christliche Menschenbild im *Aufbau der menschlichen Person* wird in einer phänomenologisch-metaphysischen Perspektive und soweit als möglich mit natürlichen Erkenntnismitteln erarbeitet, so dass die Glaubensgeheimnisse nur am Rand in die Untersuchung eingehen"; translation my own).

14. See ibid., 222: in *Was ist der Mensch?*, Stein "presents the various statements of faith in this manner: The human is a creature of God, a unity of body and soul, in which the spiritual soul is the form of the human body (WIM 6)" ("präsentiert die verschiedenen Glaubensaussagen in dieser Hinsicht: Der Mensch ist ein Geschöpf Gottes, eine Einheit aus Leib und Seele, wobei die geistige Seele die Form des menschlichen Körpers sei (WIM 6)"; translation my own).

15. Stein, *Was ist der Mensch?*, 3 ("Dieses Buch hat zum Ziel, das *Bild des Menschen* herauszustellen, das in unserer *Glaubenslehre* enthalten ist. Nach dem wissenschaftlichen Sprachgebrauch unserer Tage würde man das, was beabsichtigt ist, eine *dogmatische Anthropologie* nennen. Die Aufgabe hat sich mir bei meinen Bemühungen um eine Grundlegung der *Pädagogik* aufgedrängt Daß jede Erziehungswissenschaft und Erziehungsarbeit von einer *Idee des Menschen* geleitet und entscheidend bestimmt ist, wird niemand leugnen"; translation my own).

human personhood in order to form a solid pedagogical foundation. As one understands the nature of the human person, so one teaches accordingly. In other words, theological anthropology is the most fundamental task for education, even though it is a preliminary one. Within Stein's view, the question of divine revelation and what it has to say to us is integral to understanding ourselves as human beings.[16] Any anthropology that lacks inquiry into divinity and into potential sources of divine revelation will fall short of interpreting human being accurately and adequately.

Der Aufbau der menschlichen Person and *Was ist der Mensch?* deal explicitly with theological anthropology; however, in comparison with Stein's capstone work, *Finite and Eternal Being*, they are only preludes. This is why *Human and Divine Being* references the former works in passing but will concentrate its analysis on *Finite and Eternal Being* (completed in 1937), as well as *Potency and Act* (completed in 1931), as the two most mature and comprehensive works of Stein. Some Stein scholars within the international community focus their research on Stein's early work, including *On the Problem of Empathy* (written in 1916), *Philosophy of Psychology and the Humanities* (written in 1918–19), and *An Investigation Concerning the State* (written in 1921). These scholars tend to specialize in philosophy (rather than theology) and narrow their phenomenological research strictly to Husserl and the Göttingen Circle, and maybe go as far as early Heidegger. This is early phenomenology and, indeed, an important epoch in the history of philosophy. However, the work of Stein cannot be categorized only as early phenomenology or only as philosophy. In her mature work, Stein can

---

16. See Stein, *Letters to Roman Ingarden*, 196–97, 240, 269 (letters of December 13, 1921; November 28, 1926; and February 10, 1928, respectively): "What goes beyond the strict phenomenological sense is not so easy to accommodate. It is not just a design. We could call it *speculation* if we set aside bad memories and think of the original meaning of the word. I believe that this is *the* entrance to metaphysical questions, and certainly each philosopher in his heart is, fundamentally, a metaphysician, either explicitly or implicitly. For the one, the metaphysics is clear; for the other, it is expressed between the lines. Each *great* philosopher has his own and does not claim that it has to be accessible to everyone. It is very closely related, and in a legitimate manner, to *faith*. What Mrs. Conrad sees can probably only be seen by someone who either stands completely in the Christian world or, if not standing directly in it, is convinced of its reality . . . My position on metaphysics is not what you suspect. That is, I believe we can only build a metaphysic on a philosophy that is as critical as it is possible to be—critical, of course, also toward its own system—*and* on a positive doctrine (that is, supported by revelation) . . . I am convinced—not only according to religion but also according to philosophy—there are things that lie beyond the limits of the natural possibility of knowledge. Philosophy, understood as a science of pure, natural knowledge, as you without doubt conceive it, can just recognize this as its limits. However, then it is *philosophically* consistent to respect the limits and absurd to want to bring out something on the other side of the limits with purely philosophical means."

be seen opening explicitly more and more to theological horizons. In fact, in her September 22, 1921, letter to Roman Ingarden, in direct reference to *Philosophy of Psychology and the Humanities* and *An Investigation Concerning the State*, she writes, "I doubt that there will be any more communication with me about my works. They are from 1918 and 1919. As a matter of fact, there is hardly anything in them I want to change. They are to me about like the old skin a snake casts off. I really do not want to look at them again."[17] It is clear from Stein's own words that she had moved on to something other than the concerns and scope of her early strictly philosophical works. Her philosophical knowledge was opening onto new vistas of theological and mystical knowledge.

Even though *Der Aufbau der menschlichen Person* and *Was ist der Mensch?* were composed a decade after her conversion to the Catholic faith in 1922, they must be situated as prolegomena to her mature opus, *Finite and Eternal Being*, which she wrote out of her state of intense prayerful contemplation as a Discalced Carmelite nun. What she says in *Der Aufbau der menschlichen Person* and in *Was ist der Mensch?*, she says in *Finite and Eternal Being*, but better. Furthermore, the phenomenological movement did not stop with Husserl or with early Heidegger. It has continued to evolve and to be informed by new and innovative voices such as those of Maurice Merleau-Ponty (1908–61), Emmanuel Levinas (1906–95), Michel Henry (1922–2002), Paul Ricoeur (1913–2005), Jacques Derrida (1930–2004), Jean-Luc Marion (1946–), Jean-Louis Chrétien (1952–), et al. While this litany of more recent phenomenologists attests to the method's pregnant evolution on the soil of France in particular, these developments cannot be neglected in any discussion of phenomenology today. Yes, the danger of anachronism lingers in inviting such voices into conversation with Stein, but it is necessary to follow the progressive trajectory of phenomenology leading up to the present day and its effective application in the field of theology. *Human and Divine Being* situates Stein along this trajectory so as not to curtail the history of phenomenology or to suggest that the hermeneutic structures of Husserl alone constitute phenomenology. Stein certainly is to be grouped along with those recent phenomenologists known for their signature turn to theology and theological phenomena within their work.[18]

There is no question that *Human and Divine Being* engages in a serious polemic with the prevalent postmodern worldview, and accompanying ideologies, to be characterized as practical atheism born from material

---

17. Stein, *Letters to Roman Ingarden*, 191.

18. For more on the so-called theological turn in phenomenology, see Janicaud, *Phenomenology and the "Theological Turn"*.

reductionism.[19] Understanding existence this way reduces the human person to a random instance of atomic matter and energy that just so happens to recognize his own existence and search for his reason for being. This worldview has spawned some of the most tragic communist regimes in human history and continues to justify and reinforce systemic dehumanizing practices in economics, biotechnology, health care, and education. By disqualifying the possibility of divinity, this worldview at the same time disqualifies the possibility of collective human flourishing. It precipitates a dog-eat-dog world according to its "survival of the fittest" and "natural selection" mantras. It neglects the complete truth about human and divine being by obliterating the possibility of transcendence. It scoffs at any reference to the supernatural and insists that nature is a self-constituting, self-contained, self-referential, self-replicating matrix of matter in motion, and that is all. Altogether, its godlessness is matched only by its eclipse of the human person.

Commenting on Stein's *Philosophy of Psychology and the Humanities*, Angela Ales Bello writes that "in her polemic, especially with the positivist claim to outline a theory that gives all the conditions of possibility of a science in such a way that with the identification of a part of its structure we can proceed by extension to grasp the totality of future events, E. Stein hits upon different objectives."[20] The aforementioned worldview of practical atheism operates under the pretense that it is omniscient concerning all the conditions of not only its own possibilities, but concerning all the conditions of possibility in general and even those pertaining to the future. It commits the fatal flaw of granting that which is partial and provisional eternal status. It fails to recognize that possibility and open inquiry is what originally gave birth to all scientific enterprises and thereby has "exchanged the truth of God for a lie and revered and worshiped the creature rather than the creator."[21] For God is the condition for the condition of possibility and the impossibility of impossibility. Along with Stein, *Human and Divine Being* advocates the truth about being that is clearly evident to the intellect

---

19. For helpful treatments of the polemics between Christian faith and material reductionism, see McGrath, *Passionate Intellect*; McGrath, *Why God Won't Go Away*; McGrath, *Surprised by Meaning*; McGrath, *Twilight of Atheism*; McGrath, *Dawkins' God*; Cunningham, *Darwin's Pious Idea*; Spitzer, *New Proofs for the Existence of God*; Barr, *Modern Physics and Ancient Faith*; Cavadini, "The Anatomy of Wonder."

20. Ales Bello, *Fenomenologia dell'essere umano*, 114 ("In polemica soprattutto con la pretesa positivistica di delineare una teoria che dia tutte le condizioni di possibilità di una scienza in modo tale che dalla individuazione di una parte e della sua struttura si possa procedeere per estensione a cogliere la totalità degli avvenimenti futuri, E. Stein colpisce diversi obbiettivi"; translation my own).

21. Rom 1:25 (NAB).

because "ever since the creation of the world, [God's] invisible attributes of eternal power and divinity have been able to be understood and perceived in what he has made."[22] *Human and Divine Being* attends to that which is in order to contemplate that which Is.

The title, *Human and Divine Being*, was chosen in reference to the title of Stein's work *Finite and Eternal Being*. *Human and Divine Being* highlights the finite attributes of human being and the eternal attributes of divine being. Instead of offering an index of all being and beings, *Human and Divine Being* steers its attention toward human being in light of divine being. Most especially, it undertakes to recuperate the ontological veracity of the human soul in relation to the broader categories of spiritual being and material being.[23] Stein's work is determined to be the centrifugal center of this project in theological anthropology within today's skeptical (if not cynical) postmodern context. *Human and Divine Being* intends to renew the mystery of human being and personhood as perceived along the backdrop of divine mystery.

This book is organized according to the primary themes of Stein's oeuvre. Chapter 1 begins with a discussion of universal human vocation and the crucial potency-act hermeneutic that Stein develops to explain the makeup of human personhood. Chapter 2 describes the essence of spiritual being as the foundation of all being and the most fitting analogue for divine being. At the heart of the book are three chapters devoted to pedagogy on the human soul. The human soul is the locus of Stein's entire literary corpus as well as the centerpiece of Carmelite spirituality.[24] Comprehending the human soul is argued to be the most pressing task for theological anthropology today. If the human soul—a concept found in all of the great religious traditions throughout the world—is not taken seriously when asking what it is to be human, then we will end up with inhuman conclusions to

---

22. Rom 1:20 (NAB).

23. In commenting on the human soul in her December 10, 1918, letter to Roman Ingarden, Stein writes, "Also, what you say about me is totally appropriate. Certainly I love reality but not reality per se. Rather, I love a quite definite reality, the human soul: of the individual and of the people. What you call idealizing is perhaps more related to the fact that I am very indifferent to everything material and, therefore, I always run the risk of underestimating it. I love the ideal for its own sake—for I am also strongly inclined to the theoretical—and in addition as the single, trustworthy guiding star of our lives, without which we hopelessly go astray as has obviously occurred in the last decades. In this sense, I am a confirmed 'idealist' and my entire political activity has been directed toward creating an ideal point of view that would also be applicable in the practical world." See Stein, *Letters to Roman Ingarden*, 156.

24. See Beckmann-Zöller, "Edith Stein's Theory of the Person," 47: "Nothing occupied the philosopher Edith Stein more intellectually than the problem of a theory of the person."

our most decisive ethical questions. After establishing the fact of the human soul, the book turns to examine material being in relation to spiritual being, showing the contrast and complementarity between the two. The penultimate chapter is dedicated to Stein's dissertation work on empathy. Empathy is a dynamically important concept for theological anthropology as it goes beyond the "whatness" of the individual human being by inquiring into the intersubjectivity between persons. Finally, the book crescendoes with its last chapter dedicated to the logic of the cross as the most lucid pathway for understanding the transformation, or spiritualization, of being within the drama of cosmic redemption. It is argued that the science of the cross is the code that unlocks the enigmatic and paradoxical meaning of human being.

An observant reader may wonder why Emmanuel Levinas appears so often in a book dedicated to the work of Edith Stein. The reason is that I regard Stein and Levinas to be within the same genus of thought: theological anthropology oriented toward the ethical. Their shared Jewish heritage is ethical through and through. There is no question about this. Neither thinker elevates method, aesthetics, the question of being, or even the sense of the sacred, over and above solicitude for the other. Love and responsibility for the other is always the point. The fact that Heidegger does not figure prominently in either philosopher's work is additional evidence that neither Stein nor Levinas was enthralled with the manifestation of Being (*Sein*) from an egocentric point of view. To the contrary, for both, the question of being is always at the service of care for the other who faces me. This point is virtually self-evident given the hagiography that surrounds both of them in the wake of their courageous lives. Moreover, this is the reason I insist on beginning this book with a consideration of human vocation as an *entrée* into ontology and not the other way around. To know the nature of human being is to heed the call to responsibility for the other. Empathy takes a back seat to this call according to the call's radical alterity and its inability to be mastered or to be manipulated. This is why the chapter on empathy appears as penultimate in sequence. Had Stein lived twenty to forty years longer on this side of eternity, she would have become a Levinasian without a doubt. In fact, she lived "ethics as first philosophy" in her flesh, all the way until August 9, 1942.

The Second Vatican Council contends that "in reality it is only in the mystery of the Word made flesh that the mystery of humanity truly becomes clear."[25] Similarly, the source and inspiration for Stein's project in theological anthropology is Jesus of Nazareth, Jesus the Christ. It is Jesus, above all,

---

25. *Gaudium et spes*, 22, in Flannery, *Vatican Council II*, 185.

who reveals the true face of humanity to a world of human beings striving authentically to humanize one another. Without the enlightenment of Christ (explicitly or implicitly), the human person remains locked inside an opaque cell of agnosticism, subject to a host of ideological manipulations and unwarranted self-interests. True human freedom promotes the freedom of all persons—the coexistence of freedoms that is won to the degree that human solidarity and responsibility become the touchstone of daily behavior. Paul of Tarsus writes, "For freedom Christ set us free; so stand firm and do not submit again to the yoke of slavery" (Gal 5:1 NAB). It is Christ who has won freedom for all of humanity, liberating us from the bondage of ignorance, falsehood, sin and death. May this book, symbolically prepared on the Feast of the Exaltation of the Holy Cross, serve to promote the life, dignity and freedom of all human beings without exception or partiality.

Donald Lee Wallenfang, OCDS / Emmanuel Mary of the Cross
Feast of the Exaltation of the Holy Cross
September 14, 2016

1

On Human Vocation

Behold, I stand at the door and knock;
if any one hears my voice and opens the door,
I will come in to him and eat with him, and he with me.

—Revelation 3:20 (RSV)

Rather than begin with the question of what the human being is, chapter 1 considers how the human being is called to live. In taking our interpretive cue from Emmanuel Levinas by regarding ethics as first philosophy, we commence this project in theological anthropology. The first word is that the human being is the ethical being. This, too, is how Stein understands the peculiarity of human nature. To be authentically human is to be responsible for the other, to be responsible for all. Intersubjective existence is defined by a summons to responsibility and the call to form a communion of persons in love.[1] Paradoxically, analysis of

---

1. See Levinas, *Ethics and Infinity*, 95–101: "For I describe subjectivity in ethical terms. Ethics, here, does not supplement a preceding existential base; the very node of the subjective is knotted in ethics understood as responsibility . . . I am responsible for a total responsibility, which answers for all the others and for all in the others, even for their responsibility . . . Constituting itself in the very movement wherein being responsible for the other devolves on it, subjectivity goes to the point of substitution for the Other. It assumes the condition—or the uncondition—of hostage. Subjectivity as such is initially hostage; it answers to the point of expiating for others . . . Responsibility is what is incumbent on me exclusively, and what, *humanly*, I cannot refuse. This charge is a supreme dignity of the unique. I am I in the sole measure that I am responsible, a

human being begins by turning my attention to the other who faces me. Human being is defined, first of all, by the essence of human vocation: how am I called to live?

For Edith Stein, human vocation is comprised of a call and a response. The call issues from the divine, precisely in the other who faces me, and the human response is enabled by divine assistance. Human vocation is not simply a matter concerning choice of occupation, but rather concerns the ultimate *Gestalt*, or shape, of one's life. She writes the following to a former student of hers, Rose Magold, in a letter dated August 30, 1931: "The question of vocation cannot be solved merely through self-examination plus a scrutiny of the various possibilities. One must pray for the answer—you know that—and, in many cases, it must be sought by way of obedience. I have given this same advice several times, and those involved have arrived at peace and clarity by following it."[2] Stein suggests that shaping from within demands pliability from without. Human vocation emerges from intersubjective existence—living in community—that awakens one to possibility and development. Obedience implies a prior call. For Stein, human vocation involves a divine summons issued in and through the other who faces me. Human vocation is realized through prayer and ethical action, through contemplation and the work of social justice. In order to awaken from vocational slumber, it is necessary to heed the personal divine hail to travel eastward toward the Son of glory.[3] Only in the *imitatio Christi* does human vocation reach its full potential.

This chapter will trace the contours of Stein's portrayal of universal human vocation. First, analysis is made of the Aristotelian and Thomistic potency–act hermeneutic as developed by Stein. The relationship between potency and act serves as the lynchpin of Stein's life's work, which attempts to answer the question of being through a synthesis of Thomistic *sacra doctrina* and Husserlian phenomenology. Second, inventory is taken of the components of what Stein calls "intersubjectivity." For Stein, personal vocation does not consist in turning away from the other and toward the self but in turning outward and opening to the agency of the other. Third,

---

non-interchangeable I. I can substitute myself for everyone, but no one can substitute himself for me. Such is my inalienable identity of subject."

2. Stein, *Self-Portrait in Letters*, 104.

3. See ibid., 353: "From the transport as it stopped in the Schifferstadt railway station, early on August 7, a woman in 'dark clothing' identified herself as Edith Stein (she had acquaintances in that city) and left a message either orally or perhaps in writing: 'We are travelling east.'" This was one of the final recounted communications of Stein before her execution in a gas chamber at the Auschwitz concentration camp on August 9, 1942.

the notion and function of grace in Stein's anatomy of human vocation is assessed. In presenting a teleological vision wherein finite being stretches toward infinite being, Stein frames the question of human vocation as integral to the question of being itself. This sketch helps to understand the way in which Stein fulfilled her personal life vocation as well.

I. The Revelatory Dialectic of Potency–Act

Edith Stein embarks on her philosophical project confident that she draws from the immutable riches of *philosophia perennis*, that is, "perennial philosophy." In her preface to *Finite and Eternal Being*, Stein writes that "above and beyond the limitations of historical epochs and peoples there is something in which all those share who honestly search for truth."[4] Perennial philosophy testifies to those truths that do not change. The question of being pursues such immutable truths and it was the same question for Aristotle, as it was for Thomas, as it was for Stein, as it is for us today. At the heart of philosophical investigation always has been the question of being. What is it to be? What is being? What is the relationship between being and beings? Stein's lifelong philosophical project is marked by the struggle to understand, as fully as possible, the meaning and constitution of being (*Sein*). She finds Aristotle to be a helpful guide as he broaches the question within the heart of his *Metaphysics*: "And we think we know each thing most fully, when we know what it is, e.g. what man is or what fire is, rather than when we know its quality, its quantity, or where it is; since we know each of these things also, only when we know *what* the quantity or quality *is*. And indeed the question which, both now and of old, has always been raised, and always been the subject of doubt, viz. what being is, is just the question, what is substance [*ousia*]?"[5] For Aristotle, to know something is not to know its

---

4. Stein, *Finite and Eternal Being*, xxviii; cf. Stein, *Knowledge and Faith*, 7–8: "But *philosophia perennis* also means something else: the spirit of genuine philosophy alive in every true philosopher, in anyone who cannot resist the inner need to search out the *logos* of this world, its *ratio* (as Thomas translated the word). The born philosopher brings this spirit with him into the world—as *potency*, in Thomistic terminology. The potency becomes actualized when he meets a mature philosopher, a 'teacher.' This is the way true philosophers reach out to one another over the bounds of time and space"; and Stein, *Finite and Eternal Being*, 6–7: "The question then arises whether the reborn philosophy of the Middle Ages and the newly created philosophy of the twentieth century can possibly find a common meeting ground in the one broad river bed of the *philosophia perennis*. They still speak different languages, and the task immediately at hand is therefore to find an idiom which may serve as a means of communication and mutual understanding."

5. Aristotle, *Metaphysics* 1028b1, in Aristotle, *Complete Works*, 2:1624; cf. Stein,

color, texture, size, location, etc. (those accidental properties of a being) but to know its specific substance and the peculiar essences that together work to form the substance. Substantial differences are what distinguish one kind of being from another. Human, fish, bird, rock, tree—all such differentiated kinds of being are distinguished according to their substantial makeup. Rational life distinguishes human being; marine life (including fins, gills, and the like) distinguishes fish being; avian life (including feathers, wings, flight, etc.) distinguishes bird being; geologic nonliving existence (including lithic sedentariness, etc.) distinguishes rock being; and arborescent life (including woody stems, roots and shoots, leaves, vertical extension, etc.) distinguishes tree being. Aristotle's formulation of the question of being in terms of substance effectively peels back arbitrary layers of difference and identifies that which stands beneath a being's appearance and makes it what it is.

The question of being is primary for Aristotle, and for Stein it is the same. Stein suggests that her culminating work, *Finite and Eternal Being*, "may have grown out of this question as out of a living seed."[6] Stein finds Aristotle's hermeneutic for being, namely, the categories of potency and act, as the most helpful way to understand the mystery of being.[7] As human beings, we are able to fathom the being of existents as a perpetual process of becoming on all levels of existence. When a being becomes, it changes from a potential state of being to an actual state of being. The change from potentiality to actuality is caused by a prior actuality that acts on the latent potentiality. In biology we observe that animal cells rely on the continuous citric-acid cycle for the production of energy. Similarly, we observe that plant cells rely on the photosynthetic process for the production of energy in order to grow, develop, and reproduce. In these fundamental processes of energy production, organisms exhibit a host of potentialities that become actualized. Underlying such biological processes are the potent molecular polarities that make possible the series of chemical reactions which produce energy for the organism and allow it to attain other possibilities of its being—for example, movement, mating and nurturing its offspring. And so it is the case with all finite existents: every process of becoming begins with actuality and ends with actualized being. In contemplating the question of being according to the interpretive dialectic, potency–act, we are led swiftly

---

Potency and Act, 9: "as long as we do not understand *being* we understand nothing. Hence we should call what we are going to do here 'ontology.'"

6. Stein, *Finite and Eternal Being*, 3.

7. See ibid., 2: "With his doctrine of act and potency St. Thomas stands firmly on the ground of Aristotelian philosophy." This quotation, while directly referring to Thomas, reveals Stein's confidence in the pathways of Aristotelian thought. Also, cf. Aristotle, *Metaphysics* 1049b1–1052a10.

to the conclusion that there must be a pure, absolute and eternal actuality that is prior to all potentiality. For we observe that nothing that is potential becomes actual on its own accord but instead relies on an anterior actuality to stir its potentiality into actuality. It is this pure actuality (*actus purus*) which Thomas Aquinas calls "God."[8]

While the potency–act relationship can be construed in terms of causality (whether formal, material, efficient, or final), it runs deeper than interpretation based on causality alone would admit. Even though "a universal causal connection between all real things" exists, by penetrating into the nature of things a "*unity of a totality of meaningful existence [Sinn-Ganzes]*" is disclosed.[9] This is an observation of phenomenology. While metaphysics sets forth a comprehensive taxonomy of being, phenomenology culls together the meaning of being according to the transcendental triad of goodness, truth, and beauty.[10] Stein suggests that all existents stand together in the eternal *Logos* and therein comprise a "totality of meaning [*Sinn-Ganzes*]," and, from God's point of view, "a perfect coherence of meaning [*Sinnzusammenhang*]" obtains among the sum total of existents and their collective being.[11] The *Logos* signifies eternal, pure actuality of meaning-making and cognate recognition of this meaning. *Logos* is eternal rationality—the very rationality that had to precede the experience of finite rationality and its potential actualization. Behind "the divine plan of creation [*Schöpfungsplan*]" stands "the eternal plentitude of divine being and divine life."[12] Stein's confession of God's existence involves an act of belief in which she reaches for "the absolute hold [*Halt*]" of all that exists and by it feels herself upheld.[13] Yet she insists that there can be a universal recognition of "God" insofar as there can be a universal recognition of the necessity of pure and absolute actuality and being as such, in a word, eternal being.[14]

8. See Thomas Aquinas, *Summa theologiae* I.1.2.

9. Stein, *Finite and Eternal Being*, 112. Emphasis in original.

10. For Stein's exposition of the transcendentals in relation to the question of the meaning of being, see Stein, *Finite and Eternal Being*, chapters 5 and 6, "Existents as Such (The Transcendentals)," 277–323, and "The Meaning of Being," 325–54, respectively.

11. Ibid., 113.

12. Ibid., 114.

13. Stein, *Potency and Act*, 21.

14. See ibid., 10: "We ought not to separate from temporality the being that I am aware of as of my own being. As actual being it involves discrete points: a 'now' between a 'no longer' and a 'not yet.' But since its flowing character is split into being and nonbeing, the *idea of pure being* unveils itself to us, a being which in itself has nothing of nonbeing, in which there is no 'no longer,' no 'not yet,' and which is not temporal but *eternal*"; ibid., 20–21: "the being of finite substances is such that it has not come

For Stein, all existents are composed of an admixture of being and nonbeing, actuality and potentiality,[15] whereas God is conceived as unbounded being and pure act. For creatures, actuality and potentiality are "modes of being," while pure actuality is the divine mode of being. From the dialectic of potency–act, Stein arrives at a definition of substance: "something whose being stretches over a duration and which activates what it is in certain effects."[16] For Stein, substance is not something static but dynamic—that which unfolds over the course of an evolving temporality. All finite substances are in flux. Their being is in a constant state of becoming. The process of becoming itself is identical to the meaning of finite substance. Stein goes so far as to say that "the basis for an argument for God's existence is given [gegeben ist] in the sheer fact of being."[17] If being must be envisaged in terms of substance, and substance is an admixture of actuality and potentiality that unfolds over the course of time, God then appears as the primordial and eternal actuality that gives act to all potency. Aristotle sums up this principle well: "It is clear that actuality [energeia] is prior to potentiality [dynamis]."[18] There is no potentiality without a prior actuality,

---

to full effect. It is destined to unfold in successive activities and ever retains in itself some unfulfilledness and frailty—a 'not yet' and a 'no longer.' Its potentiality points ahead to the actuality wherein it is to fulfill itself, but it also points back beyond itself to a being that no longer unfolds in an alternating flow of actuality and potentiality but in the eternal unchangeableness of actual being. Can anything uphold [Halt geben] my frail [hinfällig] being, which touches upon genuine existence [Existenz] only from one instant to another, save true being wherein nothing of nonbeing is found and which stands changeless by itself alone, unable to have, nor needing, any other upholding [Halt]? And does not the very frailty of my own being lend certainty—not only to the idea but to the reality [Realität] of the pure, true, 'absolute [absolut]' being?"; ibid., 52: "Our—purely formal—conclusion, then, is that only a perfectly simple whole can be absolutely actual. This can only be an individual whose being is no longer separate from what it is, an individual wherein all basic forms coincide, the be-ing absolutely. There cannot be more than *one* individual that satisfies this formal definition, since otherwise the '*what*' and the 'instances' that the *what* occurs in would be separate."

15. It is important to note here that "potentiality" is not synonymous with "nonbeing"; see Stein, *Potency and Act*, 14: "We should not say, however, that insofar as they are potential they are *not*, for even potential being retains something of being in itself." This is to say that if some potential exists, it already has been actualized as such.

16. Stein, *Potency and Act*, 18.

17. Ibid., 21.

18. Aristotle, *Metaphysics* 1049b1; cf. ibid., 1049b25: "For from the potential the actual is always produced by an actual thing," and 1050a15: "Further, matter exists in a potential state, just because it may attain to its form; and when it exists *actually*, then it is in its form," and 1050b5: "But actuality is prior in a higher sense also; for eternal things are prior in substance to perishable things, and no eternal thing exists potentially"; cf. Thomas Aquinas, *Summa contra gentiles* I.16; and Stein, *Finite and Eternal Being*, 225, on three distinct meanings of actuality: "Actuality denotes: 1) the

that is, a prior actuality that gave rise to the actual potentiality in the first place. Stein claims that "every earthly reality, the entire visible creation, is in the realm of becoming [*Reich des Werdens*]. Every formed thing bears within itself possibilities of future actualization."[19] Every existent dwells in the realm of movement and change, and depends entirely on an anterior actuality for its actualization, for actuality does not emerge from potentiality but from Actuality itself: "It may be assumed, moreover, that according to the original order of creation, the movements and interactions of material elements were to aid them in forming and unfolding themselves, so that they might manifest in their entire external appearance their anchorage in the eternal."[20] Stein envisions the *creatio ex nihilo* ("creation from nothing") as an artistic masterpiece of divine composition. For instance, the teleology of atomic and molecular polarities is determined by the actuality of the created polarities themselves. Planetary orbits are predetermined by the actuality of the inbuilt laws of physics, including the fundamental forces that hold everything together as a cohesive whole. For Stein, the potency–act hermeneutic is that which unveils the primordial structure of being whose genius proceeds from eternity: "God's potency is but *one* and His act is but *one*, and His potency is brought to effect completely in this act."[21] Unlike finite existents, divine being has no potencies in need of being actualized. Otherwise, divine being would be finite and not eternal. Instead, through the analogy of being, divine potency is regarded as perfectly accomplished in the eternal actuality of divine being. Creatures, in their being composed at once of potency and act, analogously reflect eternal divine being. However, in eternal being there is nothing that corresponds to potentiality in finite being. Divine being is, by definition, always actualized, always in act. Finite created being, in contrast, is always becoming, always somewhere in between act and potency, always in the process of being actualized.

Breaking company with those who would bracket the question of God by labeling it either as a pursuit of unreachable transcendence or as an obstacle for conducting a purely neutral philosophical enquiry, Stein positions

---

imperfectly actual (i.e., the actual in the process of evolution); 2) the not yet attained end; and 3) the attained end."

19. Stein, *Finite and Eternal Being*, 247; cf. Stein, *Potency and Act*, 294: "The being of a living thing, as we described it when considering an individual plant, is not the persistence of something unchanged but a *becoming* in the sense of something shaping itself over time, and the word 'evolution, development [*Entwicklung*]' implies this."

20. Stein, *Finite and Eternal Being*, 248. Cf. Stein, *Potency and Act*, 20: "Actual being emerges from a potential being and passes into a potential being, but all potentiality is phenomenally upheld [*halten*] by actuality and it cannot uphold [*Halt geben*] actuality."

21. Stein, *Potency and Act*, 7.

divine being as the golden standard of her philosophical investigation. In fact, she posits the divine *Logos* as the meaning-principle driving the entire evolutionary process of the cosmos—physical, biological, historical, and cultural—and the ensuing task of meaning-making.[22] Not only is the personal eternal *Logos* the driving force of the evolutionary process, he is its goal: "This ever fragmentary, often misinterpreted, and sometimes completely misunderstood experience [of human unity and solidarity] receives firm support and a clear meaning from the doctrine of creation and redemption, which derives the origin of all people from one ancestor and which envisages as the goal of the entire evolution of the human race its union under *one* divine-human head, in the *one* 'Mystical Body' of Christ."[23] Here is an instance where Stein's critical philosophic thinking is extended by revelatory theological thinking. Human solidarity has its basis in a common origin, a common history, and a common destiny. In agreement with the Catholic doctrine of monogenesis—that the human species originated from a single human pair, one male person and one female person—Stein infers that humanity must have a common destiny as well.[24] The unity of

---

22. See Husserl, *Ideas Pertaining to a Pure Phenomenology*, 134: "What concerns us here, after merely indicating different groups of such rational grounds for <believing in> the existence of an extra-worldly 'divine' being is that this being would obviously transcend not merely the world but 'absolute' consciousness. It would therefore be an *'absolute' in the sense totally different from that in which consciousness is* an absolute, just as it would be *something transcendent in a sense totally different* from that in which the world is something transcendent. Naturally we extend the phenomenological reduction to include the 'absolute' and 'transcendent' being. It shall remain excluded from the new field of research which is to be provided, since this shall be a field of pure consciousness"; Stein, *Potency and Act*, 331: "Thus the individual peculiarity and the typical variations of the species are accidental outcomes from the standpoint of the entelechy [i.e., the inner forming, shaping, and unfolding principle of an organism], but from the standpoint of the *Logos* they are foreseen as possibility founded on the ordered interplay of the forces"; Stein, *Knowledge and Faith*, 9: "Both Husserl and Thomas were convinced that a *logos* is the force behind all that is, and that our understanding can uncover step by step first one aspect of this *logos*, then another, and so on, as long as it moves ahead in accordance with the principle of the most stringent intellectual honor. They differed, of course, on how far this procedure of uncovering *logos* could take them."

23. Stein, *Finite and Eternal Being*, 510. It is important to notice Stein's endnote 54 attached to this quotation—an endnote she would later experience firsthand, to the point of death at the hands of the Nazi regime: "These misinterpretations account for the one-sided exaggerations of nationalist and internationalist ideologies" (ibid., 612). In other words, the premier fault of truth is its pretension to totality in the *hic et nunc*— a pretension exhibited in both the phenomenon of political totalitarianism and that of ecclesiastical clericalism. See Paul Ricoeur's essay, "Truth and Falsehood," in Ricoeur, *History and Truth*, 165–91.

24. See Pius XII, *Humani generis*, 37: "When, however, there is question of another

the human race is secured at the bookends of origin and end. Christian revelation reinforces this reasonable philosophical conclusion in its profession of an eschatological consummate reality in which God will be all in all.[25] Christian revelation discloses the cosmic *Logos* to be Christ, the eternal Son of God made flesh. For Stein, Christ is the hermeneutic key that unlocks the mystery of the meaning of being because he is the eternal Meaning of being's meaning. Whereas Husserl's and Heidegger's philosophical projects stop short of divinity, Stein's project rests on, and culminates in, the *Logos*-principle, which is synonymous with *actus purus* ("pure act") and *esse in actu* ("being in act"). The question of human vocation, for Stein, is bound up with the question of being and, therefore, with the illuminating consequences of the potency–act hermeneutic. Universal human vocation is conceivable as being shaped from without and from within, being shaped personally and spiritually into the collective form of community.

II. Creaturely Existence as Intersubjective Becoming

Whereas God is understood as pure act for Stein, creatures are ever in a state of becoming.[26] Creaturely existence is in constant flux between actuality and potentiality. Potencies of created beings never cease to be actualized anew. Yet within this constant state of becoming creatures become co-creators with God. The divine *Logos* is operative in all of the various approaches to reality: bio-logy, psycho-logy, socio-logy, philo-logy, physio-logy, etc. Every -logy suffix points to the *logos* from which it derived and, moreover, to the *Logos* from which all *logoi* are derived. The *Logos* is the pure actuality

---

conjectural opinion, namely polygenism, the children of the Church by no means enjoy such liberty. For the faithful cannot embrace that opinion which maintains that either after Adam there existed on this earth true men who did not take their origin through natural generation from him as from the first parent of all, or that Adam represents a certain number of first parents. Now it is in no way apparent how such an opinion can be reconciled with that which the sources of revealed truth and the documents of the Teaching Authority of the Church propose with regard to original sin, which proceeds from a sin actually committed by an individual Adam and which, through generation, is passed on to all and is in everyone as his own."

25. See 1 Cor 15:28: "When everything is subjected to him, then the Son himself will [also] be subjected to the one who subjected everything to him, so that God may be all in all" (NAB).

26. Stein, *Finite and Eternal Being*, 249: "The 'process of becoming' [*Werdegang*] of the plant structure is an evolution toward a definite end, namely, the fully unfolded Gestalt with everything that belongs to it, including the ripened fruit. And this process of becoming has itself a very definite Gestalt. It has a 'temporal' rather than a spatial structure, because it involves a definite kind of progression"; cf. ibid., 223, 310, and Stein, *Potency and Act*, 283, on the teleology of evolution.

of meaning that gives rise to all subsequent discursive meanings. *Logos* is meaning, word, rationality. Every created species participating in the divine *Logos*, or *Ratio*, by virtue of its rational nature acts as a personal agent of divine creativity. On a more basic level, all individual living beings, large and small, act according to the generative life-principle which directs their becoming in an involuntary way. This Stein observes in the following passage from *Finite and Eternal Being*:

> The individual is a ministering instrument of the creator in actualizing specific forms, not merely in the manner in which dead material structures are tools, but a *creative instrument* in producing itself (in the process of growth) and in generating progeny (by means of reproduction). But the individual remains *creature* even in these creative activities. Its "creative power" (or what H. Conrad-Martius calls "creative potency") is borrowed and measured. By serving—in self-formation and reproduction—the formation, preservation, and propagation of the species and by consuming itself in these processes, the individual becomes, as it were, a "victim" of its vital task [*Lebensaufgabe*].[27]

In this poetic passage, Stein points to the kenotic "circle of life," wherein living creatures give themselves over through their "vital task" to the point of abandonment.[28] Through growth and reproduction, biological beings demonstrate an inner determination toward life and the renewal of that life. Living creatures spend themselves in service to their intrinsic proclivity for extending their lives and the lives of their offspring over the course of time and within the domain of space. In the natural process of growth and development, living beings act as ministering instruments of divine creativity, exhausting their energies and resources to achieve these predetermined tasks. While the individual living being strives naturally for the preservation of its own life, it ultimately yields to its vital task to reproduce and sustain its own kind. If this were not the case, life would cease at a certain point altogether. Without the survival of its offspring, a species becomes extinct. Stein contends that "there is in living beings a manifold of material elements held together, permeated, and molded into an organic whole by a superior, living form ... *the being of the form is life, and life is the forming of matter* in the three stages of *transformation of the structural material elements*,

---

27. Stein, *Finite and Eternal Being*, 264–65.

28. Cf. John 12:24–25: "Amen, amen, I say to you, unless a grain of wheat falls to the ground and dies, it remains just a grain of wheat; but if it dies, it produces much fruit. Whoever loves his life loses it, and whoever hates his life in this world will preserve it for eternal life" (NAB).

self-formation, and *reproduction.*"[29] Life generates life by becoming a willful victim of itself. Life begets life and to live is to evolve, to become.[30] Life signifies that form which animates matter by transforming it and uniting it within an integral individual whole. The form of life not only causes a being to be alive and to subsist as such, it also extends its ontological status of self-becoming through replication of distinct species of living organisms arranged in an organic nexus of being. Individual living beings do not exist autonomously or independently of one another. All that is alive lives in relation to other living and nonliving forms of being. Creaturely becoming takes place within a global ecosystem of becoming. The form of life constitutes a comprehensive unit of all living beings in their interconnectedness. There is no single individual living creature independent of the rest. Life is interdependent symbiotic existence. Regarding the original appearance of living creatures, from a strictly philosophical perspective, Stein prefers to leave open the question of their initial emergence: "Therefore, regardless of whether we envisage the genesis of things as a progressive evolution from chaos to cosmos or as a continuous transformation of a primordial cosmos, we are dealing with a sequence of formations and it must remain undecided whether these formations are to be conceived as temporally separated works of creation or as merged in *one* creative *Fiat!*"[31] As a critical phenomenologist, Stein leaves open the question of origins when narrowing her lens of investigation to natural phenomena. Within the scope of the natural sciences, a chronological sequence of living formations is observed. Investigation of natural processes of becoming is not concerned about the details of the supernatural act of creation which inaugurated (*creatio ex nihilo*), and continues to create (*creatio continua*), finite being altogether. This is a question for metaphysics and for theology. For a phenomenology of biological being it is enough to reflect upon the givenness (*Gegebenheit*) of finitude, creatureliness, and the processes of becoming in living existents.

In metaphysically reflecting upon the creaturely process of becoming, Stein extends the potency–act hermeneutic to its full existential potential.

---

29. Stein, *Finite and Eternal Being*, 268.

30. Cf. John 1:14: "And the Word [*logos*] *became* flesh and made his dwelling among us . . ." (NAB; emphasis added). It is this temporal process of becoming through which the divine was able to enter into complete solidarity with humanity, according to the Christian proclamation.

31. Stein, *Finite and Eternal Being*, 484–85. Cf. Stein, *Potency and Act*, 104: "Philosophy based on natural reason brings us to the act of creation which alone is able to bridge the gulf between being and nonbeing, to leap from spirit to matter. But here philosophy halts before a locked gate: creation, as taught by faith, remains a mystery for our knowledge. What is absolutely spiritual and actual calls into being its direct opposite: what is nonspiritual and potential."

Instead of pleading guilty to the Freudian accusation of wish-fulfillment in her approach to infinite being, Stein simply acknowledges the clarion metaphysical reality that Aristotle observed and articulated ages ago: "It is clear that actuality is prior to potentiality."[32] It is a statement of the obvious. However, the obviousness of actuality's antecedence to potentiality goes largely unnoticed today because metaphysics is not held to be an academic discipline of importance. In recalling timeless philosophical claims, such as this one of Aristotle, we arrive at further clarity concerning those timeless human questions: What is being? What is human being? How do we know? How should we live? This series of questions are those that commence the fields of ontology, theological anthropology, epistemology, and ethics, respectively. Without an adequate foundation in the former three fields, we will miss the mark inevitably in the latter field of ethics. Stein puts Aristotle's fundamental observation about being this way: "Actual being emerges from a potential being and passes into a potential being, but all potentiality is phenomenally upheld [*halten*] by actuality and it cannot uphold [*Halt geben*] actuality."[33] Logically, according to the *analogia entis*, this assertion leads us to the threshold of eternity—a personal eternity that appears as necessarily anterior to finite, personal, self-reflexive and co-creating creatures.[34] The potency–act hermeneutic, while it may seem old-fashioned to some, when construed according to a phenomenological tonality, offers compelling insight into the question of being and the personal creature–Creator relationship. Yet Stein goes one step further. She elucidates the phenomenon of human, personal evolution in community life—a community based on a fundamental openness to the other and openness to grace. Human beings do not become in terms of biological being alone. We are social, personal spiritual creatures and, as such, we become in communal relation to one another:

---

32. Aristotle, *Metaphysics* 1049b1.

33. Stein, *Potency and Act*, 20.

34. Cf. Thomas Aquinas, *Summa theologiae* I.2.3, in *Summa Theologiae: Questions on God*, 13: "Therefore we cannot but postulate the existence of some being having of itself its own necessity, and not receiving it from another, but rather causing in others their necessity. This all men speak of as God." For the distinction Stein makes between eternal and finite being, see *Finite and Eternal Being*, 353: "To the 'order' of the created world belongs *time*. It is that whereby the finite is in the strictest sense distinguished from the eternal. For though we have encountered a meaning of finitude which does not signify a beginning and ending in time, viz., the limitation of the diverse units of meaning with respect to their content, the demarcation of finitude from the unity *of divine* being must nonetheless be understood as a being-ordained toward temporal actualization."

> Experience tells of . . . an unfolding and development over time that makes possible, yet presupposes, a progressive opening to one another. And in such an order of becoming, we cannot imagine an entelechy unfolding in isolation from others like it unless in place of this connection with other men there were an analogous relationship with higher spirits or directly with God Himself, Who out of the infinite fullness of His being could place in the interior of each soul whatever it needs to unfold.[35]

In these words Stein reveals the phenomenal becoming of the self vis-à-vis other selves in community. A prerequisite for "a progressive opening to one another" is the phenomenon of community: a plurality of selves in relation. As human beings, we become as individuals only in relation to one another. Personal alterity is the condition of possibility for personal spiritual becoming. Spiritual opening to another personal spiritual being who faces me involves a comportment of reverence, respect, and solicitude. Words to describe such an opening include "love" and "empathy."[36] Love and empathy refer to human activities that transpire between others and have the net effect of building one another up. Authentic and healthy personal unfolding happens according to the measure of affirming responsiveness by others who face me. Without care and nurture, human development would be arrested or even undergo a kind of personal degeneration. For instance, an infant would die if responsibility for her care were not assumed by another. What Stein means by "a progressive opening to one another" is essentially a series of decisions for vulnerability—a willingness to hazard oneself before the sway of another inside the hope that this interaction will be, in the end, nurturing rather than destructive. The infant is exemplar in her radical vulnerability and dependence on others for her care. Being in a constant state of openness to others is the very nature of the infant. Stein suggests that throughout a human being's lifespan her unfolding and development are achieved to the degree of her openness. To be open to others is a free and voluntary decision inasmuch as the affirmative response of care by another is free and voluntary. It is in light of the order of becoming that human vocation assumes a universal constellation: intersubjective communion.

---

35. Stein, *Potency and Act*, 404.
36. See Stein, *On the Problem of Empathy*. Cf. Stein, *Potency and Act*, 168: "And to understand the human spirit we must ask how it is shaped as a soul in human love"; and Stein, *Finite and Eternal Being*, 454: "But to be love in the true sense, it must always be a self-giving [*Hingabe*]."

III. Universal Human Vocation: Awakening to Eternal Being

For Stein, intersubjective communion refers ultimately to the communion of saints which participates eternally in the innermost life of God.[37] Undoubtedly this language is theologically charged, but this reality also can be framed in terms of the potecy-act hermeneutic developed by Stein: if eternal actuality is disclosed in personal spiritual beings as eternal love, and the actuality of love is performed only in its consummated "union of a plurality of persons in love," then the notion "communion of saints" is the teleological consequence of eternal actuality as eternal love.[38] This is to say that the human experience of becoming within a communion of persons in loving relationship exhibits the perfection of rational, responsible, and relational being. Perfection of human being must originate in an eternal actuality of personal communal love for it to be potentially manifest in a finite instance. This is not to say that the divine is identical to an eternal actuality of perfected human being, but it does mean that whatever is experienced as a perfection of personal being is preceded in time by the pure, infinite actuality of being which encompasses and surpasses all finite perfections of being. Second, the actuality of love implies the union of a plurality of persons in loving relationship. This is to say that God is one yet more than one if God can be called the perfect actuality of love. The Christian doctrine of God as Trinity coincides with the rational metaphysics of love. Third, "communion of saints" signifies the final cause of creation.[39] The communion of saints refers to the theological mystery to which all authentic love attains. Within the human experience of love as the perfection of human activity, love, in its pure actuality, is evinced as divine origin and end of its temporal instantiation. All this is to say that the human experience of authentic love proves (1)

---

37. See Stein, *Finite and Eternal Being*, 504: "The vocation to union with God is a vocation to eternal life. As a purely spiritual form, the human soul is immortal *by virtue of its very nature* [*natürlicherweise*]. As a spiritual personal substance, moreover, the soul is capable of a supernatural augmentation and elevation of its life, and faith tells us that God *wills* to give the soul eternal life, i.e., an eternal participation in his life."

38. Ibid., 514. See further ibid., 513–14: "God created Adam and Eve in his image as spiritual personal beings. And this is why it was 'not good' that such a creature be alone, since the most sublime meaning of all spiritual-personal being is mutual love and the union of a plurality of persons in love." Cf. Song 8:6–7: "Set me as a seal upon your heart, as a seal upon your arm; / for love is strong as death, jealousy is cruel as the grave. / Its flashes are flashes of fire, a most vehement flame. / Many waters cannot quench love, neither can floods drown it. / If a man offered for love all the wealth of his house, it would be utterly scorned" (RSV).

39. For extended discussion on final causality, see chapter 3 of the present study: "The Soul as the Form of the Body."

that God is love and (2) that the communion of saints is the necessary goal of finite personal communal love.

Stein identifies God as "the plentitude of love" who "may have chosen to create for himself a special abode in each human soul, so that the plentitude of divine love might find in the manifold of differently constituted souls a wider range for its self-communication."[40] Chapters 3 through 5 of *Human and Divine Being* will uncover the rational meaning of the term *soul*, but for now it is enough to say that the human community is constituted by a diverse array of individuals who together comprise the collective reality "humanity." In relation to eternal being, named by Stein as "the plentitude of love," the variety of human souls in their individual particularity serves to extend the range of God's self-communication to personal spiritual creatures. Stein contends that God "affirms Himself in His being Who is from eternity and has never first been placed in existence. His is not only a being conscious of itself but a being approving itself [*zustimmen*] in the highest form of approval [*Zustimmung*]: love; His being is blessed self-love."[41] Because God is revealed as an eternal actuality of love, and because love implies the unity of a plurality of persons in love, God's self-love implies alterity since the divine self (God the Father) includes the divine other (God the Son) and their witness (God the Holy Spirit). Eternal actuality as eternal love only makes sense in its Trinitarian configuration, which bespeaks a simultaneous oneness of substance and fecund plurality of persons.[42] The self-communication of divine love, as communicated eternally within the divine self, gratuitously extends its self-communication to personal finite beings who become conscious recipients of this divine gift through a mutual becoming of a finite-infinite communion of persons in love.[43]

While divine love, as eternal actuality, is constant in relation to its created object—namely, finite personal spiritual beings—it can be recognized as such only by an act of awakening on the part of its recipient. In other words, a human being—as a living admixture of potency and act—must

---

40. Stein, *Finite and Eternal Being*, 506.

41. Stein, *Potency and Act*, 172.

42. Cf. Balthasar, *Theo-logic*, 2:35, 62: "In the real, difference, the 'other than myself,' is always already overtaken by a third within which I am able to apprehend its otherness in the first place ... fecundity is the law, not only of organisms, but ... also of the life of the spirit ... every I-Thou relationship between spirits can be fulfilled only in an objective third (as Hegel never tires of stressing) or in the fact that genuine *paideia* (according to Plato) is a 'begetting in the beautiful' and thus the generation of a fruit."

43. For a similar understanding of human vocation as the call to form a communion of persons, see John Paul II, *Man and Woman He Created Them*, 162–64 (9:2–3), for example, 163: "Man becomes an image of God not so much in the moment of solitude as in the moment of communion."

awaken to eternal being in order to partake of its life, resulting in an elevation of spiritual being in the life of the human person. This awakening is the most fundamental act of freedom (though executed in an intersubjective context) of which a human person is capable and is characteristic of life of the spirit. Stein's portrayal of this process is worth quoting at length:

> Man's spirit awakens to his freedom and openness; more precisely, man awakens as free and open. He does not awaken by himself, nor is he *originally* free and open by himself. But once awakened, once having his original freedom and openness, it is up to him to keep himself free and open. At the same time, it is possible for him to lose both. If he does not "keep himself on high," he can fall back into the being of nature from which he has awakened to personally spiritual being. A specific action of the will is by no means the only way to "keep himself on high." The person "keeps himself" on the higher level—by his own power and by what he is open to—to a large extent by merely "letting it happen," by not deliberately [*willensmäßig*] stopping it, and to this extent it is voluntary [*freiwillig*]. Only when his power fails, possibly when a strong pull from below leads it down into an activity of nature withdrawing it from higher activity, need he deliberately withstand the pull and keep himself on the higher level . . . [A life of grace] is possible simply because of his original openness, and it may come to his share by his merely "allowing" it, indeed even if he does not actively allow it but just fails to resist it.[44]

What Stein describes here is the life of grace in which "the innermost being of the soul is like a vessel into which flows the spirit of God (i.e., the life of grace) if the soul by virtue of its freedom opens itself to this vital influx."[45] It is important to observe that this is not a Pelagian understanding, as if human persons achieved a level of spiritual perfection on their own initiative. Rather, Stein insists that human beings are not capable of this self-surrender to divine love (which "is simultaneously a surrender of one's own self—a self which God loves—to the entire created world, and in particular to all created beings united with God") by themselves.[46] It is precisely the eternal

---

44. Stein, *Potency and Act*, 409–11.

45. Stein, *Finite and Eternal Being*, 445; cf. ibid., 504–5: "the soul is destined for eternal being . . . To say that the soul receives God means rather that it opens itself and gives itself freely to him to bring about a union that is possible only between spiritual persons. It is a union of *love*: God is love, and the participation in divine being which is granted in this union must be a participation in divine love [*ein Mitlieben*]."

46. Ibid., 457.

actuality of love that accomplishes the personal openness of being in each and every personal spiritual being since it is ultimately "a matter of *divine freedom*."[47] Yet human cooperation is necessary for divine life to enter into the human soul and remain within. The cooperation necessary can be described by the Latin word *fiat*, that is, "let it be done, so be it, amen." *Fiat* is the openness of freedom that elevates one to the divine life of love and self-surrender to the point of abandonment. Mary of Nazareth, the Blessed Virgin *Theotokos*, is the paradigmatic figure of this docility and obedience that listens for the word from the other and responds with the life-giving *fiat* of faith.[48] Just as a plant's shoot strives upwards to the light, grace is essentially the justifying "negation of the negation in freely turning toward" God, demanding a personal receptive response and resulting in "the heightening in being."[49] The "negation of the negation" refers to the willful resistance to annihilation—the resolute "no" to the degenerative process of unbecoming and the threat of nonbeing. The "heightening of being" is none other than a lifting of the human soul to the heights of actualized being through the

---

47. Stein, *Potency and Act*, 410.

48. Cf. Stein, *Finite and Eternal Being*, 516: "Just as the mutual self-giving of the parents and their common generative will prepare the existence of the child and the endowments of its future life, so the growth of the child and the forming of its body and soul demand the loving self-giving of the mother and the dedication to the task of motherhood. The paradigm of this is the *Fiat!* ('Be it done unto me') of the Mother of God (Lk 1:38). This *Fiat!* enunciates her loving self-surrender to God and to the divine will and simultaneously her own generative will and her readiness to dedicate her body and her soul to the service of motherhood"; and Borden, *Edith Stein*, 31: "As Stein presents it, the characteristic of free acts is that, while they are motivated and therefore intelligible, they are not caused and thus can arise from a personal *fiat*." This latter point Stein argues against determinist theories of human behavior.

49. Stein, *Potency and Act*, 217. Cf. 216–17: "For this liberation a free turning toward absolute being is needed . . . And just as on the part of absolute being annihilating may respond to the negation or turning away [*Abwendung*], so a heightening in being, a raising to a higher mode of being that we call 'grace,' may respond to the turning toward. The negation of the negation in freely turning toward and the heightening in being together yield *justification*"; and Stein, *Finite and Eternal Being*, 399–400: "Grace calls for a 'personal' receptive response. It is a call or a knocking of God, and the person who is thus called is to listen and to open: to open the door of his or her own self so that God may enter. The ready capacity to receive or the *potentia oboedientialis* in the more restricted and authentic sense, therefore, is a capacity to *obey*, to listen to God and to freely surrender oneself to him. The person-to-person relationship makes possible that being-one [*Eins-sein*] which can come to pass only among persons. And in the relationship between God and the free creature, being one results from the communication and communion of grace"; and Stein, *Potency and Act*, 289; and Redmond, "A Nothing That Is," on the necessity of turning toward absolute being.

process of becoming—a stretching of creaturely being into the transcendent realm, an elevation wrought by the love that knows no fear.[50]

In sum, authentic human personhood is realized in and through the opening to another—a letting of another's being come over oneself.[51] Opening to another includes both divine and human otherness. Is this way of life not precisely the way of the cross? In her study on the life and work of St. John of the Cross, entitled *The Science of the Cross*, Stein writes,

> For Christ accomplished his greatest work, the reconciliation and union of mankind with God, in the utmost humiliation and annihilation on the Cross. When the soul realizes this it will begin to understand that it, too, must be led to union with God through annihilation, a "living crucifixion, in the sensual as well as in the spiritual part." As, in the desolation of his death, Jesus surrendered himself into the hands of the invisible and incomprehensible God, so the soul must enter the midnight darkness of faith, which is the only way to this God.[52]

Insofar as one surrenders oneself to the dark night of the paradoxical phenomenon of the cross, one opens to the unfolding movement of God's grace through a responsive *fiat* that simply "lets it happen." Just as human beings retain the possibility of opening to one another to realize their full created and creative potential, so do human beings retain the possibility of opening to God, who transgresses the limits of created finitude, inviting mortal creatures to partake of immortality, of life eternal—actuality eternal, fullness of being, fullness of life: "openness is the 'open gate that God's spirit can freely

---

50. See 1 John 4:18–19: "There is no fear in love, but perfect love casts out fear. For fear has to do with punishment, and he who fears is not perfected in love. We love, because he first loved us" (RSV).

51. See Matt 5:38–42: "'You have heard that it was said, 'An eye for an eye and a tooth for a tooth.' But I say to you, offer no resistance to one who is evil. When someone strikes you on your [right] cheek, turn the other one to him as well. If anyone wants to go to law with you over your tunic, hand him your cloak as well. Should anyone press you into service for one mile, go with him for two miles. Give to the one who asks of you, and do not turn your back on the one who wants to borrow'" (NAB).

52. Stein, *Science of the Cross*, 89. Cf. Phil 2:5–8: "Have this mind among yourselves, which was in Christ Jesus, who, though he was in the form of God, did not count equality with God a thing to be grasped, but emptied himself, taking the form of a servant, being born in the likeness of men. And being found in human form he humbled himself and became obedient unto death, even death on a cross" (RSV); and Rom 6:5–8: "For if we have been united with him in a death like his, we shall certainly be united with him in a resurrection like his. We know that our former man was crucified with him so that the sinful body might be destroyed, and we might no longer be enslaved to sin. For he who has died is freed from sin. But if we have died with Christ, we believe that we shall also live with him" (RSV).

pass through.'"⁵³ Thus, for Stein, the response and disposition of openness is that which allows a personal creature to become its fully actualized self—realizing its maximum potential. The vision of the fully actualized self attests to an eschatological rendezvous between the host of personal spiritual beings and the eternal Triad of love: an eternal communal life wherein every personal soul who opens to divine life "is to be inserted as a flower in an eternally imperishable wreath."⁵⁴

Edith Stein offers the freshness of scholastic thought through its phenomenological uptake. She readily engages evolutionary thought in the line of perennial philosophy that claims to be based not on bias, presupposition or opinion, but on critical inquiry and truth as it gives and says itself. Through her faithful adherence to critical thought, Stein is able to construe the creature–Creator relationship in terms that are accessible and plausible to reason, while pointing to the necessity of a doctrine of revelation in which the whole of reality becomes a living pathway for contemplating a personal, acting, living eternity. Through the potency–act hermeneutic, recognition of the created order of becoming, and attention to the testimony of divine grace, Stein effectively argues for a configuration of human vocation that is universal—a universal yet particular *Gestalt* in which a personal spiritual being opens to the unfolding of the divine life within. One is awakened to a life of radical self-donation in which one gives oneself to the other to the point of abandonment.

And so we have begun our study on the theological anthropology of Edith Stein with the question of human vocation. Spiritual openness was found to be the key term signaling intersubjective communion of persons in love. Strongly influenced by Husserl's phenomenology, which prioritizes that which gives itself to consciousness, Stein naturally connects the philosophical category of givenness (*Gegebenheit*) to the theological category of grace. Alterity is the common denominator of gift that makes possible the unitive power of love. In relation to finite being, eternal being is portrayed as pure actual being and, more specifically via the *analogia entis*, as the eternal actuality of Meaning (*Logos*), Life (*Bios-Zoe*), and Love (*Eros-Agape*).⁵⁵

53. Stein, *Potency and Act*, 410.

54. Stein, *Finite and Eternal Being*, 508. Cf. ibid., 526: "Every individual human being is created to be a member of [the Mystical Body of Christ] . . . However, it is of the very essence of humankind that every individual as well as the entire human family are to become what, according to their nature, they are destined to be in a process of temporal unfolding, and that this unfolding depends on the cooperation of each individual as well as on the common effort of all."

55. See Stein, *Finite and Eternal Being*, 458: "For no natural knowledge of God, ascending from creatures, discloses his hidden nature or essence. All such natural knowledge—despite the analogy by which creature and Creator are linked—can comprehend him only as the totally other."

Human vocation involves the apprehensible and meaningful call to life in the spirit enacted in a communion of persons in love. Human vocation is the playing field where meaning, life, and love take on flesh. It brings what is abstract to the concrete. Vocational form is incarnate in the human body. Human vocation is sacramental. Louis-Marie Chauvet writes that the sacraments are the "Parole de Dieu au risque du corps" ("the Word of God at the risk of the body").[56] When the pattern of divine love meets the risk of frail human flesh, human vocation comes alive. This is the place where mercy is incarnate in acts of forgiveness. It is where love is spoken in acts of responsibility for the other. The human being is the responsible being. As a personal spiritual being, the human being is created, above all else, to love. Love is an act to take place between personal spiritual creatures alone, since it involves self-mastery and a total self-giving to the other and, at the same time, recognition of the other as gift through the intellect and freedom of the rational soul. According to the potency–act hermeneutic, love is enacted originally in the divine self and shared through the divine act of creation-redemption. The communion of saints is the goal of human vocation, attested by the potency–act hermeneutic of metaphysics and by divine revelation through Jesus Christ, entrusted to his Church. Stein draws from the dual font of reason and divine revelation to detect the meaning and essence of human vocation, and so must we today, unless we are content to render ourselves somehow less than human once again.

---

56. See Chauvet, *Les sacrements*.

2

Spiritual Being

Who are you, sweet Light, that fills me
and illuminates the darkness of my heart?
You who likewise lead me with a Mother's Hand,
and were you to leave me,
no further step would I go.
You are the Space,
which encompasses round my being and holds it within itself.
Dismissed from you, it sinks into the abyss
of nothing, from which you raised it to the Light.
You, nearer to me than I am to myself
and more inward than my innermost heart
and yet impalpable and incomprehensible
and has burst asunder every name:
Holy Spirit—eternal Love![1]

Truly, truly, I say to you, unless a grain of wheat falls
into the earth and dies, it remains alone;
but if it dies, it bears much fruit.

—John 12:24 (RSV)

THE INTELLECTUAL FATE OF Christian theology in the postmodern era depends entirely on a critical articulation of its pneumatology.

---

1. First stanza of "Und ich bleibe bei euch: Aus einer Pfingstnovene," by Edith Stein. See Stein, *Hidden Life*, 140–41. Modified translation my own.

If a scientific account of spirit cannot be submitted adequately, Christian theology may be banished with good reason from the sphere of serious public discourse. For the postmodern intellect demands evidence, and lack of evidence equates to lack of relevance. Among the prospective sources for developing a critical Christian pneumatology, the work of Edith Stein bears highest promise. Chapter 2 of *Human and Divine Being* will glean key insights from Stein's literary corpus in order to begin anew the science of spirit. This chapter will limit itself to exploring Stein's phenomenology and metaphysics of spiritual being in particular. First it will situate the discussion within the larger context of contemporary polemics in pneumatology. To this end, the general categories and limits of scientific knowledge asserted by various voices in the debate over the reality of spiritual being will be unmasked. Second, a broad sketch of what Stein calls the "science of the cross" (*Kreuzeswissenschaft*) will be made in order to give an account of the foundational logic undergirding her pneumatology. Third, the overarching matrix of Stein's pneumatology will be considered by sifting from her most salient texts on the subject, especially that of *Finite and Eternal Being*. And on the whole, this chapter will depict how Stein's pneumatology opens onto new vistas for a phenomenology and metaphysics of spirit in the twenty-first century.

I. Contemporary Polemics in Pneumatology

Two predominant positions exist today regarding the idea of pneumatology.[2] The first position typically couches its discourse about spirit in an amalgam of confessional metaphorical terms, all of which elude the demand for concrete evidence of spiritual reality.[3] There is nothing inherently out of place with such a confessional project, but it must be admitted that it blushes before the demands of critical public discourse in a post-Christendom world. The second position regards spirit as a fictitious construct—a residue of primitive religiosity sustained by the unenlightened masses of people who continue to enlist spirit as their top-selling opium. While biblical metaphors for spirit abound—for example, wind, breath, fire, water, dove, power, life—none of these metaphors qualifies as adequate evidence for a verifiable reality of spirit as such. Christian theology understands God to

---

2. While the term *pneumatology* typically refers exclusively to the doctrine of the Holy Spirit in the field of Christian theology, a more inclusive usage of the term will be exercised in this study. *Pneumatology* will refer to an examination of spiritual being in general.

3. One example of this approach is found in Martinez, *The Sanctifier*.

be pure spirit. Therefore, as spirit goes, so goes divinity.[4] In other words, if spirit holds no rational weight as real, then neither does God (nor angels, nor the human soul).

One of the great twentieth-century pioneers of natural theology was Pierre Teilhard de Chardin (1881–1955). Teilhard refused to foist an unwarranted antagonism between spirit and matter. He saw this rift as proceeding from a false dichotomy between religion and natural science.[5] As a paleontologist and geologist by training, Teilhard insisted that a rapprochement prevail between spirit and matter. He writes,

> At the present time many believers, to avoid the anxieties that contact with reality might renew in them, allow a veil of conventional answers to cover the mysteries of life. And scientists, engrossed in the investigation of detail or caught up by a false materialism, apparently fail to see that by virtue of their discoveries the fundamental question of the future confronts us in all our activities. Stifled by the words they have invented, men are in danger of losing sight of the problem. They have reached the point of no longer grasping the meaning of what their own experiments are discovering.[6]

---

4. See *Catechism of the Catholic Church*, 370: "In no way is God in man's image. He is neither man nor woman. God is pure spirit in which there is no place for the difference between the sexes." Throughout the entire Christian tradition, the eternal Deity is portrayed ontologically almost exclusively in terms of spirit. Cf. 1 Cor 3:17: "Now the Lord is the Spirit, and where the Spirit of the Lord is, there is freedom" (RSV); and Stein, *La estructura de la persona humana*, 209–10: "Dios es espíritu puro, en el que no hay nada de material. Es el ente en el que no hay nada de no ser: es ser puro ... Espíritu puro, ser puro, acto puro, forma pura: todo esto es en Dios una y la misma cosa" ("God is pure spirit, in him there is nothing material. He is the being of which there is nothing of non-being: he is pure being ... Pure spirit, pure being, pure act, pure form: all that is in God is one and the same thing"; translation my own); and Stein, *Der Aufbau der menschlichen Person*, 146: "Gott ist reiner Geist, in dem nichts von Materie ist. Er ist das Seiende, in dem nichts von Nichtsein ist: das reine Sein ... Reiner Geist, reines Sein, reiner Akt und reine Form: das ist in Gott alles eins."

5. I use the term *natural science*, rather than *science*, quite intentionally. Today, the word *science* is often used to refer to something entirely other than things religious. However, if we recall the etymology of the English word *science*, we are reminded that it signifies any sort of knowledge whatsoever (Latin: *scire* ["to know"], *scientia* ["knowledge"]). As pointed out in chapter 1, any discipline to which the suffix -logy refers is scientific by virtue of its intrinsic connection to the *Logos*, including (and especially!) theo-logy. In fact, we refuse to forget that during the medieval era, the time in which the university emerged in Western history, theology was regarded as the "queen of all sciences." And so it is today and always will be inasmuch as theology, above and beyond all other fields, has the aptitude to respond to the ultimate questions we human beings ask.

6. Teilhard de Chardin, *Human Energy*, 19.

Teilhard puts his finger on the pulse of the contemporary climate surrounding the relationship between natural science and religion—an ambiguous relationship that persists to this day. Many believers in particular traditions of faith cower in the face of scientific discoveries such as evidence for biological adaptation and evolution. On the other hand, many so-called scientists raise up false pretenses and brandished arguments against the seriousness of religious experiences and coherent data that point to a transcendent realm of spirit. Some have gone so far as to proclaim that religion and natural science have nothing to say to one another.

A number of recent thinkers have contributed to a growing body of literature collectively referred to as the Neo-Atheism movement. Among the representatives of this movement are Richard Dawkins, Steven Pinker, James D. Watson, Christopher Hitchens, Victor Stenger, Daniel Dennett, and Sam Harris. This movement is sustained by its claim that spirit is not, and therefore God is not. Moreover, this movement makes its onslaught on religion in the name of science. For example, in *Quantum Gods*, Victor Stenger writes that "we should see evidence for God in the cosmos, in life on Earth, and in human activities. However, using our own senses and the scientific instruments we have developed to aid those senses, we find no evidence for God or any form of supreme spirit."[7] Stenger reasons that if spirit is real, it would be observable plainly by the senses, even if through the medium of scientific instruments that extend the capacities of the senses for observing data. For those who presume to leave open the possibility of spiritual reality, Stenger's position (and that of many in the Neo-Atheism camp) can be described aptly as a crude materialism that reduces "the real" to atomic matter and energy alone. Yet, what if atomic matter and energy receive their being from a primordial giving that gives exhaustively to the point of abandonment, in turn generating finite, transient, and contingent being? Could there be a flip side to the sensible material world, itself made possible only by an elusive reality of radical self-donation? These are the questions the remainder of this chapter will attempt to investigate in light of Stein's work, which answers these questions in the affirmative.[8]

Before taking a closer look at Stein's account of spiritual being, it is necessary to recall the brilliant insights of Marianne Sawicki in regard to the nature of science and scientific discourse itself. In the sixth chapter of her book *Body, Text, and Science*, entitled "Science as Literacy," Sawicki writes that "science is possible at all, according to [Stein's] account, simply because

---

7. Stenger: *Quantum Gods*, 241.

8. Stein, *Finite and Eternal Being*, 378: "*everything material is built by the spirit*. This means not only that the entire material world was created by the divine spirit but that *every material structure is spiritually filled [geisterfüllt] and informed.*"

the bedrock that grounds all cognition is bodily life, immediately available to consciousness. Life is felt *as* the reciprocal influence and responsiveness of material, sentient, and soulful levels in their openness to intellect."[9] Sawicki depicts Stein as understanding science as a "reading of life." Stein's constant account of the complementarity between body and soul underpins her phenomenological and metaphysical assessment of the human person. While the natural sciences—for example, biology, chemistry, and physics—assume a conscious ground for every manipulation and measurement of atomic matter and energy, phenomenology brings this conscious ground into view as the centerpiece of its scientific enterprise. Because of Stein's holistic account of human being, various forms of reductive anthropologies are assuaged—for example, those that would pretend to reduce human being to a serendipitous unity of chemical processes and that is all. Instead, Stein asserts that all scientific literacy assumes an objective phenomenological alphabet of givenness according to which all data cohere and from which all data proceed. It is this self-donated bodily life of the person that grounds all cognition and thereby serves as the foundation of any and all scientific fields of study.

Sawicki writes elsewhere that "[Stein's] works on empathy and on psychology establish that natural science is indeed a cultural achievement, for it rests on the ability to isolate *caused* data by recognizing and subtracting *motivated* data from raw data. This subtractive literacy is the most basic scientific competence, and it is fundamentally interpersonal."[10] This breathtaking quote unmasks the prevailing modern-day cultural assumption that the natural sciences are robotically precise and entirely impersonal. Rather, Sawicki points out the fact that the natural sciences (and all sciences, for that matter) proceed from the careful task of distinguishing raw observable and measurable data from any motivated data that always precede and follow every experiment. This is to say that every recognized datum is perceived through multivalent layers of interpretation according to a predetermined structural order of meaning by which metacognition positions the newly acquired datum in relation to previous knowledge and presuppositions. It is clear that there is causal motivation for each and every experiment conducted. Every experiment is conducted according to motivative meanings, meaningfulness, intentions, inquiries, and goals. Accurate scientific method implies the intercultural competency of separating wish from fact. "Caused data" are obtained precisely through the process of sifting "raw data" from "motivated data." This "subtractive literacy," as Sawicki

---

9. Sawicki, *Body, Text, and Science*, 222.
10. Ibid., ix–x.

names it, is essential for adequate scientific methodology and is inherently interpersonal. It involves a dialogue between self and others, between self and one's self as another. Phenomenology arrives on the scene as the propitious science of science that possesses the aptitude for deciphering not only the difference between raw data and motivated data, but includes the ability to enact a science of consciousness itself, the science of any and all data or "givens," in a word, phenomenology. Phenomenology claims not only that a science of human subjectivity and intersubjectivity is possible—beyond that of mere epistemology—but that it is necessary as the very intellectual ground upon which all subsequent fields of science rest. Phenomenology has demonstrated sufficiently that all so-called raw data emerge from the givenness of the pure and essential data of consciousness, giving themselves in every act of intuition, that is, in each and every actual phenomenon and in each and every possible phenomenon. It is in the name of the possible—the impossibility of impossibility—and of the God who makes all things possible that Stein recuperates the apodictic basis of objective truth and the eternal nature of possibility that goes before and behind any authentic science worthy of the name.[11]

The remainder of this chapter will approach Stein's account of spiritual being per se according to the following two lines of analysis: (1) the patent cruciform logic of spiritual being as revealed through the life of Jesus Christ, and (2) the pneumatological matrix of Stein's phenomenological ontology. By investigating these two distinct moments in Stein's rational ontology and phenomenology of spiritual being, we will summarize and augment a twenty-first-century account of spiritual being positioned as primordial being, that is, the essence of the essence of being as such.

II. *Kreuzeswissenschaft*: The Science of the Cross

The uncanniness of Christian theology proceeds from its subversive and paradoxical logic—a wisdom that challenges the normative commercial dealings of worldly affairs. Secular politics and economics adhere to so-called natural norms that rule all material interactions. These include win-lose dichotomies, zero-sum games, survival-of-the-fittest mentalities, consumerism, materialism, libido, and the almighty impulse toward self-preservation. Spiritual being, however, acts according to a diametric logic in relation to the normative patterns of being in the world. Paul describes it this way in his First Epistle to the Church in Corinth:

---

11. See Matt 19:26: "Jesus looked at them and said, 'For human beings this is impossible, but for God all things are possible'" (NAB).

> For the word [*logos*] of the cross is folly to those who are perishing, but to us who are being saved it is the power of God. For it is written, "I will destroy the wisdom of the wise, and the cleverness of the clever I will thwart." Where is the wise man? Where is the scribe? Where is the debater of this age? Has not God made foolish the wisdom of the world? For since, in the wisdom of God, the world did not know God through wisdom, it pleased God through the folly of what we preach to save those who believe. For Jews demand signs and Greeks seek wisdom, but we preach Christ crucified, a stumbling block to Jews and folly to Gentiles, but to those who are called, both Jews and Greeks, Christ the power of God and the wisdom of God.[12]

For Paul, from the rational scandal of the Christian proclamation emerges its saving and transformative power. Though it is not readily apparent to conventional dealings of the world, the word of the cross crosses out the calcified logic of egocentrism in order to redeem it. Such scandalizing rationality is not therefore irrational or illogical but proves to be the iconic seedbed of logic from which germinates the entire cosmos.[13] A crucified God-man is the paradigmatic display of the logic of spirit, the logic of divinity. This is a logic according to which greatest are least and least are greatest; the meek inherit the earth; seeds, children, and pearls are paragons of majesty; kings wash the feet of their subjects; wealth is handed over to poverty; divine wisdom is taught in parable; women are on par with men; enemies are loved; sins are forgiven; truth is commonplace; listening is more important than speaking; freedom is accomplished through obedience and responsibility; infirmities are healed; life is found when lost; first are last and last are first; mercy triumphs over judgment; tables of counterfeit wealth are overturned; bread becomes body and wine becomes blood; the accused stands in the place of judgment; power is made perfect in weakness; the dead are raised to new life. In this order, the one who rules is the one who serves and the chief ruler is donned in robes of nakedness, wears a crown woven of thorns, holds a reed as his scepter, and is fastened to his wooden throne with sharp nails. According to this narrative, the unsuspected one turns out to be the hero; the underdog comes to surface as the champion. This logic demands

---

12. 1 Cor 1:18–24 (RSV).

13. Cf. John 1:1–3: "In the beginning was the Word [*logos*], and the Word was with God, and the Word was God. He was in the beginning with God; all things were made through him, and without him was not anything made that was made" (RSV); Col 1:15–17: "He is the image [*eikon*] of the invisible God, the first-born of all creation; for in him all things were created, in heaven and on earth, visible and invisible, whether thrones or dominions or principalities or authorities—all things were created through him and for him. He is before all things, and in him all things hold together" (RSV).

an exchange. To wear the new hat, one must surrender the old. It requires a conversion (*metanoia*) of mind and heart. Without such conversion, this state of affairs is held to be impossible. The logic of the cross is precisely the logic of paradox. For paradox (*para-* [beside/beyond] *doxa* [opinion/glory]) suggests the possibility of unity in plurality, of thinking more than one thing at once, of transcending the banal logic of impersonal pragmatic transaction and mechanistic operation.

In the domain of Christian theology, the logic of paradox is normative. Examples of paradoxical logic abound: the revelation of God as Trinity (three divine Persons, one divine Substance); the simultaneous transcendence and immanence of God; the doctrine of the hypostatic union in which two distinct natures (divine and human) are united in the one eternal divine Person of the Son of God; the justification of sinners; the creation of a universe *ex nihilo* ("from nothing"); the dual phenomenality of the sacrament in which the uncreated is manifest and proclaimed in the created, where the invisible is revealed in the visible, where the eternal Word (*Logos*) of God is audible in silent communion; God is conceived and born of a woman, the *Theotokos*; the eternal Son of God dies on a cross. In his book *Christology: A Biblical, Historical, and Systematic Study of Jesus*, Gerald O'Collins names the foundational principle for understanding the paradoxical ontology of Christ: "the '*communicatio idiomatum*' (interchange of properties). Since they believed that divinity and humanity were/are united in the one person of the incarnate Son of God, Leo the Great and other Church Fathers *predicated* of Christ attributes of one nature even when he was being *named* with reference to his other nature: e.g., 'the Son of God died on the cross,' and 'the Son of Mary created the world.'"[14] Because of the principle of the interchange of properties, it is possible for multiple essences to give themselves within the same being. In the case of Christ, both human and divine essences subsist, even though they are not identical to one another. Similarly, in the Eucharist both human and divine essences subsist through the transubstantiated essences of the eucharistic species. Therefore, according to the interchange of properties, the Eucharist is called "Bread of heaven, saving Drink" and "Body and Blood of Christ." The logic of the sacrament is the same logic as that of the Incarnation, Paschal Mystery, and Trinitarian life: the logic of love.

The logic of love is paradoxical because it enables two to become one while remaining two.[15] It adheres to the pattern of begetting through the

---

14. O'Collins, *Christology*, 172.

15. Gen 2:24: "Therefore a man leaves his father and his mother and clings to his wife, and they become one flesh" (RSV). Cf. Matt 19:5–6; Mark 10:7–8.

process of self-donation. In the case of marriage, for example, husband and wife give themselves to one another through sexual intimacy in order to express their covenantal love and to generate new life. Husband and wife are united in their covenantal relationship through the sacred bond of marriage, but remain distinct individuals all the while their union obtains. Are they one? Are they two? Both. Spousal unity further gives way to the unity of the family through the begetting of offspring. Are they two? Are they three? Both. Jean-Luc Marion argues that the logic of love transcends the principle of sufficient reason according to the following four qualities: certainty, possibility, knowledge of self, and alterity.[16] Authentic love is unconditional insofar as it is the only condition for loving and depends on the alterity of the other for self-knowledge. Otherness is prerequisite for love and is of its very essence. Love is paradoxical because it suggests a singular phenomenon achieved by multiple persons. More than one is necessary for the oneness of love.[17] Love's character is self-donation and self-sacrifice. Without sacrifice of self, there is no love. Giving of self describes the essence of spiritual being.

Edith Stein likewise observes that the order of existence confirms the paradoxical logic of spirit in its natural rhythm of life: "By serving—in self-formation and reproduction—the formation, preservation, and propagation of the species and by consuming itself in these processes, the individual becomes, as it were, a 'victim' of its vital task [*Lebensaufgabe*]."[18] The individual living being exhausts itself in its fundamental tasks of evolutionary becoming and sexual reproduction. To live is to die. In an involuntary way, this pattern is evinced in the natural order of biological life. However, in a voluntary way, this pattern is extended into new possibilities for personal spiritual beings within the vocation to love.[19] Christian revelation purports

---

16. See Marion, "Faith and Reason," in *The Visible and the Revealed*, 153–54.

17. See, for example, Marion, *Erotic Phenomenon*, 46: "To the question 'Does anyone love me?' an answer that is only affirmative is not enough—only the excess that surprises and surpasses would suffice. Thus, to love myself, I would have to go beyond myself, in order to respect the measure of love, which has none. I would demand of myself *an excess of myself over myself*. But who can add one cubit to his stature?"

18. Stein, *Finite and Eternal Being*, 265. Cf. Ps 19:1–4: "The heavens are telling the glory of God; and the firmament proclaims his handiwork. Day to day pours forth speech, and night to night declares knowledge. There is no speech, nor are there words; their voice is not heard; yet their voice goes out through all the earth, and their words to the end of the world" (RSV); and Rom 1:20: "Ever since the creation of the world [God's] invisible nature, namely, his eternal power and deity, has been clearly perceived in the things that have been made" (RSV).

19. See John 15:12–13: "This is my commandment: love one another as I love you. No one has greater love than this, to lay down one's life for one's friends."

that Christ became a victim of his vital task of redeeming the world, allowing his scandalous message to be inscribed in his very flesh.[20] Jesus set forth the contours of self-donating love in his preaching of the realization of the reign of God in which one must lose one's life to save it, in which the least are the greatest, in which masters are servants. It is the subversive poverty and self-divestment of Christ that redeems the world. Stein calls this recurring pattern of self-abnegation the "science of the cross" (*Kreuzeswissenschaft*).[21]

One may object at this point that the preceding prose is stacking the deck, constructing its own illusory logic instead of demonstrating sound evidence of natural logic as that found in mathematics, physics, music, and chemistry.[22] However, the logic of the cross aligns in fact with the logic revealed in nature: exactly through the phenomenon of the double negative.[23] Both grammar and mathematics bear witness to the phenomenon of the double negative wherein a negation of a negation results in a positive outcome. In other words, a debt canceled is a credit gained. The logic of the cross follows this principle: the death of Christ cancels the collective death of humanity, resulting in resurrected life.[24] Suffering becomes the antidote

---

20. See Stein, *Hidden Life*, 104, on the paradoxical logic of Christ's fruitful virginity: "This is why [the Son] came into the world. This is the divine fertility of his eternal virginity: that he can give souls supernatural life." Stein regards the intentional celibacy of Jesus to be integral to his resolute work of redemption. See again ibid., 104: "[Virginity] originates in the depths of the divine life and leads back to it again. The eternal Father in unconditional love has given his entire being to his Son. And just as unconditionally does the Son give himself back to the Father." At the same time, through the mode of celibacy, Jesus reveals himself as bridegroom of the redeemed. See Eph 5:25–27: "Husbands, love your wives, as Christ loved the Church and gave himself up for her, that he might sanctify her, having cleansed her by the washing of water with the word, that he might present the Church to himself in splendor, without spot or wrinkle or any such thing, that she might be holy and without blemish" (RSV).

21. Stein, *Science of the Cross*.

22. See Lonergan, *Method in Theology*, 91: "There is an intelligence, a *logos*, that steers through all things. It is found in god and man and beast, the same in all though in different degrees. To know it, is wisdom." The argument of this entire book hinges on this point. If there is not a common order of logic among things material and spiritual, there is no conversation to be had between the two realms of existence. Cf. Stein, *Finite and Eternal Being*, 112: "The interconnection in which 'everything' subsists in the Logos must be conceived as the *unity of a totality of meaningful existence* [*Sinn-Ganzes*]."

23. The notion of the "double negative" is my own original extrapolation on the pneumatology of Stein.

24. See Chauvet, *Symbol and Sacrament*, 527: "Thus, the Spirit is the agent of a new inscription of the Word. This word, as we have said, is the *Logos* of the cross, that is, the Word of the divine tri-unity as buried in the bitter end of humanity which is death. It is this unheard-of saying of God as God crossed out in the sub-humanity of a 'less than nothing' which the Spirit brings to the Church's body and to each Christian's body."

for suffering.[25] Death is put to death by death.[26] Since the debt of humanity is the same for all, namely, death, the credit allotted to each and every human person is equal, in turn raising all to an equal status and dignity as persons redeemed; no one receives more, no one receives less.[27] Similarly, at the core of the Christian *kerygma* is the radical vocation to discipleship of self-denial: "If any man would come after me, let him deny himself and take up his cross and follow me. For whoever would save his life will lose it, and whoever loses his life for my sake will find it."[28] This great reversal wherein one finds one's life by losing it is the uncanny constellation of Christian existence and attests to the life of spirit. For her part, Stein frames this great reversal in terms of the human will and its response to the contemplation of absolute being:

> And if the intellectual attitude to absolute being is not impeded in its effect, from it will spring the affective [*affektiv*] affirmation of absolute being as well as the practical behavior that it demands. And just as on the part of absolute being annihilating may respond to the negation or turning away [*Abwendung*], so a heightening in being, a raising to a higher mode of being that we call "*grace*," may respond to the turning toward. The negation of the negation in freely turning toward and the heightening in being together yield *justification*.[29]

---

25. See Heb 9:22: "Indeed, under the law almost everything is purified with blood, and without the shedding of blood there is no forgiveness of sins" (RSV).

26. See 1 Cor 15:22, 26: "For as in Adam all die, so also in Christ shall all be made alive . . . The last enemy to be destroyed is death" (RSV); and Song 8:6–7: "Set me as a seal upon your heart, as a seal upon your arm; for love is strong as death, jealousy is cruel as the grave. Its flashes are flashes of fire, a most vehement flame. Many waters cannot quench love, neither can floods drown it" (RSV).

27. See the parable of the Laborers in the Vineyard as related in Matt 20:1–16. Cf. Rom 5:12, 15, 17–19: "Therefore as sin came into the world through one man and death through sin, and so death spread to all men because all men sinned . . . But the free gift is not like the trespass. For if many died through one man's trespass, much more have the grace of God and the free gift in the grace of that one man Jesus Christ abounded for many . . . If, because of one man's trespass, death reigned through that one man, much more will those who receive the abundance of grace and the free gift of righteousness reign in life through the one man Jesus Christ. Then as one man's trespass led to condemnation for all men, so one man's act of righteousness leads to acquittal and life for all men. For as by one man's act of disobedience many were made sinners, so by one man's obedience many will be made righteous" (RSV); and 1 Cor 15:22: "For as in Adam all die, so also in Christ shall all be made alive" (RSV).

28. Matt 16:24–25 (RSV); cf. Luke 14:26–27 and 1 Cor 15:36: "You foolish man! What you sow does not come to life unless it dies" (RSV).

29. Stein, *Potency and Act*, 217.

For Stein, the reality of absolute being beckons to the human subject by virtue of its logical necessity. It is clear to Stein that actuality must precede potentiality, therefore leading to the indisputable logical conclusion of prime act with no admixture of potency, that is, pure act (*actus purus*).³⁰ To deny absolute being, or pure act, is in effect to submit oneself to the throes of annihilation; for absolute being is the wellspring of all being, of all potentiality and actuality. To reject the necessity of absolute being is to take hold of an abysmal lie, plunging oneself headlong into the absurdity of pure nothingness, a degenerative process of deceptive despair. However, as Stein points out, to turn toward absolute being through an affective affirmation of the givenness of absolute being is to experience a heightening of being—an experience to which the language of the Christian Testament refers as grace and justification. By affirming intellectually and spiritually the reality of absolute being, in the name of being held in existence, one receives the gift of life-in-the-spirit (*geistiges Leben*)—a gift that is received to the measure that it is given away.³¹ In other words, as Paul so eloquently puts it in his Second Epistle to the Corinthians, "We have this treasure in earthen vessels, to show that the transcendent power belongs to God and not to us . . . For while we

---

30. As observed in chapter 1, Aristotle says as much in *Metaphysics* 1049b1: "It is clear that actuality is prior to potentiality"; cf. ibid., 1049b25: "For from the potential the actual is always produced by an actual thing"; and 1050a15: "Further, matter exists in a potential state, just because it may attain to its form; and when it exists *actually*, then it is in its form"; and 1050b5: "But actuality is prior in a higher sense also; for eternal things are prior in substance to perishable things, and no eternal thing exists potentially"; and Thomas Aquinas, *Summa contra gentiles* I.16; and Stein, *Finite and Eternal Being*, 225, on three distinct meanings of actuality: "Actuality denotes: 1) the imperfectly actual (i.e., the actual in the process of evolution); 2) the not yet attained end; and 3) the attained end."

31. See Stein, *Potency and Act*, 21: "Can anything uphold [*Halt geben*] my frail [*hinfällig*] being, which touches upon genuine existence [*Existenz*] only from one instant to another, save true being wherein nothing of nonbeing is found and which stands changeless by itself alone, unable to have, nor needing, any other upholding [*Halt*]? And does not the very frailty of my own being lend certainty—not only to the idea but to the reality [*Realität*] of this pure, true, 'absolute [*absolut*]' being? I wish to claim that we must come to this conclusion *by thinking* and that the basis for an argument for God's existence is given in the sheer fact of being. This does not mean, however, that the certainty of the existence of absolute being lies immediately in the sheer fact of being. I *do have* this certainty the moment I *believe*; then I am reaching for the absolute hold [*Halt*] and by it feel myself upheld. But the certainty of faith is blind certainty; believing is not seeing. Indeed, it is doubtless possible to be conscious of God's actual being without making an act of faith in it or even to have faith in but a nonactual way." For Stein, the "spiritual life" (*geistiges Leben*) is synonymous with a Pauline notion of "life-in-the-spirit" insofar as the realm of spiritual life is the authentic realm of freedom, and where the Spirit of the Lord is, there is freedom. Cf. Stein, *Finite and Eternal Being*, 372, and 2 Cor 3:17.

live we are always being given up to death for Jesus's sake, so that the life of Jesus may be manifested in our mortal flesh."[32] This is to say metaphorically that the frailty of human being readily admits a primordial *Gründung*, or foundation, which cannot be attributed reasonably to the frail human being himself. "To give oneself up to death" amounts to an ignition of life-in-the-spirit because spiritual being is that which gives itself up out of the love for the other to the point of abandonment and personal loss, which is at the same time personal gain.[33]

The logic of the cross is the gateway to understanding immaterial spiritual reality. Without comprehending the straightforward logic of the double negative, the essence of spirit will not be recognizable as such, instead remaining at the level of phantasm. However, if one can comprehend the logic of the double negative, and thereby the logic of the cross, it is then possible to intuit the logic of spiritual being. If spiritual being can be demonstrated rationally through metaphysical and phenomenological methods of inquiry, it would be irresponsible to dismiss with haste such a proposal as mere concoction. For a cohesive logic of intelligibility exhibits its self-givenness that is not susceptible to human fabrication or alteration.[34] Rather, that which is truly intelligible proceeds from the givenness of the cosmos itself, in turn received by human understanding in its never-ending search for knowledge and truth.[35] The axiom of truth and intelligibility is not to be found in reducing to static mathematical principles that which gives itself to consciousness, as often happens in the field of analytic philosophy.[36] Instead the axiom gives itself to consciousness while remaining itself to be discovered without ceasing. The cross stands erect as not only the axiom for the inner logic of the cosmos, but as the very *axis mundi* upon which the foundations of creation rest and around which they revolve. The figure of the cross, as will be shown below, signifies the process by which absolute

---

32. 2 Cor 4:7, 11 (RSV).

33. See Galatians 5; Romans 5–7.

34. Cf. Stein, *Finite and Eternal Being*, 61: "Whatever exists in the mode of temporality does not *possess* its being but receives it ever anew as a *gift*."

35. Cf. ibid., 112: "The interconnection in which 'everything' subsists in the Logos must be conceived as the *unity of a totality of meaningful existence* [*Sinn-Ganzes*]."

36. Again, see Balthasar, *Theo-Logic*, 2:35: "Neither 'identity' nor mere 'difference' can, as Blondel has shown, express the structure of real worldly being. A logic built upon such propositions ($A = A$; $A \neq B$) is an abstract residue of the actual constitution of this being and, in that respect, performs at best the secondary function of helping us not to miss the absolute demand for decision within the relative. In the real, difference, the 'other than myself,' is always already overtaken by a third within which I am able to apprehend its otherness in the first place. The antitheses, in fact, are not indifferent but are each different for the other."

being empties itself of itself in perpetual symbiotic gestation, therein actualizing the latent potencies that proceed from its vital center.

III. The Pneumatological Matrix of Edith Stein

Now that a broad context for the relevance of Stein's pneumatology has been established, let us delve into her most compelling texts on this subject. The following three questions will be entertained: (1) How does Stein understand the relationship between matter and spirit? (2) How does spiritual being relate to the logic of the cross? (3) What is the precise relationship between created spiritual beings and uncreated spiritual being?

Stein begins her exposition of the essence of spirit by juxtaposing the non-oppositional realities of matter and spirit. She understands these contrasting yet joint realities as complementary, locating the human person at the intersection of the two. In Stein's theological anthropology, the human person is the only creature that incorporates both material and spiritual realms, thereby warranting the names "spiritual subject" and "person" in her vocabulary.[37] Further, Stein assumes the necessary task of metaphysically dissecting the human person in order to draw the distinction between matter and spirit. This is not merely a psychosomatic distinction, with psyche on one side and body on the other, but it remains necessary to qualify material and spiritual reality, respectively, on the basis of the logic that attends the created order. It is through the methods of phenomenology and metaphysics that Stein provides a sketch of a holistic theological anthropology that reveals the totality of the human person as such. By exerting the phenomenological *epoché* on human personhood, she is able to disclose the intersection at which "we live and move and have our being": the intersection of the spiritual and the material.[38] The provocativeness of Stein's project is in her boldness of working to determine the respective quiditties of matter and spirit.

---

37. Stein, *Potency and Act*, 124, 126: "Finite spirits are not from themselves; that is, they do not come into existence through their own power. But they are 'by themselves [*für sich*]'; that is, by entering into existence they are on their own. 'Hypostasis' is the specific term for this self-constancy [*Selbst-Ständigkeit*]. We shall even go ahead and restrict the word to this purely formal sense that does not include spiritualness, and we shall call what is self-sufficient, insofar as it is something spiritual, a '*person*.' We would therefore have to identify 'spiritual subject' and '*person*.' The person is what *is* spiritual originally . . . spiritual being requires a spiritual substance . . . being a spiritual substance pertains to the person."

38. Cf. Acts 17:28 (RSV).

Stein defines matter as that which fills space, is timebound, and is ontologically *in potentia*.[39] However, from the outset Stein is careful not to position matter as exclusively material since "the 'material [*materiell*]' thing is not purely material and should properly be understood in its makeup first from the viewpoint of spirit."[40] Rather, the material thing in reality is composed at once of matter *and* form—the formal spiritual component being that which gives shape to theoretical prime matter. Matter is extended in space according to its peculiar form. As bearing within itself the utmost potentiality, matter is malleable by its nature and submits to external force from without by adapting to new configurations and structures. While operating on the level of macrophysics, Stein adheres to the insights of evolutionary theory while at the same time refusing to jettison the possibilities of that which would remain incalculable by the most innovative advances in microphysics, namely, the possibilities of spiritual reality.

In contrast (and not incongruous) to material elements, spiritual being for Stein is the antithesis of matter, yet not for that reason opposed to matter:

> The common *what* [of spirit] we may take negatively as immaterial [*immateriell*]; it does not fill space, is not bound to time in the same way as a material *what* is timebound, and lacks sensible qualities. Positively, we may understand the *what* as being illumined, open, and active, or able to be illuminated, open and active. Illumination and openness in the subjective spirit mean becoming conscious of itself [*Seiner-selbst-Bewußtwerden*] and knowing [*Erkennen*], and in the objective spirit they mean becoming transparent [*Durchsichtigwerden*] and becoming-known [*Erkanntwerden*].[41]

Here Stein distinguishes between "objective spirit" and "subjective spirit." The former refers to "the spiritual that exists in dependence upon subjective spirits; it is the world of objective spirit surrounding each person and borne by the person (his 'ideas') or by the objects that are placed in existence by persons and go on existing apart from them; that is, ideas formed into matter (the person's 'works')."[42] In addition, objective spirit refers to the formal

---

39. For a more nuanced discussion of matter, including reference to that which is not limited to atomic physical properties, see chapter 6 of the present study, "The Antinomy of Material Being."

40. Stein, *Potency and Act*, 118.

41. Ibid., 223.

42. Ibid., 222. Cf. Stein, *La estructura de la persona humana*, 213: "no hay ser alguno carente de espíritu. La forma no es espíritu personal, no es alma, pero es sentido, que procede de un espíritu personal y habla a un espíritu personal e interviene en su

component of material being, as cited above. By "subjective spirit" Stein means the self-sufficient, enduring and personal being, whether human, angelic, or divine.[43] Spiritual life is characterized by intentionality, intelligibility, and personhood. Stein conceives the highest form of spiritual living as being stretched between the polarity of subject and object. "To be illumined" metaphorically refers to the capacity of intelligibility—"a knowing and being known."[44] The furthest reaches of this epistemology of spirit are still left to be determined. For it can be argued that any number of animal species can "be known" and "know" one another in the sense of recognition and memory. So what is unique about the knowing at work in subjective spirits, namely, in humans, angels, and (by way of analogy) the Deity?

First, in *Finite and Eternal Being*, Stein expands her definition of the intelligible nature of spirit that had been developed in her previous works. As "non-spatial, invisible, and intangible," spiritual being exhibits a peculiar form of "inwardness":

> While the material thing fills space in such a way that every part of the space completely coincides with a part of the thing—the thing is not wholly at any particular point, but is spread out with its total being and is as such sensorily manifest—*spiritual being is a being-in-itself* [*Sein in sich selbst*]. The spiritual has "inwardness [*Inneres*]" in a sense entirely foreign to spatial material elements. And when the [subjective] spiritual steps forth and communicates itself [*aus sich herausgehen*]—and this it does by diverse ways either by turning toward *objects* (in what Husserl calls the *intentionality* of spiritual life) or by a purely spiritual self-disclosure to other spirits and by a sympathetic entering into them or by forming itself into space (by means of informing

---

contexto vital. Está por lo tanto planamente justificado hablar de 'espíritu objetivo'" ("there is no being at all lacking in spirit. The form is not personal spirit, or soul, but it is sense, which proceeds from a personal spirit and intervenes in its vital context. One is therefore fully justified to speak of 'objective spirit'" [translation my own]). Cf. Stein, *Der Aufbau der menschlichen Person*, 147: "So gibt es kein geistloses Gebilde: geformter Stoff ist durchgeistigter Stoff. Die Form ist nicht personaler Geist, ist nicht Seele: aber sie ist Sinn, aus personalem Geist kommend und zu personalem Geist sprechend, in seinen Lebenszusammenhang eingreifend. So ist es sachlich begründet, wenn wir von ‚objektivem Geist' sprechen."

43. See Stein, *Potency and Act*, 127–28. Cf. Stein, *On the Problem of Empathy*, 96: "We found the spiritual subject to be an 'I' in whose acts an object world is constituted and which itself creates objects by reason of its will. If we consider the fact that not every subject sees the world from the same 'side' or has it given in the same succession of appearances, but that everyone has his peculiar 'Weltanschauung,' we already have a characterization of the spiritual subject."

44. Stein, *Potency and Act*, 113.

the body and by a formative molding of foreign material elements)—it remains nonetheless in itself. From its own vital center it forms itself, unifying everything that it is and everything that it appropriates. And this kind of appropriation is once more an exclusive potentiality of the spiritual.[45]

Spiritual being is being-in-itself for both objective and subjective spirit. Yet it is subjective spirit alone that is capable of intentional and sympathetic self-communication, self-disclosure, and self-informing. Objective spirit, for example, as in the case of ideal objects, is that which is given to human consciousness as the diversified eidetic forms of all beings. But it is subjective spirit that willfully appropriates all objective matter and spirit while remaining itself in its substantial constancy as personal, individuated spiritual being. Unlike material being, spiritual being is totally itself all at once. It is not spread out as a composite form with part of it here, part of it there. It is completely present in its inwardness and extends itself through intersubjective relation rather than through the calculated medium of space. It cannot be measured numerically or described in terms of sense data. Spiritual being is that center of intellectual life from which questions are asked, experiments are performed, and measurements are taken. It signifies the immeasurable one who does the measuring. Spiritual being refers to the consciousness of rational being which is awakened by a world of alterity and asks, "What does it mean?" Apart from spiritual being, no questions are asked and no meanings are recognized and reflected upon. Spiritual being is the sine qua non for intellectual life and interpersonal communication and love. Moreover, subjective spiritual being is distinct from material being in that

> the spiritual cannot take the material into its "interior" [*Inneres*]; the material is what spirit comes up against as against something foreign to itself that it cannot penetrate. Spirit on the other hand is transparent; it is transparent both for itself [*für sich*]—in the form of self-consciousness—and for something else which it takes in by knowing it. Spirit, by knowing, penetrates the other and the other penetrates spirit, for one spirit can displace itself into another spirit. Everything that happens to matter is done to it from outside; it is *passive*. But what happens to spirit comes from inside; it is *activity* [*Tätigkeit*], spirit is active [*aktiv*].[46]

According to Stein, material being is unable to penetrate the spiritual but is banished inexorably from entrance into its interior, and vice versa. This is because spirit, by its very nature, is active, whereas matter, by its very

45. Stein, *Finite and Eternal Being*, 218.
46. Stein, *Potency and Act*, 102.

nature, is passive. Passivity does not generate activity, but activity actualizes that which is passive and *in potentia*. The active transparency of spirit is due first to the basic structure of consciousness, which is from its origin a *tabula rasa*, waiting ready to receive the givenness of the external world or, more precisely, the givenness of spiritual objects. Though perception can be described in terms of empirical biological, chemical, and physical data, objective spiritual forms and subjective spiritual processes remain irreducible to sense data alone. Instead, spiritual being encompasses and informs the so-called natural sciences while at the same time transcending their technological and manipulative purview. It can be said that spiritual being transcends material being insofar as spiritual being informs material being and not vice versa. The intent here is not to call upon transcendence as an escape hatch for the seriousness of scientific inquiry. Rather, spiritual being must be said to be transcendent vis-à-vis material elements insofar as the former, by its very nature, is not bound by the same ontological properties as the latter.

The nature of spiritual being is active and interior. Spiritual being proceeds from a spiritual center, opening from the inside out. Inner life is not detectable or measurable by instruments of outward sense perception because it is not an external kind of being assuming its ontic determinations in three-dimensional space and linear chronological time. Spiritual being, instead, is the very impetus and driving force for all motivation of meaningful personal activity. It acts from the inside out and is accessible to direct thought and analysis only through an abstraction from matter. The methods of metaphysics and phenomenology make such an abstraction possible. Metaphysics probes into the abstract first principles of being and phenomenology brackets all hasty generalizations about reality in order to arrive at the objective givenness of things themselves. If there is an external world of being, there is also an internal one. If matter is the stuff of external being, spirit is the stuff of internal being. A dialectical dance of being is on display within the constant complementary interaction between spirit and matter. Spiritual being is not that which is concealed and ensconced by matter, but it is matter that is generated, made manifest, and illuminated by spiritual being. Spiritual being is not just a different kind of being than material being; spiritual being is the raison d'être of material being. Spiritual being is the medium of all personal animate life and personal communication. Every communication requires a medium or conduit appropriate for its manner of transfer and conduction. All forms of interpersonal communication involve the medium of spiritual being. Most of all, spiritual being is the ontological atrium and hearth of personal love and self-donation.

As infinite spiritual being, divine being creates a plethora of creatures both spiritual and material. According to the cosmology of the Judeo-Christian tradition, as endorsed by Stein, a hierarchy of being obtains:[47]

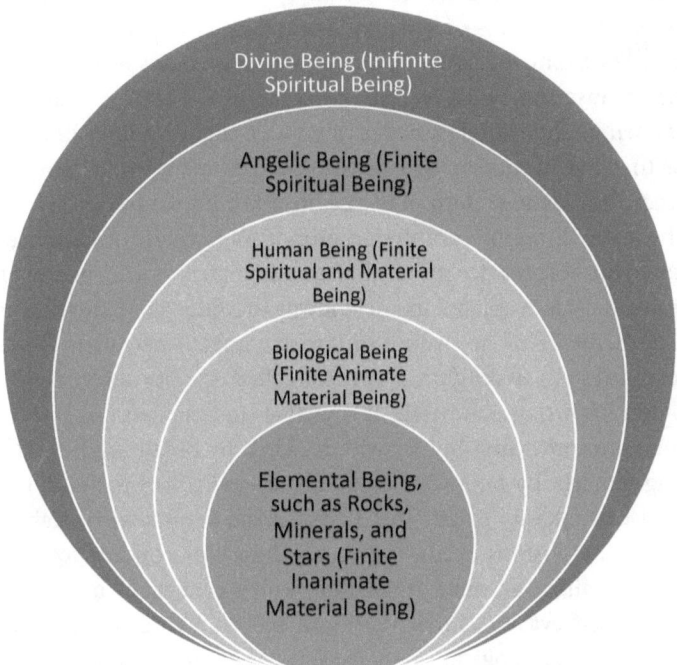

Depicting Judeo-Christian cosmology through concentric circles is apropos because the Dionysian notion of hierarchy suggests ordered, symbiotic, and complementary relationships. Sketching cosmology in this way connotes womb-ness and an interdependent matrix of created being. All that has life and being derives its existence from the spiritual source of existence,

---

47. See Stein, *Finite and Eternal Being*, 600 (endnote 48): "Today the concept of hierarchy, as it is commonly understood, has been narrowed down, so that it designates merely the graduated order of ecclesiastical ranks and functions. The concept has become static, while Dionysius uses it in a prevalently *dynamic* sense. It encompasses that divine *life* which permeates all ranks and 'estates' [*Stande*] of a sacred order which embraces and links heaven and earth"; and ibid., 411–12: "None of the angels is a self-enclosed world apart from the others. They all stand together in the 'realm' of spirits, and all are, each in his apportioned place, integrated in a communal life of a firmly ordered 'statelike structure' [*Staatsgebilde*]. This 'city of God,' as we may well call it since all the life that flows through it and all the rulership that pervades it issue from God, is the ideal archetype of all human community and social order, insofar as these latter rest on a purely spiritual foundation."

namely, divine being that is infinite spiritual being.[48] Each successive concentric circle signifies a hollowing out of being to make room for the other—a process of hospitality precipitated by the generous and graceful divine act of creation. Smaller circles imply less stature of being in relation to larger circles in terms of spiritual being and its varying degrees among creatures. For example, angels have a higher degree of spiritual being than humans because they exist as pure personal forms with no admixture of material being. Their intelligence is of a much higher caliber than humans because they live in much closer proximity to divine life and being.[49] However, according to the pattern of divine humility, higher beings are called to serve the lower. Esteem is granted in proportion to faithful response to the vocation to humble service rather than to ontological stature in and of itself.

Jean-Luc Nancy relates an ancient way to understand creation and the nature of divine being according to Jewish mystical narrative: "There is a very beautiful story in religion, in what is called a mystical form of the Jewish religion known as Kabbalah. It says that god created the world not at all by making something but by withdrawing, by breathing himself in, by emptying himself. By hollowing himself out, god opens the void in which the world can take its place. This is called the *tsim-tsum* in Kabbalah."[50] Visualizing the cosmos according to the figure of concentric circles fits with the Kabbalistic account of creation, which evokes the image of divine withdrawal, self-evasion, inhalation, and self-emptying (*kenosis*), thereby commencing an ontological cavity for created existents to take their place.

---

48. See Stein, *Science of the Cross*, 153–54: "God is pure spirit and the archetype of all spiritual being. So, really, it is only by beginning with God that it is possible to understand what spirit is; however, that means it is a mystery that constantly attracts us because it is the mystery of our own being. We can approach it, in a certain way, since our own being is spiritual. We can also approach it by way of all being to the extent that all being, which has meaning and which can be comprehended intellectually, has something of spiritual being about it. But it reveals itself to a greater depth in proportion to our knowledge of God, though it is never totally unveiled, that is, it never ceases to be mystery."

49. See Pseudo-Dionysius, *The Celestial Hierarchy*, in *Complete Works*, 156–57: "Compared with the things which merely are, with irrational forms of life and indeed with our own rational natures, the holy ranks of heavenly beings are obviously superior in what they have received of God's largess. Their thinking processes imitate the divine. They look on the divine likeness with a transcendent eye. They model their intellects on him. Hence it is natural for them to enter into a more generous communion with the Deity, because they are forever marching towards the heights, because, as permitted, they are drawn to a concentration of an unfailing love for God, because they immaterially receive undiluted the original enlightenment, theirs is a life of total intelligence. They have the first and the most diverse participation in the divine and they, in turn, provide the first and the most diverse revelations of the divine hiddenness."

50. Nancy, *Noli me tangere*, 92.

This hospitable hollowing out of self is the holy inversion of matter by the sacrificial intentionality of spiritual being, for it is not of matter's nature to willfully hollow itself out since matter per se is not conscious and self-determining being. Whereas matter is determined by that with which it comes into local contact, spirit determines itself and its deliberate course of action vis-à-vis the world which it faces. All material existents are imbued in some way with spiritual being inasmuch as they have some peculiar form. However, only those creatures that possess rational being by their very nature are personal spiritual beings, specifically humans and angels. Though human beings are composed at once of spirit and matter, angels are composed of spirit alone. From a phenomenological perspective, angelic beings are certainly a possibility. Yet the question of the necessity of angelic beings is one that must be put to metaphysics.

The above diagram on cosmology suggests that angels are in fact necessary created beings in light of the five distinct tiers or gradations of being. Finite pure spiritual beings must be not only an ontological possibility but an ontological necessity by virtue of the a priori status of form in relation to matter and of the prosopic and kenotic Trinitarian nature of God as revealed in Christ. In his book *The Sacraments: The Word of God at the Mercy of the Body*, Louis-Marie Chauvet writes that "*God reveals God in what is most different from God.*"[51] Eternal being is conveyed through finite being; eternal spiritual being is communicated via finite spiritual being. Without proximate vessels of finite spiritual being (angels), infinite spiritual being would not be able to be intuited by finite spiritual and material beings (humans). Out of divine humility, God shares the plentitude of divine being with creatures and invites them to be channels of divine self-communication, life, power, and grace. God's revelation comes by way of mediation and divinely commissioned emissaries: angels, prophets, sages, rabbis, priests, Sanhedrin, ministers, Church.[52] God is revealed precisely in what is not God within an ontological economy of mediation. While God does communicate with individual human souls in direct and unmediated ways, oftentimes God is experienced through the intercession and mediation

---

51. Chauvet, *Sacraments*, 163. Emphasis in original.

52. See Stein, *Finite and Eternal Being*, 386: "Every member of this hierarchy enjoys the divine prerogative of being a *fellow worker with God* and of allowing God's efficacious action to shine forth luminously in the member's own self." From a soteriological standpoint, this principle of mediation is so vital that the eternal Son of God became flesh in order to accomplish the redemption of humanity and the entire cosmos. See Stein, *Finite and Eternal Being*, 413–14: "[Christ] communicates his divine life to the church through the medium of his human nature. He addresses people in human language, and he has so ordered the institutional organization which serves the communication of his life that his voice can become audible to the soul by way of the body."

of another. God's nature of perfect humility and self-emptying is revealed through humble collaboration of sacred spiritual administration. Divine gifts extend throughout the created order through interpersonal media of ministry. To minister to another is to serve the other in love.[53] In her reflection on angelic being based on her study of Dionysius the Areopagite, Stein writes that angels are "the *bearers* of hierarchical acting, God's messengers, destined to bear the heavenly light throughout creation."[54] Angels serve as divinely ordained envoys of uncreated light (*energeia*, that is, actuality). Translucent to divine light, angels direct this incandescent love of God to one another and to human beings, who are likewise created in the divine image and likeness as personal spiritual beings.[55] Angels are spiritual ministers mediating things of spirit. They are the cosmic conduit for mediating the mysteries of spiritual reality.

---

53. See Stein, *Finite and Eternal Being*, 506–7: "Angels have no soul in the sense of a center of being [*Seinsmitte*] which unfolds in a temporal process of evolution by forming itself into a corporeal body and into a spiritual life. The meaning of their being is no other than the unfolding of what they are (they do not have to become what they are) in a life of pure self-giving to God: in knowledge, love, and service... Their service, however, is an actualization of their love"; Stein, *Finite and Eternal Being*, 391: "[Pure spirits] are *personally free, ministering* spirits who entertain a communion among themselves as well as with all other spiritual personal beings, and they abide in a *realm of giving and receiving love*, a realm the origin and end of which is the triune Godhead"; Stein, *Finite and Eternal Being*, 406: "The nature [*Wesen*] of angels is constantly efficaciously actual by virtue of its fullness of power [*Kraftfülle*] and in a kind of knowledge that is fully alive [*voll-lebendig*] in love and service"; and Gal 5:13–14: "For you were called for freedom, brothers. But do not use this freedom as an opportunity for the flesh; rather, serve one another through love. For the whole law is fulfilled in one statement, namely, 'You shall love your neighbor as yourself'" (NAB). Especially, see Stein, *Finite and Eternal Being*, 416–17.

54. Stein, *Knowledge and Faith*, 86. In this context, Stein also groups consecrated ministers of the Church along with angels suited for the task of bearing the heavenly light throughout creation. Cf. Stein, *Finite and Eternal Being*, 387, 389: "They are called *angels* (i.e., messengers) because they are first illumined by God and then act as mediators in passing on the revealed truths which we human beings receive... angels represent an intermediate link between created pure spirits and human beings."

55. See Stein, *Finite and Eternal Being*, 384: "God is the locus from which all that is goes forth: all natural creatures as well as all the gifts of grace and glory that are poured out over these creatures. All that is was created by the goodness of God, so that it might gain a share in divine being. This is brought about by a ray of light which issues from God and permeates the entire creation, so that every created thing and being may turn toward God and be united with him. But this illumination takes place in hierarchical gradation. The highest creatures, being nearest to God, are the first ones to be illumined by his light, to be permeated by it and turned toward God. But these highest creatures simultaneously incline toward the lower ones in order to let pour forth upon them as much of the fullness they have received as the lower creatures are capable of embracing."

Without spiritual being, material being would not exist because every instance of matter is determined by an antecedent spiritual form. Just as act always precedes potency, spirit always precedes matter. Potential material beings are conceived according to the generating power of actual forms. Aristotle, Thomas, and Stein insist on this point: no matter without form. Form is the actual causal agency of matter without which matter would not assume any coherent and subsistent shape of being. Form is the ontological progenitor and adhesive of beings. Without self-effusive formal being that generates the diversity of forms and figures throughout the universe, there would be no existents to fill the universe. Matter as such is radically potential being because it can assume a countless array of forms. What determines a specific instance of material being is the formal causation of spiritual being. Every material existent exists as a molded being. It is molded according to a predetermined form that lends matter its capacity to adhere and persist in its specific ontic constitution. Formal spiritual being is what imparts being to matter and it is divine being that gives being to all finite existents.

Following the general contours of the logic of the cross detailed above, Stein's pneumatology can be mapped directly onto such paradoxical logic. Stein writes that "the material element must be transformed in order to be revitalized. 'Out' of something, something else has to come to be. That which was there prior to the transformation is there no longer as the same that it was before. Nor has it been reduced to nothing. It has acquired a new being—a being 'in a new form'—in the thing into which it has been transformed."[56] This is the case with organic evolution and growth that is patently observable in the natural world. "The material element must be transformed in order to be revitalized." The seed is transformed in order for the stalk to sprout forth; the cell is transformed in order for the process of mitosis to occur; the person is transformed in order for a community to grow. Stein recognizes the evolutionary character of living existence whereby "the individual becomes, as it were, a 'victim' of its vital task [*Lebensaufgabe*]."[57] This process in which life begets life displays the logic of the double negative—the logic of the cross. A seed dies in order to redeem the hidden life of the sapling; a cell dies in order to call forth the entelechy of the full organism; an individual ego dies in order to participate in radical solidarity with a communion of other selves. The silhouette of the life of spiritual being serves as the impetus and driving force of all such life forms that become victims of their vital tasks. In sum, this is none other than the movement of redemption which effects an irrevocable transfiguration

---

56. Stein, *Finite and Eternal Being*, 215.
57. Ibid., 265.

of being: materiality yields to the redemptive work of divine Spirit. Spiritual being functions as the vital template for created being. Self-giving proves to be the primordial language of the cosmos, even when spoken from the heart of the rebellious cosmic resistance to such a noble vocation.

It is especially the work of her colleague, Hedwig Conrad-Martius (1888–1966), that informs Stein's intuitive presentation of spiritual life. In both *Potency and Act* and *Finite and Eternal Being*, Stein is found quoting extensively from the work of Conrad-Martius. One such key passage, concerning pneumatology, can be found in the course of Stein's depiction of the basic forms of actual being (as opposed to passive being). In contrast to corporeal being alone, Conrad-Martius describes spiritual being and the spiritual potential for human being as follows:

> On the level of spiritual being, however, a thus substantiated corporeal entity is in turn capable of transcending itself in a selfless and non-fixed [*unfixiert*] manner and—purified and freed from the mass of the limited self—to "give itself freely" to others in vital participation ... The supra-earthly, however, is the realm of fully unfolded being—a being which is actual through and through and thus abiding in the splendor of perfect selflessness (conjoined with the highest possible plentitude of essential reality!), lightness, and brightness.[58]

Conrad-Martius points to the possibility of a corporeal entity transcending itself, that is, exceeding its limits toward a kind of existence that gives itself over for the good of another. This mode of existing she calls "vital participation," signifying the gift of life that is enacted when one person gives herself over for another. This is a free and intentional giving, not abusively coerced or forced. Conrad-Martius identifies this kind of life-in-the-spirit as "supra-earthly," "the realm of fully unfolded being," "abiding in the realm of perfect selflessness, lightness, and brightness." This kind of existence indeed defies the worldly logic of commerce, namely, a what's-in-it-for-me? mentality. Conrad-Martius's employment of the metaphorical terms "lightness" and "brightness" suggests the radiance and luminosity of spiritual life that shines to the degree that it gives itself away. Spiritual being is intellectually and emotively translucent to interpersonal relationships, sense data, and intellectual objects, such as meanings, ideas, and cognitive signification. It

---

58. Ibid., 245. Cf. Stein, *Potency and Act*, 237: "Conrad-Martius stresses (speaking of the meaning of the word '*spiritus*') that the essence of what is spiritual is that it breathes, spreads its essence about itself as an aura [*Hauch*]. This 'breathing out, exhaling' or 'spiriting [*Geisten*]' wherein the be-ing gives itself away by radiating, corresponds to 'breathing in, inhaling' or a 'bodying [*Leiben*]' wherein the be-ing takes possession of its very fullness and conserves itself."

is a pattern of being observable in the nonpersonal natural order as well. For example, celestial luminaries share their light to the measure that they expend their energy and material being. Stars light up the nighttime sky at the price of their subsistent being along specific spatial coordinates. Stars shine to the level that they die. As applied to personal spiritual creatures, this is a "supra-earthly" way of being inasmuch as concern for self-preservation of the individual is displaced by concern for the welfare of the other person who faces me. My resources and my very being are unfolded and emptied outward for the sake of the other. The Christian Testament refers to this movement as love (*agape*) and self-emptying (*kenosis*).[59] Self-donation is symbolized by the cross, which stands as witness to the demanifestation of a worldly presence in favor of a presence of absence that can be called properly spiritual being.[60]

Building on the pneumatological proposal of Conrad-Martius, Stein contends that "being open for oneself and for what is other is the highest and hence also the most proper form of spirit whereto all other spiritual

---

59. For example, see John 15:12–13: "This is my commandment, that you love [*agapaō*] one another as I have loved you. Greater love [*agape*] has no man than this, that a man lay down his life for his friends" (RSV); and Phil 2:5–8: "Have this mind among yourselves, which was in Christ Jesus, who, though he was in the form of God, did not count equality with God a thing to be grasped, but emptied himself [*kenoō*], taking the form of a servant, being born in the likeness of men. And being found in human form he humbled himself and became obedient unto death, even death on a cross" (RSV).

60. See Chauvet, *Symbol and Sacrament*, 62–63: "In its role as 'shepherd of Being' (and not 'rulers of entities'), humankind has the vocation to remain vigilant against the myriad ruses which would rob it of a *distress* it is only too eager to cast off. . . . Against this supreme distress—which is the lack of distress—the absence of the god, by maintaining the distress in which humans can live and the god can come forth, is 'not a deficiency.' Emptiness is not nothing; *the absence is precisely the place from which humans can come to their truth* by overcoming all the barriers of objectifying and calculating reason. This task is burdensome. Is there anything more difficult than to hold oneself in such a 'mature proximity to the absence of the god,' than *to agree to this 'presence of absence'*? Moreover, this is a test that we do not choose for ourselves, embarked as we are on life, because the God whose absence we let die revives this absence within us as an excruciatingly painful wound." Concerning the claim that spiritual being shall not be present in the same elemental fashion as material being, but only attested to by self-donating corporeal existence, see ibid., 529: "The *sign* of the letter comes into its truth when it becomes the *symbol* of the body: Christ cannot be announced unless the letter of the cross, which the apostolic tradition deposited as a testament in the Book, pervades believers' existences and becomes a testimony." In other words, the logic of the cross, which signifies life-in-the-spirit (or personal spiritual being), is revealed in and through the self-emptying corporeal existence of those persons who willfully embrace the vocation to living a life of self-donating love. Cf. Stein, *Finite and Eternal Being*, 244: "And so we see that in its essence each and every thing bears within itself its own mystery and thereby points beyond itself."

being harks back."[61] Spiritual openness implies the ontological character of rational consciousness, even if *in potentia*, disabled or underdeveloped. It is that which is specific to personal spiritual beings, whether human, angel, or divine. Spiritual openness signifies the capacities of culture and the immediate vocation to love and responsibility. In arguably her most eloquent passage concerning the exact nature of spiritual being, Stein writes that it "remains 'within itself' while going out of itself. This going-out-of-itself pertains to the spiritual essentially. It is indicative of its being completely 'selfless,' not indeed in the sense of having no self but rather in the sense of a total self-surrender without any loss of self, a self-giving in which the spiritual reveals itself completely."[62] To recall from above, this complete self-revelation of spirit constitutes its transparency and luminosity. Instead of a hard, opaque, and dense material body that protrudes in space and time, spiritual being (by its very nature) is translucent and imperceptible in its essence by materially constructed senses, namely, sight, hearing, smelling, taste, and touch. Therefore, the nature of spirit can be said to be unnaturally natural, that is, supernatural, and thereby immaterial and, as such, the necessary inversion of materiality and autonomous self-preservation.[63] In revealing itself completely (to the point of abandonment!), spiritual reality is the absolute kenotic inversion of material reality, therein disclosing the intuition of the life-giving principle and substructure of the entire cosmic order.[64] The logic of spiritual being coincides with the logic of the cross—the

61. Stein, *Potency and Act*, 255; cf. ibid., 254: "'Being open' means being able to engage what is other than oneself, stand over against it, turn toward it intentionally."

62. Stein, *Finite and Eternal Being*, 360. Cf. Stein, *Self-Portrait in Letters*, 318 (letter to Sr. Agnella Stadtmüller, March 30, 1940): "Should we strive for perfect love, you ask? Absolutely. For this we were created. [Perfect love] will be our eternal life, and here we have to seek to come as close to it as possible. Jesus became incarnate in order to be our way. What can we do? Try with all our might to be empty: the senses mortified; the memory as free as possible from all images of this world and, through hope, directed toward heaven; the understanding stripped of natural seeking and ruminating, directed to God in the straightforward gaze of faith; the will (as I have already said) surrendered to God in love."

63. This idea of "inversion of materiality and autonomous self-preservation" is my original extension of Stein's notion of the self-surrendering and self-giving character of spirit. While Stein herself does not use the language of "inversion" per se, the description of spiritual being as an inversion of the natural attitude and of the natural way of being in the world can be inferred justly by Stein's antithetical juxtaposition of spirit and matter.

64. Again, the description "absolute kenotic inversion of material reality" is my original augmentation of Stein's pneumatology. This follows Stein's logic of "the negation of the negation." Cf. Stein, *Finite and Eternal Being*, 217: "And if the intellectual attitude to absolute being is not impeded in its effect, from it will spring the affective [*affektiv*] affirmation of absolute being as well as the practical behavior that it demands.

logic of the double negative. According to this logic inscribed within the cosmic order, life begets life as death succumbs to death. A recapitulation of transformed material reality transpires through its death and ensuing transfiguration of being. Resurrected life is the teleology of spirit—an existence that began as active spiritual being, then in turn gave itself over in the extension of a created material (though in-spired) universe *in potentia*, and finally consummates the movement of self-emptying through a return of fully actualized being in the framework of spiritual and redeemed incarnated existence.[65] Stein attributes this creative movement to the necessary origin of all actualized being: pure act, or pure spirit, which/who merits the name God. God, for Stein, according to the nature of spirit, assumes a Trinitarian form:

> The spirit in its purest and most perfect actualization is found in the total self-giving of the divine Persons, a self-giving in which each person totally divests itself of its nature [*Wesen*] and yet totally retains its nature, in which each person is totally within itself and totally in the others. The triune Deity *is* the authentic "realm of the spirit" and is thus the "supernatural" as such. And all the spirituality or spiritual endowment of creatures denotes an elevation or a "being-lifted-up" into this realm, albeit in varying modes and degrees.[66]

And just as on the part of absolute being annihilating may respond to the negation or turning away [*Abwendung*], so a heightening in being, a raising to a higher mode of being that we call 'grace,' may respond to the turning toward. The negation of the negation in freely turning toward and the heightening in being together yield *justification*." Whereas material reality is concerned solely with its self-preservation and maintenance, spiritual being is intent on inverting this brute impulsive behavior by the power of intentional self-donating love for another. In the latter, self-preservation is transfigured into other-preservation and self-maintenance is transformed into self-divestment.

65. This idea is my own. It suggests additional soteriological implications of Stein's pneumatology. See Rom 8:22–23: "We know that the whole creation has been groaning with labor pains together until now; and not only the creation, but we ourselves, who have the first fruits of the Spirit, groan inwardly as we wait for adoption as sons, the redemption of our bodies" (RSV); and 1 Cor 15:42–49: "So is it with the resurrection of the dead. What is sown is perishable, what is raised is imperishable. It is sown in dishonor, it is raised in glory. It is sown in weakness, it is raised in power. It is sown a physical body, it is raised a spiritual body. If there is a physical body, there is also a spiritual body. Thus it is written, 'The first man Adam became a living soul'; the last Adam became a life-giving spirit. But it is not the spiritual which is first but the physical, and then the spiritual. The first man was from the earth, a man of dust; the second man is from heaven. As was the man of dust, so are those who are of the dust; and as is the man of heaven, so are those who are of heaven. Just as we have borne the image of the man of dust, we shall also bear the image of the man of heaven" (RSV).

66. Stein, *Finite and Eternal Being*, 360.

While Stein is careful to delineate between the "truths of faith," the "truths of reason," and the "data of sense perception," she nevertheless attempts to reconnoiter the insights to be gleaned from the "dark light" of divine revelation.[67] According to the Christian witness, via the *analogia entis*, God is revealed as one in the divine act of spiritual being—pure act—yet three persons. Such a configuration fully performs the perfect actualization of spirit: an eternal total self-giving of spiritual persons—a perpetual divestment of oneself for the others while remaining oneself uniquely and distinct from the others. Though the human person is not infinite "pure spirit" as is God, or even a finite pure spirit as in the case of angels, human beings have the capacity to partake of infinite pure spiritual being and to undergo radical self-transformation in the form of kenotic interpersonal love, à la the pattern of divine love.[68] Though human life is open to the possibility of matriculating into the communion of life-in-the-spirit, at best it only can approximate the divine archetype:

> God is pure spirit and the archetype of all spiritual being. So, really, it is only by beginning with God that it is possible to understand what spirit is; however, that means it is a mystery that constantly attracts us because it is the mystery of our own being. We can approach it, in a certain way, since our own being is spiritual. We can also approach it by way of all being to the extent that all being, which has meaning and which can be comprehended intellectually, has something of spiritual being about it. But it reveals itself to a greater depth in proportion to our knowledge of God, though it is never totally unveiled, that is, it never ceases to be a mystery.[69]

---

67. See ibid., 27: "We accept faith on the testimony of God himself and thereby gain a certain knowledge without, however, obtaining a thorough comprehension. In other words, we cannot accept the truths of faith as evident in themselves as we do in the case of the necessary truths of reason or of the data of sense perception; nor can we deduce them logically from certain self-evident truths. This is one reason why faith is called a 'dark light.'"

68. See Stein, *Potency and Act*, 256: "Man, the whole individual of body and soul, is raised above the animal and so above himself insofar as he is animal, by something that is in him, namely, his personally shaped I with its actuality of understanding and will as well as with the potentiality belonging to understanding and will, his 'spirit [*Geist*]' ('*mens*,' distinguished from '*intellectus* [intellect]' and '*anima* [soul]'), meaning the highest form of spiritualness, yet in this sense still not 'pure spirit' since it is immersed in and bound up with that whole of body and soul which is not transparent to itself or free. Nor is it unlimitedly transparent to the spirit, nor can it be unlimitedly mastered by spirit."

69. Stein, *Science of the Cross*, 153–54.

Stein insists that one must begin with understanding God as pure spirit—more precisely, a communion of spirit—if one is to understand spiritual being at all. The dynamic of spirit, while proceeding from the innermost core of one's being, is enacted from an inwardness even more inward than one's innermost self.[70] This double inwardness could be described as an inner outerness inasmuch as it is the other (most especially the divine other) who provokes the movement of self-donating life-in-the-spirit.[71] Such an inner outerness remains mysterious since it is never fully disclosed, but can be attested only by the corporeal vanishing activity of life-in-the-spirit. A trace of presence is detectable at the liminal threshold of absence.[72] To understand correctly the nature of spiritual being, one must begin and end with contemplation of divine being, pure actuality and the uncreated Spirit of created spiritual being. Moreover, understanding divine being through Christian revelation illuminates the mystery of spiritual being as personal self-giving and interpersonal communication. Once again, for the goodness and actuality of personal self-giving and interpersonal communication to

---

70. See Teresa of Avila, *Interior Castle*, 48–49: "These interior matters are so obscure for our minds . . . You mustn't think of these dwelling places in such a way that each one would follow in file after the other; but turn your eyes toward the center, which is the room or royal chamber where the King stays"; Rom 8:26–27: "Likewise the Spirit helps us in our weakness; for we do not know how to pray as we ought, but the Spirit himself intercedes for us with sighs too deep for words. And he who searches the hearts of men knows what is the mind of the Spirit, because the Spirit intercedes for the saints according to the will of God" (RSV); and the *interior intimo meo* of Augustine, *Confessions*, 43 (III.6.11): "In seeking for you I followed not the intelligence of the mind, by which you willed that I should surpass the beasts, but the mind of the flesh. But you were more inward than my most inward part [*interior intimo meo*] and higher than the highest element within me."

71. The notions of "double inwardness" and "inner outerness" are my own, not terms from Stein's corpus. The "provocation of the other" mentioned here is inspired by the work of Emmanuel Levinas. "Inner outerness" refers to the self-giving motion of spiritual being due to the demands of the other from without who summons a person to the performance of becoming a gift of self. Also, see Tillich, *Systematic Theology*, 3:111–12, for a similar understanding of displacement of human spirit by divine Spirit: "If the divine Spirit breaks into the human spirit, this does not mean that it rests there, but that it drives the human spirit out of itself. The 'in' of the divine Spirit is an 'out' for the human spirit. The spirit, a dimension of finite life, is driven into a successful self-transcendence; it is grasped by something ultimate and unconditional. It is still the human spirit; it remains what it is, but at the same time, it goes out of itself under the impact of the divine Spirit. 'Ecstasy' is the classical term for this state of being grasped by the Spiritual Presence. It describes the human situation under the Spiritual Presence exactly."

72. See Chauvet, *Symbol and Sacrament*, 58: "Presence-as-trace; trace of a passing always-already past; trace thus of something absent. But still trace, that is, the sign of a happening which calls us to be attentive to something new still to come."

be experienced in finite temporal instances, such goodness must exist actually from eternity in order to be awakened from potentiality to actuality in the realm of creaturely becoming. Spiritual being acts according to the logic of the double negative by negating the negative concupiscence of self-preservation, self-assertion, and lustful domination (the *libido dominandi* of Augustine).[73] Instead of living according to destructive concupiscence, spiritual being takes the form of restorative self-donation, self-divestment, and erotic charity. Spiritual being is other-centered and other-inspired.

IV. Conclusion

The foregoing analysis has presented Stein's phenomenological and metaphysical approach to the question of spiritual being as an adequate response to the contemporary tendency to dismiss spirit from an empirical ontology. Since the time of the Western Enlightenment, the rational obsession with the manipulation and domination of nature has run its course and has found itself in error. To demand that spiritual being show its face in the manner of material being is to demand that a square peg insert itself into a round hole. An annihilation of spiritual being in the name of material being is as illogical as it is conceited. Spiritual being as such must subsist by its very nature as spiritual being. Likewise, material being as such must persist necessarily as material, though imbued with and dependent upon the respective spiritual forms that make material being possible.

As Stein argues above, spiritual being as such resists becoming converted into material being. Spiritual being transcends the scope of mass/energy and its predictable properties. In the same way, material being is unable to penetrate the transparency of spirit. Nonetheless, Stein has shown both material and spiritual being to coexist as complementary counterparts in the created order. In light of Christian philosophy, material reality is viewed as an essential component of the drama of salvation: material reality undergoes a redemptive inversion according to the logic of the double negative, the logic of the cross. Material reality is the soteriological substance that bears the passive potential of vital transfiguration. This is not to say that material being is annihilated and only pure spiritual being remains. Rather, it means that material being is to be transfigured by spiritual being,

---

73. See Augustine, *City of God*, 3 (Book I, Preface): "Thus, when the nature of the work here undertaken requires us to say something of it, and as occasion arises, we must not pass over in silence the earthly city also: that city which, when it seeks mastery, is itself mastered by the lust for mastery [*dominandi libido dominatur*] even though all the nations serve it."

that is, spiritualized. Christ crucified and resurrected from the tomb is what spiritualized matter looks like. The lives of the saints, too, demonstrate spirit incarnate. A consistent pattern of living characterizes the reality of spiritual being as that which puts the body at the service of the intentions of the spirit, even to its pain and demise, but above all, for the sake of its regeneration.

As human beings, we exist at the intersection of the material and spiritual realms, therein tasked with the work of corporeal kenosis, one-for-the-other.[74] As human beings we have the gifted ability to give over our bodies to contribute to the good of the other. This is not merely an exercise in sadomasochism in which "spirit" could be regarded as a code word referring to a psychological disorder. On the contrary, corporeal kenosis is a technical description of real life scenes such as a mother nursing her child, a father taking his ailing child to the hospital in the middle of the night, a man fasting in spiritual solidarity and prayer for his brethren across the globe who have nothing to eat—even more, "to give to the other taking the bread out of my own mouth, and making a gift of my own skin."[75] These real-life examples (and countless others) demonstrate the contingencies of material being on spiritual being concerning the actualization of heroic virtue in and through the flesh. The body is naturally opposed to acute pain and suffering. It is naturally opposed to its being compromised for some immaterial aspiration. Only spirit is able to forsake its own good for the good of another; only spirit recognizes the need of the other that beckons to me with a volume that overwhelms my miserable self-interests; only spirit provokes spirit to live as spirit and not as flesh.[76]

74. See Stein, *On the Problem of Empathy*, 113: "The world of the spirit . . . is no less real or knowable than the natural world. Because man belongs to both realms, the history of mankind must take both into consideration. It should understand the forms of the spirit and of spiritual life and ascertain how much has become reality." The term "corporeal kenosis" is my original invention. This term encompasses both the life-giving body (*Leib*) of spirit and the lifeless material body (*Körper*) apart from spirit. "Corporeal kenosis" calls to mind the futility of the material body apart from spirit as well as the voluntary self-emptying that characterizes spiritual life.

75. Levinas, *Otherwise than Being*, 138. Cf. ibid., 159, 182: "The equality of all is borne by my inequality, the surplus of my duties over my rights. The forgetting of self moves justice . . . It is the longest breath there is, spirit. Is man not the living being capable of the longest breath in inspiration, without a stopping point, and in expiration, without return? To transcend oneself, to leave one's home to the point of leaving oneself, is to substitute oneself for another."

76. Cf. Rom 8:1–17. The phenomenon recounted throughout the Christian Testament of demonic possession, and even the notion of "evil or unclean spirits," can be interpreted as the disordered and sociopathic activity of spiritual beings who forsake their true nature of self-donation in favor of a cancerous craving for suicidal carrion. Those persons found possessed by demons in the Christian Testament are described as exhibiting self-mutilating and sociopathic behavior—a way of acting that is directly

At the close of this chapter on the pneumatology of Edith Stein, there lingers the temptation to interpret Stein's work simply as a renewal of Neo-Platonism that calls for a shedding of corporeal reality in favor of participating in the incorporeal realm of spirit. This temptation is a serious one that challenges explicit concentration on spiritual being as opposed to material being. However, chapter 6 of *Human and Divine Being* will be devoted exclusively to material being in relation to spiritual being. By dedicating an entire chapter to material being, following three chapters discussing the human soul, we hope to represent adequately Stein's holistic ontology that regards material being as good in itself and complementary to spiritual being. Even though she leans toward Platonism in her later work, Stein in no way tries to suggest a blanket Platonic interpretation of reality or Christian faith.[77] Stein places the accent on the Platonic trajectory of thought, all the while being informed by Aristotle and Thomas, because she realizes, in the end, that it is spiritual being that causes and perfects material being. Spiritual being and material being are not on par with one another. Higher than material being stands spiritual being inasmuch as actuality always precedes potentiality. Material being is contingent on the formal actuality of spiritual being and not vice versa. The caducity of material being requires a kind of being that is not subject to the transitoriness of becoming. Ultimately, as we have seen, Stein identifies divine being as that pure actuality from which all transitory finite existents derive their being, both mass/energy (in its actual formal constitution; it would not exist otherwise) and finite spiritual beings.

Having established the peculiar nature and sine qua non role of spiritual being as such, we are positioned now to turn our attention to the reality

---

counter to life-in-the-spirit. This anti-spiritual behavior is portrayed as being instigated by the disordered spirits themselves. Cf. Mark 1:21–28, 32–34; 3:11; 5:1–20 (see here an instance of demonic spirits entering swine and provoking them to suicide); 6:13; 9:14–29. The phenomenon of suicide may mark the great imposture of the self-emptying nature of spiritual being. Instead of following the logic of the double negative, wherein self-emptying overturns death and self-gratification by a kind of dying to self, suicide adheres to the logic of the solitary negative: annihilation and destruction are its barren fruits rather than life and regeneration. Of course, one must take into consideration the frequent impact of involuntary mental illness when considering the topic of suicide with greatest sensitivity and responsibility.

77. See Stein, *Finite and Eternal Being*, xxxi: "The question may perhaps be asked why the author [that is, Stein, speaking of herself] has followed the lead of Plato, Augustine, and Duns Scotus rather than that of Aristotle and Thomas. The obvious answer is that she did indeed start out from Thomas and Aristotle. The fact that the actual discussion led in the end to certain goals which might have been reached faster and with greater ease if a different point of departure had been chosen, constitutes no sufficient reason to disavow the way which has been followed. The very difficulties and handicaps which had to be overcome on this way may prove of advantage to others."

of the human soul as a type of finite spiritual being. Chapters 3 through 5 will examine, in turn, the ontological composition of the human soul and its phenomenological revelation within human experience. It will be demonstrated that the soul is the lynchpin of Stein's theological anthropology and, therefore, the spiritual conduit of divine intimacy.

3

The Soul as the Form of the Body

May the God of peace himself make you perfectly holy and may you entirely, spirit, soul, and body, be preserved blameless for the coming of our Lord Jesus Christ.

—1 Thessalonians 5:23 (NAB)

I. The Possibility of the Human Soul

WHAT EXACTLY IS THE human soul? More precisely, what do we mean when we use the term *soul*? To what reality does the word *soul* refer? In the twenty-first century can we give an adequate scientific account of the human soul? It is these questions that have led to the present study on the notion of the human soul within the theological anthropology of Edith Stein. Upon sifting through Stein's literary corpus, it is abundantly clear that she views the human soul to be the centerpiece of the human person. In attempting "to draw the picture of the human being," the soul assumes the focal position within her two most developed works, namely, *Potency and Act* and *Finite and Eternal Being*.[1] Further, given the backdrop of the Judeo-Christian tradition, concomitant with mystical Carmelite spirituality, the uptake of the human soul's prominence vis-à-vis divine love is a natural move for Stein. However, is such a move warranted in the materialist context of twentieth-century (and now twenty-first-century) philosophy and

---

1. Stein, *Finite and Eternal Being*, 447.

theology? Does the concept of soul still hold water today or is it a term we find virtually meaningless?

Given the prevalent scientific worldview of postmodernity, the concept of the human soul has little traction in the sphere of public discourse. In fact, Stein observes as much in her introduction to *Finite and Eternal Being* as she writes of "the amazing feat which the psychology of the nineteenth century performed when it simply discarded the concept of the soul."[2] Similar to the concept of spirit, the human soul—as a category of spiritual being—has been censured effectively by contemporary critical thought. At best the soul is regarded as a symbolic term signifying the host of neurological processes in a human subject, and at worst it is despised as a heavily laden religious term that died a slow death more than a century ago. If this is indeed the case, why would Stein want to attempt to recuperate the suspicious terminology of *anima forma corporis*? The answer is to be found in Stein's peculiar brand of methodology. In fashioning a tensive dialectic between Husserlian phenomenology and Thomistic metaphysics, Stein attempts the impossible: to construct a theological anthropology that is informed at once by pure description and *sacra scientia*. She claims the impossible to be possible in the name of *philosophia perennis* ("perennial philosophy") and with the confidence of "the spirit of genuine philosophy alive in every true philosopher, in anyone who cannot resist an inner need to search out the λόγος [*logos*, mind, reason] of this world, its *ratio* (as Thomas translated the word)."[3] It is in *philosophia perennis* that Stein finds the warrant to bring together such diverse methods in such close proximity, allowing them to inform one another. Moreover, it is precisely through the rapprochement between these distinct methods that Stein places her hope in securing an accurate depiction of the psychosomatic unity of the human person. To weave together a theological anthropology via one of the two methods alone would be to end up with a truncated representation of the being that is human. To neglect the ongoing developments in philosophical method would amount to an intellectual stagnation, while to pretend that new innovations entirely supplant the wisdom of past ages would be rashly pretentious. Edith Stein "is like the head of a household who brings from his storeroom both the new and the old."[4]

---

2. Ibid., 19.

3. Stein, *Knowledge and Faith*, 6–7: "The question then arises whether the reborn philosophy of the Middle Ages and the newly created philosophy of the twentieth century can possibly find a common meeting ground in the one broad river bed of the *philosophia perennis*."

4. Matt 13:52 (NAB).

In contrast to modern ideological (and even intellectual) currents that would propose to dispense of the facticity of the human soul, Stein attempts to submit an account of the human soul that is in line with Catholic belief and coherent with the latest advances in scientific understanding. While this text, for the sake of brevity, must gloss over a thorough analysis of the concept of the human soul throughout the Judeo-Christian tradition, may it suffice to reference an emblematic excerpt from the Ecumenical Council of Vienne (1311–12) on the question of the soul in order to orient the present discussion in the direction of Stein's oeuvre. At the top of the list of the Decrees from this Council is one that seeks to confirm the orthodox teaching that the eternal Son of God assumed the fullness of human nature, body and soul, at his conception in the womb of his virgin Mother:

> Adhering firmly to the foundation of the catholic faith, *other than which*, as the Apostle testifies, *no one can lay*, we openly profess with holy mother church that the only begotten Son of God, subsisting eternally together with the Father in everything in which God the Father exists, assumed in time in the womb of a virgin the parts of our nature united together, from which he himself true God became true man: namely the human, passible body and the intellectual or rational soul truly of itself and essentially informing the body.[5]

Stemming historically from the Apollinarian controversy of the fourth century, in which Apollinaris of Laodicea maintained that the Logos of God took the place of a natural human soul of the body in the Incarnation, the Council of Vienne was concerned, in contrast, with upholding a hylomorphic conception of human nature and the doctrine that the humanity of Christ includes the assumption of the human soul as well as the body. Just as the Council of Ephesus (AD 431) confessed "our lord Jesus Christ, the only begotten Son of God, perfect God and perfect man of a rational soul and body," the Council of Vienne confirms this confession and further defines the hylomorphic nature of the human being:

> Moreover, with the approval of the said council, we reject as erroneous and contrary to the truth of the catholic faith every doctrine or proposition rashly asserting that the substance of the rational or intellectual soul is not of itself and essentially the form of the human body, or casting doubt on this matter. In order that all may know the truth of the faith in its purity and all error may be excluded, we define that anyone who presumes

---

5. Tanner, *Decrees of the Ecumenical Councils*, 1:360. Cf. Denzinger and Schönmetzer, *Enchiridion symbolorum*, 900/480.

henceforth to assert, defend or hold stubbornly that the rational or intellectual soul is not the form of the human body of itself and essentially, is to be considered a heretic.[6]

Indebted to Scholastic theology and the renewal of Aristotelian philosophy, this text affirms the metaphysical being of the soul as the essential form of the body. Without implying a crass dualism, the Council of Vienne transposes the vital biblical language of "soul" (*nephesh*, *psyche*) into its own historical intellectual context—*anima forma corporis*—thereby demonstrating the continuity of the Judeo-Christian tradition and the teaching authority of the Church. In an era when many were denying the plausibility of the concept of the human soul, Edith Stein not only concured with the fourteenth-century Decree of the Council of Vienne, she extended its application into a twentieth-century tonality. In the space below, we will trace the contours of Stein's theological anthropology that are found to be in harmony with Catholic teaching on the human soul, as well as the strictures of phenomenological investigation. The chapter will be subdivided according to the following four points of analysis: (1) a brief explanation of Aristotle's four kinds of causality, (2) an examination of Aristotle's axiomatic potency–act hermeneutic of being in relation to the notion of *logos* as a cosmic ordering principle, (3) a summary of Stein's ontology of spiritual being in relation to the soul, and (4) a consideration of the Catholic notion of the soul's redemption. By proceeding along these four touchstones, an adequate argument that positions the soul as the veritable and necessary spiritual form of the body will be furnished.

II. Aristotle's Four Kinds of Causality

In order to understand the soul as the form of the body, we must briefly outline the four distinct kinds of causality found in the work of Aristotle. One of the basic matrices of finite being is cause and effect. All scientific experimentation presupposes the logical relation and progression of causes to their respective effects. Cause and effect signify the condition for the possibility of becoming. To become is to move from cause to effect; to become is to change—to move from potential being to actual being by the power of already actualized being. All finite beings exist in a state of becoming because they are enmeshed in a perpetual network of cause and effect. Given the importance of cause and effect for all existents, one of the most necessary

---

6. Ibid., 69 and 361, respectively. Cf. Denziger-Schönmetzer, *Enchiridion Symbolorum*, 902/481.

philosophical tasks (even if a relatively preliminary one) is to examine the various types of causes in relation to their respective effects, for the types of causes are certainly multiple.[7]

In Book II of his *Physics*, and in Book V of his *Metaphysics*, Aristotle did precisely that. Therein he laid the philosophical groundwork for all ensuing discussion about cause and effect. Even though this material would be included as part of an introductory-level course in metaphysics, it is nevertheless essential to reiterate the meaning of Aristotle's classification of causes because they go largely misunderstood (or not apprehended at all) by people today. The fact is that, at least in the United States, the majority of adolescents graduate from secondary school with virtually no education in philosophy whatsoever, especially in the vital subdiscipline of metaphysics. Likewise, many adults graduate from undergraduate, graduate, and doctoral degree programs with little or no intellectual training in philosophy. The vast majority of people would be at a loss if asked about Aristotle's four kinds of causality and their significance for us today. The tragedy of this intellectual famine is evinced in the plethora of dehumanizing acts perpetrated by human beings upon one another to this day. When sound rational theory is missing, so is virtuous human activity. It is no coincidence that Aristotle's holistic understanding of cause and effect has a direct correlation to his development of virtue ethics. Authentic praxis is informed by authentic theory. One cannot act responsibly without first contemplating the cosmos.

Concerning the topic of cause and effect in the twenty-first century, categories and thought structures of the natural sciences hold sway, namely, what Aristotle calls material causality and efficient causality. Indeed, these are valid ways for understanding causality but do not exhaust its concept. Let us first examine these two types of causality in sequence, since they are most familiar, and then expose the deficiencies of thinking only in terms of material and efficient causality.

a. Material Causality

Aristotle begins his treatment of causality by defining the goal of his inquiry: knowledge. He writes that "knowledge is the object of our inquiry, and men do not think they know a thing till they have grasped the 'why' of it (which is to grasp its primary cause)."[8] Knowledge is the basis of any and

---

7. For a helpful account of the lineage of thinking causality from Aristotle to Thomas to their contemporary interpretations, see Mitchell, "From Aristotle's Four Causes to Aquinas' Ultimate Causes of Being."

8. Aristotle, *Physics* II.3, in Aristotle, *Complete Works*, 1:332.

all science worthy of the name. The foundation of science is the question, why? "Why" inquires into the origin (Greek: *arché*) or cause (Greek: *aition*) of an existent.[9] Why does such and such exist? Why is such and such here? "Why" is a question asked not enough in our day. Yet, for Aristotle, it is the premier question for the knowledge of any particular reality. Material causality inquires about "that out of which a thing comes to be and which persists."[10] He gives the example of a bronze statue originating from the copper alloy, bronze. The material statue was fashioned from already existing material. Material causality simply recognizes that all material existents were derived from previously existing material existents.

In German, Stein refers to the material cause as *woraus*, that is, "out of which." The material cause is "that *which* is transformed; in other words that *out of which* the new individual becomes, namely, the matter."[11] This is the most basic kind of cause as it merely refers to that specific matter from which a particular material existent came to be. It designates the space-filling matter necessary for the new material being to materialize. In *Finite and Eternal Being*, Stein refers to the example of the human being whose material cause is "the material elements of which the body is formed," namely, the original gametes of the parents and the subsequent material elements—via hydration and nutrition—that sustain the human organism in being and contribute to his or her successive physical growth and development.[12] At this point, well and good, but immediately the mind inquires about the causal agency of the being's becoming and not only about its material makeup. This leads to Aristotle's second category of cause: efficient.

b. Efficient Causality

Aristotle defines efficient causality as "the primary source of the change or rest" in a being.[13] Efficient causality refers to that which moves another in

---

9. For more on Aristotle's notion of origin (Greek: *arché*), see Aristotle, *Metaphysics* V.1, in *Complete Works*, 2:1599.

10. Aristotle, *Physics* II.3, in *Complete Works*, 1:332. Cf. Aristotle, *Metaphysics* V.2, in *Complete Works*, 2:1600: "that from which (as immanent material) a thing comes into being."

11. Stein, *Potency and Act*, 65.

12. Stein, *Finite and Eternal Being*, 227.

13. Aristotle, *Physics* II.3, in *Complete Works*, 1:332. Cf. Aristotle, *Metaphysics* V.2, in *Complete Works*, 2:1600: "That from which the change or the freedom from change first begins, e.g. the man who has deliberated is a cause, and the father a cause of the child, and in general the maker a cause of the thing made and the change-producing of the changing."

its being, causing the effected being to become in a new way. More basically, the efficient cause is that which changes something else. For example, a soccer ball soars into the goal be*cause* a person kicked the ball or the wind moved the ball or the force of gravity propelled the ball downhill, etc. Efficient causality, like material causality, is a simple and straightforward type of causality. It examines a practical series of causes and effects over the course of linear, chronological time. Efficient and material causality form the backbone of physics and, therefore, all other natural sciences (for example, chemistry, biology, engineering, and technology). However, with efficient causality we begin to spill over into the distinct fields of philosophy and theology. For instance, we recognize the immediate absurdity of tracing the lineage of cause and effect into the past ad infinitum. It is obvious to the sober intellect that a singular original uncaused cause must exist. This is precisely the heart of Thomas's argument in demonstrating the rational certainty of God's existence by observing God's effects: "Something in process of change cannot itself cause that same change. It cannot change itself. Necessarily, therefore, anything in process of change is changed by something else . . . So, we are bound to arrive at some first cause of change that is not itself changed by anything, which is what everybody takes to be God."[14] This is to say that mutability does not eternally proceed from mutability. The origin of change is that which is not subject to change and, at the same time, that which is delimited in no way—that which is infinite. Why is there something rather than nothing? It is be*cause* there is something in the first place, something that is not itself a thing among things, or even the sum total of all things, but that which is the source of everything else that is. In his second rational proof of God's existence, Thomas again appeals to efficient causality: "We find that there is an order of efficient causes in the observable world. Yet we never observe, nor ever could, something efficiently causing itself. For this would mean that it preceded itself, which it cannot do . . . So, there cannot be a last cause, nor an intermediate one, unless there is a first . . . So, we have to posit a first cause, which everyone calls 'God.'"[15] Likewise, Thomas forcefully argues that among a contingent, chronological series of causes and effects, we are confronted with the question of beginning: what is the first efficient cause, that not efficiently caused by anything else? The answer to this question is one of the key philosophical meanings of the term "God." And so, even within the limited paradigm of natural

---

14. Thomas Aquinas, *Summa theologiae* I.1.3, in *Summa Theologiae: Questions on God*, 25.

15. Ibid.

scientific inquiry, we are brought to the limen between the natural and the supernatural through the medium of efficient causality.[16]

In German, Stein refers to the efficient cause as *wodurch*, that is, "through which." The efficient cause is "that *by which* it is formed: the forming activity that here is the last cause."[17] As the English term *efficient* suggests the Latin term *efficere* ("to bring about, to cause, to effect, to accomplish"), efficient causality especially refers to the causal agency within a process. It asks into what is doing the causing, whereas material causality asks into the specific material being transformed in the process of change. The efficient cause is the most proximate cause that changes something other than itself. In *Finite and Eternal Being*, Stein refers to the example of the human being whose efficient cause is "the semen (or progenitor)," within an ancient Aristotelian understanding of biological reproduction.[18] In any case, according to our current knowledge of microbiology, the efficient cause of a new human life is the mother and father who unite through the conjugal act thereby conceiving a new human being through the zygotic union of their respective sexual gametes. Yet the sexual act of mother and father cannot be separated entirely from divine efficient causal agency, as we have seen above and will see further below. Efficient causality "causes some becoming, movement, or change."[19] Efficient causality is the causality of motion.

---

16. See Stein, *Finite and Eternal Being*, 110: "This paradox of the human intellect—its being distended between finitude and infinity—seems to account for the peculiar fate of the ontological proof of God's existence: Its defenders and adversaries return again and again in the history of Christian theology and philosophy. Anyone who has penetrated to the idea of divine being—the first, eternal infinite, the *pure act*—cannot remain unaware of the necessity of being which is comprised in this idea. But if that person seeks to seize it in the manner in which one seizes something in the process of cognition, it recedes and no longer appears as a sufficiently strong foundation upon which to erect the edifice of a proof. To believers who in their faith are certain of their God it seems so impossible to think of God as non-existent that they confidently undertake to convince even the *insipiens*. The thinker who applies the rules of natural knowledge shrinks back again and again from the leap over the abyss. But do the *a posteriori* proofs—the inferences from created effects to an uncreated cause—fare much better? How many unbelievers, after all, have become believers on the strength of the Thomistic proofs of the existence of God? These proofs too demand a leap over an abyss: The believer leaps across lightly, the unbeliever stops this side of the precipice."

17. Stein, *Potency and Act*, 65.

18. Stein, *Finite and Eternal Being*, 227.

19. Ibid., 227. Cf. ibid., 227: "When matter is called a cause, the implicit meaning is that the thing as a whole could not be without matter and that matter co-determines *what* the thing is. But it is not matter that gives the first impulse to the process of becoming. Unless some other principle were added, no new thing could ever originate from matter. This fact is expressed by stating that to matter is attributed only passive potency, not an active one, i.e., only the potency of suffering [*pati*] or receiving, not the

It is what initiates a process of change within a being other than its own. Thomas writes that "motion is the actuality of a being in potency."[20] Efficient causality refers to the chain of motion by which one being already in motion moves another. Motion signifies that the potential of a being to move and/or change has been actualized by a prior actualized being. Referring back to Thomas's rational proofs of God's existence, the logic of efficient causality identifies a prime mover that is itself unmoved by anything else. Inasmuch as "nothing that is not actual can actualize," efficient causality insists on a universal origin of motion and becoming that itself does not become but simply is; this origin is "is"—"to be"—itself, not one of many finite beings (or even the sum total of finite beings) in motion, but the motive actuality instigating all finite beings in their actuality and motion.

In summarizing material and efficient causality, it is obvious to recognize these two kinds of causality as forming the experimental domain of the natural sciences. The scientific methods of biology, chemistry, physics, and engineering are by definition limited to material and efficient causality since matter and material energy are the extent of their objects of study. These fields can go as far as matter and energy but no further in and by themselves. They can answer practical questions and make assertions about natural phenomena such as the role of solar energy and carbon dioxide in the process of photosynthesis or the flow of electrons and molecular reconfiguration within a chemical reaction such as in the process of sugar fermentation:

$$C_6H_{12}O_6 \text{ (glucose)} \longrightarrow 2\, C_2H_5OH \text{ (ethyl alcohol)} + 2\, CO_2$$

Chemistry can say what is changing (material causality) and how and by what it is being changed (efficient causality), but it does not ask about the essential origin of the elements, change itself, or existence itself. Such questions, concepts, and answers are beyond its purview. Chemistry can trace the process of sugar fermentation and even manipulate the process and force it to happen, but it cannot give an adequate account of why molecular polarity exists in the first place.

The natural sciences lack the grammar, concepts, and, above all, the questions that point beyond themselves as physical sciences. It is not enough to be cognizant of the material and efficient causality of various existents. We human beings naturally inquire further than this—a fact that itself attests to the realities to be detected beyond the scope of the natural

---

potency of doing or effecting anything by itself. To operate efficaciously [*wirken*] or to give a first impulse to some operation or action is, however, precisely the function of (efficient causality)."

20. Thomas Aquinas, *Sententia libri Metaphysicae* IX.1.3: "motus est actus entis in potentia" (translation my own).

sciences. These are the same realities that are the conditions for the possibility of natural science in the first place. Natural science can be performed because there is first nature as such. How are such realities that predetermine and transcend nature to be detected and rationally demonstrated? Through formal and final causality. Because material and efficient causality do not supply a sufficient reason for their own being, we look to two remaining types of causality to understand the complete causal constitution of beings in a holistic way.

c. Formal Causality

Aristotle defines formal causality as "the form [*eidos*] or the archetype [*paradeigma*], i.e. the definition of the essence, and its genera ... and the parts in the definition."[21] Indeed there exist material and efficient causes but we inevitably ask, from whence did they come? Whether on the micro or macro level, there are not formless beings but beings with form—a countless array of diverse forms of being! Yes, the beings studied by natural science are composed of matter with each being having its own efficient cause, but why and how do they exist at all in their specified shapes and operations? As it turns out, material and efficient causality are unable to answer such questions by themselves. These questions beg alternative kinds of causality that are themselves the cause of material and efficient causality to begin with. We are led back to Aristotle's foundational ontological axiom: there is no matter without form. And if matter always obtains to some specified form, we are forced to admit of a kind of causality that is formal by definition. For instance, what differentiates human from tree from insect from fish from star? Answer: formal causality. What differentiates proton from neutron from electron from gluon from pion? Answer: formal causality. What differentiates the four fundamental forces of the physical universe: nuclear strong force, nuclear weak force, electromagnetic force, and gravitational force? Answer: formal causality. What accounts for the complementary polarities within electric and magnetic fields? Answer: formal causality.

If cosmic motion is essentially derivative of molecular polarity, we naturally inquire into the origin of polarity as such. If polarity is essentially derivative of multiplicity, we naturally inquire into the origin of multiplicity and relationality as such. If multiplicity is essentially derivative of the unity of one, we naturally inquire into the origin of unity as such. In sum, we

---

21. Aristotle, *Physics* II.3, in *Complete Works*, 1:332. Cf. Aristotle, *Metaphysics* V.2, in *Complete Works*, 2:1600.

arrive at the paradox of being, the ontological difference within being: (1) the oneness of existence, and (2) finite beings—the multiplicity of existents. If there are distinct forms of existents, the ontological specificity of these respective forms must precede their ontic materialization. Even within the concept of cosmological evolution—which simply is stating the obvious, namely, that beings become in relation to one another—formal causality defines and relates the causal determination of the whole and of all parts within the whole. In other words, the very patterns of evolution are not merely happenstance—a term that itself suggests the formal causality of chance—but are predetermined by formal causality. To suggest otherwise would be to deny the essential logical relationship between cause and effect. It would be to claim that an effect is without a determining cause or that potency exists apart from prior actuality. If beings have form, it is due to formal causality.

In German, Stein refers to the formal cause as *wonach*, that is, "according to which." The formal cause is "that *according to which* [something] is formed; that is, the idea."[22] Ontology implies formal causality as the condition for the possibility of formal differentiation and subsistence. Could a particular form of being adhere in a persistent state of existence for any length of time without its formal predetermination? Such an idea makes no sense. And that is precisely the point: ideas, or forms, precede their material manifestation. Again, this fact cannot be dismissed by an appeal to the uniformity of diverse subatomic particles, for these too bear specified forms and functions, which implies anterior formal determination. Moreover, the factuality and determination of macro existents—for example, human, horse, fern, planet, universe, etc.—cannot be reduced to their aggregate parts in terms of their formal determination. The form "horse" cannot be reduced to a subcategory of being, for example, molecules, elements, atoms, subatomic particles, etc., for "horse" is a distinct individual kind of living being in relation to a plethora of other distinct individual living beings. Though it may have physical properties in common with a variety of other species—for example, mammals, quadrupeds and organic life—it is distinct in its "horse-ness" according to its specified formal constitution. This fact is significant and cannot be sidestepped by appealing to "shared-derived characteristics," "emergent properties," and the like. The reason we can identify distinct beings by linguistic referents such as cat, frog, heron, tree, rock is that each being's ontic identity is fashioned according to its ontological determinateness propagated by formal causality. Essence precedes material

---

22. Stein, *Potency and Act*, 65.

manifestation; essence causes specific material beings to subsist in their specified forms of being.

In *Finite and Eternal Being*, Stein refers to the formal cause of the human being as "being human."[23] This is not a mere tautology but attests to the fact that "the actual has its ontological ground in some enduring faculty or power (the generative act has its ground in the generative *potency*), and the power in turn has its ground in the nature or essence, i.e., in the living being-ness [*Lebewesensein*] of this particular living being (i.e., in what Aristotle calls the form of the living being)."[24] In other words, all power as potency must have its ground in the particular essence of the species. Potency does not attain to act without some prior actuality acting on the potency to transform it into a new actuality. The formal cause of human being is not evolution or natural selection. This is not to deny that the material makeup of human beings evolved to the state of its current complexity over the course of time. However, it is to deny that human being as such can be reduced to a transitory stage of the evolutionary lineage of physical beings as if there were nothing that would differentiate human being essentially from any other kind of being. It is self-evident that formal differences exist between beings to such a degree that it is implausible to reduce formal causality to material and/or efficient causality.

Similarly, the complex diversification of existents as they appear today cannot be reduced to the yawning span of time, no matter how many of billions of years fill our metanarratives of cosmic evolution. Chronological time itself does not account for formal differentiation and development. If existents change and develop it is because there is a diverse array of forms to begin with. The variety of forms of being are what change and develop through the many processes of evolutionary metamorphosis.[25] As we shall see in considering our next type of causality, namely, final causality, evolution of beings is directed to specified forms of being which are not accidental to formal causality but determined by it. The form "horse" exists today because the historical evolutionary process of the horse's being was aimed at that particular form of being all the while vis-à-vis other forms of being and environments. If this were not the case, there would be no stable form of "horse" as such today. In fact, such realities as time itself, life itself, mo-

---

23. Stein, *Finite and Eternal Being*, 227.

24. Ibid., 228.

25. See ibid., 231: "That which is before and after is grounded in something deeper which determines the entire process of evolution and leads it toward the end. And this something we have called the *essential form* [*Wesensform*]. In the essential form is alive that purposively directed power to which the *actualized essence* owes its existence if and whenever it corresponds to the end."

tion itself, evolution itself, and interdependent existence itself beg their own distinct formal causality.[26] All that which exists, including the totality of existence and its existents, owes its raison d'être to formal causality proceeding from pure actuality, that is to say, from God.[27]

Yet there are many forms we encounter that do not change over the course of time. These are the forms that ground universal rationality and objective truth. They are subject neither to revision nor to manipulation. They bear an eternal givenness insofar as they do not adapt to changing circumstances and are immutable. What fields of study deal exclusively with such forms? Mathematics, geometry, and music. To fill out the ancient quadrivium, in addition to these three fields was the field of astronomy and the apparent order and timelessness of the celestial bodies. In any case, such fields expose the purity of form in relation to their instantiations within the material order. In fact, we speak of "order" because of such order-full forms: numbers, shapes, formulas, octaves, ratios, laws, theorems, axioms, and postulates. This is the stuff of self-evidence and the very landscape of logic. In ancient Greece there was a sign above Plato's academy that read, "Let no man ignorant of geometry enter."[28] Geometry—*ge* ("land, earth") *metrikos* ("metric, measure")—is devoted to studying the inherent order and formal causality of the cosmos through attention to shape, vectors, angles, congruity, and the laws of shape. Geometry deals with the given architecture of the universe and, without the formal causality of this given architecture, we, in turn, would not be able to design or create anything. Even at twenty-five years of age, Stein writes to Roman Ingarden, "I busy myself these days with physics and mathematics (in the interest of the philosophy of nature)."[29] To understand the nature of beings, it is necessary to devote careful study to the formal causality of beings, including mathematics and the intrinsic laws of the physical order. Stein was acutely aware of the way in which formal

---

26. See Stein, *Finite and Eternal Being*, 102: "Nothing temporal, i.e., nothing whose being is becoming and passing away from moment to moment, can exist without a supra-temporal ground. Nothing temporal can exist without a timeless *formal structure* [*Gestalt*] which regulates the particular course of the temporal sequence of events [*das Geschehen*] and is thereby actualized in time."

27. See ibid., 94: "These exemplary forms have their being—according to the Augustinian interpretation of Plato's doctrine of ideas, which Thomas follows here—in the divine mind. Distinct from them are those *created forms* which have their being in things. And these created forms we must evidently understand as the *actualized* natures in things. The being they receive is the *actual* being which they have in things"; and Thomas Aquinas, *Summa theologiae* I.15.1–3.

28. See Grondin, *Introduction to Metaphysics*, 35.

29. Stein, *Letters to Roman Ingarden*, 69 (letter of May 31, 1917).

causality underpinned the peculiar individual and relational characteristics of existents.

In his erudite and helpful work, *Introduction to Metaphysics: From Parmenides to Levinas*, Jean Grondin writes of how "mathematics, more than any other discipline, teaches us that true knowledge pertains to ideal shapes and sizes rather than sensible ones ... In mathematics, one must *posit* 'intelligible' entities; the likeness of which can only be achieved through thought ... Mathematical knowledge is apodictic ... It is to this type of knowledge that belongs truth and science (*episteme*) in the narrowest sense of the term."[30] Grondin recalls the ancient philosophical observation that our most certain knowledge is that which is not able to be ascertained by sense perception but is tethered to ideal objects grasped by the mind. Ideal knowledge is more precise and truthful than sensible knowledge. Mathematical knowledge is apodictic (*apo-* ["from, of, by, with"] *deiknyai* ["to show"]) because it demonstrates the veracity of intellectual objects with absolute certainty and precision. There is no rational possibility of refuting an intellectually sound mathematical equation, for example, 3 x 5 x 7 = 105 or the Pythagorean theorem concerning a right triangle: $a^2 + b^2 = c^2$, given the self-evident first principle of noncontradiction.

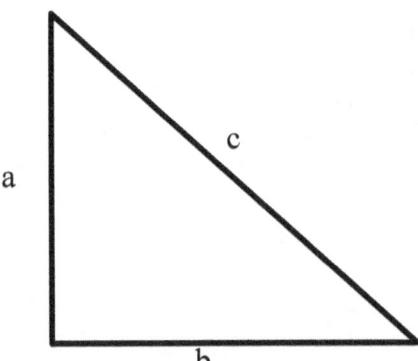

The soundness of the Pythagorean theorem depends on the underlying axioms and postulates that must be assumed to perform Euclidean geometry—for example, that the whole is greater than the part and that all right angles are equal to one another. Mathematics and geometry have their own

---

30. Grondin, *Introduction to Metaphysics*, 35.

conditions for possibility and such conditions constitute, in a sense, the formal causality of formal causes. Grondin observes that the first appearance of an unconditioned principle in the history of metaphysics is in Plato's *Republic*: "a first principle that is *not* a hypothesis ... the unhypothetical first principle of everything."[31] While hypotheses are made concerning sentient instantiations of the forms, contemplation on the relations between the forms themselves leads to positing the formal cause of all forms, namely, the unconditioned first principle of everything else. Again, mathematics "teaches us that true knowledge pertains to ideal shapes and sizes rather than sensible ones."[32] Hypothetical knowledge based on sense perception and visible images approximates certainty but extends its riskful reach from the firm foundation of apodictic ideal and intelligible knowledge of formal causes anchored in the first principle of being. Formal causality is not a matter of atoms but is that which can be abstracted from matter and serves as the condition for the possibility of distinct material forms. Just as mathematics is a precursor for measurement, metaphysics is a precursor for physics. Material and efficient causality have their origin in formal causality. Without the given principles and forms of being and logic, there would be no sense to be made of anything because nothing would have shape, proportion, essence, or meaning.

In addition to mathematics and geometry, sonorous music is based on intrinsic tonic ratios and logarithmic relationships between different pitches—for example, the unison, the minor third, the perfect fifth, and the perfect octave. For instance, the perfect octave above an A pitch tuned to the standard 440 hertz increment will sound at 880 hertz so that the sound waves oscillate at a perfect ratio:

---

31. Plato, *Republic* 510b, 511b, in Plato, *Complete Works*, 1131–32.
32. Grondin, *Introduction to Metaphysics*, 35.

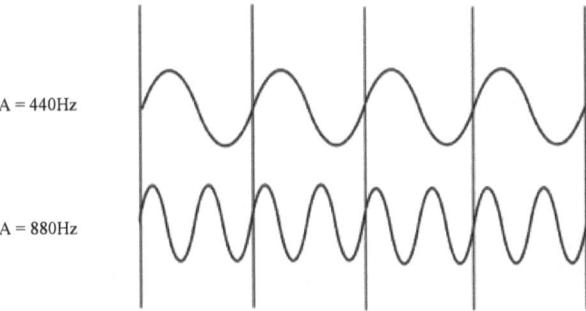

These symmetrical relationships are the basis for musical intonation, sonority, and harmony. Further, musical composition is organized according to time, thereby opening the possibility of rhythm. If music is rhythmic it is due to a perceived tempo according to which successive sound events are related. In his 1939 book *What to Listen for in Music*, American composer Aaron Copland identifies the following four elements of music: rhythm, melody, harmony, and tone color.[33] Such elements stem from the ideal mathematics of music: rhythm is the punctuation of time by creating meter; melody is the undulation of space by sound waves; harmony is the balanced logarithmic relation among various sound waves; and tone color is the timbre or quality of a particular sound determined by the presence of overtones and the specific apparatus producing the sound. The underlying formal metrics of music—the formal causality of music—serves as the basis from which all tonality and rhythm originate. All science and truth-telling is based on such apodictic knowledge as that revealed in mathematics, geometry, and music. Even the basic term *information* attests to the validity of formal causality and the givenness of ideal objects. Every phenomenon of information consists of an intangible formal component. Eidetic (*eidos* ["idea/form"]) knowledge is comprised of the formal world of in*form*ation. Formal causality, as evinced in the classic quadrivium of liberal arts studies, refers to the in*form*ation of all finite and created existents.

Formal causality refers to the anterior network of essential being according to which all finite beings are determined. Relative degrees of belief are required for all assertions of knowledge and truth. However, the degree of belief demanded to assent to the reality of formal causality is rationally

33. Copland, *What to Listen for in Music*.

little greater than that demanded to assent to the reality of material and efficient causality. True, formal causality deals with invisible, nonspatial, and nontemporal entities, while material and efficient causality deal with visible, spatial, and temporal entities. Yet material and efficient causality themselves beg the question of their reason for being in pointing subliminally to formal causality. As it turns out, formal causality is both the efficient cause of efficient causality and the spiritual cause of material causality. According to Aristotle's classic conception, all matter is formed matter. This general worldview is called hylomorphism (*hyle* ["matter"] *morphe* ["form"]). No matter is without form, though there can be form without matter—for example, in the case of angelic beings or eidetic objects.

The relation between form and matter stems from the more fundamental relation between act and potency. As act is to potency, so form is to matter. Formal causes are the actuality behind their material manifestation. For example, there must exist an actual form of bird before bird as such can be awakened into existence. Why is this so? It is because the evolutionary potential of matter to assume the form of bird as such requires a predetermined eidetic constitution before it can materialize. Act precedes potency. Again, matter does not precede form but form always precedes matter since any conception of matter—whether on a macro or micro level—is always already formed matter. Any particle, no matter how small, is always already a formed particle in relation to other micro- and macro-particles, as well as in relation to the macro-forms that are constituted by such particles, all in relation to a greater whole. For instance, what came first: the formal constitution of subatomic particles or the formal constitution of the periodic table of elements? Answer: neither because formal causality implies the simultaneous realization and interdependence of subatomic particles, elements, molecules, and larger individuated existents. Further, all of these categories imply the coexistence of unity, multiplicity, polarity, motion, energy, and spacetime. Cosmos means "order" and order implies formal causality and the actuality of determinate forms for the inert potentiality of indeterminate prime matter.

Having covered material, efficient, and formal causality, one more type of causality remains to investigate in order to arrive at an adequate understanding of being in terms of cause and effect. This last type of cause is related most directly to formal causality and can at times appear to be one and the same as it. All motion and activity in the universe beg the question of whither, that is, to what point is everything heading? Why do things act toward certain ends? What is the end of it all and what is the purpose of it all? While formal causality inquires about the question of origin or beginning, the last type of causality inquires about the question of end. This is why the fourth kind of causality is termed "final causality." Formal causality begs the question of whence, that is, from where did everything originate? Final causality begs the question of whither, to where is everything going?

d. Final Causality

Aristotle defines final causality as the "end [*telos*] or that for the sake of which a thing is done."[34] Final causality deals with the ends or goals of action. The science of final causes is called "teleology," from the Greek term *telos*, which can be translated in English as "end" or "goal." If something is in act or motion, it acts or moves toward a predetermined or intended goal.[35] A living organism adapts to a given environment (which too is constantly evolving) by developing specific traits that will promote not only its individual survival but, more significantly, the survival of its own species over the course of time. Such adaptations occur on the basis of a set purpose: subsistence of life. The cosmic order is laced with teleological attributes that determine the rhyme and reason of all cosmic activity. Whether our optic of contemplation about the universe is large or small, teleology is on display everywhere. Chemical processes happen according to the predetermined ends of molecular interaction. Interactions among various living and nonliving species of beings transpire according to the given demands of organisms such as nutrition, hydration, and reproduction. Principles such as homeostasis, inertia, unity, alterity, polarity, and complementarity determine the activity of all physical phenomena in the universe. For there to be movement there must be more than one. For there to be movement there must be one. This is to say that the interaction of a multiplicity of existents depends on the difference among respective existents and yet the unity of existence. Similar to formal causality, final causality observes that for the sake of which a thing is done. It acknowledges that all activity is purposive activity according to predetermined origins and ends. Like formal causality, final causality reaches beyond material and efficient causality by recognizing the innate goals inscribed not only in physics but in rational volition as well. The latter concept implies the uniqueness of human freedom and the fact that final causes can be consciously chosen by rational beings by virtue of intellect and self-mastery, even though the ends of action remain predetermined by the scripted patterns of the natural order. In any event, final

---

34. Aristotle, *Physics* II.3, in *Complete Works*, 1:332. Cf. Aristotle, *Metaphysics* V.2, in *Complete Works*, 2:1600.

35. See Thomas Aquinas, *Summa theologiae* IaIIae, 1, 1–8, especially article 2.

causality transcends the determinism of physics by including its totality of being and the latent possibilities implicit in its evolutionary path.

In German, Stein refers to the final cause as *wozu*, that is, "into which." The final cause is "that '*into which*' the thing is formed ... *what* the thing is becoming and later will be."[36] Aristotle uses the Greek word *entelecheia* to refer to that into which a thing is formed. Entelechy refers to the formal blueprint of a living organism's being as it is determined upon the organism's biological conception. This blueprint contains the finished product of an organism's growth, development, and natural activity. The genius of an organism's full maturity is already present in its seed and/or earliest stage of being; it has only to evolve.[37] Another term used to describe the full maturity of an organism is its "perfection." Perfection signifies the point at which the organism's growth and development has reached completion or fullness. It refers to the goal at which the organism was aiming in its growth, development, and activity all along. For inanimate objects, entelechy also applies insofar as all physical objects are in motion in their subatomic particle movements and evolution. Radioactive decay is just one of many examples in which subatomic particles undergo constant mutation and modification. The entelechy of inanimate objects is determined by formal and final causality of natural laws, such as by the four fundamental forces of the universe, by the four laws of thermodynamics, and by the inherent principles of being frequently mentioned in this book such as alterity and polarity.

In *Finite and Eternal Being*, Stein refers to the final cause of the human being as "the perfection of the human being."[38] A human being grows and develops toward maturity, from an embryonic stage to that of adulthood. Not only does the body naturally increase in size and ability over time, the soul is formed progressively to fullness and completion as well. One could say that the perfected human being is especially one who is perfected in virtue and self-giving. This is the express purpose of education (*paideia*): a

---

36. Stein, *Potency and Act*, 65.

37. See Stein, *Finite and Eternal Being*, 230: "The human being who attains to his or her end does not thereby become a *pure form* but rather a perfect image or copy of the pure form. And whether the person attains to the end or not, the person bears within the self the 'seed' of the end. The person's ἐντελέχεια—understood now as the end *structure* [*Zielgestalt*] rather than as perfection of *being*—is actuating within that person from the very beginning of that person's existence, but this ἐντελέχεια is not the only actuating force, and for this reason it may happen that its formative power cannot fully actualize itself [*sich auswirken*]. We must therefore distinguish from the pure form—which stands *above* the evolution as a guiding archetype—that vital law which actuates *in* the process of evolution itself and determines this evolution with respect to and in the direction of the end."

38. Stein, *Finite and Eternal Being*, 227.

progressive formation toward intellectual and personal perfection according to the transcendental formal causes of being, namely, the true, the good and the beautiful. Perfected being "lies ahead as an *end* and as such effects the evolution which leads this new being toward its proper end."[39] The final cause of a human being propels the evolution of the person toward his or her predetermined end both intellectually and physically. Final causality exerts a gravitational pull on a being to shape its evolution toward what it is to become. Final causality teams with formal causality in determining the intrinsic nature of a being and its existential purpose.[40] Stein further argues that "if thus the end effects the evolution, and if only something actual can actuate, the end obviously must have actuality prior to the time the movement of the evolving thing or being reaches this end and is thereby 'actualized.'"[41] It is certain that evolutionary patterns are governed by teleology, that is, final causality. Any time we attempt to give an explanation of why a particular being changed or adapted in a specific way, we inevitably point to some purposive cause of the change or adaptation. For example, in discussing the evolution of venom in some species of snakes—for example, the inland taipan (*Oxyuranus microlepidotus*)—a herpetologist may reference "natural selection" or "evolution" as the causal agent of the favorable genetic mutation in the snake that promotes the survival of the species. However, neither natural selection nor evolution per se is a material or efficient cause. Such concepts are not individual beings or among the material elements of nature. They are abstract terms that suggest a causal agency other than that which could be manipulated and measured as a finite datum in a laboratory of physical science.

Natural selection and evolution are signifiers of formal and final causality. Natural selection implies an abstract natural law by which biological species survive according to their degree of successful adaptation to their environments. Biological evolution, too, implies an abstract natural law that governs the genetic mutations of species over the course of time according to the natural tendency toward life and survival. Even though the natural sciences are confined to the boundaries of material and efficient

---

39. Ibid., 228.

40. See Stein, *Potency and Act*, 65: "We may go on—with Aristotle—to distinguish that '*into which*' the thing is formed from that *according to which* it is formed; that is, the idea and *what* the thing is becoming and later will be. 'That into which' the thing is made, if we take it to mean the concrete thing that it is to be, is not included among the causes of its becoming, for it is but its result. If we take it as the species, whose instance the individual will become, it does not differ from the *according to which* aspect, the ideal species."

41. Stein, *Finite and Eternal Being*, 229.

causality, their metanarratives seldom avoid overt appeal to formal and final causality through consistent nomenclature. Whenever an argument is made that suggests that something evolves "in order to . . . ," it is final causality to which the argument makes its appeal. Whenever we abstract from matter in our thought processes, it is formal and final causality to which our conscious deliberations attest. Abstraction consists of the eidetic objects of consciousness and their teleological manifestation in the world of being. Whenever we recognize that a particular potency is actualized, we are met with the basic ontological premise that the actual form and end caused the actualization of the potency in the act of the being's becoming. Again, to become is for a potency to be actualized—a potency that exists in the first place because it has been actualized already as a potency in relation to act.

Final causality and formal causality intersect as the two poles of becoming. These two poles are constantly present in any and every finite being, from the beginning to the end of the being's lifespan. This is so because the beginning of a being's existence (determined by the formal cause) and the end of a being's existence (determined by the final cause) coexist at every stage of the being's becoming. In light of formal and final causality, beginning is end and end is beginning: the full form of the being is the goal and the fulfilled goal of the being is its incipient form. Both formal and final causality mark the actuality of the being that is necessary for the being to exist at all. With the formal and final actuality of a being in place, a being then can become according to and into which it is designated and predestined to become. A being becomes itself according to the ontological vector running from its formal cause to its final cause—a paradoxical causality in which there are two distinct essential causes, yet one.

e. Summary of the Four Kinds of Causality

Having traced the specific attributes of the four kinds of causality according to Aristotle, Thomas, and Stein, we are now positioned to effectively understand how the soul can be construed as the form of the body. Before proceeding with this anthropological application, let us sum up the four causes in the following table:

Kind of Cause	Aristotle's Definition	Stein's Shorthand Definition	Application to Human Being as Such
Material Cause	"That out of which a thing comes to be and which persists."	*Woraus*, that is, "out of which." The material cause is "that *which* is transformed; in other words that *out of which* the new individual becomes, namely, the matter."	"The material elements of which the body is formed."
Efficient Cause	"The primary source of the change or rest" in a being.	*Wodurch*, that is, "through which." The efficient cause is "that *by which* it is formed: the forming activity that here is the last cause."	"The semen [and ovum] (or progenitor[s])."
Formal Cause	"The form [*eidos*] or the archetype [*paradeigma*], that is, the definition of the essence, and its genera . . . and the parts in the definition."	*Wonach*, that is, "according to which." The formal cause is "that *according to which* [something] is formed; that is, the idea."	"Being human."
Final Cause	"End [*telos*] or that for the sake of which a thing is done."	*Wozu*, that is, "into which." The final cause is "that '*into which*' the thing is formed . . . *what* the thing is becoming and later will be."	"The perfection of the human being."

The main point of contention that merits recalling Aristotle's four kinds of causality is the tendency in our time to view reality through material and efficient causality alone. It is helpful to reconsider Jacques Maritain's delineation between philosophical knowledge, theological knowledge, and mystical knowledge.[42] In a context of widespread materialism, consumerism, secularism, and technocracy today, oftentimes these three orders of higher knowledge are neglected altogether. A great intellectual tragedy of our time is that people are content to exist according to animalistic behavior determined by survival instinct and pragmatic questions and knowledge. Such are the guiding principles of utilitarian and mechanistic ways of being in the world. The following table, to be read from bottom to top, summarizes these five categories of thinking and knowledge:

Type of Thinking/ Knowledge	Sources of Thinking/ Knowledge	Examples of Thinking/ Knowledge
Mystical	Sacramental communion with God and other personal spiritual beings	"Take this all of you and eat of it, for this is my body given up for you."
Theological	Divine revelation	"You have created us for yourself, O Lord, and our hearts are restless until they rest in you" (Augustine, *Confessiones* I.i.1).
Philosophical	Reason	"Why do I eat? What is the meaning of eating?"
Pragmatic	Basic practical concerns on how to satisfy basic desires most efficiently and expediently	"How much does it cost? Can I get fries with that?"
Survival Instinct	Basic psychosomatic needs—for example, food, drink, pleasure, etc.	"What's for lunch?"

If indeed the human being is created in the image and likeness of God, it stands to reason that the final cause of human existence is communion with God and the entire fold of angels and saints. As a person develops through authentic education, s/he ascends upward in spiritual development toward

42. See Maritain, *The Degrees of Knowledge*.

transparent and sacrificial communion with other persons. As illuminated in chapter 1 of this book, such is the universal human vocation. There is a call that beckons before (as formal cause) and behind (as final cause) throughout the course of one's life. Unearthing the truth of formal and final causality sets the human person on the itinerary of mystical communion fashioned by responsible ethical action and a constant giving of self.

If the soul is to be recuperated as a serious and indispensable concept of our time, there must be critical retrieval of a holistic understanding of being as outlined by Aristotle, Thomas, and Stein in terms of quadratic causality. The soul can be understood clearly only according to the metaphysics of formal and final causality in relation to the physics of the body as articulated through material and efficient causality. Let us return to the theological anthropology of Edith Stein and her comprehensive account of the human being.

III. Actuality, Potentiality, and *Logos*

For Stein, the human person can be envisioned as a trichotomous interplay between body, soul, and spirit.[43] The human person is understood essentially as a spiritual being that transcends itself according to the respiratory nature of its existence, not merely on the biological level but especially on the ontological level. A respiratory (that is, spiritual) nature is revealed in the being that is human insofar as humans exhibit a spiritual actuality that consciously goes out of itself, and yet the spiritual soul of the person is at the same time shaped from without.[44] Under the potency–act rubric that dominates her work, Stein positions the material body (*Körper*) as that

43. Stein, *Finite and Eternal Being*, 363–64: "The being of human beings [*menschliche Sein*] is a composite of body, soul, and spirit. Insofar as human beings—according to their essence—are spirit, their 'spiritual life' is an outgoing life that enters into a world which discloses itself to them, while they yet retain a firm hold on their own selves. They not only 'breathe' out their essence in a spiritual manner—as does every actual formal structure—unconsciously revealing themselves, but they are, in addition, active in a personal spiritual manner. The human soul *as* spirit rises in its spiritual life beyond itself. But the human spirit is conditioned both from above and from below. It is immersed in a material structure which it be-souls and molds into a bodily form. The human person carries and encloses 'its' body and 'its' soul, but it is at the same time carried and enclosed by both." Cf. ibid., 245, 274; 1 Thess 5:23: "May the God of peace himself make you perfectly holy and may you entirely, spirit [πνεῦμα], soul [ψυχή], and body [σῶμα], be preserved blameless for the coming of our Lord Jesus Christ."

44. See Stein, *Finite and Eternal Being*, 442, 461: "This is why the natural direction of the soul life is a going-out-of-itself rather than a turning-into-itself and an abiding 'in and with itself'... The soul is spirit [*spiritus*] in its innermost essence or nature, and this spirit nature underlies the actual deployment of all its *powers* (faculties)."

which is primarily *in potentia*, while she posits the soul as the spiritual and actualizing principle of the body.⁴⁵ However, Stein also refers to the living body, that is, the ensouled body by using the German word, *Leib*.⁴⁶ The body is actualized inasmuch as it is ensouled and unfolds in its growth and development according to the vital impulse of the soul. Marian Maskulak's book *Edith Stein and the Body-Soul-Spirit at the Center of Holistic Formation* is quite helpful in its interpretation of Stein's holistic account of human being (*Menschsein*). Maskulak writes that "given the contemporary rejection of dualism, the reader may be dismayed or even affronted by the fact that Stein attributes a central and dominant role to the soul in her anthropology. But the concept of both body and soul must be held in tension with her conviction about the unity and full permeation of body and soul with one another."⁴⁷ Maskulak constantly avers in her book that Stein's theological anthropology is no facile dualism, whether Platonic, Cartesian, or otherwise. Stein's depiction of human being is clearly one that maintains the integral nature of being constituted at once as body-soul-spirit. No singular isolation of any of these three dimensions is equivalent to the complete essence of an individual human being. Maskulak goes on to assert that "Stein rejects the notion of the soul 'dwelling' in the body as in a house and holds that the Greek portrayal of the body as the prison or tomb of the soul does not do justice to the unity of the nature of the human being (*Der Aufbau der menschlichen Person*, 106). The soul so penetrates the body that it becomes spiritualized body and the spirit becomes materialized and organized spirit (*Der Aufbau der menschlichen Person*, 107)."⁴⁸ Stein's emphasis on the unity

45. While it is true that Stein's use of the term *soul* develops throughout the course of her works, I will concentrate on her use of the term in her later works but also include its usage and application from her earlier works. For the different ways Stein employs the term *soul*, see Borden Sharkey, *Thine Own Self*, 9: "Stein uses the term soul [*Seele*] in a number of different ways throughout her career ... ," and Ales Bello, "Edmund Husserl and Edith Stein." Even though I would concur with Alasdair MacIntyre that, in Stein's *Philosophy of Psychology and the Humanities*, "'soul' is not used as a theological term. It is what someone is in the depths of her or his being and 'those depths do awaken in affective and dispositional life,'" nevertheless in her later works Stein certainly understands the soul as a theological concept primarily. See MacIntyre, *Edith Stein*, 124.

46. See Maskulak, *Edith Stein and Body-Soul-Spirit*, 61–63, for the careful distinction between *Körper* and *Leib* in Stein's work. See also Borden Sharkey, *Thine Own Self*, 158n12: "To be matter-bound is, for Stein, to be a soul. If there is no matter (as in the case of pure spirits), then there is no soul."

47. Maskulak, *Edith Stein and Body-Soul-Spirit*, 9. Even the title of Maskulak's book evinces her careful attempt at presenting Stein's theological anthropology as a "holistic" one, conceiving "body-soul-spirit" as the unity and totality of the person rather than as disparate and separable parts that somehow connect to form a whole.

48. Ibid., 9.

of the human being is consonant with the fact that there is no soul as such without its intrinsic relation to a physical body. Otherwise, "soul" would be rendered "pure spirit" and would no longer refer to the human essence that always implies a living material body, formed and fashioned according to the spiritual impetus of the soul. Likewise, there is no human body as such without its intrinsic relation to a soul—the self-shaping and self-forming principle that animates the sum total of the body's vital organic processes and willful actions.[49] The human being, therefore, can be referred to as "spiritualized body" or "materialized and organized spirit"—"spirit" of course implying the rational and *imago Dei* nature of the human being.

Stein identifies the soul as the form of the body, though the soul too bears *in potentia* properties.[50] This is to say that the soul has the potential to be formed from without. As a whole, the human person remains a mystery

---

49. For a similar remark, see ibid., 72: "A particularity of the human soul as spirit is that it is naturally bound to matter."

50. See Stein, *Potency and Act*, 248: "Being moved and shaped from within is the peculiarity of living things, their mode of being; it is *life*. And the *living* inner form that gives life is the soul. The forming and shaping of the whole that the soul belongs to is the effect of bringing the potential to actuality, for the soul itself is actual and active . . . we ought to call this actual life-giving soul 'spirit'"; ibid., 289: "Act, understood as the actual being of the living soul, is life"; ibid., 342: "the soul as a whole can be called the form of this living material body [*Leibkörper*]"; ibid., 396: "I mean that the soul shapes its body not only into an organism of the human kind but into an expression [*Ausdruck*] of its own individual distinctiveness and into a tool for its specific (= individual) working"; ibid., 351–52: "*Anima forma corporis* [the soul is the form of the body]—the phrase applies to the human as well as to the animal soul . . . Just as are plants and the bodies of animals, the human body [*Körper*], too, is shaped by an inner form into an organism. Just as the animal's body [*Körper*] becomes a *living body* [*Leib*] because in it ('in' here has no spatial sense) the soul has its own inner life and is able not only to form the body but to manage it once formed in external activity, so too the living human body is as it were the scene in which and around which the life of the soul unfolds as well as the tool that extends its effectiveness beyond itself . . . In this sense, we could call the soul as a whole the form of the body and the act of its potency"; Stein, *Finite and Eternal Being*, 183: ". . . the soul functions as the *form*, the body (i.e., the besouled body) as the matter which is being formed, and the nutriment as a matter which is to receive form but is as yet unformed"; ibid., 273: "As the actuating principle in the living being—the principle which forms the living being and thus makes it actual—the soul is itself actual, but its actuation [*Wirken*] is at the same time a constant actualization of its own potentialities"; ibid., 427: "Therefore, the *human soul* is not a mean between spirit and matter, but a *spiritual creature*—not only a formed structure of the spirit, but a *forming spirit*. But the human soul differs generically from pure spirits on account of the fact that it does not cease to be a medium and a transition. As the form of the body, it forms itself into space like the lower forms. Its spirituality shows distinct traces of its being tied to matter, and its spiritual life rises from a hidden ground"; ibid., 434; Stein, *La estructura de la persona humana*, 179–90; *Der Aufbau der menschlichen Person*, 125–40. Further, Stein indicates that material being is "pure receptivity for the form" (*Potency and Act*, 288).

"never completely disclosed nor disclosable" since the self-revelation of the person as such is in a state of perpetual flux between potentiality and actuality over the course of time.[51] While Stein understands the soul to be the actualizing principle of the body, the soul itself does not "have the power to actualize what is potential in it. What is potential is bound to outside influences, so that the soul's own specific being can become actual only through an actual being that is not its own."[52] The soul is bound, above all, to pure personal actuality of spirit, namely, God. As such, the soul is the power of self-formation, propelling the living body toward the actualization of its predetermined entelechy.[53] For Stein, as for Aristotle and Thomas, the entelechy refers to the inner form of a being that is shaped from within and directed toward a goal.[54] The entelechy of an organism could be described as its inward capacity and actuating impetus for self-determination according to the predetermined shape (*Washaftigkeit*; μορφή) of its being.[55] For example, the entelechy of the oak tree is already contained in its seed, as is the entelechy of the human being present at the fusion of paternal and maternal gametes in the form of the sui generis human soul, a genetic code and all of the cellular structures surrounding this code, thereby allowing the unique

---

51. Stein, *Potency and Act*, 200: "What the person is, therefore, remains ever mysterious for him and for others, it is never completely disclosed nor disclosable. Never, that is, insofar as and as long as his being alternates between potentiality and actuality over time . . . Insofar as all that it is allows in principle for actualization in the flow of spiritual living, the person's entire core is in potency to this actualization, and spiritual actuality, conscious of itself, is its highest mode of being."

52. Ibid., 336.

53. See MacIntyre, *Edith Stein*, 122: "To have soul is to have certain kinds of power, just as to have a mind is to have certain kinds of power. To be a human *psyche* is to have the possibility of a centered self, a core self out of which the determinate powers develop."

54. See Stein, *Potency and Act*, 62, 76, 321–22, and 330–31.

55. See Stein, *Finite and Eternal Being*, 87. Cf. Stein, *Potency and Act*, 402–3: "But we should remember here that this substance, or the person's core, is entelechy. Its core has the task of constructing the entire organism of body and soul in a process of ongoing development. And this means not only progressively forming from within a given matter into which it is immersed but also appropriating the matter it needs for its *telos*, which is the fully developed individual. This matter includes first of all the space-filling matter the body needs for its conservation and growth, but it also includes the 'matter to construct' the soul . . . The full unfolding is prescribed beforehand as *telos* in the entelechy, in the person's original core." Cf. Stein, *Potency and Act*, 339: "The individual unity of the life of the soul is conditioned on the one hand by the fact that the soul is entelechy not only for the body but also for itself—I mean that the soul bears a *telos* in itself that its living strives after—and on the other hand by the fact that the soul constructs itself as an 'organism,' that is, as a whole wherein all the parts work together according to a fixed order."

person's unfurling. Stein, however, makes it clear that the process whereby the inbuilt potencies of the organism are actualized—especially in the case of personal beings—is not only a matter of the work of the entelechy:

> Our attempt to understand the meaning of "genus" and "species" led us to ascribe a definite direction to the entelechy. This direction, however, is not one that determines what it forms down to the last detail, since the outcome, the fully determined *what* of the individuals, is determined not only by the entelechy but also by the lower material forms and forces that it presupposes. Thus the individual peculiarity and the typical variations of the species are accidental outcomes from the standpoint of the entelechy, but from the standpoint of the *Logos* they are foreseen as possibility founded on the ordered interplay of the forces.[56]

Stein indicates here that the ever-unfolding development of the organism is due to both the self-determining direction of the entelechy as well as to the randomness of the material forms and forces with which the entelechy collaborates in its shaping kinesis and taxis. This does not imply, however, that all is left up to chance and complete random occurrence. Instead, Stein insists on what could be called the eternal Entelechy, or the *Logos*, which orders the cosmic order, including all possible interactions therein.

Thinking within the Thomistic tradition, the *Logos* can be identified with the notion of *actus purus*, that is, pure actuality on which all else depends for its existence and the formal divine Cause of the sum of all potencies and actualities within the cosmos. The *Logos* is also the meaning-making principle to which all meaning is tethered. Even within the realm of the possible, it is the *Logos* that makes all possibilities possible, including the unlimited possibilities of interpretation and the coherence of meanings. The diversity of entelechies within the created order attests to a formal Cause of their collective raison d'être. According to the perennial logic of Aristotle's metaphysics, the distinct forms of being always precede their potential realization. For example, the possibility of the being called "elephant" depends on a prior actualized form of elephant as such. The same goes for all differentiated species. The actualized entelechy is prior to its potential unfolding and the actuality of the entelechy is determined by a prior actuality that gave rise to the specificity of the differentiated entelechies to begin with, even if through the course of an evolutionary process of becoming in time. In fact, the possible interactions between spacetime and mass/energy—both of which are instances of radical potentiality—presuppose their actualization in relation to one another and all formal actualizations that take

---

56. Stein, *Potency and Act*, 331.

place within their matrix.[57] While efficient causality can trace the lineage between the various configurations of beings, it cannot itself account for the origin or end of these beings and their interrelatedness. Likewise, material causality only aids efficient causality in its partial discourse on the when, where, and what, but does not adequately address the question of the how, why, and who. The latter form the questions of meaning and, specifically, of personal being. It is these questions that lead to the important concern over the question of the human soul. The peculiar being of the human soul is ultimately a question of formal and final causality, that is, an inquiry into the whence and whither of personal being as such. However, comprehending formal and final causality (and therefore the soul) must never be severed from material and efficient causality (and therefore the body) since "the soul is always necessarily a soul in a body."[58]

IV. Toward an Ontology of Spirit

In order to unlock the elusive nature of the human soul, Stein calls for "an ontology of spirit corresponding to the ontology of nature," insisting that "the world of the spirit is no less real or knowable than the natural world."[59] Further, she speaks of the soul and the psycho-physical individual as "natural objects," and empathy as that which brings these objects to phenomenological view.[60] The realm of consciousness and its intentional spiritual life are

---

57. See Stein, *Finite and Eternal Being*, 231: "That which is before and after is grounded in something deeper which determines the entire process of evolution and leads it toward the end. And this something we have called the *essential form* [*Wesensform*]. In the essential form is alive that purposively directed power to which the *actualized essence* owes its existence if and whenever it corresponds to the end."

58. Stein, *On the Problem of Empathy*, 41. Cf. ibid., 49–50: "As the substantial unity announced in single psychic experiences, the soul is based on the living body. This is shown in the phenomenon of 'psycho-physical causality' we have delineated in the nature of the sensations. And the soul together with the living body forms the 'psycho-physical' individual"; Stein, *Finite and Eternal Being*, 377: "For the human soul is certainly not space-filling and sensorial in the manner of spatial material. However, it is, and in this it differs essentially from pure spirits, naturally *bound to matter* [*stoffgebunden*]. This is clearly evident from the fact that it is the *form* of the *body*"; Stein, *La estructura de la persona humana*, 189: "The union with the body is essential for the soul" (translation my own); *Der Aufbau der menschlichen Person*, 133: "Die Verbindung mit dem Leib ist für die Seele wesentlich"; and Stein, *Potency and Act*, 343: "The entire organism of body and soul should be called an individual, a unit that cannot be broken at will without being destroyed."

59. Stein, *On the Problem of Empathy*, 95 and 113, respectively.

60. Ibid., 95, and further on 95–96, defining empathy as "the perceptual consciousness in which foreign persons come to givenness for us."

constitutive of the human soul's voluntary activity. Empathy designates that outward movement toward the other that is the defining characteristic of spiritual being. To participate in the affective life of another person involves a movement of self-divesting that has been ordained already by the emotive givenness of the other. Likewise, it is the soul that both nourishes its own body and orders the process of nutrition in "animat[ing] the lifeless material elements by 'appropriating' them and thus making them part of its own being."[61] The soul, as a spiritual entity, animates and organizes the sum total of bodily processes conducted by the organism. Stein recapitulates the essence of the soul by defining it as "the supra-material [*stoffüberlegen*] form which animates a body, molding it from within, in accordance with the specific essence, in a temporal process of evolution and with the aid of extraneous structural material elements."[62] Again, Stein locates the soul as "a center of being [*Seinsmitte*] which unfolds in a temporal process of evolution by forming itself into a corporeal body and into a spiritual life."[63] The soul as such can be accessed by following the etiological lineage of all phenomena exhibited in and through the body, for they all rely on an animating principle that actualizes the conglomeration of material potencies within the body. The soul is attested in the personal spiritual interrelationality between personal subjects and their mutual spiritual formation.

Stein further identifies the uniqueness and irreproducibility of the soul as "the specific nature of the individual human soul or its *personal particularity*."[64] Even though human nature can be categorized according to a universal species, namely, the human species, each individual human soul is not to be recognized as its own incommunicable species such as in the case of individual angelic beings.[65] Stein contends that "the human

61. Stein, *Finite and Eternal Being*, 183–84.
62. Ibid., 422.
63. Ibid., 506.
64. Ibid., 432. Cf. Stein, *La estructura de la persona humana*, 180, 189: "The spiritual soul . . . is what gives to [the human person] all the character of personality and of the authentic individuality, what makes all of the strata to be penetrated by its character . . . Human souls have in common with the spirit without body personal structure and spiritual being" (translation my own); *Der Aufbau der menschlichen Person*, 128, 133: "Die geistige Seele . . . gibt dem Ganzen den Charakter der Personalität und echter Individualität und durchdringt damit alle Stufen . . . Die Menschenseelen haben mit den körperlosen Geistern die personale Struktur und das geistige Sein gemeinsam."
65. Stein, *Finite and Eternal Being*, 508. See elsewhere in her earlier work where Stein does describe the individual human being as his own species: Stein, *Potency and Act*, 407: "When we consider the soul in itself and the body as formed by the soul, each individual man is his own species, that is, each man is a spiritual person of specific distinctiveness. Yet he is no double be-ing [*Doppelwesen*]; rather, the *one* man through *one* soul is both." Cf. Maskulak, *Edith Stein and the Body-Soul-Spirit*, 80: "As stated above,

being is a spiritual person and he is shaped [*gestaltet*] as a body ... The intellectual-spiritual life of the human being differs from that of angels in that the former rises from a hidden depth and in that the formation of the corporeal body also proceeds from this hidden depth."[66] In other words, the entelechy of each individual human being unfolds over the course of time in and through the limits and finitude of corporeality and an organic community of persons. The individual human entelechy does not shine in its luminous radiance—that is, in its fully actualized self—from the start and by itself. Rather, from the hidden depth of his or her mother's womb does the entelechy of the infant begin its silent and hidden gestation. The nature of the human being is revealed as radical interdependence: "The individual human being is an embodiment of the *universal*, and this human being is a member of the whole."[67] This is to say that the term *humanity* bears within itself a duality at once pointing to the universal human nature as such and to the whole of the human community. Therefore the human soul is naturally no autonomous agent of pure self-determination but exists in symbiotic relationship with all other human souls surrounding it and shaping it. Within Stein's anthropological matrix, it is not possible to understand the reality of the human soul apart from its integral context of interpersonal relationality.

Yet even more than situating the soul as a mysterious entity ever concealed in the substratum of interpersonal relationships, Stein forges a description of the "matter [*Materie*] of souls" by way of analogy. Just as all material things exhibit sensible accidental qualities that allow us to characterize matter according to its various substantial forms, so does the soul exhibit sensible accidental qualities in the shape of human action. The acts that we perform in and through the body each constitute "'a piece of the soul's life.'"[68] Human acts carry with them a sensible mode of detection which permits a certain empirical verification of the soul as such. Is not the human soul, after all, at the heart of the subject of study for behavioral psychology? All human behaviors can be traced back to the center of the personal particularity of the individual who performs them. The impetus

---

the hallmark of being a person is possessing something incommunicable which the person shares with no one else," and Borden Sharkey, *Thine Own Self*, 44: "Each soul is a particular and unique mirror of God and reflects his glory in a unique way ... We are created 'wholly personally,' and [Stein] suggests that in each soul, God creates a unique dwelling place. We do not live simply to propagate the species, sending the human form on to another generation."

66. Stein, *Finite and Eternal Being*, 506. Cf. Berkman, "Edith Stein," 7: "Stein saw her life, and all human character at large, as grounded in mystery, articulating a view of the person's innermost being as rooted in a hidden fertile darkness."

67. Stein, *Finite and Eternal Being*, 509.

68. Stein, *Potency and Act*, 339.

of all human action springs from the determination of the soul's being in its action and reaction vis-à-vis other human souls. Further, Stein compares the "matter of the soul [*seelische Materie*]" to corporeal matter in the following ways:

> Just as in corporeal matter a definite amount of matter belongs to each substantial form, so a definite amount of "life power or force [*Lebenskraft*]" belongs to each soul. Just as corporeal matter fills space with its qualities, so the life of the soul fills time with its qualities. Just as the soul as entelechy causes living matter to gather into the form of the individual, into a self-contained organism, so too it gathers its "life" into an individual unity.[69]

In the first comparison, Stein likens the *Lebenskraft* of the soul to the quantitative matter belonging to each substantial corporeal form. The notion of *Lebenskraft* is akin to Henri Bergson's *élan vital*—a kind of vital force that undergirds the whole of the cosmic order, but in the case of the human soul is a predicate of its very being. Whereas substantial forms consist of the exact amount of matter belonging to each particular form, the human soul is composed of a definite quantity of *Lebenskraft* that determines its potencies of action and can be measured by observing the individual and aggregate acts of the person. The meaningful acts of the person provide evidence of the acting principle within the person. In the second comparison, Stein relates the qualitative aspects of corporeal matter as it fills space with the qualitative aspects of the soul as it fills time. But how does the soul fill time if not in its meaningful approach to the other as well as in its meaningful journey to its innermost core? If time measures the rate of movement of objects in space in the domain of physics, time likewise measures the quality of movement of souls in relation to one another in metaphysics. Time takes on a qualitative meaning through the play of psychological intercourse. In other words, time is invested with meaning to the degree that personal souls act in relation to one another through mutual formation. Time is not so much a rule of measure as it is the created and ever-unfolding expanse of relationship between spiritual souls. In the third comparison, Stein again uses the language of entelechy to relate the organic unity of soul and body. Yet she goes beyond the typical psychosomatic composite being of metaphysics in order to incorporate the symbolic structure of human existence as a living subject among other living subjects. The soul gathers its "life" into an individual unity by weaving together its manifold textured meanings into a coherent and intelligible tapestry of individual personhood—a personhood that is at once individual and communal. Through the soul's

69. Ibid.

power to remember the past and to organize experiences and events into an organic whole—even if accessible only through fragmentary recollection—the integrity of an individual life is elevated to the heights of contemplation.

V. The Rational Soul and Its Redemption

How is the human soul different than plant and animal souls, that is, nonhuman beings that likewise exhibit an animating principle within themselves? Stein follows the Aristotelian and Thomistic distinction between vegetative souls, sentient souls, and rational souls. First, Stein distinguishes the character of living things from the nonliving: "Living things [*Lebewesen*] obviously receive their qualities progressively from within—they are shaped and reshaped—over the entire duration of their being *as* living things, whereas non-living things are 'finished' from the beginning of their existence and are not further shaped and reshaped unless 'set in motion' by outside forces."[70] Stein appeals to entelechy as the inner vital principle that shapes an organism from the inside out. In the case of nonliving beings, such as a rock or water or oxygen, an internal entelechy is certainly nonexistent as such beings are determined exclusively from without and from the purely circumstantial outcome of their change of form and appearance. This is not to deny the diversity of forms of solids, liquids, and gases but to assert the cardinal difference between living and nonliving beings: self-formation. Stein contends that "being moved and shaped from within is the peculiarity of living things, their mode of being; it is *life*. And the *living* inner form that gives life is the soul. The forming and shaping of the whole that the soul belongs to is the effect of bringing the potential to actuality, for the soul itself is actual and active."[71] Again, in the case of nonliving beings, their potential quantities, qualities, modalities, and relationalities (in the Kantian sense) are actualized entirely from without. Yet within living beings is observed a generative actualizing principle that brings what is potential within the organism to actual existence.

Second, Stein confirms the classic distinction between vegetative, sentient, and rational souls. Plants demonstrate a genuine vegetative soul in that they perform the vital operations of growth and development from an internal entelechy, reproduction, and metabolism. Animals exhibit not only a kind of vegetative soul in sharing all such properties with plant life, but evince further life characteristics: movement and sensation. The animal soul is actualized through the processes of the vegetative soul as well as the

70. Ibid., 248.
71. Ibid.

additional processes of locomotion and bodily sensation (including the sensation of various appetites). Therefore the animal soul can also be called a sentient soul. Finally, the rational soul is on display in human beings alone and is characterized by intellectuality and freedom. Intellectuality refers to being that is conscious of itself "not in the dullness of the senses ... but in freedom and clarity."[72] Stein defines intellectual being as "being illumined and being open."[73] While these terms ring a rather metaphoric tone, they signify those life properties that are unique to human beings:

> "Freedom" here refers to the possibility as it were to detach oneself from oneself and to face oneself as foreign, as an object. And "clarity" means the possibility of "intuiting" oneself, knowing oneself. "Oneself" refers first to the subject that lives in its "acts" and also to this living. "Being open" means being able to engage what is other than oneself, stand over against it, turn toward it intentionally ... Being open for oneself and for what is other is the highest and hence also the most proper form of spirit whereto all other spiritual being harks back.[74]

To clarify, Stein describes the freedom of rationality as essentially the freedom of self-reflection, or self-reflexive being. In conscious freedom, humans have the capacity to abstract from themselves and understand that they are in the process of understanding. Such metacognitive capacities delineate human being from all other forms of animate being. Human beings are able to know not only about things outside of themselves, but also are able to know themselves with clarity both as individual personal subjects and as historical personal subjects. Language (and not merely a mode of species communication), history, and culture are constitutive of what it is to be human. As rational beings, humans recognize the meaning of not only the objects of their psychosomatic needs (such as food, drink, copulation) but recognize the menagerie of meanings that are generated from the dynamic relationships among all of their purposeful actions. The interrelationality of human activity generates meanings that extend beyond the isolated meanings of individual acts. The capacity to open one's self intentionally to what is other than oneself is also peculiar to human life.[75] This "openness" refers not

---

72. Ibid., 254.

73. Ibid. Cf. Stein, *Finite and Eternal Being*, 72: "It pertains to the nature of man that he has a body and a soul, that he is endowed with reason and free will."

74. Ibid., 254–55.

75. Ibid., 264: "In man, however, we may equate core and soul since what makes up his individual being and shapes him inside and out is at the same time open in his inner life for himself and open for taking in the world spiritually. It is his distinctive human soul that makes man a spiritually personal be-ing, that makes him a person. The soul

merely to sensation of that which is not oneself but to the conscious activity of personal spiritual being: the virtue of self-mastery exercised from the core of a personal being able to channel and integrate all urges and desires according to ultimate ends of action. The rational soul rises above instinctual behavior by ascending to the heights of interpersonal being, living not only according to the self-consumed *conatus essendi* (that is, the "struggle of being") but living for the other in the form of radical self-donation. In light of the uniqueness of the universal human vocation, Stein is able to say that "the human soul is the form of the body not by virtue of its lower powers, which it shares with plant and animal souls, but by virtue of its total unified essence or nature, in which are also rooted those higher powers which are the distinguishing mark of the human soul and which place it in close proximity to the pure spirits."[76] In fact, Stein takes up a claim made by her colleague, Hedwig Conrad-Martius, that there is a split between a "soul of nature" and a "soul of spirit" within the human soul: "We should not think of 'two souls,' however, but of man's 'soul of spirit' taking over what the animal's 'soul of nature' does."[77] This is to say that there remains the possibility of transcending nature precisely in and through nature and entering into the realm of supernatural living. The human soul bears within itself the potential to be actualized by the life-giving Entelechy of the divine Spirit.

For this reason, the human person can aptly be described as "at once animal and angel."[78] It is the human soul that "mediates between spirituality and bodily sentient being [*Leib-Sinnenhaftigkeit*]."[79] The human soul shares all of the characteristics of the vegetative and sentient souls but surpasses both in its rational and spiritual capacities. Human souls have the capacity to be regenerated and elevated by the divine Spirit, thereby sharing in

---

makes his entire organism of body and soul different from the animal's. For by such a spiritual, personal soul dwelling in them, body and soul are in a way spiritually open and free, and hence shaped personally."

76. Stein, *Finite and Eternal Being*, 377. Cf. Stein, *Potency and Act*, 256–57: "Man, the whole individual of body and soul, is raised above the animal and so above himself insofar as he is animal, by something that is in him, namely, his personally shaped I with its actuality of understanding and will as well as with the potentiality belonging to understanding and will, his 'spirit [*Geist*]' ('*mens*,' distinguished from '*intellectus* [intellect]' and '*anima* [soul]'), meaning the highest form of spiritualness, yet in this sense still not 'pure spirit' since it is immersed in and bound up with that whole of body and soul which is not transparent to itself or free. Nor is it unlimitedly transparent to the spirit, nor can it be unlimitedly mastered by spirit."

77. Stein, *Potency and Act*, 407.

78. Ibid., 406. Cf. Stein, *Finite and Eternal Being*, 371: "People are neither brutes nor angels, because they are both in one."

79. Stein, *Finite and Eternal Being*, 371.

the personal life extending from the eternal communion of divine Persons. The human being is not simply a sophisticated animal among animal species since humans exercise a peculiar spirituality that nonhuman animal species do not.[80] This human spirituality is evinced in all that makes up culture—for example, art, law, music, sciences, politics, education, cooking, agriculture, manufacturing, economy, language, literature, religion and rituals—as well as in the pinnacle of human virtue: free and conscious self-giving that becomes sacrificial and heroic. Spiritual being is that which consciously divests itself to the point of abandonment. Yet the human being is not only a spiritual being (as are the angels) since humans are composed of a material body along with a spiritual soul.[81] The human being is the one who unites the spiritual (that is, referring specifically to actuality, rationality, and personhood) and material realms of being. In this way is the human person a sacramental being par excellence: "The body [speaks] a 'language' testifying in the most diverse ways to things of the soul."[82] This is to say that

80. This assertion is confirmed by the teaching of the Second Vatican Council in its groundbreaking document, *Gaudium et spes*, 12, 24: "Believers and unbelievers are almost at one in considering that everything on earth is to be referred to humanity as its centre and culmination. But what is humanity itself? ... For scripture teaches that humankind was created 'in the image of God', with the capacity to know and love its creator, and was divinely appointed with authority over all earthly creatures, to rule and use them and glorify God ... Indeed, when the lord Jesus prays to his Father that 'they may all be one ... , even as we are one' (Jn 17, 21–22), disclosing prospects unattainable to human reason, he indicates a certain similarity between the union of the divine persons and the union of God's children in truth and love. And this similarity indicates that the human, the only creature on earth whom God willed for its own sake, can attain its full identity only in sincere self-giving" (English translation taken from Tanner, *Decrees of the Ecumenical Councils*, 1075–76, 1083–84).

81. Cf. Stein, *Finite and Eternal Being*, 462: "At this time we must again remind ourselves that the being of the human soul is not exhausted in its spiritual life. If we go back to the human root of being, we find a threefold direction in its unfolding: the forming of the body, the forming of the soul, and the unfolding in spiritual life. All this is done by the formative power of the soul, although this power (in its threefold formative efficiency) is *one* ... What is formed by this power is a human body, a means and field of expression for a free spirit ... This formative power is alive in the body and forms itself in the manner in which an animal soul is formed, and yet quite differently, since the life of the senses in its entirety is united with and formed by the spirit. And this formative power of the soul rises to a spiritual life of equal rank with the life of the pure spirits, but this spiritual life, nevertheless, has its own particular form, because it is rooted in bodily-sensory life. In this manner the separate realms of the created world are joined in human beings in the unity of an essence or nature, while outside human beings they are linked only by a causal nexus and by an interconnection of meaning."

82. Stein, *Knowledge and Faith*, 123. Cf. ibid., 99, 124: "This world with all it discloses and all it conceals, it is just this world that also points beyond itself as a whole to him who 'mysteriously reveals himself' through it. It is *this* world, with its referrings that lead us out beyond itself, that forms the intuitive basis for the arguments of natural

the human body reveals and attests to the underlying and invisible spiritual soul. The body expresses and makes visible the soul. The soul, in turn, attests to its rootedness in the divine Spirit, for the created soul is not itself the reason for its own existence. Stein insists that "the traditional tri-partition of body-soul-spirit must, however, not be interpreted as if the human soul were a third realm interposed between two other realms subsisting without the soul and independently of one another. Rather, it is in the medium of the soul that spirituality and bodily sentient being meet and intertwine."[83] The human being lives at the intersection of the visible and invisible realms, exhibiting a double phenomenality within the singular human phenomenon. This paradoxical mode of existence is the condition for the possibility of genuine self-giving and sacrifice. Only the self-possessed, self-conscious, and self-reflexive being is able to make of himself or herself a gift to the other. Only the personal being is able to love with the love of persons—to love with the divine love extending from the eternal Trinity of Persons. The human being turns out to be the crux of a cosmic redemption since the human being unites both the material and spiritual realms of being in himself or herself.

In the human being, spiritual being works to redeem both matter and spirit, both body and soul. The observable nature of material being is that which tends toward degradation, disorder, and disintegration, in a word, entropy. Entropy increases in proportion to the rate of the dissolution of ordered being. The natural interplay between energy and matter, according to physics, is a cosmic process moving toward static being with a uniform temperature throughout the universe, called a thermal equilibrium. In this static state, no work is able to be done and perpetual motion is deemed impossible. In other words, an absence of thermal differentiation results in the impossibility of work and the transfer of energy. The dynamism of being and the diversity of its forms all seem to be on their way to mass extinction, according to the inherent principles of thermodynamics.[84] This is observ-

---

theology . . . Conceiving a body in its physical aspect [*Körper*] as human [*Leib*] means regarding everything about its shape and movement as 'expression,' taking everything 'outside' as a symbol of something 'inside'"; and Stein, *On the Problem of Empathy*, 92: "As we consider expressions to be proceeding from experiences, we have the spirit here simultaneously reaching into the physical world, the spirit 'becoming visible' in the living body."

83. Stein, *Finite and Eternal Being*, 371.

84. Yet it is puzzling to note the vast intrinsic order in the universe. Advancements in cosmic order depend on an increase in potential energy, but an increase in potential energy itself depends on an increase in kinetic energy. This is to say that the potency of a molecular system stems from an energetic actuality that itself is not subject to entropic decay. For how else could we account for the impeccable order in the universe

able in the evolution of stars and in the cycles of life and death among all living beings. All biological life forms come in and out of existence, struggling for survival and self-preservation through the processes of metabolism, growth, development, and movement. Yet none of these processes can preserve the life of the individual being indefinitely. Only the process of reproduction perpetuates the biological life of the species in space and time, but the parental life form expends itself through the course of this process, becoming "a 'victim' of its vital task [*Lebensaufgabe*]."[85] Each life form is like a firework that issues its brilliance for a time and then wanes into self-extinction, not in the form of annihilation, but through a diffusion of material being and energy into the immediate biosphere.

The human soul and its desires attest to something beyond this futile fate of disintegration and decay. Human souls are charged with a trajectory beyond mortality and finitude—a trajectory whose scope has been set from the beginning on eternity. The human soul recognizes its vocation and destiny to be an eternal rendezvous of life. Personal existence refuses to assent to the lie that it is for a time and that is all. Rather, personal being hearkens to the voice of the infinite, which urges it to hope against hope and to recognize its inbuilt eternity.[86] Crude anthropology rises to a theological anthropology imbued with the truthfulness about existence—the fact that something does not originate from absolute nothingness and that actuality is prior to potentiality. Such self-evident principles modestly undress the vestiges of *philosophia perennis* in order to gaze with wonder upon the mystery of an existence that is at once material and spiritual. Without formal and final causality, material and efficient causality would wither away in an instant. Serving as Stein's point of departure for her grand project in theological anthropology, the soul's position as the form of the body ignites a faithful and accurate account of the composition of the human person. It is the very fragility and vulnerability of human being, living as it does at the intersection of the material and spiritual realms of existence, that reveals the mystery of "love divine, all loves excelling" (to quote Charles Wesley's 1747 hymn). The human person bears the potency and testimony to the

---

in the face of the observable natural force of entropy? If all mass/energy is on its way to chaos, how do we account for the ordered rivalry of chaos? Work is that which revolts against the alleged final causality of entropy and chaos. If this is indeed the case, what exactly is the unnatural (supernatural?) principle that resists the inclination to chaos and instead expends great amounts of energy as a champion for order, constantly warring against disorder? If a cosmic reversal of entropic decline is possible, what might this possibility look like?

85. Stein, *Finite and Eternal Being*, 265.
86. See Rom 4:16–18 and Wallenfang, "From Albert Einstein to Edith Stein."

radical movement of redemption, reversing the natural tendency toward entropy and, through a holy inversion, extending the vital sacrificial task into eternity, ever old and ever new. The human person is that unique being that incorporates both degenerating matter and regenerating spirit, opening the possibility of matter's regeneration inasmuch as it is united to spirit hypostatically.[87]

VI. Conclusion

This chapter began with a consideration of the possibility of the human soul, given the doctrinal trajectory of Catholic teaching and the boundless scope of phenomenological investigation. The question was posed, what traction does the concept of the human soul have in an intellectual milieu charged with implicit preponderance for recognizing material being alone? Next, it was argued that by tapping into *philosophia perennis* the human soul can be conceptualized as the spiritual form of the body. Any material being demands an account of its a priori form, or entelechy, which determines its ontological unfolding from the inside out—especially in the case of organic living beings. Second, we turned to the classic dialectical hermeneutic of being, actuality-potentiality. According to this rational worldview, all beings are in a constant state of becoming—a dynamic movement from potential being to actual being. We were led, once again, to posit a primordial locus of actual being, that is, pure actuality. Along with an eternal pure actuality is the principle of order, coherence, intelligibility, and meaning, called the *Logos*. Through this schema of reality the soul can be understood as the formal principle of the body, interiorly actualizing the organism's ordered evolution of individual being. Third, we considered Stein's project of developing an ontology of spirit alongside a typical ontology of natural material being. As a spiritual substance, the human soul must be understood according to the index of spiritual being, even if relying on the aid of analogies taken from the realm of material being. By setting forth a compelling ontology of spirit, Stein is able to further the comprehensibility of the human soul in relation to the entire created order.

Finally, we turned our attention to the specific contours of the rational soul and the Christian proclamation of its redemptive vocation. Stein posits

---

87. The logic of hypostatic union is at the soteriological crux of Christian theology. Especially codified at the Ecumenical Council of Ephesus in 431 AD, the doctrine of Christ's hypostatic union is the sine qua non of human (as well as cosmic) redemption. This process of matter's inversion that we are describing here is equivalent to a corollary hypostatic union whereby human nature is united to divine nature through the resurrection of the body and soul by the power of God's Word and Spirit.

the defining characteristics of the rational soul as freedom and intellectuality. The human person is found existing at the intersection of animal being and angelic being, yet taking up a distinct existence from nonhuman animal species and angelic species. Sharing in the rational life of the eternal Spirit, human beings are destined for life eternal, which includes the integral redemption of human being, body and soul. The human soul itself is not the source of its spiritual renewal and regeneration, but is shown to be the receptive spiritual vessel of the vital work of the Holy Spirit. By the power of the divine Spirit, the progressive entropic decline toward null being is reversed and the soul is elevated to the heights of divine Life and Being. The work of the Holy Spirit occurs especially at the margins of existence in the impetuses of formal and final causality. Material being is assigned the vocation to partake of spiritual being in its radical inversion informed by the pattern of sacrificial self-giving.

On the whole, Edith Stein provides a most plausible account of the human soul. This study has examined only one facet of this account, namely, the soul as the form of the body. Drawing from both classic Greek and Latin philosophical traditions, as well as from Catholic theology, Stein is able to counter the rash tendencies of modern thought in neglecting the phenomenological givenness and metaphysical necessity of spiritual being. As a spiritual phenomenon par excellence, the human soul is unable to be comprehended exclusively by categories of material being but must be rendered intelligible by categories of spiritual being, which themselves precede any sort of material existence. Without a careful examination of spiritual being as such, including the manifestation of formal and final causality, the human soul will continue to be regarded as unreal and irrelevant.

4

The Soul as Inner Life and as Substantial Image of God the Father

> It is a shame and unfortunate that through our own fault we don't understand ourselves or know who we are. Wouldn't it show great ignorance, my daughters, if someone when asked who he was didn't know, and didn't know his father or mother or from what country he came? Well now, if this would be so extremely stupid, we are incomparably more so when we do not strive to know who we are, but limit ourselves to considering only roughly these bodies. Because we have heard and because faith tells us so, we know we have souls. But we seldom consider the precious things that can be found in this soul, or who dwells in it, or its high value.
>
> —Teresa of Avila, *Interior Castle*, 1.2[1]

The words of Teresa of Avila still ring true for our time today. Contemporary normative anthropologies have excised the human soul as a serious concept for study. Instead, Edith Stein maintains the reality of the human soul in terms of its spiritual being and its certain manifestation in and through the body. Building on chapter 3, chapter 4 will trace two additional primary avenues through which Stein presents the human soul: (1) as the inner life of the human person, and (2) as the substantial image

---

1. Teresa of Avila, *Interior Castle*, 34.

of God the Father. By considering these crucial aspects of Stein's holistic theological anthropology, we will present a rational basis for speaking of the human soul in the twenty-first century.

I. Conscious Spiritual Being

In addition to designating the soul as the form of the body, Stein also describes it as the inner life of the human person. The soul is that which cannot be understood sufficiently by the natural sciences alone, for there is an innerness to personal life that cannot be accessed by instruments of outward sense perception. All outward perception depends on a hidden ground for its external observations. The one who perceives is ever removed from that which is perceived. The one who perceives constitutes a human subject who lives from an inwardness that cannot be extracted or manipulated by the corporeal senses. This inward self exhibits many properties, designated by such terms as consciousness, affectivity, intellect, memory, will, and personality. Stein writes, "Among the things we perceive with our outer senses are 'having life' and 'having soul.' Life and soul are 'seen along with' what we actually see in our outward perception, but they can never be seen in the proper sense from the outside. They are nevertheless truly experienced from the 'inside,' and what we conceive along with the outer world can in a certain way come to dovetail with what we experience inwardly."[2] Stein claims that we are able to intuit lived experience (*Erlebnis*), and especially the inner workings of consciousness, at the center point of an ensouled body. Whatever we observe in our outward perception always runs concomitant to an inward recognition of conscious meaning-making and empathetic experience. Our inner hidden and subjective experiences are no less real than our outer objective experiences. In fact, both types of experience act as complementary to one another. The inner life of the human person is the condition of possibility for meaningful outward perception, while outward perception serves as one of the primary means by which the inner self is formed. While the soul can be identified as integral to human life and being, it cannot be quantified, measured, or manipulated in a laboratory of natural science. As Stein insists, "The soul as a spirit is positioned in a realm of the Spirit and of spirits. She, however, possesses her own structure. She is more than a simple form that animates the body, more

---

2. Stein, *Knowledge and Faith*, 99. Cf. Stein, *La estructura de la persona humana*, 81: "'Having soul' means to possess an interior center, in which it perceives as crashing all that comes from without, and from which proceeds everything that manifests itself in the behavior of the body as coming from within" (translation my own).

than the *interior* of an *exterior*. Rather, within her there lies an opposition between internal and external."[3] It is difficult to speak of the human soul in terms of natural science based only on external sense observation. The realm of natural science is confined to the radically potential dimensions of spacetime and mass/energy, while the human soul can be circumscribed by none of these. The soul is not merely an object among objects and can be reduced neither to pure interiority as separated from an exterior world nor to an external datum of sense perception. Distinct from the externality of corporeal objects and the corporeal senses that can perceive these objects, the soul exhibits an interior life that is not identical to any external object, external corporeal senses, or the sum total of these.

Instead, one of the primary properties of the soul is consciousness, which "as a correlate of the object world is not nature, but spirit."[4] The soul, belonging to the order of conscious spiritual being, is that which has "stepped out of the order of nature and faced it."[5] The soul is that inner life of

---

3. Stein, *Science of the Cross*, 153. The end of the quoted text is followed by endnote 1, which reads, "Here one must recall that in these distinctions we are using a spatial image for something that is not spatial. Actually, the soul 'has no parts, and there is no difference as to inward and outward.' Cf. *The Living Flame of Love* by John of the Cross, 1.10." Cf. Stein, *Potency and Act*, 153: "The spirit or soul is not an extended thing, nor is the understanding a spatial part of such a thing. The understanding is not a kind of drawer we can shove things into. It is not a material body that can be molded and impressed with forms like visible, tangible shapes." Cf. Stein, *Finite and Eternal Being*, 373: "The soul is the 'space' in the center of the body-soul-spirit totality . . . As spiritual soul it rises above itself, gaining insight into a world that lies beyond its own self—a world of things, persons, and events—communicating with this world and receiving its influences. As *soul* in the strictest sense, however, it abides in its own self, since in the soul the personal I is in its very home. The soul as the interior castle—as it was pictured by our holy mother Teresa—is not point-like as is the *pure ego*, but 'spatial'"; ibid., 433.

4. Stein, *On the Problem of Empathy*, 91. Cf. Stein, *Finite and Eternal Being*, 370: "In the human soul personal erectness has become a fact. Here the *inner* life has become conscious being. The I has been awakened, and its vision moves in an outward and inward direction. The I is capable of viewing the multitude of external impressions in the light of its understanding and of responding to them in personal freedom. And *because* the human I is *capable* of doing this, people are spiritual persons, i.e., *carriers* of their own lives in a preeminent sense of a personal 'having-oneself-in-hand.'" Cf. also Cassirer, *Philosophy of the Enlightenment*, 89: "We can never imagine deriving the conscious from the unconscious, for in so doing we should have asserted a real creation out of nothing. It is quite absurd to think that the origin of the soul can be explained in terms of a combination of atoms, none of which possesses either sensation or intelligence, or any other psychological quality. Hence there is no alternative but to assume consciousness as an original phenomenon, in the atoms themselves; we cannot assume consciousness emerges from atoms as a creation, but that it develops within the atoms and rises to higher and higher degrees of clarity."

5. Stein, *On the Problem of Empathy*, 91. Cf. Stein, *Finite and Eternal Being*, 375: "The awake and conscious ego-life is the entrance portal to the soul and its hidden

the human being that, while existing alongside the natural world of objects, is not to be counted among the various objects that it never ceases to face as a genuine other. As personal consciousness, the soul demonstrates an intentionality that symbolically orders the world in which it lives and thereby exercises its "spiritual actuality, conscious of itself, [which] is its highest mode of being."[6] The being of the soul is the core of the human being, intending a world from the inside out. Mette Lebech gives a helpful summary of Stein's depiction of the ego-life in *On the Problem of Human Dignity* as she writes,

> As the origin of experience the I is absolutely individual: not in a qualitative sense, but because it is itself-and-no-other. Its individuality is not added to it, as it simply is the "otherwise indescribable, qualityless subject of experience," and so the I constitutes itself, or is constituted by itself, as the pole of structured experience. There is no constituted experience without such a pole; it is the "unity of a stream of consciousness." We may identify, upon reflection, the "bearer" of this stream as the "soul," and what seems to pertain to the stream we may identify as pertaining to it, such that acuteness of senses (apparent in perceptions) or energy (apparent in mental life and conduct) are constituted as qualities of the soul.[7]

---

life, just as the life of the senses is the entrance portal to the body and its hidden life. The awake and conscious life is the entrance portal because it is a manifestation of that which takes place in the soul, and it is an actualization [*Auswirkung*] of the soul's essence. Everything I consciously experience issues from my soul. It is an encounter of my soul with something that 'impresses' it."

6. Stein, *Potency and Act*, 200. Cf. ibid., 257, 258 (including footnote 220), 340: "Lastly, in this inner life the soul's very depth opens up, and albeit (according to Conrad-Martius's discourse on 'the soul') the soul remains a 'ground beyond' which does not fully enter its actual life, nevertheless what the soul is in itself lights up in its inner life. And as we have seen, it is possible for the soul to pass into a form of being wherein it is entirely actual, hence entirely illumined. We also saw that the free activity of the I, what is specifically personal, proceeds from its 'interior.' From here, too, the real [*real*] unity of soul and body evinces itself ... The child does not *know* what it is nor what it is like inwardly. It is given over wholly to its actual living, radiates itself therein without restraint, and this is precisely why the aura it gives off is so strong ... Children differ greatly, however, in how much their 'depth' is involved in their actual living; we should sharply distinguish this involvement or non-involvement from the kind we are reflexively aware of. I daresay, though, that on average children also live 'with their whole soul' more than adults do ... The life of a soul is the life of the subject that has the soul ... the acts of the soul—as in man—have the form of intentionality." Moreover, Stein indicates the potential perfection of the highest mode of being human: "Whoever truly wants, in blind faith, nothing more but what God wills, has, with God's grace, reached the highest state a human being can reach" (*Science of the Cross*, 166).

7. Lebech, *On the Problem of Human Dignity*, 243–44.

Individual human consciousness, signified by the "I," reveals its absolute and incommunicable character in how it serves as the immutable reference point for every noetic intention and noematic intuition.[8] The individual I is not the product of anything else, but gives itself as the spiritual axis of all perceptible, intelligible and coherent experience. A unity of perception, memory and cognition is formed from the conscious stability of the rational self. As bearer of a steady stream of consciousness, the soul is designated as the immediately imperceptible house of perception. Within the common experience of perception, we are confronted by an underlying spiritual sinew that holds all material neurological sinews together, thereby forming an organic mental whole. The touchstone of rational coherence is the soul. In other words, Stein regards the soul as the doubly intangible condition for the possibility of perceiving all that which is tangible and intangible. Case in point, the soul is evinced in the mental act of considering the essence of intangibility—an abstraction of an abstract concept that cannot in any way be attributed to the aggregate of neuroelectric impulses of the brain, which of themselves exhibit an exclusively concrete and nonconscious character per se. While the soul, as the inner life and substantial core of the human person, employs the physical faculties of neurological matter to perceive the sensate physical world, it nevertheless attests to its predetermined self-constitution and vital actuality precisely in acts of cognition that abstract themselves and the host of intuitive essences from their concrete manifestation in the material realm of atomic matter and energy.[9] The soul shows itself to be the dark ground and primordial substrate for every perception and mental act. It even has the potential to transcend the abstract character of eidetic mental acts through its supernatural responsiveness to divine intimacy. For instance, the phenomenon of love is experienced not so much as an abstract idea but as a living relationship between spiritual personal beings, whether human, angelic, or divine.

In submitting a phenomenological description of consciousness, Stein brings together the wealth of both Thomistic metaphysics and Husserlian phenomenology. In vital dialectical tension, Stein harnesses the generative power of reason working "from above" (as in Thomas) and "from below" (as in Husserl). For his part, Thomas begins with self-evident first principles and a particular brand of divine revelation, while Husserl, in contrast,

---

8. See Stein, *Finite and Eternal Being*, 31–60 (especially 46–60) for her careful description of the "pure ego" and its modes of being.

9. See ibid., where Stein defines "essences" (*Wesenheiten*) as "preconditions of experiential units" (66), "timeless meaning[s] ... condition[s] of the possibility of all knowledge" (102), "units of meaningful existence" (105), and "elements of being [*Seinselemente*]" (153).

commences his descriptive exercises with consciousness bracketed from working assumptions about that which is to be perceived. In her analyses, Stein unpacks the phenomenological givenness of the human soul vis-à-vis a metaphysical assessment of being.

II. Getting at the Heart of the Matter

The integral inner life of the soul is portrayed by Stein as including both mind and heart. Her analysis takes seriously the psychosomatic constitution of the human person in the fullness of her objective and subjective dimensions. On one hand, Stein stresses consciousness as a preeminent trait of the soul, while on the other hand she regards the heart (in both a physical and spiritual sense) to be the innermost center of the ensouled body and, therefore, of the human being:

> [Intellectual life] affects the bodily organs, the heartbeat, and the rhythm of breathing, the individual's sleep and digestion. He "thinks with his heart," and his *heart* is the actual *living center* of his being. And even though the heart signifies the bodily organ to whose activity bodily life is tied, we have no difficulty in picturing the heart as the inner being of the soul, because it is evidently the heart that has the greatest share in the inner processes of the soul, and because it is in the heart that the interconnection between body and soul is most strikingly felt and experienced.[10]

The human soul is at once bound to intellectual life, affectivity, and the body, forming an organic personal whole. Intellectual activity has not only a neurological center but a cardiological center as well. There is an indissoluble bridge between mind and heart, and this bridge is encompassed by the soul. The psychological state of a person directly affects his or her physical state. The cardiac center of the person gives itself as the domain of the most interior chambers of the soul.[11] Just as the heart pulsates involuntarily according to the electric stimuli from the sinoatrial node and the parasympathetic (automatic) nervous system, so does the soul pulsate involuntarily as the hidden riverbed of the ongoing stream of consciousness stimulated by exterior

---

10. Ibid., 437–38.
11. Cf. ibid., 433: "We have repeatedly described the soul as a sort of 'space,' and we have spoken of its 'depth' and its 'surface.' The same idea is expressed in the metaphor of the *castle of the soul*, a castle that has outer and inner chambers as well as an innermost abode. The 'I' inhabits this castle, and it may choose to reside in one of the outer chambers, or it may retire into that nearer and innermost abode."

and interior psychosomatic perceptions. All conscious life unfolds outward from the center of the person, even as it is informed by external sensory data. Beginning as a single-celled organism, the entelechy of the human being ever unfolds as from a hidden center—from not only the biological nucleus of the cell, but also from the psychological nucleus of the entire person as body, soul, and spirit. Stein goes on to posit the innermost center of the soul as "the 'most spiritual' part of the soul."[12] Likewise, it is from the innermost center of the soul that there issues "that *radiation* of the personal essence or nature which is an involuntary spiritual emanation of the personal self . . . the more a human being is at home in the interiority of its soul, the stronger is the body impregnated with this inner life and 'spiritualized' by it. Here, then, is the true center of the being of body, soul, and spirit."[13] In other words, the unique personality of the human being issues from his or her soul and charges the body in an involuntary manner. The personal spiritual self radiates through every fiber of the body to the degree that one is at home in the inner habitation of the soul. As one retreats further into the interior castle of the soul, one at the same time ascends further upward to God and further outward to neighbor. The incommunicable and unrepeatable personality of the individual emanates outward in the measure that the personality is fashioned inward, in the hidden spiritual terrain of the soul.

For Stein, it is impossible to understand the nature of the human soul apart from its indissoluble relationship with God, who is pure Spirit and the archetype and actuating pattern of all created spirits, including the type of spiritual being that is the soul. While the general form of the human soul can be divided into three distinct actualities—the understanding, the sense appetite, and will—these alone do not reflect entirely the soul's holistic constitution.[14] As already mentioned, the soul further consists of the formative involuntary entelechy of the body, as well as the voluntary capacity for self-mastery and self-possession that masters the very actualities of the soul,

---

12. Ibid., 441.

13. Ibid. Cf. Stein, *Letters to Roman Ingarden*, 259–60: "An infinite world opens up something entirely new when you once begin to live the interior instead of the exterior life. All prior realities become transparent; the genuine sustaining and motivating strengths become perceptible. Previous conflicts become trivial! The individual comes to understand a life filled with passion and blessedness that those living a worldly life do not know and cannot grasp, something that from the outside appears as the most uneventful day in a totally inconspicuous human existence. And how strange it appears when you live among those who see only the superficial and never notice anything else in the world around them" (letter of November 8, 1927).

14. See Stein, *Potency and Act*, 381–83, for a discussion of the three actualities of the soul: understanding, sense appetite, and will.

namely, understanding, sense appetite, and will.[15] This is to say that by vital participation in God's uncreated Spirit, spiritual souls master themselves through the process of self-surrender to the uncreated Spirit. A human soul can master and possess itself only in and through that spiritual being that is not identical to the soul, namely, the divine Spirit. It is a paradox in which the soul masters and possesses itself to the degree that it surrenders itself to God. Stein contends that "this surrender is the highest act of her freedom" and "here it must be considered that the autonomous action of the soul apparently diminishes the more she nears her inmost self. And when she arrives there, God does everything in her, she no longer has anything more to do than to receive."[16] Receptivity and passivity characterize the maturation of the soul's hidden life. They also signal the goal of interpersonal communion among human beings: an awakening to the ethical. Exteriority and transcendence grow in proportion to the dilation of interiority and immanence. Ethics and contemplation are counterparts within the unified trajectory of human vocation.

The transition from living as a sensual person to embodying an ethical attitude is marked by a supernatural awakening to an "attitude of one who wants to recognize and do what is morally right."[17] The character of "supernatural" awakening cannot be emphasized enough, for "the conscience of the one who lives in this certainty of faith can no longer quiet itself by following its own best knowledge. It must strive to recognize what is right in God's eyes . . . only in seeking for the divine will can human beings truly reach their goal."[18] Even the natural spiritual soul must undergo a metamorphosis and assume the character of supernatural spiritual being, not by prescinding from the material body but by conforming the material body to the self-giving and life-giving shape of spiritual being, manifest and proclaimed in the form of sacrifice. Only the personally free being can comport himself or herself voluntarily to the meaning and demands of sacrifice in the precise definition of the term.[19] Acts of sacrifice are the supreme testimony to spiritual being. Sacrificial acts reveal the utmost possibilities of the human soul: to exhaust oneself for the sake of the other. The itinerary of the soul's journey inward is disclosed in the performance of the body's outward

---

15. See ibid., 352–53, on the notions of self-possession and self-mastery. Cf. ibid., 242: ". . . the base of a man is shifted into his spirit, and so he can have his soul and master it."

16. Stein, *Science of the Cross*, 162.

17. Ibid., 164.

18. Ibid., 165.

19. Cf. ibid., 163–64, for a brief discussion on the spiritual prospect of self-denial and sacrifice.

display of love, extended toward the furthest reaches of the world and to the direst circumstances of the other.

Interpersonal communion in love is the goal to which the inner life of personal spiritual creatures is ordered. Ethics, simply put, is the field in which the proposed narratives of authentic love are tried and tested. Stories of human lives are woven from the loom of the human heart. All meaningful action proceeds from the desires of the heart and the determination of the will. Ethics outlines a territory that exceeds the competence of the natural sciences, including behavioral psychology. A posteriori studies are unable to account for the shrouded a priori self-conscious determinations of action, concealed as they are in the inner life of the soul. It is only by way of metaphysics and phenomenology that the most foundational principles and ethical phenomenality of the soul can be brought to light. According to metaphysics and phenomenology, all roads lead to God—both in terms of actuality (metaphysics) and possibility (phenomenology). For metaphysics, God is pure actuality, and for phenomenology, the idea of "God" signifies the heights of possibility, even if some phenomenologists want to call it by some other name or to de-nominate divinity in the name of divine possibilities. Supernatural phenomena are inaccessible by instruments of natural sense perception alone, but demand spiritual penetration to arrive at their detection; like discovers like. Only spiritual beings can recognize spiritual phenomena, and only methods that constitute the science of spiritual phenomena can render accurately the nature and life of such phenomena. Metaphysics and phenomenology bear the methodological competence to identify and explicate the inner life of the human person and its intimate relationship to ethical action with clarity. In pioneering the blend of these two methods, Stein is able to unearth the givenness of the human soul and its attested being in the realm of ethics.

III. The Substance of Spiritual Being

The difficulty with attempting to furnish a scientific description of the human soul is that it does not fit neatly within the parameters of the natural sciences, which limit themselves to the various forms of physical energy—for example, radiant, thermal, chemical, electric, nuclear and mechanical—and material objects that the human ego is able to face, measure and manipulate. As Husserlian phenomenology demonstrates, however, the most foundational empirical analysis will be a science of consciousness that performs a critical appraisal of all (immanent) data within consciousness rather than of those (transcendent) data outside of consciousness.[20] Phenomenology ultimately inquires about the spiritual objects that infiltrate consciousness, for example, colors, textures, sounds, shapes, ideas, concepts, sensations, meanings and images, thereby extracting raw data of a universal character. For instance, the shape of the triangle gives itself to consciousness as a universal datum: three lines intersecting and forming three respective angles. The triangular shape may take many forms and figures in the external world, but within consciousness it is regarded as an absolute datum—as a pure noema for noetic consciousness. The triangle is a spiritual object within consciousness, which includes the imprint of its shape within memory and imagination, but even more refers to the immutable givenness of its shape from an essential whence to consciousness.

Spiritual objects are of a different nature and substance than material objects. They are not locatable in space and cannot therefore be observed and measured in spatial dimensions, for example, height, length, width. Neither is their breadth or dearth verifiable by measurements of weight, mass, or material freight. Spiritual objects are not, for this reason, to be ruled out of the realm of possibility in a priori fashion. Instead, their very possibility is protected by the rights of phenomenology—by the rights of any phenomenon to give itself as such—and their actuality is secured by the logic of metaphysics. Stein contends that "spatial material structures—both dead and living—do not exhaust the range and scope of what is termed *ousia*. For self-dependent, autonomous existents are also found in the realm of the spirit. And, indeed, according to what has previously been said concerning the *first existent*, it is evident that the name *ousia* applied to it in the highest and strictest sense, because the first existent possesses an infinite 'preeminence' of being over and above all finite existents."[21] Stein insists that

---

20. See, for example, Husserl, *Idea of Phenomenology*, 28–29: "*Immanent here means then genuinely (reell) immanent in the cognitive mental process*. But there is still another transcendence whose opposite is an altogether different instance, namely, *absolute* and *clear givenness, self-givenness in the absolute sense*. This givenness, which rules out any meaningful doubt, consists of a simply immediate 'seeing' and apprehending of the intended object itself as it is, and it constitutes the precise concept of evidence (*Evidenz*) understood as immediate evidence . . . transcendence is both the initial and the central problem of the critique of cognition . . . Nothing transcendent must be used as a presupposition . . . For every mediated warrant goes back to something immediate; and it is the unmediated which contains the riddle . . . the theory of cognition has, *neither at the outset nor throughout its course*, any license to fall back upon the content of the sciences of a natural sort which treat their object as transcendent. What is proved is the fundamental thesis *that the theory of knowledge can never be based upon any science of the natural sort, no matter what the more specific nature of that science may be*." Cf. Husserl, *Ideas Pertaining to a Pure Phenomenology*, 78–104 (§§38–46).

21. Stein, *Finite and Eternal Being*, 275. Cf. ibid., 275: ". . . *substance*, i.e., an actuality

we can intuit the precise nature of spiritual being, or the substance of spirit. Not only is this analysis to be applied to spiritual objects of consciousness, but to consciousness itself through the terminology of "soul."[22] Spiritual objects can be intuited as such only by a spiritual subject.[23] Yet what is the specific substance of the spiritual subject? In other words, what is the precise substance of the spiritual soul? How might this created spiritual substance reflect the eternal substance of the first existent? Here is where the analysis must tread very carefully. The principle of the *analogia entis* must not be forgotten. God, spoken of in terms of substance and of the first existent, is not to be regarded simply as an extension and highest proportion of created substances and existents. First of all, God is supremely other and therefore ontologically different from finite existents in the most radical way.[24] The idea of God itself defies definability and comprehension and must be understood as either (1) a limit concept (as in Kant), (2) the most radical possibility—the possibility of impossibility (as in phenomenology), or (3) the first existent and the highest degree of substance, of course by way of analogy (as in metaphysics).[25] Stein adopts the latter two understandings of God, in dialectical tension between one another. For Stein, God is not solely a limit concept that marks the natural boundary of reason. Rather, God is ascertainable intellectually and able to be known with certainty via rational demonstration. Stein concurs with Thomas that we do not know what God is in God's essence, but we can know that God exists with certainty

---

resting upon itself and both encompassing and unfolding its own essence. *Essentia is* the *nature* belonging irrevocably to the being of this actuality as the foundation of the quidditative determinateness of such an existent."

22. Stein, *Potency and Act*, 354: "And the soul can carry out an activity wherein the body no longer seems to play any role at all, when the soul is not concerned with the body itself nor through it with the sensible world but with purely spiritual objects . . . and the soul itself, which is capable of such an actuality [of spiritual acts], appears to be a purely spiritual substance."

23. Ibid., 385: "Through this empty form, the soul is open in three ways: it is sensibly receptive, intellectually directed to objects, and innerly open to spiritual contents."

24. Stein, *Finite and Eternal Being*, 447: "In the case of lower creatures we have seen the similitude with the divine archetype primarily on the side of the form, because matter—in the dual sense of that which fills space and of the determinable indeterminate—is with respect to God the totally other. Only as formed matter does matter partake of the Godlikeness of created things and beings."

25. It is important to note that Stein regards analogy as the hermeneutical key for theology. See Stein, *Finite and Eternal Being*, 607–8, endnote 126: "the *law of analogy* which in my opinion is the basic law of all theological thinking. This law makes it impossible to transfer to God the categories of the finite completely unchanged. In God there are neither states of the heart nor qualities. Everything that is attributed to him must be understood analogically . . . And that which is separated in creatures is one in God."

by reasoning about God's effects.[26] Secondly, we can experience God personally through divine condescension and self-revelation as personal and relational. We are invited by God to call God by name: Father, Son, and Holy Spirit. Even more, Stein posits the human soul specifically as the substantial image of God the Father.

Stein argues that the human soul is "a substantial unity which, entirely analogous to the physical thing, is made up of categorical elements and the sequence of categories... This substantial unity is 'my' soul when the experiences in which it is apparent are 'my' experiences or acts in which my pure 'I' lives."[27] Among the persistent substantial properties, or categorical elements, of the soul are its personal individuality, and other psychic categories such as its unique causality and personal pliability. In addition, Stein points to three levels of its fundamental structure: substance, potency, and act. According to Stein, "filling time is characteristic of [the substance of the soul], and hence it is something that endures and fills its duration with a stock of qualities that persists throughout changes."[28] This is to say that, all the while the soul undergoes various changes, in every temporal instance where that which is potential is actualized, the soul's substance subsists and remains the same.[29] In comparison, the nature or substance of human being subsists throughout the course of the individual's life, independent of circumstance, stage of development, or manifestation of abilities. The peculiar nature of each and every existent is determined by its pre-set entelechy, which defines its nature and substance from the start. In light of Aristotle's distinction between substance and accidents, the substantial unity of the soul is akin to God the Father inasmuch as the unity of the divine substance is always in reference to the Father, for example, when one professes that the Son is consubstantial (*homoousios*) with the Father, and the same consubstantiality applies to God the Holy Spirit as well. The substance of the soul remains constant while its accidental properties fluctuate according to its interaction with other extrinsic substances. The divine substance is constant with respect to the diversified persona of the Godhead, which too are constant in the case of divinity. A creature's being is not contingent on its accidental properties and the caducity of its material makeup. A living creature's specific kind of being is determined by its peculiar animate substance of being evident at its existential and ontological inception.

26. Cf. Thomas Aquinas, *Summa theologiae* I.2.1–3.
27. Stein, *On the Problem of Empathy*, 40.
28. Stein, *Potency and Act*, 337.
29. Ibid., 262–63: "For the soul's potency and essence cannot possibly be identical, since its essence is simple but its potencies are many, corresponding as they do to its acts... The potencies are not part of the soul's essence but of its power as a whole."

For example, the inception of the human being is clearly at biological conception—the fusion of paternal and maternal gametes.[30] Upon this event of reproductive conception, the full entelechy of the unique individual person gives itself and begins to unfold through the processes of DNA replication and cellular division (mitosis).[31] Human nature, as a distinct species of being, is realized substantially in its fullness at the epiphany of the newly formed individual person, even as a single-celled totipotent organism.[32] All subsequent processes within the maternal womb (for example, implantation) play a subsidiary role as they work to promote and sustain the life and substance of the newly fashioned infant. Simultaneously with the inception of the individuated material body of the person originates the substance of the soul.[33] The soul does not predate the body in terms of its specificity, but comes on the scene, as it were, at the fusion of paternal and maternal nuclei, upon the complete formation of the zygote nucleus. Just as the nucleus of the cell is at the core of the cell's vital processes, physical constitution, and individuated ontological identity as a genuine other distinct from the mother and the father, so is the soul the spiritual nucleus of the entire person.

The substance of the soul cannot be reduced to the material substance of the body, just as the physical body cannot be reduced to the spiritual soul.[34] The body and soul together constitute the nature of human being and

---

30. Stein, *Finite and Eternal Being*, 515–16: "Every soul is directly or immediately created by God ... the new creature has a particular individuality of body and soul from the first moment of its existence in the maternal womb, a particular individuality which, though akin to that of the parents, is nonetheless something quite different. It must be considered, furthermore, that the new human being is from the first moment of its existence the carrier—albeit not a free, conscious carrier—of its own being and initiates its own evolution. It takes in nourishment, it grows, and it forms itself. Must we not assume, then, that the soul too, even in this earliest stage, receives impressions and initiates its own formation [*Ausgestaltung*]?"

31. Even in (1) the case of identical twins that originate from a single zygotic cell that divides into two distinct beings, or (2) the case of tetragametic chimerism in which two originary zygotic cells fuse into one, the human soul—as nonspatial—is united with the distinct material body at its inception. In the case of identical twins, a distinction of two souls would at least have to be made upon the inception of the second individual zygotic cell. In the case of tetragametic chimerism, it can be assumed plausibly—in the light of the notion of the soul as entelechy and its definitive teleology—that there is an individual soul that informs the two originary zygotic cells simultaneously, with the divine foreknowledge that the two zygotic cells will at a precise point fuse together as one unified being. The latter case is no different than a singular soul informing a plurality of cells in flux that constitute the human body.

32. See Condic, "When Does Human Life Begin?"

33. See Stein, *Finite and Eternal Being*, 274: "The soul comes out of nothingness and yet bears within itself the power for being."

34. The argument that attempts to reduce the human self/soul/person to the body

together comprise the quidditive determinateness of the human existent. However, the soul itself, falling within the category of spiritual substance, can be abstracted from its indigenous corporeality as a spiritual object for consciousness. Stein insists that the human soul exists always and necessarily in a body, but still we are able to speak of the soul in a sense in which it can be viewed as a distinguished spiritual substance in itself.[35] This task of abstraction is all the more important if we are to entertain the possibility of the postmortem soul existing in its vital specificity apart from the body.

IV. The Analogy of Material Being

In order to avoid speaking in such a way that becomes too removed from the natural world of material objects, Stein employs the concrete language of material being in order to speak of a concrete science of the soul by way of analogy:

> Just as the soul's being, as we described it, is "formed matter" (life having qualities and specified for acts), its substance (whose being is life given qualities) is also formed matter = power having

---

alone is undercut by the fact that the vast majority of the human body is regenerated several times throughout the course of a mature human lifespan. This is to say that the physical body is not contiguous with itself over the course of the body's temporal formal existence. The human body is always in a state of flux and becoming. Most anthropological material reductionisms today make their case in the name of neurobiology, arguing that all of the attributes of the so-called soul can be traced to neurological processes within the human brain as their source. Yet this argument, too, is rendered untenable in light of the recent discoveries of neurogenesis occurring naturally within the brain. Neurological matter is, similar to other somatic cells, subject to change and regeneration—a fact that calls into question the hasty anthropological interpretation that posits the subsistent self upon non-subsistent cellular matter. In other words, the whole self is much greater than the sum of its ever-fluctuating material parts. It is nonsensical to reduce the self to the organized activity of neurotransmission. The subsistence and continuity of the unique self cannot be reduced to its material components alone because the material components come and go while the self's entelechy remains the same—the entelechy as the actualizing agency of latent potencies of material being in its precise configurations and matrical properties.

35. See Stein, *Finite and Eternal Being*, 367, 597 (endnote 27): "Whatever is bodily [*leiblich*] or of the body is never *merely* so. What distinguishes the body [*Leib*] from a mere physical body (*corpus*) is the fact that the body is be-souled. Where there is a body, there is also a soul. And conversely, where there is a soul, there is also a body. A physical body without a soul is nothing but a *corpus* [*Körper*] and no longer a living body [*Leib*]. A spiritual nature [*Geist-wesen*] without a corporeal body is a pure spirit, not a soul ... The separation of body and soul in death is the scission [*Durchschneidung*] of a natural unity and does not destroy the intimate interconnection between the two, although both suffer a certain diminution of their nature."

qualities. The soul's power without form does not have actual being any more than space-filling matter in the sense of *materia prima* without form has being. But neither could the form, if it lacked power, have actual being since *this* form is formal in the sense of an empty form and the first formed power is substance.[36]

As precisely as possible, Stein describes the substance of the soul as power (*Kraft*) having qualities. The substance of the soul is depicted as the actual power of the organism's entelechy since the entelechy is at once power and form. The power of the soul cannot be separated from the qualities of the soul, such as understanding, sense appetite, and will.[37] Just as the thought of prime matter is purely theoretical and could not take place in reality (because prime matter is pure potency with no admixture of actuality), so too power, as the core of the soul's substance, would not be manifest as such without its constitutive qualities. The manifest qualities of the soul—for example, understanding, sense appetite, and will—attest to a substantial ground of their being that remains even more abstract than these abstract qualities.[38] The soul's substance is what stays the same during the ongoing processes of metamorphosis and variation within itself and within the body.[39] Stein

36. Stein, *Potency and Act*, 385. About the way in which Scripture depicts angels through material symbols, Stein writes, "The intentional object [*das Gemeinte*] can be grasped only by means of these images, but this intentional object nevertheless remains wholly different from the image by means of which it becomes conceivable. And this remains true even when that earthly thing [*das Irdische*]—experientially familiar to us—by means of which we try to gain access to the supra-sensible and supra-natural, pertains to the realm of the soul or the realm of the spirit" (*Finite and Eternal Being*, 385).

37. See *Potency and Act*, 189–90.

38. See Stein, *Finite and Eternal Being*, 369: "Following the lead of H. Conrad-Martius, we have regarded it as a particular characteristic of the *soul* to be the *center of the being* [*Seinsmitte*] of the animate existent [*Lebewesen*] and the hidden source from which this existent draws its being and rises to its visible form."

39. See Stein, *Potency and Act*, 124–26: "Finite spirits are not from themselves; that is, they do not come into existence through their own power. But they are 'by themselves [*für sich*]'; that is, by entering into existence they are on their own. 'Hypostasis' is the specific term for this self-constancy [*Selbst-Ständigkeit*]. We shall even go ahead and restrict the word to this purely formal sense that does not include spiritualness, and we shall call what is selfsufficient, insofar as it is something spiritual, a '*person*.' We would therefore have to identify 'spiritual subject' and '*person*.' The person is what *is* spiritual originally . . . If we take 'substance' for what activates its being in certain effects and—where it is something variable—persists throughout its variations, we intend something more than what selfsufficiency implies, even though without this something selfsufficiency is not possible *realiter* . . . A spiritual substance is a spiritual subject having a *what* of a definite content . . . The life of the I is stimulated at [*an*] something outside, at 'objects [*Gegenstand*]' that 'come to consciousness.' But the I is not an empty form that life is put into from without; its life rather comes from itself. Hence something exists

refers to substance of the soul as the "soul of the soul" and speaks of the living soul as "an act of the organism ... what gives being to the organic object as a whole, indeed the characteristic being that we call 'life' ... Act, understood as the actual being of the living soul, is life."[40] The substance of the soul, as power having qualities, exhibits a spiritual center of constant actualization of the organic being in its life. Once the organism dies, the soul's substance no longer is operative within the body. Upon death, the body commences an irreversible biological process of unbecoming: deterioration, decay, decomposition. However, Stein does not regard the soul as a sort of pure actuality in the finite world:

> Divine being is for us the *pure act*, in comparison with which all finite being—in different measure and degree—is partly potential and partly actual. This also applies to the soul. As the actuating principle in the living being—the principle which forms the living being and thus makes it actual—the soul is itself actual, but its actuation [*Wirken*] is at the same time a constant actualization of its own potentialities. This supremacy of the soul over all merely potential being is implied in the term "*potent potency*" [*Kraft*-*Möglichkeit*].[41]

In other words, the actuality of the soul is to be understood in relation to the constant actualization of its pluripotent potencies. "Potent potency" amounts to the finite actuality exercised by the soul. Not only does the soul bear countless potentialities to be actualized, it actualizes many of its own potencies in view of its final causality and by the power that is its very spiritual substance. If potency is that which lacks actual being (thereby assuming a negative character in relation to the positivity of actual being), "potent potency" can be viewed as a negation of negation wherein actual being gives itself. Another way of saying "potent potency" is "non-actual non-actuality," or "actual actuality"—not *pure actuality* but a constant actualization (a powerful potency) of potential being. Theoretically speaking, prime matter is pure potentiality, whereas spiritual being is the actual being that always precedes material being. Prime matter could assume this form or that form

---

that takes effect in living, and this something must have its own qualities and it must bestow qualities, although the objects whereat conscious life is stimulated *also* give qualities to the stream of consciousness. So we cannot imagine any being of the I where the I lacked substance; spiritual being requires a spiritual substance. Consequently, we may answer our question in this way: being a spiritual substance pertains to the person. Person denotes not just the form of the object in the spiritual region, but at the same time the need for an individual substance to fill this form."

40. Ibid., 289.
41. Stein, *Finite and Eternal Being*, 273.

depending on the formal actuality that causes it to take its specific shape of being. Prime matter alone—as it can be conceived theoretically—is pure potency or possibility. Only the powerful potency as finite actuality can give specific forms to this prime matter. It is the soul that actualizes the life of the individual being, including its corporeal and spiritual properties, forming the unity of the human person. And it is the pure actuality of divine Being that actualizes the actuality of the finite soul.

V. The Analogy of Divine Being

As the life-giving principle of the organism, the soul is at the same time the actuating agent of its own potentialities. As immaterial and nonspatial (though naturally living as a single nature along with the material body) the substance of the soul is the very actuating agent of both soul and body. As an individuated power having qualities, the soul's substance is manifest in its qualities, though these qualities themselves do not constitute their own substances and self-possessing powers. Individual human beings stem from the uniqueness of individual human souls, all of which partake of the same human nature but each of which constitutes an unrepeatable sui generis existence.[42] In sum, for Stein, the substance of the soul is the actuating principle of both soul and body, while the body stands in relation to the soul as entirely dependent material potentiality in need of being actualized by the soul.

Stein designates three realms of actual being: (1) material being as "that which maintains itself in a self-enclosed structure," (2) the being of the soul as "that which tends toward formation," and (3) spiritual being as "that which freely gives and diffuses itself."[43] The soul exhibits a threefold

---

42. See ibid., 272–73: "Finite being has an *essence* and it has the *power of self-being* [*Macht zu seinem eigenen Sein*]. This power is a *dynamic potentiality* in the sense that all finite actuality is constantly on the way toward its being and is therefore essentially temporal. When we designated *substance* as 'autonomous [*selbsteigen*] existent,' we meant to indicate that this kind of existent owns 'itself' or is its own self and thus has its own essence and being. However, we understood being as the actualization [*Sichauswirken*] of the essential form, i.e., as the actualization of those potentialities which have their foundation in the essence (including temporality and the 'power of being an independent self' [*Macht zum eigenen Sein*]) . . . *The specific being of living beings is distinct from both body and mind (spirit) by virtue of the fact that living beings must first acquire possession of their essence or nature*. That which is alive [*das Lebendige*] is distinguished from purely material natures because it has a 'center' of its own being, i.e., a *soul* or what we may call a 'be-souling principle' (if we want to reserve the term *soul* for that personal soul which does not make its appearance until we arrive at the individually and *personally* formed human totality)."

43. Ibid., 274. Cf. ibid.: "The form toward which material elements as such tend is the form of the body. The form for which the mental (or spiritual) as such craves is the

The Soul as Inner Life and as Substantial Image of God the Father

power of formation: "the forming of the body, the forming of the soul, and the unfolding in spiritual life. All this is done by the formative power of the soul, although this power (in its threefold formative efficiency) is *one*."[44] The substance of the soul—this singular power having qualities—is the actualizing force of life and meaning; it is the substratum of all corporeal form and cellular processes. Stein traces the origin of the soul's substance to the first existent that is pure actuality and therefore must be understood as pure spirit, even if by way of analogy. The soul, as the source of life for the living organism, "has in God its primordial archetype, because the divine life from eternity draws creatively from the source of its own self and wells up from its own depth. If the divine life were rigid and unmoved, it would not be *life*, and it is not only life but *the* life, and all earthly life is nothing but its remote image."[45]

The human soul can be understood as the spiritual heart of the *imago Dei*. Drawing creatively from the source of its entelechy, the soul wells up from its own depth and bears itself outward in a bodily manifestation. The soul's power is constantly dynamic as personal potent potency rather than as some empty, static, and meaningless substance. It is the power of the soul that generates its inner life that unfolds temporally in its spiritual life (*zoe*) and corporeal life (*bios*), the latter through mitosis and the gradual teleological formation of the organism.[46] More specifically, Stein draws an

---

form of the mind (or spirit). The soul principle [*das Seelische*], however, being 'creative' and 'underground' [*unterirdisch*], does not actualize itself in a third kind of fullness of content [*inhaltliche Fülle*], but in a form that is either material or spiritual. What we customarily call *living beings* are *substances* whose being is the progressive formation of a material body out of the soul principle. That which is alive is never finished. It is forever on the way to its own self, but it bears within itself—i.e., within its soul—the power of forming itself." Cf. ibid., 245.

44. Ibid., 462.
45. Ibid., 361.
46. For the eschatological implications of final causality relating to living human being, see Ratzinger, *Introduction to Christianity*, 304–5: "If the power of love for another were so strong somewhere that it could keep alive not just his memory, the shadow of his 'I', but that person himself, then a new stage in life would have been reached. This would mean that the realm of biological evolutions and mutations had been left behind and the leap made to a quite different plane, on which love was no longer subject to *bios* but made use of it. Such a final stage of 'mutation' and 'evolution' would itself no longer be a biological stage; it would signify the end of the sovereignty of *bios*, which is at the same time the sovereignty of death; it would open up the realm that the Greek Bible calls *zoe*, that is, definitive life, which has left behind the rule of death. The last stage of evolution needed by the world to reach its goal would then no longer be achieved within the realm of biology but by the spirit, by freedom, by love. It would no longer be evolution but decision and gift in one."

intimate connection between the three basic forms of created being—material being, the being of the soul, and spiritual being—and the triune Deity:

> To the Father—the primordial creator—from whom everything derives its existence but who himself exists only by and through his own self, would then correspond the being of the soul, while to the Son—the "born-out" essential form—would correspond all bodily being. And the free and selfless streaming forth (of the Holy Spirit) would have its counterpart in the activity of the spirit, which merits the name *spirit* [*Geist*] in a special sense. We might then see a triune unfolding of being in the entire realm of reality.[47]

Here Stein establishes a most meaningful correspondence between the fruits of reason and the illumination of divine revelation. The triune structure of the soul's formative power, as well as the trichotomy of actual being, directly accords with the Trinitarian form of divine revelation in the Christian tradition. By rationally understanding the pattern of Christian faith, one is better able to understand the creedal rationality of the structure of personal being, for "faith has its reasons and scientific reason has its beliefs."[48] In such analyses, the truth of metaphysics, phenomenology, and divine revelation coincide. Faith and reason act as two lungs breathing in the pure air of truth. By way of analogy, Stein conceives the human soul as an image of God the Father who from eternity is begetting God the Son. The eternal actuality of God is revealed as an eternal begetting of the divine *Logos*, the preexistent Word of the Father. This word at once communicates truth, goodness, and beauty. The logic of divinity is nothing less than the veracity of truth, the delight of goodness, and the radiance of beauty. As primordial creator of the universe, the character of God the Father is revealed most precisely as the *causa sui* and the unity of essence and existence. While the divine substance is the same among the three Persons of the Trinity, the doctrine of the divine processions sheds light on the distinct figure of God the Father as the prosopic archetype of the human soul in its indivisible relation to body and spirit. The personal identity of

---

47. Stein, *Finite and Eternal Being*, 361. Cf. ibid., 463: "The threefold formative power of the soul must be regarded as a tri-unity, and the same is true of the end product of its forming activity: body—soul—spirit. If we attempt to relate this tri-unity to the divine trinity, we shall discover in the soul—the wellspring that draws from its own sources and molds itself in body and spirit—the image of the Father; in the body—the firmly designed and circumscribed expression of the essence or nature—the image of the eternal Word; and in the spiritual life the image of the divine Spirit."

48. Marion, *Visible and the Revealed*, 145.

God the Father is revealed only through the divine processions of Son and Spirit, of *Logos* and Love, of Meaning and Power.

Stein likens God the Son to all bodily being since material corporeality is the "born-out" form of spiritual being. This is not to imply that there is an eternal finite materiality within the infinite Godhead. Rather, through the *analogia entis*, a direct correlation can be made between the eternal procession of God the Son and the nature of material being as such. The logic of the laws of physics and metaphysics themselves originates within the eternal *Logos*, from whom there proceeds, and in which there actualizes, "a perfect coherence of meaning [*Sinnzusammenhang*]" and "a totality of meaning [*Sinn-Ganzes*]."[49] The divine procession of the Son is the personal and gratuitous self-communication of Godself to the created universe. All coherence of meaning, all logic and intelligibility, and all rational form and truth issue from the eternal *Logos* that is the loving discourse of divinity. To be born outward in generous and sacrificial self-donation is the pattern of divine kenotic self-giving. As Albert the Great, teacher and mentor of Thomas Aquinas, wrote, "It is characteristic of the greatest love to give itself as food" and it is in this food that God manifests his whole sweetness to us.[50] The mystery of the Incarnation reveals most poignantly the "born-out" form of spiritual being. Consisting of a double generation—one divine, the other human—the immaterial and eternal *Logos* manifests itself to the created universe in becoming flesh in time and space as the Incarnate Word. His material manifestation depends entirely on the anteriority of immaterial spirit, in this case and in particular, the pure and eternal actuality that is the preexistent *Logos*. Yet God the Son does not stop his voluntary kenosis at his virginal conception. He goes even further by offering his flesh to his followers as food and drink in the Eucharist. His desire is to continue to bear himself outward in and through the Church as Word and Sacrament.

God the Spirit, according to Stein, is marked by its free and selfless streaming forth. The Holy Spirit goes by the nomenclature of spirit because this divine Person exhibits the character of spirit par excellence. The activity of the Holy Spirit is constant self-diffusion that wields the power

---

49. Stein, *Finite and Eternal Being*, 113. Cf. Stein, *Potency and Act*, 112, 331: "Ideas are—on this view—archetypes of things and the things are their likenesses or copies. But the ideas owe the fact that they have the power to call their likenesses into existence and to form the matter into copies of themselves to their being in the *Logos*, who makes them alive [*lebendig*], hence effective as well . . . Thus the individual peculiarity and the typical variations of the species are accidental outcomes from the standpoint of the entelechy, but from the standpoint of the *Logos* they are foreseen as possibility founded on the ordered interplay of the forces."

50. Albertus Magnus, *Commentary on the Gospel of Luke*, 22, 19, in *Opera Omnia*, 23:672–74. Translated in Paul VI, *Liturgy of the Hours*, 1560.

of inverting the natural tendencies of material being and spiritualizing it. Material being tends toward consumption and self-preservation, selfishly fixated on its *conatus essendi* (that is, its "struggle for being"). Its cardinal concern is to prolong its own existence over and against the existence of the rest. Spiritual being, on the contrary, is other-centered. Its concern is to promote the well-being and flourishing of the other through passionate sacrifice and loving service. Spiritual being gives itself over to the other to the point of abandonment; invisible and immaterial by nature, it is entirely selfless and self-transparent, with a purely righteous and virtuous intentionality in its self-divestment: "For in [Wisdom] is a spirit intelligent, holy, unique, manifold, subtle, agile, clear, unstained, certain, never harmful, loving the good, keen, unhampered, beneficent, kindly, firm, secure, tranquil, all-powerful, all-seeing, and pervading all spirits, though they be intelligent, pure and very subtle."[51] Along with the meaningful *Logos*, the Holy Spirit is the very power of regeneration. Just as the רוּחַ (*ruah*) swept over the primordial waters at creation, it is the Holy Spirit who likewise gives life (ζῳοποιέω) through the regenerating waters of baptism while the flesh is of no avail on its own, merely material and unspiritual.[52] The Holy Spirit lends the pattern, power, and authority of radical self-donation to both body and soul, thereby opening the way to redemption for created finitude and mortality.

For Stein, God the Father is identified as the primordial creator of the universe, creating all precisely through the eternal processions of Son and Spirit, of Word and Breath, of Meaning and Power, of Order and Kinesis. The Father, in relation to Son and Spirit, is the hidden Substratum of the

---

51. Wis 7:22b–23 (NABRE).

52. See Gen 1:1–2; John 6:63; Jude 17–20: "But you, beloved, remember the words spoken beforehand by the apostles of our Lord Jesus Christ, for they told you, 'In the last time there will be scoffers who will live according to their own godless desires.' These are the ones who cause divisions; they live on the natural plane [ψυχικοί], devoid of the Spirit. But you, beloved, build yourselves up in your most holy faith; pray in the holy Spirit" (NAB); Rom 6:4: "We were indeed buried with [Christ Jesus] through baptism into death, so that, just as Christ was raised from the dead by the glory of the Father, we too might live in newness of life" (NAB); Rom 8:5–6, 14: "For those who live according to the flesh are concerned with the things of the flesh, but those who live according to the spirit with the things of the spirit. The concern of the flesh is death, but the concern of the spirit is life and peace ... For those who are led by the Spirit of God are children of God" (NAB). Cf. Stein, *Finite and Eternal Being*, 445, 464: "And the spirit of God is meaning and power ... In the last analysis, therefore, every *meaningful* demand which is made upon the soul with obligatory force is a *word of God*. For there is no *meaning* that does not have its eternal home and abode in the *Logos*. And anyone who willingly receives such a word of God simultaneously receives the divine power to comply with the demand ... All creatures have a triune structure as substances that stand upon themselves and that are filled with meaning and power. And all self-dependent structures pertain to a triune (body—soul—spirit) unfolding of their being."

Godhead, "from whom everything derives its existence but who himself exists only by and through his own self."[53] The kenosis of the Spirit testifies to the Son while the kenosis of the Son testifies to the Father. The kenosis of the Father runs in the opposite direction, exhibiting a self-attestation through the divine processions of Son and Spirit. Scripture reveals God the Father primarily as the mysterious One, the incomprehensible One, as dark Abyss that is paradoxically Foundation.[54] And so Stein identifies the soul as corresponding most similarly to God the Father, since the soul is the hidden spiritual ground, or substance, of the totality of the human person. Just as God the Father metaphorically signifies the relational point of reference for the unity of the divine substance, the soul signifies the ontological and personal unity of the individual human being. As entelechy and actuality of the body, the soul is the animate principle from which the entire person derives his or her existence. As proximate formal and final cause of the human being, the soul reflects the Father as uncaused Cause. It is the soul that is associated most apparently with God the Father, given the trichotomous structure of the human being: body, soul, and spirit.

VI. Conclusion

In sum, soul, body, and spirit mirror the nature of divinity as revealed in Christ. From eternity, both Son and Spirit proceed from the Father, and the Spirit proceeds from both Father and Son. Joseph Ratzinger articulates the meaning of *imago Dei* very well: "The true God is, of his own nature, being-for (Father), being-from (Son), and being-with (Holy Spirit). Yet man is in the image of God precisely because the being for, from, and with constitute the basic anthropological shape."[55] The unity in plurality evident within the self, enmeshed within a community of persons, reflects the unity in plurality of interpersonal relationships and the unity in plurality within God. As Stein suggests, soul, body, and spirit together correlate with the Trinity: a singular divine Substance and a plurality of divine Persons. To recapitulate, the soul most directly correlates with God the Father as the substantial and immutable ground of the person; the body coincides with

53. Stein, *Finite and Eternal Being*, 361.

54. See Exod 3:14: "God replied to Moses: I am who I am. Then he added: This is what you will tell the Israelites: I AM has sent me to you" (NABRE); Deut 6:4: "Hear, O Israel: The Lord our God is one Lord" (RSV); Judg 13:18: "The angel of the Lord answered him: Why do you ask my name? It is wondrous" (NABRE); Ps 139:12:"Darkness is not dark for you, and night shines as the day. Darkness and light are but one" (NABRE).

55. Ratzinger, *Truth and Tolerance*, 248.

God the Son as the "born-out" essential form of the person; and the spirit coalesces with God the Spirit that is characterized as the free and selfless streaming forth of divine life. The soul is the substantial seat of personal being, bearing within itself the capacity to be elevated according to the divine Spirit and thereupon spiritualizing the merely natural struggle for being in body and soul.[56] This is to say that the soul itself either can live in the spirit or die in the flesh; the soul may yield voluntarily to the natural corruption of the body, exacerbated by its chronicle of inclinations and appetites, or it may surrender itself voluntarily to the higher faculties and movements of its finite spiritualized soul that are anchored in the infinite divine Spirit.[57] The soul—as a substantial power having qualities, as a substantial receiver and weaver of meanings, and as the substantial source and object of interpersonal love—is the substantial image of God the Father.

In providing a description of the inner life of the human person, and in drawing the analogy between the spiritual soul and material being and the analogy between the spiritual soul and divine being, Stein sufficiently presents a picture of the human soul that reduces it neither to material being nor to a meaningless and empty conceptual placeholder. Through the joint efforts of metaphysics and phenomenology, Stein accurately depicts the human soul in its spiritual substance and in its particular being in relation to the body and to divine Spirit. Stein's work effectively counteracts the postmodern tendencies to reduce the human being to categories of material being alone. A holistic theological anthropology is proffered that greatly contributes to a truthful answer to the question, what is it to be human? Chapter 5 of *Human and Divine Being* will proceed to recollect the soul in Stein's work according to one final image: the soul as spiritual vessel.

---

56. Cf. Stein, *Finite and Eternal Being*, 364: "The human soul *as* spirit rises in its spiritual life beyond itself."

57. Cf. ibid., 444: "The soul's being appears anchored in divine being."

5

The Soul as Spiritual Vessel

> We consider our soul to be like a castle made entirely out of diamond or of very clear crystal, in which there are many rooms, just as in heaven there are many dwelling places. For in reflecting upon it carefully, Sisters, we realize that the soul of the just person is nothing else but a paradise where the Lord says he finds his delight.
>
> —Teresa of Avila, *Interior Castle*, 1.1[1]

As alluded to in previous chapters, within today's intellectual climate, the human soul tends to be regarded as an antiquated nuisance to critical thought. Material reductionism has won the day, leaving spiritual notions such as the soul on the periphery (if anywhere at all) of a postmodern evaluation of human being. Nevertheless, in spite of such limiting patterns in contemporary thinking, is it possible to consider the ancient idea of the human soul anew? Given the precedent set by Edith Stein, this task is not only possible but intellectually responsible and necessary. The whole of Stein's work presents a defense of spiritual being in general, including the particular spiritual being of the soul. She approaches the question of the human soul from several angles: (1) the soul as the form of the body, (2)

---

1. Teresa of Avila, *Interior Castle*, 33. For Stein's reflection on the notion of the soul as "interior castle" in the work of Teresa of Avila, see Stein, "Die Seelenburg," in *Welt und Person*, 39–68. Stein originally intended this essay to be an appendix to *Finite and Eternal Being*.

the soul as the inner life of the human person, (3) the soul as the substantial image of God the Father, and (4) the soul as a spiritual vessel of divine Love. By tapping into the Carmelite charism of solitude and interiority, Stein illuminates the spiritual being called "soul." The present chapter will examine only the last of these rubrics through which Stein construes the human soul: a spiritual vessel of divine love.

I. *Entrée* into Divine Love

Of all the images through which Edith Stein conceives the being of the human soul, the most beautiful and poetic, as well as the most akin to Carmelite spirituality, is the soul as a vessel of love. First, we remember that the primary nature of a vessel is to receive its welcome contents. In the case of the human soul, what it opens to receive is the Spirit of God: "The innermost being of the soul is like a vessel into which flows the spirit of God (that is, the life of grace) if the soul by virtue of its freedom opens itself to this vital influx."[2] Like attracts like and it is the spiritual essence of the soul that attracts the spiritual essence of divinity to itself. In *Der Aufbau der menschlichen Person* Stein writes that "the 'soul of the soul' is something spiritual and the soul as a whole is a spiritual being whose peculiarity is to have an innerness in the center from which it must go out to encounter objects, carrying home to itself what it gains from without, and from which it can even donate to the outside."[3] Stein's depiction of the soul proceeds from the harmonic resonance of phenomenology and metaphysics working together to bring into view the ontological and noetic meaning of the soul. From the phenomenological viewpoint, Stein observes that the soul refers to the innerness of consciousness from which everything else is perceived. Without such an internal reference point for eidetic perception and meaning-making, distinct essences of consciousness would not be recognizable nor would rationality exist. The soul constitutes the logical interface of the

---

2. Stein, *Finite and Eternal Being*, 445. Cf. Stein, *Potency and Act*, 410–11: "Only by God entering and 'passing through'—theology calls what enters '*grace*'—is man 'born of the spirit' after having already been created by God as a personal spiritual being [*Wesen*] . . . And in virtue of this higher being, which is his personally spiritual being, a 'being born of the Spirit' (a life of grace) is possible for him. It is possible simply because of his original openness, and it may come to his share by his merely 'allowing' it, indeed if he does not actively allow it but just fails to resist it."

3. Stein, *Der Aufbau der menschlichen Person*, 162: "Die 'Seele der Seele' ist etwas Geistiges und die Seele als Ganzes ist ein geistiges Wesen, dessen Eigentümlichkeit es ist, ein Inneres zu haben, im Zentrum, von dem sie ausgehen muß, um Gegenständen zu begegnen, in das sie heimträgt, was sie von draußen gewinnt, und aus dem sie selbst auch nach außen spenden kann" (translation my own).

self in relation to all intellectual objects facing the self, including the very notion of "self" to begin with. Sarah Borden Sharkey reinforces this point as she observes how "Stein claims that our experience is one of coming to recognize a personal structure existing in some sense prior to our conscious experience of it. It is this personal core that is developed or unfolded in one's interior life, and this is part of the inner world in relation to which the I takes a stance."[4] As the (metaphysical) formal spiritual substrate of the person, and as the (phenomenological) conscious axis of all rational perception, the soul constitutes the personal I of the human subject. The "I" refers to the center point of the self that faces both the inner and outer worlds of relation, perception, and meaning. Borden Sharkey's observation highlights the fact that the "I" predates our conscious recognition of its existence. In other words, the "I" gives itself prior to its own self-recognition, thereby attesting to the enigmatic character of the soul as the pneumatic hidden ground of the person. Because of its spiritual constitution, the soul is at work forming the being of the person as the actualizing agency of both life (as vegetative/sentient soul) and rationality (as rational soul).

Moreover, Stein mentions the possibility of self-donation by the soul because of the soul's inherent spiritual character. If the human being were matter alone, there would be no potential to voluntarily give up oneself for another. Matter alone acts according to the intrinsically deterministic laws of nature, whereas the spiritual soul is met with the possibility and vocation of acting in a way that defies natural inclinations toward consumption and self-preservation, namely, the potential to act in a supernatural and transcendent manner. Transcending the exigencies of material being, the soul bears the vocation to extend itself outward in radical self-donation in response to the vulnerable interdependence of spiritual being. Likewise, as spiritual vessel, the soul retains the potential of bearing divine life within itself in the Person of the Holy Spirit who shares the divine substance of God the Father and God the Son. This is to say that the indwelling of the Holy Spirit implies the consubstantial indwelling of Father and Son within the domain of the human soul.

One of the primary conditions for the soul to receive the influx of the divine Spirit is "emptiness and quiet."[5] Just as an earthen vessel cannot receive its contents unless it is first emptied and open, so the soul is unable to receive the precious indwelling of God's Spirit without first emptying itself of all that is not the Spirit and without first quieting and stilling its anxious

---

4. Borden Sharkey, *Thine Own Self*, 47.
5. Stein, *Finite and Eternal Being*, 443.

wanderings.⁶ The soul prepares itself for its divine Guest who offers the power of transformation and regeneration that the soul does not possess on its own. Similarly, Paul writes in his Second Letter to the Corinthians, "But we hold this treasure in earthen vessels, that the surpassing power may be of God and not from us."⁷ The express power to which Paul refers is the Holy Spirit, the very power and bond of love (*vinculum amoris*) within the Godhead, for "the cycle of the intra-divine life completes and closes itself in the Third Person who is gift, love, and life."⁸ The soul need only open to this vital influx of divine gift, love, and life in order to receive it, but to open one's self is to empty oneself. Greatly influenced by the Carmelite charism and spiritual heritage, Stein knows well both the twofold dark night as articulated by John of the Cross—the night of the senses followed by the night of the spirit—and the demands of the inner chambers of the soul as expounded by Teresa of Avila in *Las Moradas*. Kenosis is the primary requisite for the soul to become an open spiritual vessel of divine love, the indwelling of the Holy Spirit. Yet this is a loving kenosis in which the measure of withdrawal into one's innermost self is at once the measure of outward concern for the other. Teresa of Avila coveys this paradoxical double movement in her exposition of the seventh dwelling places in *Las Moradas*:

> This is what I want us to strive for, my Sisters; and let us desire and be occupied in prayer not for the sake of our enjoyment but

---

6. Cf. Ps 131: "Lord, my heart is not proud; nor are my eyes haughty. I do not busy myself with great matters, with things too sublime for me. Rather, I have stilled my soul, like a weaned child to its mother, weaned is my soul. Israel, hope in the Lord, now and forever" (NABRE).

7. 2 Cor 4:7 (NAB).

8. Stein, *Finite and Eternal Being*, 351. Cf. ibid., 399: "Grace is the means to unite God and creatures and to make them one. According to what it is in God, grace is the divine love or the divine being, as *bonum effusivum sui*, i.e., a goodness which effusively diffuses or imparts itself while maintaining itself undiminished. According to what it is in creatures, grace is what creatures receive in themselves as imparted divine being, an imparted similitude of the divine nature, and as such limited and created, but replenished by the inexhaustible source of infinite divine being, and capable of unlimited growth"; ibid., 419–20: "But because love is the highest kind of freedom, a giving of self as the act of one who fully possesses himself (i.e., a *person*)—in the case of God, however, the act of a person who is and loves not in the human manner, but who is love or whose very being is love—the divine love must itself be a Person: the Person of Love. And when Son and Father love each other, their mutual self-giving is simultaneously the free act of the Person of *Love*. However, love is *life* in its highest perfection. Love is being which eternally gives itself without suffering any diminution, and it is thus infinite fecundity. The Holy Spirit is therefore the *gift* as such: not merely the mutual self-giving of the Divine Persons to one another, but the self-giving of the deity *ad extra* [*nach aussen*]. The Holy Spirit thus comprises in itself all the gifts of God to his creatures."

so as to have this strength to serve ... Believe me, Martha and Mary must join together in order to show hospitality to the Lord and have him always present and not host him badly by failing to give him something to eat. How would Mary, always seated at his feet, provide him with food if her sister did not help her? His food is that in every way possible we draw souls that they may be saved and praise him always.[9]

In this passage Teresa draws from the tenth chapter of Luke's Gospel in presenting Martha and Mary as the complementary personifications of spiritual perfection. Martha is busy with serving—symbolic of outward service of the other—while Mary sits beside Jesus at his feet to listen to him—paradigmatic of the spiritual itinerary of interiority. The nature of love is all-pervasive, spreading itself in every possible direction and dimension. Love stretches out to the human other to the degree that it reaches within toward the divine other. Interiority and exteriority are mutually complementary components of one and the same love. We are led at this point to inquire again into a more specified understanding of divine love.

First, it is necessary to recognize divine love as both erotic and agapic.[10] The former side of love may be associated with the interior disposition of Mary and the latter with the exterior acts of service of Martha. In any case, it is clear that the love of God revealed in Christ is a love that gives all, to the point of abandonment. It is at the same time fixated on the beloved while loving in a radically disinterested way. A term closely aligned (if not practically synonymous) with kenosis (that is, "self-emptying") is self-giving. Stein argues that "the innermost essence of love is self-giving [*Hingabe*]. God who is love generously gives himself to those creatures whom he has created for love."[11] In other words, self-giving is the very nature of divinity. Pure actuality is pure personal self-giving. Stein describes the eternal life of God as a unity in plurality in which a Trinitarian self-giving of persons obtains since "God is *love* and that love is a free self-giving of an I to a Thou, and a union of both in a We."[12] Reflected in the Song of Songs, three parties

9. Teresa of Avila, *Interior Castle*, 437. Cf. Teresa of Avila, *Way of Perfection*, in *Collected Works*, 2:155: "This is a great favor for those to whom the Lord grants it; the active and the contemplative lives are joined. The faculties all serve the Lord together: the will is occupied in its work and contemplation without knowing how; the other two faculties serve in the work of Martha. Thus Martha and Mary walk together."

10. See Pseudo-Dionysius, *Divine Names*, in *Complete Works*, 82: "So they call him the beloved and the yearned-for since he is beautiful and good, and, again, they call him yearning (*eros*) and love (*agape*) because he is the power moving and lifting all things up to himself"; and Benedict XVI, *Deus caritas est*, Part I.

11. Stein, *Finite and Eternal Being*, 416.

12. Ibid., 419. Cf. ibid., 454: "Love is the being of God, the life of God, the essence

participate eternally in in this mutual self-giving: the Lover, the Beloved, and the Witness to their Love, as the divine persona of Love itself. The eternally begotten Son is the eternal Object of the Father's affection and the Son forever chants the praises of the Father in their diverse unity. Further, God the Spirit proceeds from both Father and Son as personal Witness, Fruit, and Gift of their mutual exchange of Love.[13]

As a Trinity of Persons, divine Love is manifest and proclaimed with a Trinitarian structure. God the Father, as the primary unconditioned first principle (*prote ousia*), is conceived as the very substance of love. God the Son, as the primordial archetype and paradigm of all meaning and existence, is rendered as the meaning of love. God the Spirit, as the power of all life and creaturely being, is revealed as the actualizing power of love. The reality of love gives itself according to the Trinitarian structure of substance, meaning, and power.[14] In turn, as the vessel of love, "the soul in and by itself may be regarded as an image of the triune God. As a personal spiritual nature [*Wesen*] its stands upon itself, is filled with meaning and power, and forms itself in accordance with its meaning."[15] As the *imago Dei*, the human soul stems from the actualizing nature of spiritual being, in particular, the pure actuality of divine Spirit. The soul is a fitting vessel for divine Love as it exhibits the synchronous attributes of substance, meaning, and actualizing power. Self-giving that issues from a personal spiritual being can be received and reciprocated only by a personal spiritual being. Within the whole of the created and uncreated order, the mutual self-giving of persons is reserved for God, angels, and human beings since only angels and human beings genuinely resemble the divine image in their spiritual personhood. Human beings are distinct from angelic beings in that they also encompass material being as essential to their nature, whereas angels do not include materiality in their essential being. As a fertile effusion of divine glory, authentic creaturely love is always divine Love. The term *love* does not describe just a state of affairs or the quality of an action or an intense desire or affection, although it does relate to all such notions. In the context of

---

of God. It is fully adequate and proportionate to each of the Divine Persons as well as to their unity"; and 1 John 4:8, 16 (*Theos agape estin*).

13. For an insightful analysis of these themes as related to Sanjuanist spirituality, see Michael Waldstein's introduction to John Paul II, *Man and Woman He Created Them*, especially 23–34. Waldstein's "Sanjuanist Triangle" (24) is a very helpful heuristic device through which to make meta-connections between the works of John of the Cross and John Paul II's theology of the body catecheses. The similarity in thematic material between the literary corpus of John Paul II and that of Edith Stein is striking.

14. See Stein, *Finite and Eternal Being*, 418–20, 447–48.

15. Ibid., 448.

Christian theology, love refers above all to the divine nature that is at once (by way of analogy) personal Substance (*ousia*), Meaning (*logos*), and Power (*energeia/entelecheia*).

II. The Meaning of Self-Surrender

Within Stein's theological matrix, there is no potentiality (*dynamis*) in God because God is pure actuality (*energeia*).[16] The human soul, on the other hand, exhibits a constant flux of potentiality and actuality. As mentioned in chapter 2, according to a traditional account of creation within Kabbalah, "god created the world not at all by making something but by withdrawing, by breathing himself in, by emptying himself. By hollowing himself out, god opens the void in which the world can take its place. This is called the *tsimtsum* in the Kabbalah."[17] Just as God hollows out Godself for the universe to take its place in the created void, the soul too must hollow out itself in order for God to take his place at the vacant center of the soul's microcosm. In breathing in its potentiality, the soul metaphysically invites the pure actuality of divine Love to fill it as an open vessel. In emptying itself of its status as self-sufficient substance, as self-legislating meaning, and as self-asserting power, the human soul selflessly gives itself up to the substance, meaning, and power of divine Love to fill it and make it new. This self-emptying, according to Stein, is an occasion of radical self-surrender:

> For Love, as we know, is in the last analysis and in its ultimate meaning a surrender of one's being and union with the beloved. Therefore, the one who does God's will learns to know the divine spirit, the divine life, and the divine love, i.e., that person learns to know God himself. For by doing what God demands of us with total surrender of our innermost being, we cause the divine life to become *our* own inner life. Entering into ourselves, we find God in our own selves.[18]

---

16. Stein, *Potency and Act*, 19–20: "Pure being is pure act wherein nothing is merely potential; it does not start and stop, but *is* immutably from age to age . . . [God's] being is *actus purus*—implying that all that this something is, is constantly coming to effect actually. Hence in God's being there is no possibility that has not taken effect, no possibility determined to something that has yet to be. 'Potency' here is but possibility brought to effect, *potentia in actu* [potency in act]. Nor is there any room for a plurality of potencies in a substance that takes effect in *one* act. So substance, potency, and act in God, we must say, coincide *realiter* [really], even though in our idea we should keep them apart."

17. Nancy, *Noli me tangere*, 92.

18. Stein, *Finite and Eternal Being*, 447. Cf. ibid., 453: "Love is a self-surrender to the loved good. And such self-giving in the true sense is possible only where a person

The meaning of "surrender" is to yield to the will of God, but even more, to deliver—to give back—to the One who has come to bring liberty and absolution. God the Father, through God the Son and God the Spirit, offers the possibility of an eternal union of Love that is a Gift to be received in the measure that it becomes a Gift returned and given away to others. To complete its circuit, divine Love incorporates the beloved into itself, not by annihilating the otherness of the beloved, but by affirming the otherness of the beloved in a genuine unity in difference. The beloved makes of herself a gift back to the divine Lover who created her as gift in the first place. Therefore, "as the love with which the lower loves the higher it is more in the nature of desire and primarily disposed to receiving. As the love with which the higher loves the lower, it is more in the nature of a free giving out of personal superabundance."[19] Receptivity marks the primary character of finite love and the vocational disposition of the Bride of the Lamb of God who takes away the sins of the world. In surrendering herself to her divine lover, the Bride (who is the Church) renders unto God that which God has given her according to God's absolute initiative and superabundant generosity. Just as God gives all without remainder, so is the beloved of God called and invited to give all of herself back to the One who created her for Love—in other words, to make a genuine gift of herself. Nothing less is required of the beloved for a genuine union to obtain between Bride and Bridegroom. Just as Adam and Eve first "knew" (יָדַע) one another and thereby conceived Cain, so must the beloved know her divine Lover in pure nakedness and transparency, opening in complete receptivity to the Gift of the divine Giver, Christ the Bridegroom, Visage and Voice of the Father.[20] The finite soul becomes the house of the infinite Gift, which is possible only if the soul willfully avails its vacant center to the One who is at once its Origin and Destiny.

Even though the soul is called to a radical self-surrender of love, "human beings are incapable [of this] by their own nature."[21] The power of self-surrender issues from the pure actuality of eternal being, that is, from God's life-giving and regenerating Spirit: "To be an image of the eternal, the spirit

---

is the object of love, so that love in the full and authentic sense proceeds from person to person . . . Self-surrender aims at union [*Einswerden*], and it attains to its perfection only when the gift of oneself is accepted by the beloved person. To be perfect, love thus demands a mutual self-giving of persons. And only in this kind of self-giving can love be affirmation [*Jasagen*] in the full sense, since it is only in self-giving that one person discloses or reveals himself to the other."

19. Ibid., 454.
20. See Gen 4:1 (RSV).
21. Stein, *Finite and Eternal Being*, 457.

must be directed toward the eternal. It must *embrace* the eternal in *faith*, retain it in *memory*, and lovingly seize it with the *will*."[22] The finite soul itself is not the eternal or the power of the eternal, but must open itself to this influx of eternal power and glory in order to serve as a humble vessel of divine Love. Just as Christ emptied himself to the point of abandonment—culminating in his God-forsaken death on the cross—so, too, the human soul must empty itself to the point of abandonment by embracing the cross of self-abnegation and self-donation. Just as Christ became a transparent icon of God the Father, so, too, the soul must give itself over as a translucent alabaster vessel of Christ: "[The soul] surrenders its self to the will of the Father, who generates in the soul anew, as it were, the Son. The soul unites itself with the Son. It desires to disappear in him, so that the Father may see in the soul nothing but the Son."[23] This is not to say that the unique individual soul is annihilated in its being conformed to the image of Christ. Rather, the soul is made its true self in being incorporated into the mystical Body of Christ. This incorporation is, after all, its very raison d'être and the soul teeters on its annihilation by refusing its noble vocation: "In this activity against God, he lives from his own power and, if he persists in being in this way, he must in the end exhaust his power. His actual being must lead to nonbeing, that is, to that empty, powerless, *null* being of which we spoke earlier: the being that will continue to be maintained without its own substance and potency."[24] Null being may very well be another name for hell—an existence without life, a soul folded in on its self, frozen and destitute without any vital influx of divine actuality since it has closed itself off rebelliously to such a wonderful Gift. Hell is the wasteland of everlasting slavery—the self, enslaved to debauchery; the other, a slave to the self. It is a world of consumption and vice, a world closed to spiritual vitality, a world subject to the entropic wages of futility.

The kingdom of the blessed, on the other hand, is the realm of "heightened spiritual activity" and the land of love, the "heights of freedom."[25] The *fiat* of creation is the *fiat* of redemption:

22. Ibid., 456.

23. Ibid., 458. See Matt 26:7: "A woman came up to him with an alabaster jar of costly perfumed oil, and poured it on his head while he was reclining at table" (NAB). See also Luke 7:37–38; Mark 14:3; John 12:1–8. Note that alabaster is a translucent material, similar to depicting the soul as a translucent spiritual vessel that sheds the light of its divine contents. Moreover, in the Gospel accounts, the alabaster jar is broken by the woman who anoints Jesus, suggesting both translucence and surrender of brokenness in order for the contents to be shared.

24. Stein, *Potency and Act*, 411.

25. Ibid., 398; Stein, *Finite and Eternal Being*, 446. Cf. *Finite and Eternal Being*, 454: "There is nothing that is freer than love, for love commands not only some individual personal urge or impulse, but the personal self in its totality."

> *Dixitque Deus fiat lux et facta est lux*
> *Et Vidit Deus lucem quod esset bona*
> *Et divisit lucem ac tenebras*
>
> Genesis 1:3–4

> *Dixit autem Maria*
> *Ecce ancilla Domini*
> *Fiat mihi secundum verbum tuum*
>
> Luke 1:38

> *Et Verbum caro factum est*
> *Et vidimus gloriam eius*
> *Gloriam quasi unigeniti a Patre*
> *Plenum gratiae et veritatis*
>
> John 1:14

> *Pater noster qui in caelis es*
> *Sanctificetur nomen tuum*
> *Veniat regnum tuum*
> *Fiat voluntas tua sicut in caelo et in terra*
>
> Matthew 6:9–10

The Genesis text relates the originary creative Word of God, who is the Son—the divine *Logos*—through whom the universe was created. It is the *fiat* of this word that generates the entire cosmos in all its life and fertility, beginning with the primordial radiance of light. God regards this light, and all that is created, as good since all springs from the eternal goodness of God. The division of light and darkness signifies the difference between actuality and potentiality. Darkness is naught without its contingent relation to the light. Darkness signifies an absence of light—an abyss waiting to be filled by luminous brightness. The light is good because it allows everything to come into view and it is the source of warmth and initiator of the biological process of photosynthesis. Light signifies the pure actuality that is from eternity. The generative energy of light from celestial bodies—today understood as the process of nuclear fusion and its productive radiant and thermal energy—is that which opens the possibility of all organic life forms to take their place in existence. However, the process of nuclear fusion itself attests to a prior actuality that generates the twofold physical dimension of spacetime and mass/energy. The physical reality, as admixture of potentiality and actuality (and, theoretically speaking, which is pure potentiality), gives witness to a noncontingent, immutable, uncaused spiritual Reality in which existence itself is undoubtedly its very essence.

Pure actuality commences creation with a punctuating *fiat* that ushers in the totally other in relation to God: created finite spacetime and mass/energy, as well as potential actuality, namely, finite spiritual being. The one who claims that any sort of potentiality is prior to actuality has misplaced his intellect along with its covenantal tethering to truth. For the possibility of the possibility of possibility already depends on an actuality of possibility as such. The creative *fiat* of God initiates the impossible in relation to God: that which is not God. God, who is the full actualization of all good possibilities (that is, of all possibilities), empties the center of her eternal Life in order for the created cosmic offspring to be generated within. It turns out that the genius of motherhood is an image of divine Life par excellence and directly relates to our second selected passage from the Gospel of Luke.

Mary's *fiat* faithfully responds with all uprightness to divine Goodness which extends the maternal vocation to her as the glorious pathway of salvation.[26] As Augustine of Hippo observantly put it, "But without you God made you ... In some way, therefore, God made you without you, but God does not justify you without you."[27] Mary affirmatively responds to God's will on behalf of all humanity, welcoming the divine Life within the womb of her flesh as well as the womb of her soul. Unlike Lucifer and the renegade angels with their defiant *non serviam*, Mary embraces the vocation to serve. Calling herself the servant of the Lord (*ancilla Domini*), she models for all humanity the proper response to the God who created us to serve; for to love is to serve. Mary's finite *fiat* echoes the infinite-become-finite *fiat* of God's creative Word. The voluntary and loving inversion of God's eternal actuality opens the possibility of the impossible in relation to God, namely, potentiality: "for nothing will be impossible [οὐκ ἀδυνατεῖ] for God."[28] Creation is the act of God that introduces potentiality into the eternal tide of actuality.

---

26. Stein, *Finite and Eternal Being*, 516: "Just as the mutual self-giving of the parents and their common generative will prepare the existence of the child and the endowments of its future life, so the growth of the child and the forming of its body and soul demand the loving self-giving of the mother and her dedication to the task of motherhood. The paradigm of this is the *Fiat!* ('Be it done unto me') of the Mother of God (Lk 1:38). This *Fiat!* enunciates her loving self-surrender to God and to the divine will and simultaneously her own generative will and her readiness to dedicate her body and her soul to the service of motherhood. Is it even possible to conceive of the relationship of the Mother of God to her child otherwise than as a loving embrace with the whole power of the soul?"

27. Augustine of Hippo, *Sermo 169*, 11, 13 (PL 38, 923): "Sed sine te fecit te Deus ... Qui ergo fecit te sine te, non te justificat sine te" (translation my own).

28. Luke 1:37 (NAB).

The actuality of potentiality is God's *fiat* to humanity; the potentiality of actuality is humanity's *fiat* to God.

The third featured biblical text, taken from John's Gospel, utilizes the same language in the original Greek version as the other texts: γίνομαι (*ginomai*), which can be translated "to become, to come into being, to take place, to happen, to arise, to receive" and even "to marry" (see Rom 7:3–4). Instead of the subjunctive form of *facio*—*fiat*—the Latin translation of John 1:14 renders the passive indicative form of *ginomai* as *factum est*. The significance of this text is that it highlights the fruit of the Marian *fiat*: "Most blessed are you among women, and blessed is the fruit of your womb."[29] Mary's *fiat* results in the literal conception of the Christ-child in her womb (*factum est*). In order to become what it was not, the eternal Word had to be heard and welcomed by that which was not God, yet, at the same time, to be heard and welcomed by that which was most like God. Mary is at once not God and yet most like God in her spiritual personhood, impeccability, upright freedom, docility and transparency. Indeed, most blessed is she among all women and men of all times and places. Through Mary is the course of truth and glory completed as the eternal generation of the Son extends to a finite generation of a creature. The *fiat* of Mary's affirmative response to the divine summons opens the transposition into the *facio* of the Incarnation. As filial divine procession, the bodying forth of the *Logos* first occurs through the divine act of creation and secondly transpires through the *fiat* of Mary. The eternal glory, grace, and truth of God are revealed in the Word made flesh. This mystery is praised most poetically in the ancient Akathistos hymn to the wondrous *Theotokos*.

The last chosen biblical text, taken from Matthew's Gospel, conveys the primacy of the *fiat* in the life of all would-be followers of Christ: *fiat voluntas tua*—thy will be done. This is the interior disposition of the soul who seeks God as its welcome Guest. Just as Mary expresses her irrevocable and unwavering Yes in response to the divine Yes of creation, so is every human being invited by God to respond to the offer of salvation with an unrelenting Yes. The paradox of this response is how the unyielding Yes takes the form of yield and surrender. Stein claims that "every human soul is destined to become a spiritual vessel" and that "Mary realized this destiny of the human soul in the most perfect manner."[30] The human soul's yielding to the divine *Logos* is expressed in the verbal form of the *fiat*. Stein notes that just as the Litany of Loreto calls the Mother of God a *vas spirituale*, so every human soul is called to become a spiritual vessel similarly by opening

---

29. Luke 1:42 (NAB).

30. Stein, *Finite and Eternal Being*, 608 (endnote 126).

to the vital power of divine logic, meaning, and substance.[31] Mary serves as the model of spiritual perfection for humanity: "And since it was to be [Jesus's] nourishment to do the will of his heavenly Father (Jn 4:34), the mother whose nature was to be his first nourishment had to give herself over to the will of the heavenly Father with the whole power of her soul."[32] The *fiat* of the Lord's Prayer is realized perfectly—actualized—in Mary's life and womb. The blessed fruit of her womb is the eternal *Logos* who became (*facio*) flesh through the reciprocal freedom of Mary's Yes (*facio*). In the figure of Mary we behold the definitive meaning of love as self-giving in the form of receptivity to the gift and return-gift.[33]

As self-giving, love "is a receiving into the innermost core of being and simultaneously a response issuing from the center of interiority."[34] The substance of the soul, as demonstrated above, underlies the conscious life of the ego. A spiritual depth can be felt beneath the constant stream of consciousness—an "innermost essence of the soul [that] becomes manifest externally."[35] This is the sacramental relationship between body and soul in which the invisible spiritual soul is manifest in and through the visible physical body. However, it is the innermost being of the soul that is the "'abode of God' ... capable of receiving into itself the Spirit of God ... destined for eternal being."[36] As early as her dissertation work, *On the Problem of Empathy*, Stein is found positing the givenness of the zero point of the living body—"a 'zero point of orientation' which my living body surrounds."[37] In her earlier work, this zero point of the living body is equivalent to the ego-center of consciousness in which there is no notable distance between any portion of the living body as an organic whole in relation to the ego. Yet in her later work Stein underscores the depth of the innermost being of the soul as that which "is the *how* ($\pi o\tilde{\iota}ov$) of the essence itself and as such impresses its stamp on every trait of character and every attitude and action of human beings, and it is the key that unlocks the mystery of the structural formation of the character of a human being ... all bodily processes (if they

---

31. Cf. Stein, *Potency and Act*, 399: "... openness belongs to spirit as such; to the infinite spirit belongs universal openness, and to the finite spirit (hence to man, too) belongs an openness of a particular kind and pointed in a particular direction"; and Stein, *Finite and Eternal Being*, 364, 463: "The human soul *as* spirit rises in its spiritual life beyond itself ... [The soul] steps forth from itself (transcends itself) in its spiritual life."
32. Stein, *Finite and Eternal Being*, 517.
33. See Chauvet, *Sacraments*, 117–27.
34. Stein, *Finite and Eternal Being*, 467.
35. Ibid., 502.
36. Ibid., 504.
37. Stein, *On the Problem of Empathy*, 43.

are really *bodily* [*leiblich*] and not merely corporeal [*körperlich*]) are simultaneously soul processes."[38] Through the agility of metaphor Stein discloses the reality of the soul in its sacramental character. True interpersonal love rests at nothing short of the innermost depth of the person. The center of the person, which is the person's soul, is the target and home of spiritual love. For human beings, such love is expressed sacramentally in and through the body. The union of body and soul forms a singular human nature in which the life of the soul is the life of the body. If "the most sublime meaning of all spiritual-personal being is mutual love and the union of a plurality of persons in love," then the human soul—as the free, rational, and spiritual center of the person—is the condition of possibility for such love and communion of persons.[39]

Love desires to enter into the center of the other's being and to be enveloped by the other. In spousal love, through the unfolding of sexual intercourse, the masculine enters into the feminine while the feminine envelops the masculine. An interpenetration of persons occurs, creating a most intimate expression of love. A procreative *perichoresis* (*circumincessio*) obtains within this empathetic communion of persons. The teleology of love is fecund and generative. The final causality of love is ordered toward communion and procreation, while the formal causality of love is the essence of spiritual being. This is evinced in the eternal begetting of the Son of God and in the phenomenology of spousal love. In human procreation, an infant is conceived within the body of the mother, commencing his or her existence within her vital center. Spousal love becomes personified further in the life of the child as he or she takes up residence within the personhood of the mother: person inhabits person. The mother envelops the child as she enveloped her spouse in their intimate communion of love. Fatherhood is characterized as the bodying-out of love from which issues an outward and productive gift of life. The symbolic language of the masculine body follows the contours of spirit that empties itself to the point of abandonment and exhaustion, extending itself (and propelling itself) toward the beloved in an initiatory expression of gift. Like the mother, the father is called to serve. He is to be the servant of the servant, emptying himself in daily service of his spouse and children. As husband, the father makes of himself a total gift to his family, conscientiously and constantly bonding himself to his household in covenant relationship. The essence of spirit is servanthood—to become a constant gift of self for the other. The human soul is charged with the vocation to receive the divine Gift within the center of its being and, in turn,

---

38. Stein, *Finite and Eternal Being*, 501–2, 513.
39. Ibid., 514.

to become a radical gift of self for others in and through, and at the risk of, the body.

In summary, the soul is a spiritual vessel of love inasmuch as it alone is able to receive love in a personal spiritual way. No conglomerate of chemical processes is able to receive love as such because genuine interpersonal love is a phenomenon among spiritual beings and cannot be reduced to the interplay of energy and atomic matter. Love surpasses the domain of physics insofar as it proceeds from the heights of metaphysics and even that dark province that transcends metaphysics. Yet love utilizes the field of physics in order to reveal itself in its vulnerability, humility, and otherness. Divine love, as revealed in Christ (and especially in his incarnation in the womb of Mary), is paradoxical giving in which greatness is manifest in littleness, in which power is perceived in weakness, in which divinity is proclaimed in humanity, in which redemption is experienced in suffering, and in which life is revealed in death because love raises the dead to new life. Since love is pure spirit and personal—most especially revealed as the Third Person of the Trinity, the Holy Spirit—personal spiritual being is the only kind of being capable of receiving love. According to divine revelation and upon contemplating the natural order, the only two kinds of beings that bear the capacity to recognize, receive, and reciprocate divine love are pure spiritual beings called angels, and human beings who exist at the intersection of spiritual and material being. It is due to their rational souls that human beings have the capacity to be personal recipients of divine love. The interior castle of the soul is truly the abode of God wherein the soul opens to divine Gift as a womb of divine Life.

III. Afterlife of the Soul and Union with God

Having traced an anatomy of the human soul according to Stein's conception of it, we will now turn to the great obscenity of the soul's separation from the body at death and yet its prospect for permanent union with God. In order to treat these questions, we will proceed along the following three lines of Stein's portrayal of the postmortem soul: (1) metaphysical analysis of the phenomenon of death, (2) examination of the hypostatic union of Christ, and (3) investigation of the meaning of the soul's permanent union with God. By considering these three facets surrounding the question of the status of the soul following death, we will arrive at a portrayal of the beatific vision as it concerns the indefatigable vitality of the soul beyond the grave.

a. Death

To this point the soul has been regarded as forming an indivisible union with the body. Within Stein's theological anthropology, however, we may inquire into the relationship between soul and body upon the death of the human subject. If the soul and body constitute an integrated whole, which is the human person as such, how can we conceive of a separation of soul from body without destroying the integrity of the unified psychosomatic person? Following Thomas Aquinas, Stein regards the soul to continue to subsist following the death of the biological organism because it maintains the incorporeal operation of understanding (*intelligere*).[40] Stein writes that "because the soul has neither its only nor its true being in the informing [*Hineingestaltung*] of the body (since the soul is capable of living independently in separation from the body), the soul in and by itself may be regarded as an image of the triune God. As personal spiritual nature [*Wesen*] it stands upon itself, is filled with meaning and power, and forms itself in accordance with its meaning."[41] We have noted earlier the soul's *imago Dei* as substance, meaning, and power. Since the soul—in its understanding—is able to abstract from its material and bodied-forth self, it cannot therefore be reduced to the brain or to any subsection of the organic physical body.

The soul ever transcends its corporeal manifestation and expression. While sensation is a phenomenon dependent upon the bodily faculties—for example, eyes, ears, nose, tongue, neurons—the operation of understanding cannot be reduced to the sensate faculties alone, including the brain, for the respective substances and essences of finite beings are not perceived according to the senses but according to abstraction from the senses.[42] In

---

40. See Thomas Aquinas, *Summa theologiae* I.75.3.

41. Stein, *Finite and Eternal Being*, 448.

42. See Thomas Aquinas, *Aquinas's Shorter Summa*, 74: "... a recipient must be lacking in that which is received. The intellect is capable of knowing all sensible natures. Therefore, if it knew through the medium of a bodily organ, that organ would have to be entirely lacking in sensible nature; but this is impossible." This is to say that if the intellect were a color, how could it understand color as such; if the intellect were a neuron, how could it understand the neuron as such; if the intellect were a material object, how could it understand material objects as such? Rather, the intellect is an immaterial substance distinct from those material components that it informs and from which it abstracts: "The intellect in act is the object actually understood" (ibid., 78). There must be an intellectual actuality that is anterior to all sensible perception and interpretation. For what else interprets all that which the bodily senses perceive? Neurons and the brain as a whole are contingent components of the physical body. They are lifeless without their organic relation to other vital processes such as circulation and respiration. Further, neurological matter transmits no information to thought other than that which is perceived by the senses. Yet to where does neurological matter transmit its information

classic Aristotelian metaphysics, as well as in Thomistic scholasticism, passive reason (possible intellect) is receptive to intelligible forms while active reason (agent intellect) organizes and operates upon the intelligible forms. Metaphysical contemplation transcends biochemistry insofar as the understanding soul is able to abstract from all biochemical processes, even if the physical senses supply the intellect with the raw formal material for imagination. One surely must admit that the formal material itself precedes the senses as the senses only gather up the givenness of the pure forms, for example, circle, blueness, two. Understanding even surpasses imagination as the intellect is able to abstract from imagination in recognizing the givenness of the diversity of forms revealed in the created order—for example, sounds, colors, numbers, shapes, and noematic ideas. The rational soul—that is, the intellect—cannot be reduced to neurological matter because the latter is a composite material organ while the former gives itself as singular, simple, and immaterial. In particular, the agent intellect stands apart from matter in its ability to abstract universal forms from matter and to face matter. The agent intellect (in its unity with the possible intellect) is the actualizing rational entelechy, synonymous with the term *soul*. The corporeal senses are channels to the soul, but composite senses do not constitute the soul as such. Whereas the senses (including neurons) constitute a network of receptors imbued with potency, the soul is both the formal and final causality of the body—as actualizing principle of the body—and the interpretive agency of all bodily processes. It is self-evident that sensate potentialities cannot themselves be the source of actual understanding.[43]

---

to become meaningful and intelligible if not to the spiritual intellect? The known itself does not know per se. Only the knower knows a known. Any corporeal material involved in the processes of sensation and knowing is not equivalent with the knower as such, but serves as a medium for knowing and understanding: "We must realize that forms in corporeal things are particular, and have a material existence. But in the intellect they are universal and immaterial. Our manner of understanding brings this out. That is, we apprehend things universally and immaterially. This way of understanding must conform to the intelligible species whereby we understand. Consequently, since it is impossible to pass from one extreme to another without traversing what lies between, forms reaching the intellect from corporeal objects must pass through certain media. There are the sense faculties, which receive the forms of material things without matter . . . However, the forms of things received into the sense faculties are particular, for we know only particular objects with our sense faculties. Hence man must be endowed with senses as a prerequisite to understanding" (ibid., 77).

43. Even to posit an objective reality as such already implies a subjective (nonobjective, immaterial) reality that is doing the positing of the objective reality "out there." The subjective dimensions of human existence certainly cannot be circumscribed by, or reduced to, the objective dimensions of human existence. Any attempt at defining "the real" as such already attests to an anterior subjective reality that abstracts from "the real" in order to verify it. Any objective material reality exists insofar as it can

Intentionally severing physics from metaphysics results in a worldview that reduces the whole of reality to material and efficient causality alone, as if reality is composed solely of energy and matter and their mutual interaction. Do energy and matter themselves account for their formal and structured composition? Do energy and matter combined exhibit a pure actuality and self-givenness from eternity? The material reductionist would answer such questions in the affirmative. However, right reason refuses to play the fool to the deceptions of material reductionism. Contemplative reason recognizes the interlocking relationship between potentiality and actuality. Energy and matter—as we know today from Albert Einstein's mass-energy equivalence equation, $E = mc^2$—are convertible one into the other, always maintaining a constant measure of mass (and/or energy) within the physical system. Since matter is theoretically pure potency—for it could take this form or that form depending on that which acts on it—and since energy is convertible into matter and vice versa, then neither energy nor matter accounts for its own existence in the form of pure actuality. We must ask, what is the actual basis of existence itself? To deny the self-evidence of the fundamental scientific hermeneutic of potency–act is, at the same time, to dispense with a holistic comprehension of the cosmos—yes, this ordered expanse of the universe that testifies unceasingly to its physical and metaphysical givenness. Even

---

be distinguished as other than the mind, by the mind. The givenness of all material objects depends on that to which it is given, namely, consciousness, which itself cannot be reduced to just another material object or even a network of material objects. The ontological difference between matter and mind (soul) transcends and outstrips the model of material and efficient causality of dialectical materialism in which quantitative changes pass into qualitative changes at some critical point of material evolution. Consciousness is not merely the product of material and biological evolution (even if regarded as somehow qualitatively different from basic matter), but is rather an attribute of the very source of human becoming that is the substantial spiritual human soul. One who attempts to argue that potentiality is prior to actuality fails to trace the origin of existence far back enough: to the beginning. Any intelligible sense of beginning must posit actuality prior to potentiality or else there is no beginning, in which case there is no existence, which is certainly not the case. In the beginning was relationality and it was this relationality that was the actuality that generated all subsequent components of existence, both spiritual and material. This primordial relationality has been revealed gradually to humanity by divine initiative and self-communication and ultimately revealed through Jesus Christ as the Most Holy Trinity: one God, three Persons. As quantum physics has made plain today, even the most elementary particles—namely, atoms—are themselves comprised of a host of subatomic particles—for example, quarks, leptons, and gauge bosons, according to the current Standard Model of elementary particles—which exhibit even more fundamental structural polarities and potencies than those observed on the macro-atomic level. The fact that there is something rather than nothing, coupled with the fact that there is more than one within this something, points to a paradoxical infinite reality that is both one and many as pure actuality. The universe is charged with the vestiges of the triune God.

the question of the human soul is ruled "out-of-bounds" by the intellectual treachery of material reductionism. Why inquire into a kind of being whose possibility is denied a priori? Instead, Stein argues that

> the being of the spiritual soul is detachable from all sensuality and corporeality. We are able to conceive of an "inner life" of the soul that persists even in separation from the body and after the cessation of all sense impressions. In this manner we envisage the life of the soul after death and prior to the resurrection of the body. And in this manner the soul lives—according to the testimony of the mystics—in those ecstatic states in which the soul is enraptured [*entrückt*], in which the senses are non-receptive to any external impressions and the body in death-like rigidity, while the spirit acquires in contemplation its greatest vitality and attains to the plentitude of being.[44]

For Stein, the transcendence of the soul beyond matter is due to its immaterial and nonspatial interiority. Natural science is concerned with objects "out there," that is, outside of the "I," while metaphysics and pneumatology are concerned with the spiritual life within, which cannot be quantified or measured by the physical laboratory dimensions of spacetime and mass/energy. Whereas death indicates the cessation of biological processes within the physical organism—for example, circulation, respiration, metabolism, neurotransmission—the life of the soul subsists following biological death by virtue of its character of formal intellect that is not prone to corruptibility as is the body.[45]

In the secret center, or zero point, of the body does the soul withdraw from the sensible world and begin its movement outward in expressing itself through the body. Likewise, the phenomenon of ecstasy attests to the activity of the soul that is not itself contingent on the physical body. Spiritual contemplation of the luminous darkness of divine simplicity, and communion with the totally other in relation to the created dimensions of potentiality, take leave of matter as long as matter is not subject to the laws of the spirit. For the soul is "a personally formed spirit capable of receiving into itself divine life. And this is why every human soul can be elevated to a height that

---

44. Stein, *Finite and Eternal Being*, 441. Cf. Stein, *On the Problem of Empathy*, 47: "An 'I' without a body is a possibility. But a body without an 'I' is utterly impossible."

45. See Thomas Aquinas, *Aquinas's Shorter Summa*, 68–69: "But beings that are supreme among created entities approach most closely to likeness with God. They have no potency with regard to existence and non-existence; they have received everlasting existence from God through creation . . . existence always follows form. Since the substances in question are subsisting forms, they cannot be separated from their forms, and so cannot lose existence. So they are incorruptible."

makes it capable of dominating its body and its own nature . . . the soul may then be elevated from its natural bondage [*Gebundenheit*] to the body and to itself, to a position in which it freely rules over the body, over itself, and over the divine life with which it is filled."[46] Stein is not suggesting a Platonic discarding of the physical body but a spiritualization of the body in which both body and soul are transformed according to the power (*energeia*/*entelecheia*) and authority (*exousia*) of the divine Spirit. The heights of freedom are reached by the humility of divine condescension. Body and soul are not at odds with one another in their integral unity. Death is only a prelude to the eternal union of body, soul, and spirit: "The separation of body and soul in death is the scission [*Durchschneidung*] of a natural unity and does not destroy the intimate interconnection between the two, although both suffer a certain diminution of their nature."[47] The soul is not finally at home apart from the body and the body is naught without the formal actuality of the soul. The teleology of both body and soul—of human nature—is anchored proleptically in the eternal union of the material body, the spiritual soul, and the divine Spirit: the consummate communion of angels and saints alive in the unity of the Godhead. However, this teleology itself is generated by its inverted archetype of the mystery of the Word made flesh.

b. The Hypostatic Union of Christ

The soul is not entitled to eternal beatitude and bliss due to its metaphysical composition alone. Rather, it is because of divine gift that the soul is created, awakened, and redeemed—all by the merits of Christ. It is ultimately an intricate Christology that undergirds the multifaceted structure of Stein's theological anthropology. Stein's Christology is entirely staurological, or cross-centered. In line with the Carmelite charism, Christ can be

---

46. Stein, *Finite and Eternal Being*, 461–62. Within this passage Stein draws the distinction between soul and spirit: "The division between the *soul* being (i.e., the body-bound being) and the *spiritual* being (i.e., the God-centered being) of the human soul is found in the soul's very essence or nature." Cf. Stein, *Science of the Cross*, 153–55: "[Within the soul] there lies an opposition between internal and external . . . In her ascent to God, the soul raises herself above herself or is raised above herself. But at the same time, by this more than by anything else she actually attains her innermost center. That sounds contradictory, but corresponds with the facts and is grounded in the realm of the spirit's relationship to God . . . A created spirit can only ascend to [God] by transcending itself. Whatever ascends to him descends at the same time, by that very act, into its own center or resting place . . . The higher [the soul] ascends to God, the deeper she descends within herself: the union is consummated in the innermost soul. In the deepest ground of the soul."

47. Ibid., 597, endnote 27.

understood only according to the logic of the cross, that is, the logic of simply sublime paradox. Very basically, according to the logic of the cross, God became human so that human beings could become united eternally to God.[48] First, God accomplished the impossible by creating that which is not God. Second, God accomplished the doubly impossible by becoming that which is not God in order to redeem that which is not God. The otherness of God vis-à-vis humanity is not annihilated in the incarnation of God the Son, but subsists in perfect union with his assumed human nature. The key to redemption is the unity that obtains precisely in and through ontological difference. Likewise, in resurrected life, individual human beings lose neither their human nature nor their incommunicable personhood as they participate in the divine nature by divine union, and all this comes as gift from God.

The logic of the cross is where kinesis is because kenosis was and will be. In other words, any physical kinetic energy is due to a prior self-emptying of divine being that freely generates mass/energy. Further, the bookends of kinesis, as it transpires in spacetime, are anterior formal causality and posterior final causality—two causalities that are intimately bound to one another so much so that beginning is end and end is beginning. Divine self-emptying simultaneously begins and consummates. As covenantal self-emptying, divine Life has fashioned an oath that swears that it will swear the same forever as it swore in the beginning.[49] The doctrine of Christ's incarnation implies that the eternal Son of God both united himself to created mass/energy (the body) and to created spiritual being (the soul). Through the early ecumenical councils, especially the Council of Ephesus in AD 431, the magisterial teaching authority of the Church came to understand the divine nature and the human nature of Christ to be united hypostatically in the one Person of the eternal Son of God insofar as his divine nature subsisted—or "stood under"—his assumed human nature without

---

48. See Irenaeus, *Adversus haereses*, Book V, Preface: "the Word of God, our Lord Jesus Christ: who, because of his infinite love, became what we are so that we would be perfected into what he is himself" (Verbum Dei, Jesum Christum Dominum nostrum: qui propter immensam suam dilectionem factus est quod sumus nos, uti nos perficeret esse quod est ipse). Translation my own.

49. See Heb 13:8: "Jesus Christ is the same yesterday, today, and forever" (NAB); Rev 1:8: "'I am the Alpha and the Omega,' says the Lord God, 'the one who is and who was and who is to come, the almighty'" (NAB); Rev 22:13: "'I am the Alpha and the Omega, the first and the last, the beginning and the end'" (NAB); Rev 1:17; 21:6; Isa 41:4; 44:6; 48:12; Exod 3:14. It is also important to note that the Hebrew word for the verb "to swear" is שָׁבַע (shava), which means "to seven oneself" or "to bind oneself by seven things." This is the covenantal form of swearing which implies eternity in the number seven where the beginning is the end and the end is the beginning. See Gen 21:24, 27; 24:7; Deut 6:13; 1 Sam 20:17; Ezek 16:8.

separation or admixture. In becoming fully human (along with being fully divine), Christ assumed the entire human nature, body and soul. Because of his radical solidarity with humanity, and because of the fullness of divine life within his human soul, "the true life-giving or life-awakening spring is the soul of Christ, because this soul bears within itself the plenitude of the divine spirit and because this soul in the boundless freedom of the divine Person of Christ has full command over its plenitude of life ... even in making this plenitude efficaciously actual in other souls."[50] Stein argues here that the human soul of Christ is the essential medium through which divine life is channeled to all other human souls. Other than the human soul of Christ, no human soul is capable of awakening itself or giving itself life, neither originally as created nor finally as redeemed. The human soul of Christ is the *axis mundi* whereby all human souls receive the plenitude of the divine Spirit. Because the eternal Son of God hypostatically took on human flesh—body and soul—all human beings are summoned to take on divinity hypostatically by the "surpassing power of God" that is circulated through the supreme actuality of the soul of Christ.[51]

Since human beings exist at the intersection of material being and spiritual being, the incarnation of Christ perfectly includes the ontological totality of the created order. Christ indeed recapitulates and sums up the whole of creation in his incarnate Being:

> everything was created in the image of the Son of God and ... the Son, by his incarnation, entered into the total context of the created universe ... grace flows from the head into all the members: not only into human beings, but into all creatures. As

---

50. Stein, *Finite and Eternal Being*, 461. In this divine giving, "the spirit of God is beyond all measure, and when he gives himself, he does not bind himself to the measure of the being to whom he gives. Although it is true that the comprehensive capacity of the finite spirit is limited and thus incapable of receiving into itself the infinite, its comprehensive capacity is strengthened by that which is imparted to it, so that the limits of its being filled and being elevated are not restricted to any finite measure" (ibid., 462). Cf. ibid., 461, 519–20: "The soul of Christ has command over all created spirits. It has the power of calling departed souls back into the soulless body and of expelling evil spirits from the dominion they have conquered ... No closer and stronger union of separated natures is possible than that union in one Person as it was consummated by the incarnation of the Word. By virtue of the incarnation, human nature—first of all, in Christ himself—is filled with divine life to a degree proportionate with the divine will. By virtue of the personal freedom with which the God-Man has sovereign command over his two natures, he may allow the divine life to overflow into human life or he may restrain this influx. But by virtue of this influx, Christ is a *life-giving spirit* from the very first moment of his human existence ... The union of the two natures in Christ is the basis of the union of other human beings with God."

51. 2 Cor 4:7 (NAB). Cf. Stein, *Finite and Eternal Being*, 519–20.

> the entire subhuman nature was implicated in the fall of man, it is also to share in the restoration of man wrought by redemption... For humankind is the portal through which the Word of God entered into the created world. Human nature has received the Word, and the Word is linked in a special way with human beings, by virtue of a unity of common descent—not with subhuman nature and not with angels. As the head of humankind, which combines in itself the higher and lower reaches of being, Christ is the head of creation in its totality.[52]

Even though Christ's incarnation effects an inclusive cosmic solidarity with all of creation—so much so that all of creation partakes of salvation—a sui generis link is fashioned between God and humanity.[53] Human nature, as it includes within itself both material being and spiritual being, is the pivotal nature at the center of the universe through which salvation enters and accomplishes its task. As Tertullian wrote in his *De resurrectione carnis*, "truly, the flesh is the hinge of salvation."[54] It was necessary for the eternal and invisible God to assume the human nature—body and soul—in order to achieve a perfect and genuine union between God and creation. The paradoxical nature of humanity—at once vulnerable and powerful—is the very nature that encompasses the diverse natures of the universe: material, vegetative, sentient, rational, and spiritual. In particular, material being, consigned to entropic decay and futility, is set to be redeemed through Christ and through its gradual spiritualization. Material being is destined to be at the service of spiritual being and its constant pattern of self-donation if it is to be at all in the time of eternity. Human being, as at once material and spiritual, is the locus of the drama of cosmic redemption. Psalm 8 reflects the anthropological center of the cosmos:

> When I see your heavens, the work of your fingers,
>
> the moon and stars that you set in place—
>
> What is man that you are mindful of him,

---

52. Stein, *Finite and Eternal Being*, 527.

53. See Rom 8:18–23: "I consider that the sufferings of this present time are as nothing compared with the glory to be revealed for us. For creation awaits with eager expectation the revelation of the children of God; for creation was made subject to futility, not of its own accord but because of the one who subjected it, in hope that creation itself would be set free from slavery to corruption and share in the glorious freedom of the children of God. We know that all creation is groaning in labor pains even until now; and not only that, but we ourselves, who have the firstfruits of the Spirit, we also groan within ourselves as we wait for adoption, the redemption of our bodies" (NAB).

54. Tertullian, *De resurretione carnis* 8, 2: "adeo caro salutis est cardo" (translation my own).

> and a son of man that you care for him?
> Yet you have made him little less than a god,
> crowned him with glory and honor.
> You have given him rule over the works of your hands,
> put all things at his feet.[55]

The psalmist's wonder at the paradoxical nature of human being is evident. On the one hand, humans appear to be so small and insignificant within the vast expanse of the universe—so frail and vulnerable, yet on the other hand, humans (as rational creatures) wield an intrinsic command over all other creatures in Earth. Human beings truly are created in the *imago Dei* and this image is fulfilled perfectly in Christ, who is "the image of the invisible God, the firstborn of all creation. For in him were created all things in heaven and on earth, the visible and the invisible . . . He is before all things, and in him all things hold together. He is the head of the body, the church . . . For in him all the fullness was pleased to dwell."[56] Because of the Son of God's hypostatic union with human nature, human beings are empowered by the life-giving soul of Christ to participate in the process of cosmic redemption. The human soul becomes the gateway of salvation "and when it opens itself in its innermost being to the influx of divine life, the soul (and through it the body) is formed into an image of the Son of God."[57] In becoming configured to Jesus of Nazareth, true God and true man, according to the pattern of his self-giving and self-emptying life, human beings sacramentally are incorporated into the mystical Body of Christ, thereby incorporating the totality of created being along with them. As enmeshed within the created order—both materially and spiritually—human beings serve as the lynchpin of salvation's circuit. The spiritual efficacy that issues from the soul of Christ extends to human souls as co-creators of the world's reparation, and "then 'streams of living water' emanate from [the soul]—streams which effect a renewal of the face of the earth out of the Spirit. The human spirit, when it is permeated and guided by the Divine Spirit, recognizes in the divine light—underneath all the disfiguring veils—the original form of the created world and becomes capable of cooperating in the task of its restoration."[58]

---

55. Ps 8:4–7 (NABRE).
56. Col 1:15–19 (NAB).
57. Stein, *Finite and Eternal Being*, 463.
58. Ibid., 463–64. Cf. Beckmann-Zöller, "Edith Stein's Theory of the Person," 62: "Questions of salvation belong to being human. These cannot be solved by empirical or rational inference. Answers from a 'superior mind' are required . . . Humans, created by God, are called to be co-creators, that is, they must give the world form and structure, which is only possible if they understand and obey God's call."

This disfigurement of the world brought about by postlapsarian humanity is refigured according to the revelation of Christ, at the heart of which is the universal human vocation to become children of God by adoption.[59] Christ, as legitimate Son of God, freely enters into covenant relationship with humanity, calling us his brothers, his sisters, his friends.[60] Human beings thereby become adopted sons and daughters of God, summoned to eternal life within the pulsating heart of divinity, through their personal and communal *fiat* in free response to divine gift. At the twilight of life, the soul stretches across the abyss between chronological meter and the tempo of eternity by the power of God extended through the incarnate soul of Christ.

Not fully consummated in the temporal growth and development of the body, which is subject ultimately to corruption, is the entelechy of the soul. Rather, the final goal to which the soul reaches is its hypostatic union with God that ushers in a radical inversion of universal entropy, including the spiritualization and resurrection of the body.[61] Because the Incarnate Word assumed human flesh—both body and soul—humanity is to be redeemed in its totality, body and soul. There is an ancient Chaldean prayer, the Lakhu Mara, which puts it this way:

> To you, O Lord of the universe, we proclaim our confession,
> and we glorify you, Jesus Christ, because you are the resurrection
> of our bodies and the savior of our souls. You indeed, Lord, are
> the resurrection of our bodies and the good savior of our souls
> and the everlasting keeper of our life, and we are bound to thank you,
> adore and glorify you at every moment, O Lord of the universe through
> all ages.[62]

Lex orandi, lex credendi: the law of prayer is the law of faith. This prayer poignantly articulates the holistic redemption of the human person: body and soul. As "Lord of the universe," Christ the Lord redeems the entire universe. God has bound himself to the universe upon creation and extends this bond into the resurrected new creation. The anthropological implications of salvation in Christ are at once cosmological. Union with God is not a selfish and solipsistic desire of an individual soul, but in such a union

---

59. See Rom 8:14–17 and Gal 4:5–6.

60. See John 15:15: "I no longer call you slaves, because a slave does not know what his master is doing. I have called you friends, because I have told you everything I have heard from my Father" (NAB).

61. See Stein, *Finite and Eternal Being*, 518: "The resurrected Christ, the King of Glory, is the paradigm and the head of the human race—the end form [*Zielgestalt*] to which every human being is ordained and from which it receives its meaning."

62. Apostolic Penitentiary, *Manual of Indulgences*, 87.

is implied a communion of spiritual persons as family. The Son of God's hypostatic union with human nature is not merely an abstract metaphysical proposition that self-congratulates the prowess of the mind, but it conveys a personal and communal vocation to each and every human soul "to be inserted as a flower in an eternally imperishable wreath."[63] Every soul has its own unique place reserved for it in this eternal rendezvous of familial and consanguine destiny. The soul's union with God is a union of love that freely gathers all of the elect in a consummating banquet of spiritual persons within the entire nexus of the created order.

c. The Hypostatic Union of the Soul with God

In order to understand the meaning of the soul's union with God, it was first necessary to outline the meaning of the hypostatic union of the Son of God with human nature. We observed that the efficacy of spiritual union between humanity and God comes through the human soul of Christ that is united supremely with the divine nature. Yet we must press on still further and inquire into the precise phenomenality of the soul's union with God according to Stein. First, as shown above, the soul, "as a spiritual-personal substance—is nearer to God than all nonpersonal structures and capable of being united with him."[64] Moreover, in the union of body and soul "we have an inner junction which can no longer be understood in any spatial sense."[65] This point is immensely important as it reinforces the way in which spiritual realities deflect any attempt to reduce them to the dimensions of material being, namely, spacetime and mass/energy. Stein insists that the inner junction between body and soul cannot be understood according to such limiting dimensions of potentiality alone, but must be conceived in terms of actuality and spirit.

---

63. Stein, *Finite and Eternal Being*, 508. Cf. ibid., 507–8, 510: "It pertains to the essence of the human being that the individual is a *member* of the human race and that this individual realizes himself as a whole (with all the possibilities implied therein) in a *humankind* [*Menschheit*] in which the individuals inhere as 'members of one another' [*Glied zu Glied*] . . . The individual human being is in his content not merely a particularization of something more universal, but a member of a whole that realizes itself as a *vital unity* [*Lebenseinheit*] and that can achieve its unfolding only in the vital context of the whole, in its particular place and in cooperation with the other members . . . by our contacts with foreign members of the human race our own being is enriched and perfected."

64. Ibid., 519.

65. Ibid., 459.

This is no *deus ex machina* argument but instead corresponds to the given intellectual truth of being and becoming, of matter and form, of physics and metaphysics, of phenomenology and first principles. There are persons and there are not persons, and where there are persons, there is rational spiritual being. However, the unitive inherence of body and soul is surpassed by the union of soul and divinity:

> For the soul forms itself into the body as into a foreign medium, as into a generically different material element. God and soul, on the other hand, are both *spirit* and interpenetrate or permeate each other as only spirit and spirit can interpenetrate, i.e., by virtue of a free and personal self-giving which, though it presupposes a difference of being, is nonetheless—despite the infinite distance between uncreated and created being—an essential communion [*Wesensgemeinsamkeit*] that makes possible an *entering* into one another in the true and full sense. The spiritual nature [*Geistnatur*] of the soul is presupposed for its union with God (i.e., for its life of grace and glory). In this union the soul ascends to a height of being that places it side by side with pure spirits. But the soul is distinguished from pure spirits in that this union (the life of grace and glory) is in the case of the soul an "ascent" or an "elevation."[66]

Here is the crux of redemption where the soul does not seek to take leave of the body but to elevate and spiritualize the body. The human being's union with God is primarily a spiritual phenomenon that is accomplished in the inner life of the person. The benefits of this spiritual union of the soul with God follow the interpenetration of created and uncreated spirits. A phenomenology of spiritual union would note the intentional disposition of personal consciousness that freely, willfully and docilely assents to the gentle sway of divine grace. In this paradoxical union, intimacy obtains as much as distance through absolute self-giving. The human soul ascends to the realm of divine self-giving by divine grace extending from the soul of Christ, resulting in an essential communion of solidarity between creatures and creator. Even though human souls ascend to the realm of being akin to pure spirits, the uniqueness of the human soul's union with God is in its redemptive character. A spiritual ascension is required of the soul that itself foreshadows the resurrection and ascension of the body as it reunites with the soul. The actualizing renovation of spirit must precede the ensuing actualization of the physical body in the transfigured form of resurrection and ascension into the heart of divine life eternal. Without a prior elevation

---

66. Ibid., 459–60.

of the soul, the resurrection and ascension of the material body is not possible, for prior to potentiality is actuality. Redemption of the forming principle—namely, the soul—must occur before a regeneration of that which is informed. Nevertheless, the perennial question for human beings remains: Does the soul conform to the worldly nature of material being or to the divine super-nature of spiritual being?[67]

In her collection of notes intended for the publication of a study on the question, "What is the human being?" Stein relates the following: "From the generality of the debt then follows the generality of the criminal state: All humans since Adam's fall, by their descent, are deprived of friendship with God and thus the supernatural life. All are enslaved to physical death. And all are worse in body and soul than Adam before the Fall . . . Just as the human intellect according to its natural power cannot be trusted, as if it could avoid the error and find the truth, so the natural will is of itself unable to avoid sin and to do what is right."[68] As part of her attempt to determine an adequate theological anthropology in light of Catholic doctrine for the sake of effective pedagogy, this text reveals Stein's recognition of the significance of original sin for understanding the human person. With the annulment of the supernatural life in which the physical faculties of the body are conducted entirely by the prerogatives of the spirit, human beings are infected with concupiscence by the hereditary condition of sin and opposition to God. Furthermore, even the natural human will is predisposed to falsehood and evil apart from the divine initiative of grace. In effect, the postlapsarian tendencies of natural material being are contrary to supernatural spiritual being.

Whereas spiritual being lives according to a constant giving and emptying of self for the sake of the other, material being caves in on itself like a supernova whose core collapses into itself, resulting in a vacant and degenerate black hole. Material being is consumed by its concern for

---

67. See Jude 17–20: "But you, beloved, remember the words spoken beforehand by the apostles of our Lord Jesus Christ, for they told you, 'In the last time there will be scoffers who will live according to their own godless desires.' These are the ones who cause divisions; they live on the natural plane [ψυχικοί], devoid of the Spirit. But you, beloved, build yourselves up in your most holy faith; pray in the holy Spirit" (NAB).

68. Stein, *Was ist der Mensch?*, 67–68: "Aus der Allgemeinheit der Verschuldung folgt dann die Allgemeinheit des Strafzustandes: Alle Menschen seit Adams Fall entbehren von Geburt an Gottes Freundschaft und damit das übernatürliche Leben. Alle sind dem leiblichen Tod verfallen. Und alle sind an Leib und Seele schlechter als es Adam vor dem Fall war . . . Wie der menschliche Verstand seiner natürlichen Kraft nicht zutrauen darf, daß er den Irrtum meiden und die Wahrheit finden könnte, so ist der natürliche Wille aus sich allein nicht imstande, die Sünde zu meiden und das Rechte zu tun" (translation my own).

self-preservation, self-maintenance, and self-assertion. It adheres to an egocentric logic of "survival of the fittest," and the fittest achieve their fitness at the expense of the other. The irony of material being is that it feverishly attempts to preserve its life only to lose it in the end. Yet the paradox of spiritual being is that it voluntarily and lovingly loses its life in order to save it.[69] For spiritual being, to live truly is to give oneself away to the other in radical love and self-donation. Spiritual being welcomes suffering for the sake of the other and invites suffering the other, that is, letting the other disrupt the myopic prerogatives of matter's insatiable desire to consume. Spiritual being inverts consumption according to the threefold pattern of self-denial: in the form of poverty, chastity, and obedience, and in the form of prayer, fasting, and almsgiving. Spiritual being irrevocably gives itself away in loving service to the other. Matter must be humbled in order to be spiritualized. The *humus* ("earth, ground, soil, dirt") of humanity must undergo a subversive self-humiliation in order for its re-creation to take place. As Stein puts it, "By virtue of its spirit nature [*Geistnatur*], humankind is called to a communal life that—after having grown from a temporally, spatially, and materially determined soil—eventually annuls the limitations of time and space."[70] The limited dimensions of mass/energy and spacetime must give way to their expansion, not in terms of material magnitude, but in proportion to the littleness and transparency of spirit where the greatest is the least.[71]

Union with God does not imply an annihilation of mass/energy and spacetime, but demands a nullification of the limitations of finitude. Finite realities are destined to be transformed into infinite Reality. Just as through his hypostatic union with human nature did the Son of God transgress the boundlessness of infinity by binding himself as Husband to the home of his Bride, the Church, so do human beings transgress the boundaries of finitude in order to be bound eternally and covenantally to the heavenly home of the Bridegroom. The parameters of mass/energy and spacetime constrain the yearnings and reaches of spiritual being. In the realm of becoming, spiritual being groans in such a way as Thérèse of Lisieux in her spiritual anguish of love: "Ah! my Jesus, pardon me if I am unreasonable in wishing to express my desires and longings which reach even unto infinity . . . To satisfy me I need *all* . . . Nevertheless even because of my weakness, it has pleased You, O Lord, to grant my *little childish desires* and You desire, today, to grant other desires that are *greater* than the universe."[72] The deepest desires of the hu-

---

69. Cf. Mark 8:35; Matt 16:25; Luke 9:24; John 12:25.
70. Stein, *Finite and Eternal Being*, 508.
71. Cf. Matt 20:16, 26–27; 23:11–12; Luke 9:48; 22:26.
72. Thérèse of Lisieux, *Story of a Soul*, 192–93 (Manuscript B, 2ro–3ro). Cf. Rom

man soul attest to their origin and fulfillment in that which is greater than the universe. Appropriately, Augustine's *cor inquietum* ("unquieted heart") can find rest only in its permanent union with the Sacred Heart of Jesus.[73] Such a union does not eradicate thereby the fundamental ontological difference between creatures and creator:

> Divine being is neither augmented nor diminished nor changed in any other way by its union with human beings. The soul, to be sure (and therefore the entire human being), undergoes a radical transformation in this union, and it yet persists in its own being and does not become part of the divine being. But this union may nonetheless be designated as even more intimate and as an inner junction in a more genuine sense than the union of soul and body.[74]

In other words, the prosopic and ontological alterity between God and humanity is not dissolved into some homogenous and ubiquitous substance in which there is no longer any distinction among persons. To the contrary, human beings subsist in their created human nature and in their individuality in their union with God just as the three divine Persons share the divine nature in and through a distinction of Persons. Human beings live in the image and likeness of God in sharing a universal nature while existing as a plurality of persons, destined to become a communion of persons in an eternal exchange of love. Unity obtains inasmuch as otherness subsists, for what would there be to unite if all were the same?

IV. Conclusion

To this point, the intricate reality of the human soul has been explicated according to the theological anthropology of Edith Stein and her profound conception of the soul as the vessel of love. Through this primary image of Stein, we were able to provide a paradigmatic sketch of the soul through physical and metaphysical discourse, as well as through metaphoric discourse. It was apparent that metaphoric discourse is perhaps the most appropriate discourse for a reality like the human soul since its being does not fit neatly into the limited strictures of material being. Secondly, we

---

8:26–27: "In the same way, the Spirit too comes to the aid of our weakness; for we do not know how to pray as we ought, but the Spirit itself intercedes with inexpressible groanings. And the one who searches hearts knows what is the intention of the Spirit, because it intercedes for the holy ones according to God's will" (NAB).

73. See Augustine, *Confessiones* I.i (1).
74. Stein, *Finite and Eternal Being*, 459.

considered the prospect of an afterlife for the soul and the possibility of attaining interpersonal communion with God. By reflecting on the phenomenality of death and the mystery of the hypostatic union of the Son of God with human nature, we were able to entertain what might be meant by the human soul's union with divine life with some degree of relative adequacy.

Throughout this study a palpable polemic can be detected between a shameless theological anthropology and the skeptical doctrine of material reductionism. In the postmodern context such a polemic cannot be avoided. In societies where the question of God is banished from public teaching and learning on a daily basis, an intellectual apologetic must be made in defense of possibility at least, if not actual truth as clearly revealed through reason and the epistemological reaches of faith. Life must be breathed into that truncated anthropology that adamantly refuses to inquire into being in all of its fullness. To indoctrinate young people with a worldview that bars the doors to divinity and to the realm of spiritual being is to do the greatest disservice to the human mind and its demands of intellectual transparency. Is it really religion that is the cardinal breeder of war throughout human history, or is it our inability to openly and empathetically communicate with one another? If we intentionally lock out the divine from our worldview, do we not lock out simultaneously the other? This study aims at contributing to the humanizing of humanity if indeed humility is the essence of what it is to be human.

At the heart of this study, Mary the Mother of God was portrayed as the pinnacle of humanity and the heights of spiritual freedom. Her constantly affirmative response to the other paved the way for salvation to enter the world. To understand the true being of the human soul, with its inseparable relation to the body, one must seek to understand the contours of Mary's graceful life as she perfectly fulfilled the universal human vocation to become a sincere gift of self. Apart from the example of Mary, empowered by the Host-life within her, we are utterly at a loss in understanding what it is to be human.[75] After all, how can one understand what it is to be human apart from understanding the human soul? An anthropological construal without the human soul is no anthropology at all; it is merely a view of the material husk all the while neglecting the spiritual kernel of being. Humanity understood without reference to the soul or to spiritual being is, in the end, a dehumanizing conception of the human person. To remove the human soul from the human is to remove personhood from the person, and the human soul can be comprehended only in reference to the incomprehensible God who deigned to reveal divine incomprehensibility to us through that which

---

75. See Houselander, *Wood of the Cradle, Wood of the Cross.*

is comprehensible. It is the sacramentality of the human body that manifests and speaks the being of its innermost life, the human soul. In the final analysis, Edith Stein may be portrayed as a champion of the sacramentality of the human body.

6

The Antinomy of Material Being

Beginning with an inquiry into universal human vocation, *Human and Divine Being* has presented a summary and interpretation of Edith Stein's foundation of human being (and all forms of being): spiritual being. In particular, chapters 3 through 5 gave an account of the human soul as the spiritual core of the person. However, is not the human being composed of both spiritual soul and material body? It is now time to consider the peculiar attributes of material being in light of spiritual being. Any discussion of material being without prior discussion of spiritual being would be very difficult indeed, for spiritual being precedes and grounds all material being. But it is necessary to reflect on the unique characteristics of material being in conversation with natural science. That is the aim of the present chapter. Before garnering together the specific traits of material being, let us recall Stein's pioneering methodology that gives us confidence to do so.

In her two *magna opera*—*Potency and Act* and *Finite and Eternal Being*—Edith Stein proposes a most innovative account of material being in relation to spiritual being. The present study will seek to elucidate Stein's intuitive conception of matter and its distinct properties within the cosmos. Taking into account both modern atomic physics and ancient Aristotelian philosophy, Stein unearths an ontological description of matter with perspicuous clarity and exactness. At a time when natural scientists, philosophers, and theologians alike struggle to understand the precise being of matter, Stein's insights come as a welcome aid to comprehending the division and unity given in the created order.

As a lucid metaphysician who employs the tools of phenomenology, Stein carefully anatomizes the human being without breaking the totality of human being as such. Through the application of the phenomenological reduction, she is able to isolate and probe the distinct components of the human person without landing in a truncated physicalist reductionism to objectivity or in an unanchored psychological reductionism to subjectivity. Instead, Stein constantly maintains the totality of the human person while illuminating the variety of unequivocal facets that comprise the individual: body, soul, and spirit. The human soul is construed as a type of spiritual being and the human body is categorized as the material being of the person. Both body and soul bear the perpetual potential of being spiritualized by the divine Spirit, thereby transfiguring the naturalness of the psycho-physical individual into a supernatural existence. This distinction between natural and supernatural, between flesh and spirit (à la St. Paul), between the world and heaven, and between pure potency and pure act is essential for understanding the intrinsic relation between body, soul, and spirit which takes place within the human form.

Stein's method, which in fertile antinomic tension combines metaphysics and phenomenology, describes and analyzes the complementary dimensions of human life, both inward and outward. Phenomenology functions to repel easy anthropological reductionisms, whether in favor of matter alone or subjectivity alone, by exacting a reduction upon all a priori reductionisms. As Jean-Luc Marion has argued, "so much reduction, so much givenness."[1] This is to say that the givenness of a phenomenon will come into clear view to the degree that the phenomenon is reduced to its originary givenness. In the present case, any presumed anthropological constructions are bracketed and set aside in order to get at the pure givenness of the human person. Where more recent phenomenological proposals have insisted on the bracketing of traditional metaphysics in order to access the originary phenomenon (such as in the work of Heidegger, Marion, and Levinas), Stein permits metaphysics to draw near to phenomenology in order to harvest the fruits of their dialectical dance. By enlisting traditional metaphysical language, categories, and concepts within a phenomenological method of investigation, Stein submits a picture of reality that concedes neither to bland circular tautology (with metaphysics alone) nor to unbridled relativism (with phenomenology alone). The genius of her method is due to the providential unfolding of her life: Jewish family and faith, philosophical erudition and atheistic critique, Catholic conversion and Thomistic enlightenment. Stein's life itself encompassed the poles of faith and reason, of theology and philosophy, of religious

---

1. Marion, *Reduction and Givenness*, 203. Cf. Marion, *Being Given*, 14–18.

assent and rational deliberation. Her developed worldview also included the two great forms of religious expression: manifestation and proclamation.[2] Stein was accustomed to dialectical confrontation and the fruitfulness of genuine unity engendered by complementary difference.

To answer the perennial question—"What is it to be human?"—Stein inquires about the precise meaning of human being according to phenomenological description and ontological constitution. She investigates through the metaphysical categories of being, substance, essence, matter and form, as well as the phenomenological categories of givenness, appearance, meaning, hermeneutics and affectivity. Metaphysics does not fully possess the competence to interpret phenomena such as love, joy, fear, the other, or the person; neither does phenomenology have the aptitude to pronounce a definitive judgment as to what is ultimately true since it functions only to describe plausible possibilities rather than define certain actualities. Therefore, in order to describe the human person in his or her totality, and to arrive at the essence of the human being, both phenomenology and metaphysics are needed.

Chapter 6 of *Human and Divine Being* is concerned solely with Stein's descriptive ontology of material being (vis-à-vis spiritual being) in order to understand the foundational relation of the body to the soul. Much care is needed to avoid presenting a reductionistic view of Stein's theological anthropology. It can be reduced neither to material being nor to spiritual being alone. Further, Stein's account of human being cannot be labeled "Cartesian dualism," wherein the soul and body are separated to the degree of becoming alien to one another. Instead, Stein presents the human being as an integral organic whole of body, soul, and spirit. The task of distinguishing between the soul and the body, and between the soul and the spirit, is an important one for a project in theological anthropology, as it allows for a descriptive analysis of the unique properties of each.[3] The fundamental distinction between spiritual being and material being is essential to recognize and to comprehend. Without making this distinction, an even more problematic depiction of the human being follows: reductive monism, as if the person were matter alone or spirit alone. In modern times, the former

---

2. See Ricoeur, *Figuring the Sacred*, 48–67; Tracy, *Analogical Imagination*, 193–229; and Wallenfang, *Dialectical Anatomy of the Eucharist*.

3. See Heb 4:12: "Indeed, the word of God is living and effective, sharper than any two-edged sword, penetrating even between soul and spirit, joints and marrow, and able to discern reflections and thoughts of the heart" (NAB). This biblical text indicates the exactitude necessary to dissect the human person according to his or her totality of being, thereby revealing the distinct qualities of the primary dimensions that constitute the human person as such, namely, body, soul, and spirit.

of these reductive monisms is standard fare as advances in neuroscience, blended with ideological currents of atheism and secularism, contribute to the worldview of material reductionism, which reduces all characteristics of the so-called soul to chemical processes within the brain. The present analysis will show such a position to be hastily minimalistic, intellectually irresponsible, and imprecise. As at once body, soul, and spirit, the paradoxical nature of the human being must be assessed according to the paradoxical state of created being: spiritual and material.

In order to provide nuanced analysis of material being as put forth by Stein, this chapter will move along four lines of development. First, key terms will be clarified in order to establish a working vocabulary for the entire chapter. Second, with all of the key terms in place, we will proceed to an ontological examination of matter in terms of physics and metaphysics. Third, having achieved an accurate ontological description of matter, we will apply these findings to a scrutiny of the human body in its sui generis configuration. Finally, we will consider the possibility of matter's redemption and regeneration with a view toward eschatology. In taking these successive steps toward exploring the essence of material being in the work of Edith Stein, we will justify the relevance of Stein's theological anthropology, especially concerning the physical body, for today.

I. Clarification of Terms

Before relating the ontological structure of material being, first it is necessary to sort out the specific key terms Stein uses when speaking of matter. There are two different German words that can be translated as "matter": *Stoff* and *Materie*. While these terms are virtually interchangeable, *Stoff* refers to a "piece" or "item" of matter, and *Materie* refers to "what receives content and is paired with 'form' as what gives content (this is the scholastic usage). For Theresa [sic] Benedicta, however, not all matter is physical or 'space-filling' since all created things are material in some sense."[4] This latter

---

4. Walter Redmond, "Translator's Note," in Stein, *Potency and Act*, xi. See ibid., 77, for Stein's description of matter occurring in the "immanent sphere": "In the immanent sphere, too, we encounter a 'matter [*Stoff*]' that has potential being with respect to the diverse forms it can enter, and indeed in several senses. We may see sense data as matter formed through mental conceptions into acts of perception, memory, or imagination [*Phantasie*]. But we can also understand the 'matter' of our inner living as the life of the I welling up and formed by its shifting contents into different 'living experiences.' The one harks back to the other. We can grasp sense material [*material*] only through the spiritual activity that processes it, yet it becomes graspable as something that can be actual without this intellectual forming, that is, as 'bare sensation.'"

point is paramount to understand. In twenty-first-century natural sciences, matter is regarded exclusively as that which is composed of atoms. Stein maintains a broader application of the term *matter* to refer to the aspect of potency in all created existents insofar as all creatures are on their way of becoming, that is, perpetually in a state of movement from potentiality to actuality due to the eternally pure actuality who is God.[5] Therefore we are able to speak of a materiality of spiritual substances such as souls or angels at least in an analogous sense compared with atomic matter.

However, Stein tends to use the term *matter* (*Materie*) to refer to that which is "posited solely by the creative act, and its *what* as that which is absolutely potential and nonspiritual."[6] Spiritual being is associated with the formal principle of an existent while material being is correlated with the pure potentiality and atomic composition of the existent. Atoms can be configured according to this or that form but the atoms (or their sub-particles) alone do not prescribe for themselves their macro-formal configuration. To argue to the contrary would be to contradict the second law of thermodynamics, thereby denying the natural tendency of matter to decompose and disintegrate according to the trajectory of thermal equilibrium. Neither the Stoic notion of ὁρμή (*horme*) ("impetus, impulse, urge") nor the Spinozan idea of *conatus essendi* ("struggle of being") nor the Darwinian theory of "survival of the fittest" can in itself account for the ontological diversity of beings and their stunning formal variety. Miniscule atoms and their sub-particles do not admit of their own raison d'être or self-determination of macro-configuration into various species. Reason points to the formal and final causality to which all motion, growth, development, shaping and evolution are indebted.[7] This is the precise fundamental difference between actuality and potentiality. It would be nonsensical to argue that atoms (or any subatomic particle set) bear a pure actuality because clearly they do not.[8]

---

5. See Stein, *Finite and Eternal Being*, 172 (referring to Aristotle): "... matter by itself does not suffice to explain becoming"; and ibid., 186: "For Aristotle, ὕλη is the *raison d'être* of the undeniable experiential phenomenon of *becoming*."

6. Stein, *Potency and Act*, 115. Cf. ibid., 103: "... the being of matter is conceivable only on the basis of a creative act. To understand this origin lies beyond our power."

7. See ibid., 298: "*Prima materia* can receive the first form that gives it being only from the first being. First being is the *first cause*, and creation is the *first causality* [*Kausalität*] underlying all else. Earthly causality does not involve initial forming but only transforming."

8. Even beyond the clear limitations of natural science's parameters of competent investigation, the realm of meaning certainly transcends mere physicality and chemical reactions. Even more, the speech of the most meaningful meanings undoubtedly transgresses the boundaries of animalistic being and the egocentric tasks of self-preservation

Stein follows Thomas in calling matter "'pure potency' because it is receptive of all 'forms,' that is, of all the species of sensible things, and because it acquires no actual being at all until it receives some species or other. Thus we can form a *concept of the form* of matter [*Materie*] as what is purely potential."[9] Stein likewise follows Thomas's distinction between matter that fills empty forms (*imprimere*) and matter that is brought to actual being by taking in form (*indere*): "The first word [*imprimere*] recalls how matter [*Stoff*] is shaped into a work of art from without and the second [*indere*] how a living thing is provided with an 'inner form' that shapes it from within."[10] This latter concept refers to the notion of entelechy: the vital inner form of a living organism that serves as the formal and final cause of the organism's specific unfolding. For inanimate objects, matter is shaped from without as in a work of art—here matter can be thought of as filling predetermined empty forms as in a mold. In contrast, yet similarly, living creatures are shaped from within due to the entelechy at work at the outset of their conception and ensuing germination and gestation.[11]

Strictly speaking, "the *material thing*, is the existent [*Existierendes*] in the proper sense; it is that wherein matter and form when united receive actuality in the sense of *real* [*real*] *being* . . . the 'material [*materiell*]' thing is not purely material and should properly be understood in its makeup

---

and consumption. The phenomenological conclusions of Emmanuel Levinas convincingly have shown this to be the case. See, for example, Levinas, *Ethics and Infinity*, 122: "I mean to say that a truly human life cannot remain life *satis*-fied in its equality to being, a life of quietude, that it is awakened by the other, that is to say, it is always getting sobered up, that being is never—contrary to what so many reassuring traditions say—its own reason for being, that the famous *conatus essendi* is not the source of all right and meaning." According to a material reductionist worldview, all meaning can be reduced to base instincts of survival. However, experiences such as sacrifice, forgiveness, continence, and self-denial attest to logical meaning that clearly transcends the prerogatives of matter and its self-sufficiency, self-preservation, and insatiable appetite for consumption. The realm of meaning exceeds and renders inadequate the claims of material reductionism.

9. Stein, *Potency and Act*, 76.

10. Ibid., 115.

11. Stein uses the example of the kaffir lily to demonstrate the manifestation of the organism's entelechy: "The kaffir lily developed like this from the inside out; nothing else had to be done . . . The shape before us has in itself something of an inner necessity, and the becoming that we watched as it developed seemed to aim at this result and to find its fulfillment therein. Here, too, an individual has emerged that *realizes* an 'idea.' The idea is not brought to the matter from outside and formed into it; there is no 'unorganized'—implying 'unformed'—matter at all. The growth of the matter here is at the same time a growth into the shape that is its goal. We actually 'watch' the shaping from inside out, and so we are inclined to speak of an 'inner form' or 'entelechy [*Entelechie*]' (insofar as the shaping from within is directed to a goal)" (ibid., 62).

first from the viewpoint of spirit."[12] Here Stein affirms the hylomorphic constitution of all created existents: real being is composed of matter and form, united in actualized existence. The formal component of the thing proceeds from spiritual being—that which is ever unseen and yet constantly actualizes the pure potentiality of pure matter.[13] The form of an existent, whether as a filling of an empty form [*imprimere*] or as the unfolding of an inner form [*indere*], shapes matter according to a predetermined species. Even if species formally adapt to climate and physical surroundings, the emergent properties of organisms adhere to original specific configurations of ontological difference, for example, horse or tree or star or ant or human, etc. Evidence of evolutionary lineage of material being does not itself contravene the radical ontological distinctions among existents. In other words, all existents are not virtually the same simply because they are composed of the same stuff/matter. The individual substances of existents are drastically different from one another due to their respective forms that are assigned to matter by the prerogatives of spiritual being.

A further word must be said on the cautious relationship between the terms *matter*, *mass*, and *energy*. Since Albert Einstein's (1879–1955) watershed postulate, $E = mc^2$, we now understand energy and mass to be mutually convertible, one into the other. Mass can be converted into energy (such as in the process of nuclear fusion) and energy can be converted into mass (such as in the process of synthetic particle collision). Similarly, we know through quantum mechanics that light acts both as a particle (photon) and a wave. The paradoxical and transient natures of mass/energy and light, respectively, suggest that defining a term such as *mass* requires knowledge of its inherent duality, that is, that mass is convertible into energy and in some instances may act more as a wave than as a particle. Even more, some particles (such as photons) are regarded as massless because they travel at the speed of light and a rest mass (invariant mass) cannot be observed of them directly. With this in mind, we carefully advance to delineate between matter, mass, and energy. Stein defines pure mass as "the boundless stuffing [*das masslos Füllende*] and the totally unformed that, taken by itself, is never actual. Pure mass shares this non-actuality and the incapability of existing by itself with Aristotelian prime matter."[14] Mass can be understood as a particular quantity of formed matter that is extended in spacetime as

12. Ibid., 117–18.

13. See ibid., 420: "Traditionally, this aspect of the thing's makeup [*Aufbau*] that cannot be grasped qualitatively is called 'matter [*Materie oder Stoff*].'"

14. Stein, *Finite and Eternal Being*, 195. Cf. Stein, *Potency and Act*, 8: "Pure potentiality is the mode of being of bare matter [*Materie*]; hence, like matter, it does not occur in fact. In God there is no potentiality in this sense."

an observable sentient and objective phenomenon located outside of the human subject (that is, outside of the conscious self, the one making the observation). Formed matter, in turn, is the stuff of which a particular object is composed. Yet matter, we know, is comprised of subatomic particles that can be divided asymptotically. That is, every detectable particle can always be subdivided further. The current Standard Model of particle physics theorizes there to be sixteen different subatomic particles—categorized as quarks, leptons, and gauge bosons—which make up the totality of the atom. All this is to say that, even when speaking about matter in the most common way, we are dealing with a very fluid phenomenon. Matter typically is conceived as physical stuff that fills space but, as Colin McGinn has recently opined, space is internal to continuous matter.[15] This means that space can be viewed as an integral component of matter itself since space intertwines with atomic particles to constitute mass together.

Neither mass nor matter is a concept that refers to a static reality; rather, they indicate dynamic multivalent substances that are in a constant state of flux, perpetually changing their configurations according to their interaction with other forms of matter and energy around them. Especially in the case of living organic species, the living body remains in an unceasing process of change, cellular replication and renovation. Over the course of time, the living body virtually replaces its entire cellular composition, even multiple times. Because matter is dynamic and innately transmutable in form, material being must be conceived not as a rigid and static kind of entity but as a reality always on the move, driven about by an actuality outside of itself.[16] Since energy, too, is convertible into mass, this prime actuality

---

15. See McGinn, *Basic Structures of Reality*, 41. Cf. Stein, *Finite and Eternal Being*, 195–96, 198: "*Material* stuff-structures [*Stoffgebilde*], i.e., structures of massive weight, are not only *filling* space but also *tied* to space, and their formation proceeds from the external toward the internal. Pure apparent-units (which have light as their material element) are produced in space by something external to them without filling space or maintaining themselves in space in their own right. *Vital* stuff-structures are placed into space by some internal force . . . Material elements differ among themselves by virtue of the particular mode in which they fill space. Of essential significance for the total structure of the material world are the *three basic modes of filling space* which in natural science are known as *states of aggregation*: the *solid*, the *liquid*, and the *gaseous* state." Cf. ibid., 217–18, 237: "The material thing fills space in such a way that every part of the space completely coincides with a part of the thing—the thing is not wholly at any particular point, but is spread out with its total being and is as such sensorily manifest . . . We encounter matter [*Stoffe*]—as elements, mixtures, and combinations—in 'pieces' or 'quantities,' such as, for example pieces of gold or quantities of water."

16. See Stein, *Finite and Eternal Being*, 194–95: "Massive weight [*Massenbeschwertheit*] does not at all represent the primordial state of external nature. The primordial state, i.e., the truly 'natural' in external nature, is the inner unity of force and material elements, the free, efficacious realization [*das Sichauswirken*] of force in space-filling

must not be identified as energy since energy itself is prone to change and exhibits the property of potency. The fundamental difference between the purviews of physics and metaphysics, respectively, cannot be overlooked. Physics is limited as a method and lacks the faculties to peer into the full ontological constitution of reality, dealing only with ontic formulations and manifestations. McGinn argues as much when he writes that "physics is structural, and it can get by without entering into the question of what matter ultimately is . . . Energy is just as enigmatic as matter, being known only structurally."[17] Physics, by itself, is not able to fathom the enigma of beings, let alone being. The road of material being—which includes the infrastructure of potential and kinetic energy in contingent relation to mass—leads us back to the self-evident first principle of metaphysics: actuality is always prior to potentiality.[18] This premise leads us to pure actuality that certainly is not to be identified with mass/energy within the field of spacetime since the matrix of mass/energy is imbued radically with potentiality. Spiritual being is a precondition of material being, just as form is a precondition of matter.[19] Now let us propose a sketch of the ontology of matter in relation to spirit.

---

material formations [*Stoffgestaltungen*]. The breaking apart of *Kraft* and *Stoff*, the 'breaking away' [*Herausfallen*] of the material elements from this unity, which turns them into pure mass, is a reversal of the primordial ontological state. Pure mass, therefore, cannot be conceived as an eternal, not-become prime matter. Nor can it be conceived as nontransitory. For even if external nature in its actual present state is massively weighted [*massenbeschwert*] this state is by no means immutable . . . *Stoff* is never without *Kraft*. In the case of dynamic constitution, material elements are effectuated by force and *inwardly* ruled. In the case of atomistic constitution, mass is subjected to aggressive forces that work from the outside, and it cannot be conceived apart from these forces . . . No initial state of the world is conceivable in which *pure mass*, entirely unformed, could have filled space. In order to be, pure mass needs a hold which it cannot give to itself. It is 'held' by those forces which rule it and form it."

17. McGinn, *Basic Structures of Reality*, 60, 64. Cf. ibid., 172: "The *reason* energy is measured to be the same over time is that it is the same *thing* over time: the *explanation* of measurement constancy is ontological constancy." This is to say that only metaphysics can get at the ontological substratum of reality, while physics is confined (according to its preset methodology) to measure the ontic qualities of beings—for example, size, weight, duration, molecular composition, and velocity (all to degrees of relative adequacy). Metaphysics is able to penetrate the ontic exterior showing of beings by employing the categories of consciousness, cognition, first principles, causality, substance, accidents, essence, spiritual and material being, act and potency, and the recognition of ontological difference, that is, the difference between existence as such (*esse*) and existents (*entia*) that participate in existence.

18. See Stein, *Potency and Act*, 71: "Consequently matter, even were it from eternity, would always have been mutable, that is, not absolutely actual but at least partially potential. But then it is conditioned and upheld in its being by absolutely actual being."

19. While Stein posits "an inseparable unity of matter and form," she further holds

II. Ontology of Matter

Stein defines matter as "that which is absolutely potential and nonspiritual" because "matter can only come into existence as formed by concrete species."[20] Matter therefore can be thought to be the very antithesis of spirit. As pure potency, theoretically speaking, matter stands in stark contrast to the actuality of form, spirit, and, most especially, God as pure act and Spirit. In relation to God as pure act, prime matter is the radical other. While it might trouble our materialistic sensibilities today to continue to render God as wholly immaterial, it would be entirely irrational to do otherwise.[21] We must continue to assert that there is nothing material in God insofar as God is pure act, and matter, by definition, is charged with potency. Though it is difficult to segregate matter from spirit, since "the things we deal with in our experience are units of spirit and matter, matter formed by spirit," it is necessary to subdivide reality metaphysically in order to account for the demarcation between potency and act.[22] If this metaphysical partitioning of

---

that "*every material structure is built by the spirit.* This means not only that the entire material world was created by the divine spirit but that *every material structure is spiritually filled [geisterfüllt]* and informed" (*Finite and Eternal Being*, 254, 378). For more on this argument, see my essay "From Albert Einstein to Edith Stein: Understanding the Resurrection of the Body vis-à-vis Natural Science," 209–44.

20. Stein, *Potency and Act*, 115. Cf. ibid., 298: "A thing is what it is through its form. When it consists of form and matter, the matter (taken as *prima materia*) is actually nothing by itself, for it is first shaped into something by the form that it takes into itself."

21. See, for example, Webb, *Jesus Christ, Eternal God*, 282, 286: "As Hans Schwarz suggests in a brilliant essay on this issue, 'The God who is reduced to invisibility, intangibility, and elusiveness hardly differs from being no God' [Hans Schwarz, "God's Place in a Space Age," *Zygon* 21 (1986) 355] . . . Today, when outer space is increasingly open to us for exploration both mental and physical, we are in need of a new theology of place. Otherwise, cosmic neutrality can easily slip into cosmic nihilism, with God haunting the West at the margins of an empty technological utopianism . . . The exchange within Jesus is nothing that is added to the Trinity. God can become incarnate because God is always spirit on its way to matter and matter receiving spirit, and the joy of this sharing is the love that is the Holy Spirit." Webb's postmodern project in Christology fails to tether itself to the metaphysical dialectic of potency–act, thereby falling into irrational claims such as this one. Regarding God as invisible, intangible, and elusive need not end up in an annihilation of God. A robust understanding of personal spiritual being leads, on the contrary, to a most perfect communion between human beings, angelic beings, and divine Being. There is no reductionism involved in affirming God as pure actuality. Instead, this affirmation prevents the recent tendency of material reductionism that would anthropomorphize God to the point of attributing material (potential and finite) properties to the divinity.

22. Stein, *Potency and Act*, 229. Cf. ibid., 116: "We ought not to conceive of matter [*Materie*] as an item of matter [*Stoff*] present to us and formed into an object by outside mechanical agency; any item of matter that we know by experience, of course, is already formed."

reality is not performed, we risk conflating the whole of the real to only one of its integral parts.

With a view to the whole of reality, Stein asserts the origin of matter and the incapacity of philosophy to grasp conceptually this origin:

> Philosophy based on natural reason brings us to the act of creation which alone is able to bridge the gulf between being and nonbeing, to leap from spirit to matter. But here philosophy halts before a locked gate: creation, as taught by faith, remains a mystery for our knowledge. What is absolutely spiritual and actual calls into being its direct opposite: what is nonspiritual and potential. Matter represents the utmost in potentiality ... matter is brought to actual being by taking in form.[23]

For Stein, natural reason is not able to comprehend the very act of creation but nevertheless demands its necessity in light of the ontological difference between being (*esse*) and beings (*entia*), as well as the clear distinction between potency and act that is detectable in this created state of becoming. Even though the act of creation is completely enigmatic for human knowledge, existence itself and all created existents attest to absolute spiritual being and to pure actuality, for no existent can claim for itself its own origin and actuality. Neither can the sum total of mass/energy account for its primordial conception and birth into being. Instead, mass/energy defers the question of origin by transferring it either to metaphysics or to agnosticism. Agnosticism answers nothing meaningful or intelligible, while metaphysics supplies an answer at once clear and decisive: pure act and spirit. Spiritual being is not just a negative verbal placeholder for the so-called opposite of material being, but the term signifies the fullness, plentitude, and perfection of being as that which gives itself to the point of fecund abandonment. Yet all created beings—spiritual and material—depend on an original and eternal actuality to enter into existence and to be held in existence over the course of time. Material being, in particular, inasmuch as it is intrinsically nonspiritual and potential, is constituted as the radical other—the direct opposite—of spiritual being. Stein contends that "everything that happens to matter is done to it from outside; it is *passive*. But what happens to spirit comes from inside; it is *activity* [*Tätigkeit*], spirit is active [*aktiv*]."[24] In other

---

23. Ibid., 104.

24. Ibid., 102. Cf. ibid., 101, 105, 116, 301: "Matter acquires actual being only by taking on qualities [*Qualität*] ... Pure, 'lifeless' matter differs from living matter in that whatever is done to it, all additional formings that it can undergo, come from outside. Nonliving matter does share with living matter the fact that they both come into existence with a 'determination' prescribing beforehand what can happen to it from without; that is, they come into existence as a thing with a determined '*nature*'

words, matter relies entirely on the formative activity of spiritual being for its general existence and particular shape. Matter, as a theoretical concept, is the radical other of God, who is pure actuality and Spirit. Matter is precisely that which God is not from eternity.

One might wish to argue that the radical other of God is evil. Such an argument would only hold in a Manichaean theological view in which there are two diametrical creative forces, or deities: one good and the other evil. However, from a Judeo-Christian perspective evil is not its own oppositional force to the good Deity. Evil is merely a deprivation (to varying degrees) of the Good.[25] Pure actuality is the Good. All created beings participate in the eternal Good to the measure that they are given actual being and persist in a state of becoming by being actualized further in their being. As indicated above, matter participates in the eternal Good insofar as it is formed matter. Any matter that actually exists does so because it has been informed by a formative actuality by a creative impulse from an immemorial elsewhere. If God is to be construed as pure act, then the opposite of God may be conceived as pure potency, which is theoretically *materia prima*. The very event of creation—the event wherein something that is precisely not God is welcomed into being (*ex nihilo*)—rests on *materia prima* as the entirely other vis-à-vis God. Stein suggests that "there are two different poles opposed to pure being": "the null being of the spirit that lacks substance" and "the sheer potentiality of pure matter."[26] Since angelic beings are not composed of atomic matter—that is, pure spiritual beings—one must reckon a null being of the spirit that lacks substance alongside *materia prima* as the condition

---

... the thing's being, the formed matter, is not completely undetermined potentiality, but *a potentiality in determined directions* ... Matter differs from the nonbe-ing by being *determinable*. This determinability, in contrast to the nonbe-ing, implies something positive, although in comparison to definite being it implies something negative as well; I mean that it is undetermined ... Matter is not determined, but determinable, in position, shape, and size (that is, spatially). It must be determined in order to come into existence."

25. See, for example, Pseudo-Dionysius, *Divine Names* 4.18–35, in *Complete Works*, 84–96.

26. Stein, *Potency and Act*, 413. Cf. ibid., 104–5: "We said earlier that potential being lies between being (that is, pure, absolutely actual being) and nonbeing, or that it is at once being and nonbeing. We were not thinking of some third thing between being and nonbeing, nor a mixture of both. We meant rather that there are degrees of being and corresponding levels or degrees of potentiality; I mean degrees of nearness to pure being. *Materia prima* is on the lowest rung on this scale of be-ings. Here it is pure potentiality, not actual being present *beside* potential being—as in the case of formed matter ... Determinability is the readiness to receive forms or species. Receiving means passing from the absolutely potential being of *materia prima* to the higher mode of being of formed matter that includes something of actuality; it means that a particular be-ing, a material thing, emerges."

of possibility for the creation of finite pure spiritual beings, or angels. These two empty and pure formal possibilities of being serve as the precondition and null essence of that which is not God. Matter, in a word, is that which is not God—that which is purely *in potentia*.[27] Stein goes on to clarify that "matter stands to form as what is unformed, to act as what is potential, and to spirit as what is unopened [*unerschlossen*]. Matter may have these features without filling space. Every limited be-ing must have matter, even the so-called 'pure spirits' insofar as they are finite spirits."[28] The term *matter* is used by Stein as a concept that entails the created primordial chaos—pure potency or *materia prima*—in which formed matter is to open and to take its place.[29] The original act of creation implies a sudden, irrevocable, and redoubled othering commenced by the Godhead. There is, first of all, the eternal othering between Father, Son, and Spirit. With the act of creation originates a second and subsidiary othering whereby something brand new arrives on the scene of eternal begetting and self-giving: matter. If God is pure spirit then matter is the very antithesis of pure spiritual being inasmuch as the act of creation invites the other-than-God to exist. This other-than-God is formed in two senses: (1) "it must be formed by the species that determines the thing to its content (the form of the *essence* [*Wesensform*]," and (2) "by the form of the individual, into which the matter, as formed by the species, enters."[30] This is to say that all material being comes to be from the formal actuality and causality of specific essences and the process of individuation. In order for a specific essence to be actualized, it must be manifest in an individual being. Without individuation, no essence could be revealed vis-à-vis other essences in the created order. However, for living organic creatures composed of body and soul (whether vegetative, sentient, or rational souls), "something material [*stofflich*] exists before life and the vital forming process from within begin, and something material remains behind after the life that was therein ceases to be."[31] This "something material"

---

27. Ibid., 414: "This absolutely potential something that is necessary for a thing to be able to be without being pure act we call '*matter* [*Materie*].'"

28. Ibid.

29. See Gen 1:1–2: "When God began to create heaven and earth—the earth being unformed and void, with darkness over the surface of the deep and a wind from God sweeping over the water" (JPS Tanakh translation). Cf. Stein, *Potency and Act*, 395: "To be sure, matter must have a certain disposition in order to receive any substantial form at all, but within certain limits there is room for much diversity."

30. Stein, *Potency and Act*, 421.

31. Ibid., 285.

that gives itself before and after the ensouling of the living organism is specifically atomic matter that fills space.[32]

Stein envisions a network of material nature that is governed by predetermined laws of physics and takes place within the manifold dimensions of spacetime: "But if we understand 'formed' as well as 'matter' materially [*material*], 'formed matter' denotes a definite area of being. If we use 'material form' as space-filling matter, then everything belonging to this category is connected by laws [*gesetzlich*] through the order of empirical origin in a network: in the network of *material nature*."[33] In the natural sciences, matter is posited exclusively according to this network of material nature observable by the five senses and measurable by aggregate sense data. Within Stein's worldview, however, atomic matter is only one sense of matter alongside other senses as shown above, for example, spiritual matter, ideal matter of consciousness, and theoretical *materia prima*. Stein argues that atomic matter is always formed matter, otherwise it would not assume its place in existence. The hydrogen atom, for example, is an instance of formed matter. A single electron orbiting a single proton is already involved in a network of material nature, with subatomic particles asymptotically composing the respective forms of electron and proton from within and, in addition, an innumerable host of other atoms and molecules determining the activity of the temporally solitary hydrogen atom from without. Even the element hydrogen as such, with its peculiar properties, is a physically manifest form in relation to other differentiated manifest forms. Hydrogen is hydrogen as such insofar as it is not helium, oxygen, carbon, nitrogen, gold, etc. Though all elements are composed of the same atomic and subatomic particles, each element stands out in contrast to the rest by virtue of its formal determination and configuration.[34]

---

32. See Pius XII, *Humani generis*, 36: "The Teaching Authority of the Church does not forbid that, in conformity with the present state of human sciences and sacred theology, research and discussions, on the part of men experienced in both fields, take place with regard to the doctrine of evolution, in as far as it inquires into the origin of the human body as coming from pre-existent and living matter—for the Catholic faith obliges us to hold that souls are immediately created by God." Cf. Denzinger-Schönmetzer, *Enchiridion Symbolorum Definitionum et Declarationum*, 3896.

33. Stein, *Potency and Act*, 326.

34. Stein, *Finite and Eternal Being*, 213–14: "*Form*, finally, we call the 'scaffolding' [*Gerüst*] of the entire thing (as well as the parts of the scaffold), considered in relation to what imparts to it content and determines it as *this* individual thing ... What enters into the thingly form as its content is formed matter, i.e., something which fills space in a particular way by being structurally conjoined to form a unified whole, and manifesting itself externally in sensible appearance. What makes this formed matter a thing of such and such specific qualities we call its *essential form* [*Wesensform*]. The Wesensform is—in contradistinction to the *empty form* [*Leerform*]—precisely what

It would be carelessly reductionistic to conflate all material existents to universal homogeneous miniscule particles while at the same time refusing to admit the particular manifest elemental and ontological (individuated being-specific) forms that together comprise a diverse array of beings in symbiotic relation to one another. Further, it would be a most serious categorical mistake to condense all living creatures into a singular ontological status. There is a clear ontological demarcation between living creatures and their specific forms of being based on the classic categories of the soul: vegetative, sentient, and rational. Differing degrees of consciousness, life-activity, and self-reflexivity unmistakably distinguish living species from one another. In particular, such characteristics define the absolute distinction between the human species and all other nonhuman species, or more generally, between personal spiritual creatures and nonpersonal nonspiritual creatures. For Stein, the height of created finite being is "that of finite spirits or persons."[35] Within the Judeo-Christian tradition, as well as within rational philosophical deliberation, the nomenclature of personhood is reserved for God, angelic beings, and human beings. Finally, let us turn our attention to the material human body and its import for understanding material being in relation to human being.

III. The Human Body and the Possibility of Its Regeneration

Stein considers the human being as a trichotomous unified composite of body, soul, and spirit. As living entelechy of the body, the soul both forms the body from within and is itself formed through the medium of the body from without.[36] Stein claims that "the entire organism of body and soul

---

imparts content—a content, to be sure, for which it is essential to become enclosed in this empty form. There is then an inner connection between these two forms, and the process of filling must not be conceived in the manner in which a receptacle may be filled with any kind of content."

35. Stein, *Potency and Act*, 414.

36. See ibid., 327: "The *entelechy* is the substantial form of living matter. It is the act of the matter which it enters and to which it gives being, that distinctive mode of being that we call 'life.'" Cf. ibid., 402: "But we should remember here that this substance, or the person's core, is entelechy. Its core has the task of constructing the entire organism of body and soul in a process of ongoing development. And this means not only progressively forming from within a given matter into which it is immersed but also appropriating the matter it needs for its *telos*, which is the fully developed individual. This matter includes first of all the space-filling matter the body needs for its conservation and growth, but it also includes the 'matter to construct' the soul . . . As the body can fall short of its *telos* and diverge from it for want of the matter it needs for its construction, so too the soul."

should be called an individual, a unit that cannot be broken at will without being destroyed" as "to each organism belongs its *own* 'piece of matter' and to each its *own* life power as the 'matter' of the being of its soul, and each is separate from all the others through the form of subjectivity."[37] The individuality of each human being is due to the incommunicable character of individuated subjectivity. No ego is synonymous with another ego. Every ego maintains its individual uniqueness vis-à-vis other egos. While the matter of one's body can be transferred and grafted into another body—such as in the case of organ transplants—subjectivity itself is nontransferable. Amidst the radical symbiotic matrix of living beings in relation to nonliving beings, human subjectivity reveals the impenetrable and unrepeatable sui generis character of each and every human soul.

To underscore this point, Stein draws the distinction between the material body (*Körper*) and the living body (*Leib*), which is propelled according to the voluntary and involuntary operations of the soul. She writes that "the living body (*Leib*) in contrast with the physical body (*Körper*) is characterized by having fields of sensation, being located at the zero point of orientation of the spatial world, moving voluntarily and being constructed of moving organs, being the field of expression of the experiences of its 'I' and the instrument of the 'I's' will."[38] This description of the living body's characteristics can be summed up by the word *subjectivity*. The ego marks the zero point of orientation from which the rational soul abstracts from the world and from the living body itself. Self-reflexive consciousness of subjectivity can neither be located according to spatial coordinates nor abstracted any further from itself. It assumes the zero point of orientation for the entire organism and exercises its determinative volition in and through the living body. Upon death,

---

37. Ibid., 343. Cf. ibid., 414–15: "Persons, too, have their matter (what we called their 'life power') as well as their essence which forms this matter, and they need all this for their full being."

38. Stein, *On the Problem of Empathy*, 57. Cf. Stein, *Potency and Act*, 351: "Just as the animal's body [*Körper*] becomes a *living body* [*Leib*] because in it ('in' here has no spatial sense) the soul has its own inner life and is able not only to form the body but to manage it once formed in external activity, so too the living human body is as it were the scene in which and around which the life of the soul unfolds as well as the tool that extends its effectiveness beyond itself . . . The personally formed human soul animates the body and controls it from a center wherein it is gathered into itself and leads its own life that does not affect the body at all or rather only in a quite secondary way." Cf. Stein, *Finite and Eternal Being*, 422–23, 426, 462: "The living body [*Leib*] in this sense is this particular physical body [*Körper*] which is animated and formed by the soul . . . The being of the body denotes the possession of a thoroughly formed essence or nature . . . the life of the animal soul remains tied to and conditioned by the body . . . [whereas] a human body [is] a means and field of expression for a free spirit."

what was once an ensouled living body becomes a nonliving corpse (*Körper*). Without a living soul the physical body is left to the natural processes of decay and decomposition, its integral constitution no longer sustained by the voluntary and involuntary drives of the spiritual soul.

For the living body, "the body is formed then as the scene of what plays in the soul and as the organ for engaging the outside world . . . In this sense, we could call the soul as a whole the form of the body and the act of its potency."[39] Just as every material particle, element, molecule, and object is constituted by peculiar forms, so too the human body is informed by the formal actuality of the human soul. As the material structure that is molded by the form of the soul, and as "that which maintains itself in a self-enclosed structure," the living body (*Leib*) is "the 'outborn' structure of the essence or nature" of the human being.[40] This is to say that the soul expresses itself in and through the body. Human nature is disclosed through the outborn spatial structure of the body. From the external manifestation of the physical body, the invisible and spiritual soul is communicated and thereby receptive to communication from without.

Moreover, Stein differentiates between the becoming of material structures and the becoming of living beings: "But whereas the material structure *comes to be* finished, the living being is never finished. It is a being that is renewed again and again, a being that forms itself continuously and that is thus with respect to itself at once determinative and determinable (in need of being determined)."[41] Any material element—for example, sodium, iron, phosphorous—reaches a state of completion upon its differentiated atomic configuration. Sodium, once sodium, has fully realized its maximum potential to be sodium. No further modification, growth, or development is needed. Its material structure is finished and need no longer become what it was formally destined to be. Living beings, on the other hand, are in a constant state of self-formation from within and from without—being at once determinative (that is, forming themselves from within) and determinable (that is, being formed from without). Personal spiritual beings remain ever unfinished. To become perpetually through the process of intersubjective communication attests not only to the idea of the infinite, but to an eternal communion of loving persons from which every experience of love

---

39. Stein, *Potency and Act*, 352. Cf. ibid., 352–53: "But man is not altogether given over to the reactions of his body; he is rather their *master* (albeit not without restriction). He can repress reactions begun involuntarily, he can bring his body into play as he pleases in this way or that, and thus shape his body itself . . . the body is subject to free shaping."

40. Stein, *Finite and Eternal Being*, 463.

41. Ibid., 270.

originates and finds its ultimate fulfillment and finality—a finality that is at once a new start.

One might object that this vision of perpetual becoming is inadequate to the phenomenon of death. Does not death bring the process of personal becoming to a halt? Does not death deal the individual living organism an impassable blow of finality that is precisely an end and only an end? Is not the pretense of impassibility met with the stark reality of impassability—the unmistakable passion that tragically confronts the hopeful yet futile dream of eternal life as personified by Gilgamesh, as embodied by Jesus of Nazareth? To answer such questions in the negative demands a source that not even death can terminate. For Stein, the Christian doctrine of creation comes to bear on these questions directly:

> According to the view of the emergence of the world in Christian philosophy, which follows the creation account but differs from other theories of natural philosophy, the Creator did not first form a preexisting [*vorausexistieren*] matter [*Materie*] but created matter and the many different shapes wherein it occurs at the same time. That is, He shaped the matter itself, *by* creating it, into concrete individuals according to a fullness of ideas of all kinds. So matter [*Stoff*] would exist in this case but not preexisting matter. The concrete individual would owe its actuality to the creating "*fiat* [let there be]" alone. This is a calling into existence [*Ins-Dasein-Rufen*] by the absolutely Actual from something nonbe-ing beforehand, an imparting of being.[42]

Within the Christian paradigm of cosmic origin, God creates *ex nihilo* (that is, "from nothing"). Material being is actualized instantaneously through the plethora of concomitant forms that shape matter in variegated ways. A genuine other emerges vis-à-vis God but only in proportion to the measure of actuality given by divine initiative. All created beings derive their existence from the divine *fiat* that summons creatures into the living cosmic order. Divine life and being are shared with newly formed creatures that once had no life or being. God, as the absolutely Actual, is the raison d'être (*Logos*) for every created existent. Upon reflecting on the Christian doctrine of creation, it is none too difficult to imagine a re-creation of living creatures following temporal death. Yet how should one envision such a regeneration of living creatures in relation to the physics and ontology of material being as such? In particular, how should one envision the regeneration of individual human beings whose composite material being is disintegrated

---

42. Stein, *Potency and Act*, 59–60.

(in most cases) in its postmortem state and reintegrated into other forms of material being, for example, air, earth, and other living creatures?

Stein proposes that "external nature can be 'redeemed,' that is, it can be raised to its original state."[43] By "external nature" Stein means the external manifestation of mass-particles that are constituted by "the inner unity of force and material elements, the free, efficacious realization [*das Sichauswirken*] of force in space-filling material formations [*Stoffgestaltungen*]. The breaking apart of *Kraft* and *Stoff*, the 'breaking away' [*Herausfallen*] of the material elements from this unity, which turns them into pure mass, is a reversal of the primordial ontological state."[44] Stein argues that pure mass, entirely unformed, is inconceivable since each and every existent is generated from nothing by formal actuality. Even the idea of pure potency comes to mind through the actuality of the idea itself. Stein insists that "*Stoff* is never without *Kraft*."[45] Does this separation of *Stoff* from *Kraft* not describe the intellectual tendency today to disregard completely the veracity of formal and final causality? Is material reductionism not based on the fundamental belief that *Stoff*—pure mass—is eternal apart from its intrinsic unity as a diverse relational matrix of distinctively formed material atomic particles, elements, beings, and ecosystems? As if an originally chaotic and random atomic soup (which already implies form and order, by the way) over the course of time (which too implies form and organization) spontaneously developed into the innumerable complexity of beings that exist today, only thereafter itself (voluntarily?) to undo this process of ontological augmentation and return to a primordial state of entropy and nondiversification! Such an idea is equivalent to claiming that disorder precedes order, that potency precedes act, and that essentially nothing precedes something. Nothing could be more intellectually backwards and bankrupt. Stein asks, "Is matter to blame for the fact that things lag behind the pure form?"[46] Her conclusion: certainly not! Stein contends that "only in the 'fallen' state can matter—cut off from the original unity—impede pure formation [*Ausgestaltung*]."[47] In other words, unity precedes disunity, form precedes matter, essence precedes hylomorphic species, and the actuality of order precedes the unbecoming of

43. Stein, *Finite and Eternal Being*, 194.
44. Ibid.
45. Ibid.
46. Ibid., 240.
47. Ibid. Cf. ibid., 236: "It should be pointed out in this connection that pure mass is not to be conceived as something primordial but rather as something resulting from the disintegration of an original unity. Matter which is brought forth from and molded by living forms becomes pure mass as soon as it is taken out of that essential unity which binds it to the molding forms, so that it falls prey to space."

disorder. At some definite point in time, something must have "gone wrong" to bring about the state of affairs that exists today because entropy in no way could precede an organized and orchestrated teleology of existents and life forms, including the process of biological evolution. The theory of evolution presupposes a formal impetus toward life, organization, and order. Whether that uncreated impetus is called "nature" or "god(s)" is a matter of semantics. In either case, the linguistic referent signifies an uncaused cause—that which determines in advance the evolutionary genius observed throughout the universe. However, philosophically and theologically speaking, if one wishes to use "nature" as a substitute for "god(s)" within a postmodern metanarrative of material reductionism, let's at least come clean about the matter. Nature as such did not "give birth" to itself. Even its own etymology suggests otherwise, for *nascor* means "to be born" and that which is born is born of something other than itself. And so we come full circle back to pure actuality that refers to something other than the sum total of the mutable existents of nature, namely, pure spiritual being, itself immutable and the logical condition for the possibility of material being and its diversification of finite, contingent, and individuated forms.

Stein insists that "from a strictly philosophic point of view, the 'fallen' state can be understood only in terms of a possible metamorphosis of nature."[48] The onset of entropy must be understood as a malady introduced at a certain historical moment within the ontic trajectory of the cosmos. This is not to deny the fact that viruses, bacteria, and the like are ordered entities as well. However, this is to say that the metamorphosis of nature toward its own decline contradicts the holistic order of nature and the symbiotic and interdependent coherence of its respective existents. A preternatural and perfect symbiotic order of nature must be admitted in light of the potency–act rubric of ontology. An inherent antagonism within the natural order from the beginning is implausible because the very principle of antagonism implies a struggle against something else. If all natural living beings innately struggle against death, decay, and disorder, nature per se does the same. Nature's struggle is not against itself but against its own demise. Yet nature's demise has become its very identity and legislation, such as that of the second law of thermodynamics, that is, the gravitational pull toward entropy. The state of nature today suggests that nature somehow turned against itself, thereby violating and compromising the holistic integrity of its being. Ironically, nature's struggle against entropy is at once its struggle against God—pure actuality and the perfection of being. Inasmuch as nature struggles against entropy in the mode of "sur-

---

48. Ibid., 240.

vival of the fittest" and "natural selection," it at the same time wages war against the vocation to self-donation.[49] Enter the doctrine of original sin: "The theological doctrine of original sin ... offers us a firm basis which permits us to relate the actual state of the world to people's rebellion against God and to discover a link between the perversion of the original order of human nature and the fallen state of the world as a whole."[50] The

---

49. See Levinas, *Ethics and Infinity*, 120–22: "[But if one fears for the Other and not for oneself, can one even live?] This is in fact the question one must ultimately pose. Should I be dedicated to being? By being, by persisting in being, do I not kill? . . . In society such as it functions one cannot live without killing, or at least without taking the preliminary steps for the death of someone. Consequently, the important question of the meaning of being is not: why is there something rather than nothing—the Leibnizian question so much commented upon by Heidegger—but: do I not kill by being? . . . what is most natural becomes the most problematic . . . being is never—contrary to what so many reassuring traditions say—its own reason for being, that the famous *conatus essendi* is not the source of all right and all meaning."

50. Stein, *Finite and Eternal Being*, 240. Cf. ibid., 584 (endnote 221): "In a theological perspective, this fall might be linked with the fallen state that is a consequence of original sin. The 'fallen' state of external nature is then a grandiose symbol of the fallen state of human beings. It should be added, however, that such an interpretation is not supported by any specific dogmatic declaration, although many Scriptural passages seem to point in that direction"; 248: "It may be assumed, moreover, that according to the original order of creation, the movements and interactions of material elements were to aid them in forming and unfolding themselves, so that they might manifest in their entire external appearance their anchorage in the eternal. This form-language of material elements cannot be expressed in words, nor can its meaning be conceptually grasped, but it is still unmistakably visible and audible in the towering mountains, in the waves of the sea, and in the raging storm no less than in the gentle breeze. The fact that the forces and events of nature often cause grave disturbances, mishaps, and the destruction of natural structures, has its reason and cause in the fallen state of nature. And yet a glimmer of the original order is still discernable. Even now the world is a cosmos rather than a mere chaos . . ."; 250: "To explain these defects, we must have recourse to external circumstances—aside from and in addition to the fundamental defect, namely, the *corruption* of all material elements after the fall, i.e., the falling away of *mass* from its union with its essential form. In the case of living beings, on the other hand, a formative power superior to the material elements stands over against some foreign matter. Here a given matter is indeed radically transformed, i.e., changed into other material elements, vitalized, and integrated with the unified corporeal structure"; 256: "Presupposed in this entire complex of circumstances is the 'fallen' state of nature. A body that would be alive in the true and full sense of the term would not be tied to 'dead' structural elements at all and would therefore not be vulnerable to death. Such a body would be formed out of the soul and commensurate with it, without absorbing any material elements. On the other hand, where 'dead nature' serves as the substructure of what we call *life*—what in reality, however, is merely a faint copy of the true life—those transmutations from death to life and from life to death are found"; 267: "But even in the evolution of plants there are not lacking certain impediments and malformations which interfere with the total fulfillment and actualization of the *pure form* in the vegetable kingdom as it is actually constituted. Plants, too, are of the realm

Judeo-Christian narrative of salvation history locates human beings at the center of the cosmic drama of rebellion and redemption. It is no mystery that as go human beings, so goes Earth. We have immense power to promote either the good of the planet or its destruction. The human being is the responsible being—responsible for everything, responsible for all. This sheer fact alone attests to the vulnerable communion that obtains in Earth and to the direct impact of humanity's action in relation to nonhuman existents. When we render natural waterways unswimmable and uninhabitable, when we annihilate one another and our surroundings with nuclear weapons, when we eradicate a plethora of unique living species in the name of profit, when we render a mother's womb hostile to life—all such actions bring about the cosmic ecological malaise that we experience today. The doctrine of original sin, in its essence as an inherited condition toward decline, refers to all such acts and similar ones that precede us, envelop us, and become the prepense patterns of our personal willing and way of being in the world. Left to ourselves, we inevitably self-destruct, even (and especially) in the name of progress.

For the question of human being, all this is to say that sickness, injury, and death together mark a reversal of the primordial irenic ontological state of human being. The disintegration of body and soul—the fissure of *Körper* and *Leib*—implies a great unnatural obscenity wherein the totality of the human person is ruptured and degraded radically. However, according to the privilege of possibility in phenomenology, it is conceivable for the onset of death and decomposition to be transfigured. If such an unnatural process is to be reversed, "the material element must be transformed in order to be revitalized."[51] It remains an open possibility for the corporeal structure of the human being to be refashioned in a similar way as it was created originally. A noncontingent pure actuality is required to reverse the entropic process of anatomic corruption. If that which is corruptible is to clothe itself with incorruptibility, and that which is mortal is to clothe itself with immortality, it must be an impossible work wrought by the same divine Actuality that fashioned the universe in the beginning.[52] Following death a new *fiat* must be issued, summoning the flesh of incarnate personal spiritual beings to a spiritualized existence. The flesh itself must take on the character of perpetually actualized spiritual be-

---

of fallen nature and are thus, as it were *sub ratione peccati* (stained by original sin), although the paradisiacal innocence of pure nature appears in this stage less impaired than on higher levels of being. The vegetable kingdom thus reveals the universal condition as well as the unity of the entire created universe."

51. Ibid., 215.

52. See Gen 1:1—2:25; John 1:1–18; 1 Cor 15:54.

ing. Instead of inclining toward dissipation, the body must be conformed entirely to the power of spiritual being whose life cannot be extinguished by virtue of its indissoluble share in divine Actuality through an intimate relation of alterity. Any creature that has been imbued with personal spiritual existence is incapable of falling out of individual existence since such a creature has been welcomed into eternal relationship with the supereternal Trinity of Persons.

Just as the "fallen" state of nature is characterized by nature turning against itself, while at the same time turning against God, the cosmic elixir must undo the onset of what could be called the logic of negation by a subsequent negation of negation.[53] In effect, the divine nature must turn against itself in order to redeem and reverse the lethal process of cosmic degeneration. Similar to the way antivenin serum is produced by the original venom being injected into an animal in order to harvest the antibodies to be applied to a human snake bite, the divine nature had to submit to the venomous effects of sin and death in order to furnish the antidote of grace into the human experience. Benedict XVI says as much in his first encyclical letter, *Deus caritas est*, when he writes that "God's passionate love for his people—for humanity—is at the same time a forgiving love. It is so great that it turns God against himself, his love against his justice . . . so great is God's love for man that by becoming man he follows him even to death, and so reconciles justice and love . . . [Christ's] death on the Cross is the culmination of that turning of God against himself in which he gives himself in order to raise man up and save him. This is love in its most radical form."[54] Benedict, in exquisite fashion, describes the paradoxical nature of divine love that willfully enters the terrain of forgiveness by overturning the tables of justice according to the power of merciful transcendence. The logic of the double negative is the logic of the cross. By crossing out the grand cosmological No—the No of nature against nature, the No of self against the other, the No of the world against God—God effectively introduces the soteriological Yes back into the created order. It comes by way of invitation and gift. It is not a coercive or mechanical Yes, but one hailed by the filial Yes of God the Son to God the Father in the bond of the Holy Spirit manifest and proclaimed in Christ's incarnate life, death, and resurrection. The filial Yes of God the Son is at once the divine No against creation's No in the form of the revelatory God-forsakenness of God the Son on the cross. By divinity turning against

---

53. See chapter 2 of the present work, "Spiritual Being," for further discussion on the logic of the double negative as it relates to the Christian doctrine of salvation.

54. Benedict XVI, *Deus caritas est*, 10, 12.

divinity, nature's voluntary (and subsequent involuntary) turn against nature is negated and thereby reversed into the perfect integrity of the original created order in which there exists no hostility of material being toward spiritual being. Cosmic redemption must begin with the source of voluntary animosity toward God and the other: human nature and, in particular, the human body.

In order for the flesh of unique individual persons to be re-actualized, the principle of actualization needed to become fully united with that which was to be re-actualized. The incarnation of the eternal Son of God instigated the irreversible movement of redemption whereby all human flesh is regenerated in alignment with its primordial irenic ontological state. A recapitulation is necessary in which the ontological and teleological perfection of humanity is consummated within the inner life of the Trinity. Stein refers to God the Son as "the 'born-out' essential form" of the Godhead, which corresponds to all bodily being.[55] The resurrection of Jesus Christ inaugurates the redemption of all human flesh and of the entire material and spiritual network of the cosmos. Through the hypostatic union of the incarnate *Logos*, followed by the resurrection and ascension of the Body-Soul-Spirit of the God-Man, a chain reaction is set in motion that will include the bodily resurrection of all human beings ever conceived in the flesh. Entropic decay, which tends toward null being, can be inverted only by its antinomy: pure Act. Entropy is the result of a waning actuality within the energetic and anatomic potencies of material being. In other words, when material being is deprived of the various instantiations of spiritual being—in its array of formal manifestations—then diversified material being inevitably will dwindle toward cosmic death and extinction. Apart from the pure Actuality revealed in the *Logos* become flesh, entropy indeed would be the final word on existence that would result in virtual nonexistence. However, if Christ truly has been raised from the dead, then through his radical solidarity with humanity is opened the pathway of regeneration. Material being is destined to be redeemed in the same way as it originated through the divine act of creation: *fiat*.

In examining the specific description of material being submitted by Stein, we were able to clarify the relation of material being to spiritual being and to suggest the plausible possibility of the revitalization of material being in the form of resurrection. Stein's work constitutes a viable bridge between metaphysics and the natural sciences through the innovations of the phenomenological method. By comprehending the precise relation of material being to spiritual being, a holistic theological anthropology

---

55. Stein, *Finite and Eternal Being*, 361.

can be developed that marshals the most current advances in the natural sciences, philosophy, and theology. The logic of resurrection coincides with the logic of the natural order in the form of paradoxical continuity of being.

7

Empathy and the Other

> The Desire for Others that we feel in the most common social experience is fundamental movement, pure transport, absolute orientation, sense.[1]

IN 1916, EDITH STEIN completed her doctoral dissertation, *Zum Problem der Einfühlung* ("On the Problem of Empathy"), under the direction of Edmund Husserl, who likewise was intrigued by the phenomenon of empathy. As Stein states at the beginning of the second chapter of her work, "All controversy over empathy is based on the implied assumption that foreign subjects and their experience are given to us."[2] For Husserlian phenomenology, the question of empathy centers on the possibility of empathy's givenness to consciousness of the human subject. In other words, can empathy be considered as a particular instance of givenness and, if so, how is the givenness of empathy to be described? Such are the questions that occupy Stein throughout the deliberations of her dissertation project.

Given the tightly knit fabric of Stein's theological anthropology—conceiving the human person as body, soul, and spirit—there looms the important task of inquiring into the relationship between the self and the personal other. For instance, what is the relationship between individuality and community, between autonomy and interdependence, between solitude and fraternity? As it turns out, a Steinian view of the human person is one

---

1. Levinas, *Humanism of the Other*, 30.
2. Stein, *On the Problem of Empathy*, 3.

that is derived from an organic communion of selves rather than from a psychosomatic inventory of the solitary self. Stein's theological anthropology is imbued with a communitarian tonality that describes the ontological totality of human personhood as one in which persons are "revealed in original experiencing or in empathetic projection" rather than as experiences constituted as objects.[3] In order to probe into the meaning of empathy and of the other within Stein's holistic understanding of the human person, we will examine the following three lines of thought: (1) consideration of the veritable paradox of alterity, (2) investigation into the essence of empathy, and (3) reflection on the precise relationship between the individual human soul and the experience of the personal other. By moving from the general idea of alterity to the more specific phenomenological and metaphysical attenuations of empathy, we will sum up the indispensable place of the other within a Steinian account of the human person created in the *imago Dei*.

I. The Paradox of Alterity: An Ode to Otherness

The greatest provocation of ipseity is alterity. Yet alterity is at the same time the most fertile source of vitality for the self. The self is precisely not the other and the other is definitively not the self. However, it is the other who makes the self as such possible in the first place. One is able to recognize oneself as distinct only in an anterior relation to another self. In other words, the alterity that obtains within the self through the process of self-reflection is determined formerly in the self's relation with the other, most especially with the personal other. As Emmanuel Levinas has made clear so deftly, the relationship between the self and the personal other (*l'autrui*) is always already an ethical one. The command of the other on me to be responsible for her is issued always in advance. It meets me before I arrive on the scene, incessantly calling me to the scene where I meet the other in the proximity of an intersubjective yet asymmetrical relationship. The other affects me without respite, stirring me into a compunctious disposition wherein I recognize my negligent history of irresponsibility and am at the same time spurred on toward the redemptive possibility of serving the other in love—not according to moral generosity but as demanded by the preponderance of ethical exigency. Paul Ricoeur likewise confirms Levinas's proposal of an ethics of responsible freedom, granted in a nuanced tenor, as he writes,

---

3. Ibid., 109.

> It is finally on the ethical plane that the affection of the self by the other displays the specific features that belong as much to the properly ethical plane as to the moral plane of obligation. The very definition of ethics that we have proposed—living well with and for others in just institutions—cannot be conceived without the project of living well and being affected by solicitude, both that which is exerted and that which is received.[4]

Both Levinas and Ricoeur admit that the other affects the self with a sense of solicitude, that is, with a causation of disquiet, perturbation, anxious care and concern. In a state of radical passivity the other affects the self and the self is forever subject and beholden to the face of the other. For Levinas and Ricoeur, to live well with others is not to remain undisrupted by the other but to be pricked perpetually into upright action by the other and on behalf of the other. Solicitude is the condition for the possibility of justice and, moreover, of love. Ricoeur refers to the affectivity of solicitude coming upon the self from without as well as from within. As will be shown further below, the other refers not only to a phenomenon occurring outside the self and crashing in on the self, but the other also refers to that which gives and speaks itself from within the core of the self in figures such as the absolute, conscience, and God.[5] Solicitude is determined both from without and from within; it can be exerted as well as received. In either case solicitude refers to the disruptive call of the other to the self that confirms that love relaxed is no love at all.[6]

The paradox of alterity is at once the paradox of the self, for the self is one yet composed of more than one. Stein refers to "a life beyond our own, although it includes ours."[7] She recognizes the self as inextricably bound

---

4. Ricoeur, *Oneself as Another*, 330.

5. See Nabert, *Le désir de Dieu*, and Ricoeur, "The Hermeneutics of Testimony," in Ricoeur, *Essays on Biblical Interpretation*, 119–54.

6. See Teresa of Avila, *Interior Castle*, 435: "... whoever does not increase decreases. I hold that love, where present, cannot possibly be content with remaining always the same"; and Thérèse of Lisieux, *Story of a Soul*, 257–58: "... for a soul that is burning with love cannot remain inactive. No doubt, she will remain at Jesus' feet as did Mary Magdalene, and she will listen to His sweet and burning words. Appearing to do nothing, she will give much more than Martha who torments herself with many things and wants her sister to imitate her. It is not Martha's works that Jesus finds fault with; His divine Mother submitted humbly to these works all through her life since she had to prepare the meals of the Holy Family. It is only the *restlessness* of His ardent hostess that He willed to correct."

7. Stein, *Self-Portrait in Letters*, 9: "You see, I can no more be in love with Germany than with myself for, after all, I am myself it, that is, a part of it. Peoples are 'persons' who have life, who are born, who grow, and who pass away. It is a life beyond our own, although it includes ours. Therefore, one cannot reasonably inquire whether they

together within a whole that is a society of persons—a community of others. The self is constituted as a vital member of an organic communion of persons. John Donne, in a similar way, echoes this reality in the seventeenth meditation of his *Devotions upon Emergent Occasions*:

> No man is an Iland, intire of itselfe; every man is a peece of the Continent, a part of the maine; if a Clod bee washed away by the Sea, Europe is the lesse, as well as if a Promontorie were, as well as if a Mannor of thy friends, or of thine owne were; Any mans death diminishes me, because I am involved in Mankinde; And therefore never send to know for whom the bell tolls; It tolls for thee.

Donne poetically maintains that no human being is an island unto herself, but rather that every person is knitted within the entire living tapestry of humankind. The bell of which he speaks certainly is in reference to death, but even more so to the summons to be responsible for the personal other who commits me to ethical account. This is no vocation to evade but one in which I realize that I am enriched by the other without end and that the meaning of the other's death is both an affront to my duty toward her and a deduction from the totality of my very own self and from the happy web of the entire human family.

Without the other the self withers and dies. An infant within his or her mother's womb attests to the radical dependence of the self on the other. Biologically interconnected through the media of umbilical cord, uterus, and amniotic fluid, the infant and the mother share a common bond of life through their most proximate and sanguineous relationship. The phenomenon of empathy proceeds from this originary relationship of prosopic intimacy. It is where the lived experience (*Erlebnis*) of the other becomes the lived experience of the self. Empathy is the event in which the pathos of the other is suffered simultaneously, or borne, by the self. Though originating in the lived experience of the other, the empathetic experience of the other's lived experience is impregnated paradoxically within the self. The emergence of the other's experience within the self manifests and proclaims that which precisely has not originated primordially within the self. Empathy reenacts the paradoxical relationship between the self and the other, verifying the ethical responsibility of the self for the other inasmuch as the other affects me beyond the shadow of a doubt. The moment the lived experience

---

'should' be great or small; i.e., whether we ought to do something about it, for we have as little power within that sphere as cells have in deciding whether the organism they constitute should grow or decrease" (letter to Roman Ingarden, February 9, 1917).

of the other no longer affects me is the moment at which I die, even if it is a death that I live.

Derived from the German term *Einfühlung*, empathy is the paradoxical lived experience of the self whose source material is the lived experience of the other.[8] This is to say that the singular experience of the self is composed simultaneously of the lived experiences of both self and other. In this case empathy is much more than a vague "feeling about" or "feeling in relation to," but is rather the innermost affectivity of the self as engendered by the innermost affectivity of the other through the noetic medium of intuitive consciousness. Empathy is the de facto experience of the other affecting me—an experience over which I have neither control nor jurisdiction. The paradox of empathy is extended to this fact in which my innermost lived experience is my own yet not originally my own. Stemming from the elemental experience of "wombness," that is, the intimate relation between the infant *in utero* and his or her mother, empathy is rooted characteristically in the feminine genius. In her essay entitled "Spirituality of the Christian Woman," Stein describes empathy as a "feminine gift" that enables woman "to participate, understand, and stimulate; she does so outstandingly as an assistant worker, interpreter, and teacher."[9] Woman is attuned naturally to the other due to her intrinsic and inborn disposition of perceptiveness and empathic attentiveness to the other. As John Paul II has pointed out on numerous occasions, especially within the whole of his *Theology of the Body* corpus, the feminine genius is manifest and proclaimed by the peculiar hylomorphic constitution of woman and through her distinct psychosomatic signification: receptivity to gift.[10] In other words, woman

---

8. The German term *Einfühlung* is related to its root terms, *fühlen*, "to feel or sense," and *Fühlung*, "contact or to be in touch with." Empathy, therefore, is essentially the receptive interior contact with the other and proceeds originally from the lived experience of the other and emerges within the self as given to consciousness inwardly.

9. Stein, *Essays on Woman*, 115. Cf. John Paul II, *Mulieris dignitatem*, 22, 31: "The Bible convinces us of the fact that one can have no adequate hermeneutic of man, or of what is 'human,' without appropriate reference to what is 'feminine.' There is an analogy in God's salvific economy: if we wish to understand it fully in relation to the whole of human history, we cannot omit, in the perspective of our faith, the mystery of 'woman': virgin-mother-spouse... The Church gives thanks *for all the manifestations of the feminine 'genius'* which have appeared in the course of history, in the midst of all peoples and nations; she gives thanks for all the charisms which the Holy Spirit distributes to women in the history of the People of God, for all the victories which she owes to their faith, hope and charity: she gives thanks for all *the fruits of feminine holiness*."

10. See John Paul II, *Man and Woman He Created Them*, for example, 21:5 (212): "The whole exterior constitution of woman's body, its particular look, the qualities that stand, with the power of a perennial attraction, at the beginning of the 'knowledge' about which Genesis 4:1–2 speaks ('Adam united himself with Eve'), *are in strict union*

is the form of being human that embodies and thereby reveals genuine receptivity to the other, especially on display in the vocation to authentic motherhood. For woman, empathy assumes a literalness not experienced by man, namely, the experience of bearing the other, body and soul, within oneself. The natural body language of motherhood serves as the touchstone for authentic empathy. For example, genuine empathy is manifest in effective listening—a charism that Stein recognized in her sister, Rose: "Using her exceptional gift of empathy, Rose would captivate persons whom she valued. As she was a consummate listener, one was drawn to confide in her. In intellectual matters her grasp of another's thoughts was rapid and facile; and she could then participate in a discussion on the topic with remarkable

---

with motherhood ... of the feminine body in its typical expression of creative love ... These words express the whole theological depth of the function of begetting-procreating. The body of the woman becomes a place of the conception of the new human being. In her womb, the human being takes on its characteristic human appearance before being brought into the world"; ibid., 40:2 (287): "The eternal 'feminine' (*das Ewig-Weibliche*)—just like, for that matter, the eternal 'masculine'—tends even on the level of historicity to free itself from mere concupiscence and seeks a place of affirmation on the level proper to the world of persons"; ibid., 109:1 (558–60): "'*You are all-beautiful, my friend*, and there is no spot in you' (Song 4:7). The bridegroom ends his song with this word, leaving all metaphors behind, in order to turn to the only one, through whom the 'language of the body' seems to express the '*integrum*' of femininity and the '*integrum*' of the person ... Both the femininity of the bride and the masculinity of the bridegroom speak without words: *the language of the body* is a language without words." Also see John Paul II, *On the Genius of Women*, for example, 27–28: "In fact, woman has a genius all her own, which is vitally essential to both society and the Church. It is certainly not a question of comparing woman to man since it is obvious that they have fundamental dimensions and values in common. However, in man and in woman these acquire different strengths, interests, and emphases and it is this very diversity which becomes a source of enrichment. In *Mulieris Dignitatem* I highlighted one aspect of feminine genius, that I would like to stress today: woman is endowed with a particular capacity for accepting the human being in his concrete form (cf. no. 18). Even this singular feature which prepares her for motherhood, not only physically but also emotionally and spiritually, is inherent in the plan of God who entrusted the human being to woman in an altogether special way (cf. ibid., no. 30)"; and John Paul II, *Mulieris dignitatem*, 4: "Thus the 'fullness of time' manifests the extraordinary dignity of the 'woman.' On the one hand, this dignity consists *in the supernatural elevation to union with God* in Jesus Christ, which determines the ultimate finality of the existence of every person both on earth and in eternity. From this point of view, the 'woman' is the representative and the archetype of the whole human race: she *represents the humanity* which belongs to all human beings, both men and women. On the other hand, however, the event at Nazareth highlights a form of union with the living God which can *only belong to the 'woman*,' Mary: *the union between mother and son*. The Virgin of Nazareth truly becomes the Mother of God"; *Mulieris dignitatem*, 18, 30; and Calcagno, *Philosophy of Edith Stein*, chapter 4: "Empathy as a Feminine Structure of Phenomenological Consciousness," 63–79.

fluency."[11] To listen well is a sign of authentic empathy and the condition for the possibility of investment and growth in human relationships. Open confiding in another is determined by the degree of listening and empathy demonstrated by the other. Without effective empathy, people close off to one another and are reluctant to trust one another. Empathy not only refers to a phenomenological experience, but it ascends to the rank of a virtue due to the role it plays in fostering peace and solidarity among human beings. Peace is achieved through the paradox of empathy and the sustained dialectical relation between oneself and another in which the other takes his or her place within the receptive noetic inner core of the self. In the end, solicitude is found to be the very foundation of a society held together in solidarity, one with the other.

II. The Essence of Empathy

In her doctoral dissertation, Edith Stein aims at defining the essence of empathy through the method of phenomenology. This project was completed in 1916, well before she became enthralled with Thomistic metaphysics, so it lacks any metaphysical approach to the question of empathy in terms of scholasticism. It is solely a phenomenological exploration. Nevertheless, Stein's investigation exemplifies a textbook analysis in the school of Husserlian phenomenology. She defines the subject matter with lucid precision, openly considers counterpositions to her argument, and sustains a critical analysis of empathy and its concomitant sub-phenomena through the key terms of givenness (*Gegebenheit*) and feeling (*Gefühl*). Sarah Borden Sharkey, in her biography on the life and work of Stein, rightly asserts that "Stein places the distinction between the *act of experiencing* and the *content experienced* at the center of her discussion of empathy."[12] This move follows the classic phenomenological distinction between noesis (the act of experiencing) and noema (the content experienced). It is important to recall that the noesis-noema distinction is not to be confused with the Kantian noumenon-phenomenon distinction that phenomenology directly challenged. This is to say that for phenomenology, "since intuition gives in the flesh, the Kantian caesura between the (solely sensible) phenomenon and the thing-in-itself [i.e., noumenon] must disappear."[13] The distinction between the self's act of experiencing and the content experienced that originated in the lived experience of the other makes possible the act of

11. Stein, *Life in a Jewish Family*, 125.
12. Borden, *Edith Stein*, 28.
13. Marion, *Visible and the Revealed*, 56.

empathy in which the other's experience becomes a living content within my own act of experiencing.

Antonio Calcagno similarly observes Stein's centralization of the phenomenon of empathy within her approach to understanding the phenomenology of community. He writes, "Stein treats community under two important aspects (*Abschattungen*), namely, ontologically and from the viewpoint of consciousness. She first tries to describe what an experience of community would look like in consciousness, that is, how we experience it phenomenologically. Second, she describes the object of consciousness, namely, the ontic essence or structure of community."[14] Building on the work of her dissertation in *Philosophy of Psychology and the Humanities*, Stein approaches the lived experience of the community by reiterating the pure ego as the zero point of orientation of consciousness while at the same time considering the possibility of an individuated ego to expand to form an empathetic collective *nos*, or "we."[15] In terms of the ontic essence of community, Calcagno further relates that, for Stein, "community is defined through the category of life, as a 'living through' of the experience of one in the other in solidarity."[16] As Calcagno infers, the definition of community cannot be reduced to the pure ego life of the self, but demands an inclusive hermeneutic of mutual empathetic intersubjectivity between self and other engendering a solidarity of persons sharing in the unity of communal life. Even though "Stein distinguishes empathy from the communal experience she is analyzing in the *Philosophy of Psychology and the Humanities*," as Calcagno carefully points out, she nevertheless suggests an intimate connection between the two.[17] In essence, the elemental structure of communal life is determined by the more fundamental structure of empathy as generated from the heart of the self-other relationship.[18] In order to unlock the possibility of an experience in which the other dwells in the same, or one in which the same dwells in the other, let us examine the various ways in which Stein defines empathy.

---

14. Calcagno, *Philosophy of Edith Stein*, 29.

15. See Calcagno, "Thinking Community," 35: "There is a particular lived experience, Stein argues, that is unique to the experience of the community—the experience of the 'we.'" Further, see Calcagno, *Lived Experience from the Inside Out*.

16. Calcagno, *Philosophy of Edith Stein*, 35.

17. Ibid., 32.

18. On the difference between Husserl's and Stein's phenomenological loci, see Calcagno, "Thinking Community," 41: "Husserl insists on the primacy of the interior life, the life of the ego, whereas Stein admits that this is an important step but would also want to give the communal life greater value by describing its own legitimate epistemological sphere."

To begin her pursuit, Stein defines empathy in a basic way as "the perceiving [*Erfahrung*] of foreign subjects and their experience [*Erleben*]."[19] This basic definition lays out the essence of empathy: a living experience of the lived experience of another person within the self. Commenting on Stein's dissertation, *On the Problem of Empathy*, Angela Ales Bello writes, "The important role of empathy is manifest in the understanding between people on the spiritual level; that level . . . manifests itself in all its fullness in the context of the will."[20] Ales Bello underscores the fact that, in its essence, empathy is a spiritual phenomenon since it involves personal spiritual beings. More specifically, empathy occurs via the will because the self both voluntarily vacates itself in its approach to the other and voluntarily attunes itself to the experience of the other, welcoming the other's lived experience to take its place within the heart of the self's lived experience. Stein clarifies the essence of empathy according to the following definitions:

1. "Acts in which foreign experience is comprehended"[21]
2. "An act which is primordial as present experience though non-primordial in content"[22]
3. "An experience of our own announcing another one"[23]
4. "The basis of intersubjective experience [that] becomes the condition of possible knowledge of the existing outer world"[24]

These definitions of empathy work to throw light on the phenomenon by uncovering its givenness and meaning layer by layer. Beginning with the understanding of empathy as a basic act in which any foreign experience is comprehended, Stein proceeds to posit empathy as the sine qua non through which knowledge of the outside world—that is, outside of the self—is made possible. Let us consider each of these definitions in sequence.

---

19. Stein, *On the Problem of Empathy*, 1.

20. Ales Bello, *Fenomenologia dell'essere umano*, 119 ("Il ruolo importante dell'empatia si manifesta nella comprensione fra le persone a livello spirituale; tale livello, [connesso già a quello precedente,] si manifesta in tutta la sua ampiezza nell'ambito della volontà"; translation my own).

21. Stein, *On the Problem of Empathy*, 6.

22. Ibid., 10.

23. Ibid., 19.

24. Ibid., 64.

1. "Acts in which foreign experience is comprehended"

First, empathy refers specifically to comprehending the lived experience of another self. It is not merely the perception of any foreign element outside of the self—for example, an object, idea, sound, etc.—but the sure experience of another's experience even though the experienced experience does not originate with the self. In fact, Stein is careful to indicate that empathy is not outer perception, although it is closely related to perception in that empathy, too, deals with a presence in the here and now: "Perception has its object before it in embodied givenness; empathy does not."[25] The key difference between empathy and outer perception is that the former is dealing with a given datum which is not experienced originally by the self through immediate sense data, whereas in outer perception the given datum is experienced originally and directly by the self in and through the living body (*Leib*). This initial definition of empathy provides a basic understanding of its concept: acts, or living experiences, in which the lived experience of another self is given to consciousness.

2. "An act which is primordial as present experience though non-primordial in content"

This second definition of empathy sheds further light on the distinction between what Stein calls primordial givenness and non-primordial givenness. She asserts that "all our own present experiences are primordial ... but not all experiences are primordially given nor primordial in their content."[26] The term *primordial* refers to that which is most originary and incipient within the self, or within consciousness. In the case of givenness, there are varying degrees of incipience. For instance, through the witness of another, I may be able to access an event even if I was not present at the event. The event itself would not be given to me in a primordial way but instead through a non-primordial givenness mediated by the testimony of another. I would perceive the event only by way of secondary imagination with no direct access to the event in its original (primordial) givenness to my immediate conscious perception. Similarly, Stein describes empathy as an act that is primordial as present experience though non-primordial in content. This is to say that "the subject of empathized experience ... is not the subject empathizing, but another."[27] In empathy the lived experience of the other is pri-

---

25. Ibid., 19.
26. Ibid., 7.
27. Ibid., 10. This distinction gets at the fundamental difference between empathy

mordial for him or her, while this same lived experience of the other is given to me in a non-primordial way in terms of its content. My lived experience of empathy is primordial as a genuine present experience occurring in my own consciousness, but the content of the experience is non-primordial for me since it was experienced first by the other and its original presence is derived from the elsewhere of the other's lived experience.

The paradoxical nature of empathy, insofar as it contains in itself the primordial givenness of the self's ownmost experience and the non-primordial givenness of the content of the other's original lived experience, assumes a new human subject altogether: not I, not you, but we. In empathy, Stein writes, "I intuitively have before me what they [i.e., the others outside of the 'I'] feel. It comes to life in my feeling, and from the 'I' and 'you' arises the 'we' as a subject of a higher level."[28] In other words, the experience of empathy creates an entirely new order of subjectivity by transcending the I-you dichotomy without dissolving it. The "I" and "you" remain distinct yet integrate with such intimacy as to form a new level of subjectivity in the "we." In Stein's view, "The unified act [of empathy] does not have the plurality of the individuals for its subject, but a higher unity based on them."[29] Empathy, as a given phenomenon, is lived and expressed through the paradoxical phenomenality of containing within itself a singular subjectivity composed of the unity of the lived experiences of two distinct subjects. With the experience of empathy originates the collective subjectivity of the "we."

3. "An experience of our own announcing another one"

The third definition Stein gives for empathy points to the experience of attestation within the self. Though Stein does not use the terminology of

---

("in-feeling") and sympathy ("with-feeling"). The content of empathy is non-primordial while the content of sympathy is primordial. Stein makes clear that the transition from empathy to sympathy is made once the other's lived experience becomes the self's personally lived experience. Stein refers to the example of joy. If I perceive that the other is joyful about some particular state of affairs, I may empathize initially with the joy of the other. However, if I, too, become joyful about that same state of affairs directly, the joyful experience is caused in the same fashion as it is in the other by the state of affairs rather than by the experience of the other's expression of joy. In this case it is more properly called "sympathy" instead of "empathy" since the state of affairs provokes the experience of joy in the "I" directly. See ibid., 14–16.

28. Ibid., 17.

29. Ibid., 122 (endnote 28). Cf. ibid., 18: "But 'I,' 'you,' and 'he' are retained in 'we.' A 'we,' not an 'I,' is the subject of the empathizing. Not through the feeling of oneness, but through empathizing, do we experience others. The feeling of oneness and the enrichment of our own experience become possible through empathy."

"attestation," she further describes the phenomenality of empathy as "the experience back to which knowledge of foreign experience points."[30] Within the self, empathy performs the function of attestation. Empathy always refers to a lived experience that originates from an elsewhere in relation to the self. As neither imitation, association, inference by analogy, nor inner perception, empathy is accomplished through an attitude of "turning toward or submerging ourselves in the foreign experience."[31] Consciousness of the "I" must follow the pathway between the primordial present experience of the self to the non-primordial content of the other's lived experience. The primordial present experience of the self must apprehend the given testimony of the content of the other's lived experience as this content is announced to the "I" in the form of a call or witness. Empathy is essentially the experience that is lived after the other as "the foreign individual is announced" to the self.[32] Again, it is the other who first lives an experience primordially and directly while the "I" in turn experiences the same content of the other's original experience, though in a non-primordial way, since "feelings can be comprehended in their purity."[33] The original feeling of the other—whether pain, joy, sorrow, elation, etc.—can be experienced in me to the very same degree as experienced by the other inasmuch as the empathized experience palpably announces the given content of the other's lived experience.

Stein avers that every "I" manifests a zero point of orientation that the living body surrounds.[34] This means that all experiences of the "I" are given to consciousness as to a zero point of orientation that cannot be reduced to any anatomical component of the living body (*Leib*), let alone the physical body (*Körper*) as such. All things are experienced from the perspective of this zero point of orientation, including the experience of one's own living body. The zero point of orientation is coextensive with the Scholastic concept of the agent intellect that effectively abstracts from, and faces, everything else. Beyond the categories of primordial givenness and non-primordial givenness, Stein suggests a third category—namely, con-primordial givenness—which refers to the kind of givenness "where what is not perceived can be there itself together with what is perceived."[35] Take the example of a coin. Upon perceiving the "heads" side of the coin,

---

30. Ibid., 19.
31. Ibid., 23. Cf. ibid., 24–34.
32. Ibid., 34. Cf. ibid., 34: "Just as our own individual is announced in our own perceived experiences, so the foreign individual is announced in empathized ones." Cf. ibid., 69, 70, 93, and Stein, *Philosophy of Psychology and the Humanities*, 93.
33. Stein, *On the Problem of Empathy*, 50.
34. See ibid., 43.
35. Ibid., 57.

the "tails" side is co-given insofar as "this givenness of the one side implies tendencies to advance to new givennesses. If we do this, then in a pregnant sense we primordially perceive the formerly averted sides that were given con-promordially."[36] Con-primordial givenness allows one to perceive hidden facets of that which is given by virtue of the given facets that remain temporarily latent and in potentia but nevertheless given within the whole experience of givenness.

Con-primordial givenness is relevant to the question of empathy since it allows "the foreign living body [to be] 'seen' as a living body."[37] From my unique zero point of orientation I interpret my own living body as a physical body. Intellectually, I am able to position my physical body at a distance from my imcommunicable zero point of orientation, but I cannot abstract any further from my zero point of orientation because it is the source and ground of every perception and thought that is my own. Stein indicates that sensual empathy is made possible "by the interpretation of our own living body as a physical body and our own physical body as a living body because of the fusion of outer and bodily perception."[38] I am able to intuit the givenness of the other's living body according to the con-primordial givenness of the other's living body. First, however, I must have been able to intuit the givenness of my own living body as a physical body from the standpoint of my zero point of orientation.

In the same way, I am able to receive the givenness of the other's living body through the phenomenon of empathy. In fact, as Stein suggests, a new zero point of orientation is realized in empathy just as a new human subject is created through empathy: "I retain my 'primordial' zero point and my 'primordial' orientation while I am empathetically, non-primordially obtaining the other one ... But this orientation, as well as the empathized sensations, is con-primordial, because the living body to which it refers is perceived as a physical body at the same time and because it is given primordially to the other 'I,' even though non-primordially to me."[39] Again, the paradoxical intermingling of primordial and non-primordial givenness produces a trilectical con-primordial givenness, thereby establishing a new

36. Ibid.
37. Ibid.
38. Ibid., 58. Cf. ibid., 67, 87.

39. Ibid., 61–62. Cf. ibid., 63–64: "From the viewpoint of the zero point of orientation gained in empathy, I must no longer consider my own zero point as the zero point, but as a spatial point among many. By this means, and only by this means, I learn to see my living body as a physical body like others. At the same time, only in primordial experience is it given to me as a living body ... The perceived world and the world given empathetically are the same world differently seen."

and original zero point of orientation, in effect disorienting the primacy of my own primordial zero point of orientation by taking it up into a world not given to myself alone. Through empathy the given content of the other's lived experience in his or her living body is in turn given to me non-primordially, yet within the primordiality of my own lived experience, therefore resulting in a paradoxical and con-primordial experience of the other as a living body experiencing his or her own primordial experiences. The experience of the other's primordial experiences takes place through empathy in which an experience of my own announces another one.

4. "The basis of intersubjective experience [that] becomes the condition of possible knowledge of the existing outer world"

In this fourth definition, Stein claims that empathy is the basic form and condition for experiencing anything that comes from the outer world, that is, outside of the self. This means that without the fundamental experience of empathy, we would not be able to know anything from the outside world since empathy is required for the intuitive fulfillment of givenness and the full experience of intersubjective expression.[40] In fact, empathy is the sine qua non for self-knowledge because the givenness of the self is delivered through the interplay between empathy and inner perception. Stein contends that "it is possible for another to 'judge me more accurately' than I judge myself and give me clarity about myself."[41] The self becomes more transparent to itself through intersubjectivity and especially through the other's experience of me. The other's experience of me is given to me as a living seed. Even after its initial apperception, the other's experience of me continues to exert its influence on my self-understanding from its hidden life of interpersonal signification in the depths of the soul in the form of memory. While the other's experience of me takes place primordially in the other (and outside of me), the content of his or her experience is then given to me non-primordially as a kernel within my primordial experience of the non-primordial content of the other's experience of me. Alterity and empathy are that which allow a self to be given to itself and permit the other to be comprehended as a genuine other.[42]

For Stein, empathy gives access to the realm of feeling and to the world of values. Even though empathy is not to be equated with spiritual

---

40. See ibid., 82.

41. Ibid., 89.

42. See ibid., 109: "As my own person is constituted in primordial spiritual acts, so the foreign person is constituted in empathetically experienced acts."

understanding, it is what "makes it possible for us to relive the spiritual life of the past" and what opens the possibility of "comprehending or intending the value of a person," in a word, love.[43] Because all spiritual life is intersubjective, only empathy engages the memory that allows for the interpersonal spiritual life of the past to come to surface in consciousness. Without empathy we would not have access to spiritual life, that is, the intersubjective life between personal beings that consciously transcends the facile and unconscious world of objects. Only spiritual creatures are able to comprehend and intend the value of a person since "spiritual" implies intellectuality and freedom—the very conditions necessary to exercise the feeling of value that is "the source of all cognitive striving and 'what is at bottom' of all cognitive willing."[44] Spiritual life consciously strives for the highest value—especially the value of a person, that is, to love—in a world that gives a host of meanings of unequal value and significance. Acts of empathy are those that correlate unambiguous feelings with emergent values that serve as the basis for all meaningful willing and acting.

Stein brings her analysis of empathy to a close by reflecting on self-knowledge and accurate knowledge of the other. First, she writes that "only he who experiences himself as a person, as a meaningful whole, can understand other persons."[45] Personal and holistic self-knowledge is necessary for understanding others, and to understand one's self requires the exercise of empathy. I must strive to understand myself through the givenness of myself mediated to me by the empathetic acts of the other. In addition to inner perception, my own self is given to me through the ways in which others experience me. I am able to access others' experiences of me through empathy, and once I acquire sufficient knowledge of myself as a person as a meaningful whole, then I am able to understand other persons as meaningful wholes as well. Understanding persons (including the self) as meaningful wholes implies surpassing the competing reductionisms that threaten to

---

43. Ibid., 95, 102. Cf. ibid., 92. For an in-depth treatment of an ethics of values, see Scheler, *Formalism in Ethics and Non-formal Ethics of Values*. The first volume of Scheler's *magnum opus* appeared in 1913 and the second volume in 1916, the same year in which Stein's doctoral dissertation was completed.

44. Stein, *On the Problem of Empathy*, 108. Cf. ibid., 112: "As the realization of the spiritual person, the psycho-physical individual can be called the 'empirical person.' As 'nature' he is subject to the laws of causality, as 'spirit' to the laws of meaning"; and Stein, *Philosophy of Psychology and the Humanities*, 158.

45. Stein, *On the Problem of Empathy*, 116. Cf. ibid., 110: "We find not only that the categorical structure of the soul as soul must be retained, but also within its individual form we strike an unchangeable kernel, the personal structure . . . The levels of the person do not 'develop' or 'deteriorate,' but they can only be exposed or not in the course of psychic development."

subordinate the meaningful network of persons to some political or scientific ideology, or to an egotistical projection of self-aggrandizement. Perhaps the world is not there to exalt me after all. Stein recognizes the temptation of reducing the world to the feeble self as she writes, "If we take the self as the standard, we lock ourselves into the prison of our individuality. Others become riddles for us, or still worse, we remodel them into our image and so falsify historical truth."[46] The danger of becoming locked into the prison of one's individuality raises the stakes for cultivating an empathetic worldview. Proper empathy demands an optic conversion in which the all too natural *incurvatus in se* is inverted, promoting the face of the other to shine with its unique radiance. According to the phenomenological perspective, the "natural attitude" must be bracketed effectively and the phenomenon be reduced in order to stay all falsifying reductionisms in their menacing advance. By turning our attention to the other through empathy, "what is 'sleeping' in us is developed."[47] Our true selves are awakened through the constancy of riskful encounters with the other and the fruitful progress of empathy. Likewise, the true self of the other is awakened and affirmed also in his or her personal dignity and unrepeatable uniqueness.

III. The Individual Soul and the Other

Having traced the meaning and interconnection of Stein's four definitions of empathy, we finally turn our attention to the two basic modalities of the other: (1) the other without and (2) the other within. So far we have gained a preliminary understanding of the otherness involved in empathy from without as well as from within. We have witnessed Stein's claim that "empathetic experiences are . . . central to being a person."[48] This implies that an analysis of empathy is indispensable for an adequate theological anthropology. It remains to be clarified what specific contours unfold upon examining the particularity of the human soul in relation to the givenness and the call of the other. We will examine the three basic relations between the soul and the other, implicitly informed by a Levinasian description of alterity even though focusing on the peculiar contributions of Stein. These three basic relations between the soul and the other are (1) the soul in relation to the other in general (Levinas's notion of *l'autre*), (2) the soul in relation to the

---

46. Ibid., 116. Cf. Marion, "The Marches of Metaphysics," in *Idol and Distance*, 1–26, and Marion, *God without Being*, to understand further the phenomenon of reducing the iconic alterity of the other into an idolatrous mirror of the self.

47. Stein, *On the Problem of Empathy*, 116.

48. Borden, *Edith Stein*, 29.

personal other (Levinas's notion of *l'autrui*), and (3) the soul in relation to the voice of the other within the self, that is, conscience, and even prophecy.

a. The Soul in Relation to the Other (*l'Autre*) in General[49]

To begin with, Stein purports that "any reception into the inner soul involves the growth and unfolding of the soul itself" and that "the full unfolding is prescribed beforehand as *telos* in the entelechy, in the person's original core."[50] While bearing an intentional will calibrated according to the distinct value structures of being, the soul is receptive in its very nature. The unfolding of the soul's potential depends on outside influences yet this potential itself is given beforehand as entelechy, or the inner form of the ever developing person. Not only does the other person affect the soul in its ongoing state of becoming, all alterity outside of the self, which the self encounters, affects the soul and its formation. Similar to a lump of clay, the accidental shape and character of the soul (but not its immutable substance) is altered according to the plethora of others who approach the soul and toward whom the soul strives. The soul is inherently malleable as a spiritual being. One's immediate environment serves to cultivate the soul as within a womb.[51] All material and spiritual goods influence the soul's progress on its way to the perpetuity of character formation. Every other that comes in contact with the soul leaves an indelible trace, for good or for ill.

Destined for vital intellectual activity, the soul is the existent with which the "transcendental determinations [namely, the true, the good, and the beautiful] which characterize existents as such in relation to, and in congruity with, other things ... establish a relationship."[52] Beauty, for instance, "has such a mysterious hold on the human soul."[53] The soul is tethered to the value of beauty according to its inbuilt thirst for perfect and saturating beauty. Beauty lifts the soul as a warm wind beneath the pinions of a majestic eagle in flight. The soul, more fragile than pinions, cannot help being moved in relation to forces from without. However, the soul acts as the vigilant gatekeeper of its own interior domain as "nothing that it is not open

---

49. The distinction between the other (*l'autre*) in general and the personal other (*l'autrui*) comes from the work of Emmanuel Levinas. See Levinas, *Totality and Infinity*, 24. This is an important distinction to apply to the work of Stein, even retrospectively, since it helps delineate the different faces of alterity in the abstract and in the concrete.

50. Stein, *Potency and Act*, 403.

51. Cf. Stein, *Finite and Eternal Being*, 424: "The more or less perfect unfolding of the animate creature's essence or nature depends on its environment."

52. Ibid., 291. Cf. ibid., 294.

53. Ibid., 322.

to can enter its interior."⁵⁴ As Teresa of Jesus envisions the spiritual structure of the soul with many inner dwelling places, the soul voluntarily moderates that which enters its innermost center. On the whole, "the soul cannot live without receiving ... nourish[ing] itself with those contents which it makes its own in an experiential spiritual manner—as the body nourishes itself with those structural material elements which it absorbs."⁵⁵ All that is other in relation to the soul has the potential to shape the soul through embodied spiritual contact. Stein maintains there to be two primary sources of the soul's development: (1) involuntary formation and (2) education or personal formation.⁵⁶ The soul in relation to the other in general deals with the first of these sources—the constant involuntary formative effects on the life of the soul that do not cease throughout the entire course of life. Let us now proceed to examine the soul in relation to the personal other through whom emerges "the inception of a genuine intellectual life" through the process of pedagogy.⁵⁷

b. The Soul in Relation to the Personal Other (*l'Autrui*)

Concerning the soul's relation to alterity, it is the personal other especially who wields influence on the formation of the soul. Stein writes that "the experience of the being of the soul develops on the sensible and intellectual levels in the mutual dependence of the experience of the self and the experience of the other."⁵⁸ The soul does not develop sensibly and intellectually by coming in contact with an object-world alone but must be stimulated intellectually by other spiritual beings in the context of a communal relationship. Upon the intellectual awakening of the "I" (*das Ich*), one enters into the field of self-determination and meaningful ethical action.⁵⁹ As demonstrated above, the realm of feeling and the world of values open through empathy and the perichoresis of intersubjectivity. Persons mutually interpenetrate through the phenomenon of empathy as they grow in self-knowledge and authenticated knowledge of the other. Empathy proves that "when the soul is affected by the distinctiveness of another man, it can take this

---

54. Stein, *Potency and Act*, 403.
55. Stein, *Finite and Eternal Being*, 373.
56. Ibid., 428.
57. Ibid.
58. Stein, *Knowledge and Faith*, 124.
59. See Stein, *Finite and Eternal Being*, 428.

distinctiveness into itself in a certain way and grow by so doing."[60] Through being affected by the other, the soul is changed forever at the mercy of the other's influence. The pedagogical nature of intersubjectivity, especially as realized within the adult-child relationship, continues throughout the entire span of life. We constantly teach one another—this is certain. We instruct one another through the witness of our speech and our actions. It is this process of personal instruction that either molds or poisons the human soul. A miseducation in love and personhood is the death of the human soul, but an authentic testimony to true love and to the good is life and beautiful existence for the soul.

Through enriching education "the innermost essence of the soul also becomes manifest externally. We 'feel' the ineffable soul's essence also in our communication with others."[61] Pupils become teachers and teachers become pupils. Students who have had their souls enriched through authentic pedagogy wear the joy and gratitude of their enrichment "on their sleeves," so to speak. That is, the enrichment of the soul is expressed externally. The witness to truth exacted by the teacher is in turn attested by the student. Further, the invisible essence of the soul is certainly felt—through empathy—in the course of our interpersonal communication with one another. And what is meant by "communication" if not the exchange of a call and a response? Stein infers from successive acts of empathy that "what takes place in the being-moved of the soul has to do not with a natural process but with a *call* and *response*" in which "the person is expected to 'take a stand' with respect to its own position—either negating it or freely affirming it."[62] The transition from a sensual attitude to an ethical attitude—"the attitude of one who wants to recognize and do what is morally right"—"may not even be possible in a natural way, but only on the basis of an extraordinary *awakening*."[63] Call and response are terms belonging to the realm of spiritual personal beings and cannot be understood according to an ignorant worldview of material reductionism. Sense and perception is one thing, ethics and responsibility is another. Undergoing a conversion from a purely sensual attitude to a solicitous ethical attitude (if one dare make this painful

---

60. Stein, *Potency and Act*, 402.
61. Stein, *Finite and Eternal Being*, 502.
62. Ibid., 439.
63. Stein, *Science of the Cross*, 164. Cf. Ratzinger, *Introduction to Christianity*, 350: "It is a question of a 'dialogic' immortality (= awakening!); that is, immortality results not simply from the self-evident inability of the indivisible to die but from the saving deed of the lover who has the necessary power: man can no longer totally perish because he is known and loved by God. All love wants eternity, and God's love not only wants it but effects it and is it."

transition) requires an unnatural—or better, supernatural—attunement to the call of the other. One is summoned to take a stand, to stake out one's ground with respect to the acute call of the other, not in an arbitrary way but in such a manner that it concerns the whole of one's precious life because the other's life, too, is precious. Everyone is called to the witness stand to state one's relation to the other. Is it one of responsibility or indifference? With this question in mind, we may inquire ever further into the exact form of proclamation whereby the call of the other is heard. Let us turn then to an examination of conscience as the premier venue through which the call of the other is heard.

c. The Soul in Relation to the Voice of the Other within the Self: Conscience

When met with the term "voice of the other," one immediately may conceive of an audible sound of the other's voice proceeding from mouth to ear. However, within a phenomenological analysis of the call of the other, we are dealing with language, expression, and words certainly, but most of all with a peculiar form of language that does not proceed from ears to mind. Instead, the call of the other refers above all to a language that is issued in the depths of consciousness, from the heart of the soul. How is it that the other can speak from the inner chambers of consciousness, although he or she appears to me from without? Jerome, Peter Lombard, Thomas Aquinas, and Bonaventure all speak of the notion of synderesis, a term derived from Greek meaning "to preserve, guard or observe." It refers especially to the voice of the other within the soul that guides the soul in upright ethical action. Synderesis stems from the belief that there are principles of right and wrong that do not originate exclusively from the self or from a community of selves. Rather, an ethical imperative confronts the self and constantly demands that the self give an account of it. Thomas defines synderesis as that which inclines to good only, and as a habitual impulse for doing good, to which belong the first practical principles of reason that guide us in virtuous living.[64] Within the Catholic tradition, conscience is viewed more specifically as the law of God that assigns the human person its most authentic vocation even before the person comes on the scene.[65] Conscience signifies the voice of the other within the self—an elsewhere speaking from within.

---

64. See Thomas Aquinas, *Summa theologiae* I.79.12.
65. See *Catechism of the Catholic Church*, 1776–1802.

Stein, too, regards conscience as a voice or call that "recalls the I again and again to its proper place and condition and demands that the I answer for its actions and gain an understanding of their effects and consequences. For all actions leave a trace in the soul, which is differently disposed before and after the act."[66] Conscience is the voice of accountability within the self, incessantly examining all personal acts and their moral character. It is the judgment seat that allows the I to understand the meaning and ramifications of all of its personal acts. Each personal act functions as a shaping mechanism of the soul as the soul itself is manifest and expressed in each and every personal act. Conscience, as the standard of virtue and interrogator of vice, signifies the paradox of empathy in which the other can be recognized unambiguously within the self. Conscience calls me to account for the fate of the other, the state of myself, and the exigency of the absolute.[67] Yet in order to hear clearly the voice of conscience, "the life of the soul must be *drawn* into itself, and this is brought about by the *demands* with which the soul meets and by the *voice of conscience*. But quite naturally the urge and pull toward the outside will always be stronger, so that abiding within is usually of short duration."[68] The voice of the other within the soul requires that the soul enter into its innermost chambers—especially through the classic spiritual itinerary of purification, illumination/meditation, and contemplation—so that the soul will be attuned and awakened intimately to the needs of the other and to its incomparable vocation to serve the other in love.

IV. Conclusion

Through this reflection on empathy and the other in the work of Edith Stein, we have unearthed her careful inspection of the phenomenon of empathy in its multifaceted dimensions. The basis of empathy was shown to be alterity, and the paradoxical nature of alterity was brought to light in order to trace the etiological roots of empathy. To come full circle, created in the *imago Dei*, the human person is sustained and enriched vitally through empathy. Just as God the Father, God the Son, and God the Spirit live in eternal empathetic relation to one another, so too are human beings called by God and by one another to live in an open and translucent attitude of facing

---

66. Stein, *Finite and Eternal Being*, 442.

67. See, again, Nabert, *Le désir de Dieu*, and Ricoeur, "The Hermeneutics of Testimony," in Ricoeur, *Essays on Biblical Interpretation*, 119–54, for an explication of the concept of "the absolute" in relation to the ethics of interiority.

68. Stein, *Finite and Eternal Being*, 442–43.

one another in loving vulnerability. Authentic love bids the soul to open in radical risk to the in-breaking of the other in order for love to complete its circuit and for fear to be dispelled. In moving toward the other, the soul must still itself simultaneously and enter into its innermost depths in order to hear the voice of conscience openly and to reap the fruits of empathetic encounter. Let us close with the anthropological pattern set forth by Psalm 131. Beginning with the solitary self, filled with trepidation, moving to the warm scene of mother and child, and concluding with the communal character of the people of Israel, this sacred poem of King David profoundly paints a picture of the child of empathy—the pupil who waits with loving trust for the Other:

> O Lord, my heart is not lifted up,
> my eyes are not raised too high;
> I do not occupy myself with things
> too great and too marvelous for me.
> But I have calmed and quieted my soul,
> like a child quieted at its mother's breast;
> like a child that is quieted is my soul.
> O Israel, hope in the Lord
> from this time forth and for evermore.[69]

---

69. Ps 131:1–3 (RSV).

8

The Logic of the Cross

The message of the cross is foolishness to those who are perishing, but to us who are being saved it is the power of God.

—1 Corinthians 1:18 (NAB)

THE MEANING AND POWER of the cross is what sets the Christian faith apart from all other religions of the world. Signified by the term *cross* is expiatory suffering, that is, suffering on behalf of the other in order to atone for the sins and destitution of the other. The cross also signals the act of substituting oneself in the place of the other in order to liberate the other. It goes without saying that the cross refers above all to the passion and death of Jesus of Nazareth outside the wall of Jerusalem some two thousand years ago. If Jesus truly reveals what it is to be human through his life, his teaching, and, above all, his paschal mystery, then surely the cross serves as the hermeneutical key to understanding the human paradigm in relation to the divine Trinity.

As we rapidly proceed into the twenty-first century, the term *suffering* tends to be interpreted as having a negative connotation. Suffering is regarded as that which should be eradicated at all costs. The term *suffering* is conflated often with the term *pain*, together interpreted as a meaningless and irksome phenomenon that just needs to go away as expediently as possible. However, the message of the cross presents a formidable challenge to the pretentious impassible lifestyle of self-sufficiency. Through the signification of the cross, the etymological roots of the term *suffering* are recuperated: in Latin, *sufferre*, "to bear up, to endure." What does suffering bear up if not the other person? Is this not the happy vocation to love? John of the Cross says as much when he writes that "love is not tried by ease and satisfaction."[1] Suffering is none other than the vocation to make room for the other at the expense of one's own self-satisfaction. The exigency of this vocation is initiated by the call of the other and to suffer the other requires something supernatural—that is, something that does not originate with the human being, who is entirely finite and natural. In speaking of the transition from the active night to the passive night of the soul, Edith Stein writes that "one can deliver oneself up to crucifixion, but one cannot crucify oneself."[2] In other words, the other is necessary for the logic of the cross to run its course. At the heart of the proclamation of the cross is the admission that a power is required that comes from outside of the self—even more, outside of humanity—to humanize and to redeem. In a word, the cross manifests and announces grace.

"Grace," derived from the biblical Greek term χάρις, in its most basic sense refers to the concept of gift. Pure gift is that which is given freely in a completely gratuitous way on the part of the giver. The gift is precisely that which its recipient could not procure by his or her own initiative and willpower for himself or herself. Grace connotes the unexpected, the undeserved, the unmerited, the uncontrollable. Christ's vicarious offering of himself unto death on a cross of wood expresses divine grace to a degree that even surpasses the divine act of creation from nothing (*ex nihilo*). That the eternal God would become human flesh in order to regenerate this flesh redoubles the grace of created existence. Created being, after degenerating

---

1. John of the Cross, *Degrees of Perfection* 9, in *Collected Works*, 729.

2. Stein, *Science of the Cross*, 49. Lest the meaning of the "logic of the cross" be misunderstood at the outset, it is important to draw the distinction between meaningful and redemptive suffering and what Levinas calls "useless suffering." See Levinas, *Entre Nous*, 91–101. Levinas writes here that "the justification of the neighbor's pain is certainly the source of all immorality" (ibid., 99). Indeed there is much abusive suffering perpetrated by human beings against one another, which must be checked immediately. The logic of the cross does not imply an affirmation or condoning of all human suffering, such as that horrifically met by the Jewish people, in particular, during the German Holocaust from 1940 to 1945. Neither does the logic of the cross seek to glamorize the crucifixion of Jesus of Nazareth by glossing over its tragedy and horror. Rather, the logic of the cross illuminates the vocation of the self—me—to suffer for the sake of the other through my radical responsibility for him. The logic of the cross argues that to be responsible for the other implies suffering the other, for the other, with the other. In terms of the scapegoat theory of René Girard, I nominate myself as the scapegoat out of sacrificial love for the other. See Girard, *The Scapegoat*. In terms of Levinas's theory of substitution, I willingly accept the call to substitute myself in the place of the other. See Levinas, *Otherwise than Being*, 99–129.

at the behest of human dereliction, is imbued with the seed of resurrected life through Christ. Through the incarnation of Jesus of Nazareth, creation becomes charged with the actualizing potency of life eternal issued in the form of a nuptial covenant between personal beings, human and divine.

Upon entering the Order of Discalced Carmelites, Edith Stein viewed herself as the spouse of Christ. She understood the meaning of the cross and wrote about it frequently. We could not tender adequately an account of the theological anthropology of Edith Stein without concluding with a brief reflection on the place of the cross in a Steinian (and, moreover, Christian) understanding of what it is to be human. Turning our attention to the whole, we realize that the cross is not an arbitrary addendum to a project in Christian philosophical theology that would serve to decorate some more important topic. Rather, the cross is the imperative and integral lens through which to view finite and eternal being in their complex interplay. Apart from the cross we are unable to make the most meaningful sense of the mysterious adventure called "human."

In order to arrive at a clear comprehension of what is meant by the logic of the cross, we first will attempt an earthy snapshot of the life of Edith Stein in searching for the meaning of the cross in her personal life. Second, we will consider the meaning of the dark night of solitude emerging from Carmelite spirituality in relation to the logic of the cross. Third and finally, we will summarize the distinct character of the logic of the cross by enumerating and describing some of its primary traits. Through these three successive steps we will discover the decisive bearing the message of the cross has for knowing what it is to be human.

I. Edith and the Cross

Born on the Day of Atonement, October 12, 1891, Edith Stein "was especially attracted to the ritual of this particular holy day when one refrained from taking any food or drink for twenty-four hours or more, and [she] loved it more than all the others."[3] Raised in a Jewish family, Edith was schooled in the ethics of alterity, the dignity of sacrifice, the disciplines of penance, and the priority of the stranger.[4] As attested in her autobiographical account,

---

3. Stein, *Life in a Jewish Family*, 71.

4. See, for example, where Edith speaks about "the old Jewish custom that, instead of keeping for oneself the first of each kind of produce one rather gives them away" (ibid., 40). Edith Stein will be referred to as "Edith" for the remainder of the chapter in order to underscore her personal familiarity with the logic of the cross and her lived experience of suffering and martyrdom.

Edith relished the art of giving up for the sake of the other.[5] Edith—her name meaning "prosperous in the strife"—"found it an intriguing kind of sport to overcome hindrances that were apparently insurmountable."[6] She readily leaned into a challenge, whether coming from her studies, from family life, or from her occasional bouts with depression and a depreciated feeling of self-worth. In the midst of "nasty human experiences," Edith contended, "true, the world might be evil; but if the small group of friends in whom I had confidence and I strove with all our might, we should certainly have done with all 'devils.'"[7] Edith endured tragedy—for example, the sudden death of her father from heat stroke when Edith was only two years of age—and yet witnessed the unrelenting perseverance of her mother and others in her circle of family and friends who refused to back down from persecution and hardship. She came to recognize a bigger picture in life: "a life beyond our own, although it includes ours."[8] From a young age Edith recognized the interdependence of created existence and the vital interpersonal dimensions of communal life.

Due to her critical and probing mind, Edith drifted away from her Jewish faith during her teenage years only to regain this faith with its Christian extension at the age of thirty. However, in the year 1917, at the age of twenty-six, Edith received the devastating news of the death of her mentor and friend, Adolf Reinach, in battle. Upon visiting his wife, Anna, Stein was perplexed that she was not in despair. As a newly made Christian, Anna radiated with the hope to be reunited with her husband in eternal life. This experience influenced Edith profoundly, so much so that toward the end of her life she commented to her friend Johannes Hirschmann, "It was my first encounter with the Cross and the divine power that it bestows on those who carry it. For the first time, I was seeing with my very eyes the Church, born from her Redeemer's sufferings, triumphant over the sting of death. That was the moment my unbelief collapsed and Christ shone forth—in the mystery of the Cross."[9] Edith was so struck by Anna's faith and hope in the face of darkest tragedy that the same flame of faith and haven of hope began to awaken in her. Edith's fascination with the power of the cross would con-

---

5. See, for instance, ibid., 235–36: "My guiding principle was always: give in, in all that is not unjust." Also, commenting on her disinterested service in the Red Cross during wartime, she writes that "I placed myself unconditionally at their disposal" (ibid., 298).

6. Ibid., 152.

7. Ibid., 216–17.

8. Stein, *Self-Portrait in Letters*, 9 (Letter to Roman Ingarden, February 9, 1917).

9. Posselt, *Edith Stein*, 49. English translation taken from Herbstrith, *Edith Stein*, 56.

tinue to grow throughout the rest of her life. Baptized on January 1, 1922, after reading the autobiography of Teresa of Jesus, Edith eventually would enter the Order of Discalced Carmelites to give herself over completely to the cross of Christ. Even thinking back to her student years at Göttingen in 1913–14, Edith recalls a bare hill on campus "crowned with three windswept trees which always reminded [her] of the three crosses on Golgotha."[10] Proleptically and prophetically, the cross became significant to Stein before she began to decipher its definitive meaning for her life and for the world.

Adopting the phrase "how one may go about living at the hand of the Lord" as her *ceterum censeo* ("However that may be, I think . . .") with which she concluded every speech she gave, Edith challenged each would-be follower of Christ: "Do you want to be totally united to the Crucified? If you are serious about this, you will be present, by the power of His Cross, at every front, at every place of sorrow, bringing to those who suffer comfort, healing, and salvation."[11] It is the cross of Christ that binds one without relief to the cause of the other. A magnificent vocation to love wells up from the kenotic sanguinity of the cross, inspiring faith to trust in God alone for the provision of all life's needs and empowering one to live a life of heroic virtue. One who lives according to the pattern of the cross overcomes fear by love, supplants doubt with faith, and flies untethered from the memory of tragedy with hope.

To follow Christ, and especially to be united with Christ crucified, demands the daily crucifixion of sin and self-aggrandizement. To follow Christ is to become attuned so acutely to the plight of the other that one even experiences amnesia concerning one's own death.[12] The cruciform life, set in particular relief in the religious life, is distinguished by "the total surrender of the whole person and his or her entire life to the service of God."[13] To become "crucified with Christ" is to give one's life up for the sake of the other to the point of abandonment.[14] Very often this is accomplished very quietly and without much pomp and circumstance. Prayer is the first and most constant way to give of oneself in loving empathy to the other.

---

10. Stein, *Life in a Jewish Family*, 242.

11. Ibid., 435. Cf. ibid., 423, and Stein, *Self-Portrait in Letters*, 87 (letter to Sr. Adelgundis Jaegerschmid, April 28, 1931).

12. This comment is inspired especially by the philosophy of Levinas, for example, cf. Levinas, *Is It Righteous to Be?*, 121–29.

13. Stein, *Essays on Woman*, 52.

14. See Gal 2:19–20: "For through the law I died to the law, that I might live for God. I have been crucified with Christ; yet I live, no longer I, but Christ lives in me; insofar as I now live in the flesh, I live by faith in the Son of God who has loved me and given himself up for me" (NAB).

To permit the other to trouble one's conscience night and day is to live the cruciform life in perpetual solidarity with the other. Moreover, to live according to the Evangelical Counsels of poverty, chastity, and obedience is to live a life dedicated to and responsible for the other.

Many times we may feel that we are unable to influence others directly, yet Edith reassures us that "after every encounter in which I am made aware how powerless we are to exercise direct influence, I have a deeper sense of the urgency of my own *holocaustum* . . . Let us help one another to learn more and more how to make every day and every hour part of the structure for eternity."[15] When Edith was enclosed within Carmel, it was for the sake of others and for the Other from whom all otherness is derived. Prayer is always directed to the other, even in the case of praying for one's self. Edith readily admits *sed Deus dat incrementum*—"but God gives the increase"—and realizes that she must decrease in order that he might increase.[16] And this is precisely the logic of the cross: "whoever exalts himself will be humbled; but whoever humbles himself will be exalted."[17] This is a paradox indeed, but there is a consistency of this paradox that runs as a crimson thread through the whole of scripture.

Through prayer we are able to bear not only our personal cross in life, but we are empowered to take up the crosses of others as well. Edith

---

15. Stein, *Self-Portrait in Letters*, 60 (letter to Sr. Adelgundis Jaegerschmid, February 16, 1930). Cf. ibid., 101 (letter to Anneliese Lichtenberger, August 17, 1931): "You are not the only one to make mistakes day after day—we all do it. But the Lord is patient and full of mercy. In his household of grace he can use our faults, too, if we lay them on the altar for him. '*Cor contritum et humiliatum Deus non despicies* (A contrite and humbled heart, O God, you will not scorn)' (Ps. 50). That, too, is one of my favorite verses"; and 1 Cor 3:5–9: "What then is Apollos? What is Paul? Servants through whom you believed, as the Lord assigned to each. I planted, Apollos watered, but God gave the growth. So neither he who plants nor he who waters is anything, but only God who gives the growth. He who plants and he who waters are equal, and each shall receive his wages according to his labor. For we are God's fellow workers; you are God's field, God's building" (RSV); and Stein, *Letters to Roman Ingarden*, 86: "I have great difficulty finding this feeling of absolute powerlessness in myself. Perhaps that is because with very little effort I accomplish things with others. However, sometimes we must have the courage to accurately express powerlessness in order to heal the naïve trust we have in our will and ability—something I definitely possessed earlier" (letter of February 12, 1918).

16. See 1 Cor 3:7 and John 3:27–30: "John [the Baptist] answered and said, 'No one can receive anything except what has been given him from heaven. You yourselves can testify that I said [that] I am not the Messiah, but that I was sent before him. The one who has the bride is the bridegroom; the best man, who stands and listens to him, rejoices greatly at the bridegroom's voice. So this joy of mine has been made complete. He must increase; I must decrease'" (NAB).

17. Matt 23:12 (NAB). Cf. Luke 14:11; 18:14.

confirms this idea as she writes, "I thought that those who recognized it as the cross of Christ had to take it upon themselves in the name of all. Certainly, today I know more of what it means to be wedded to the Lord in the sign of the Cross. Of course, one can never comprehend it, for it is a mystery."[18] Such a heroic testimony! Edith assures us of the possibility of taking up the cross on behalf of those who are ignorant of its life-giving majesty. That I can vicariously substitute myself on behalf of the other before the divine summons of responsibility opens the way for atonement and salvation through communal solidarity. Christ's incarnation is the source of this collective redemption performed by the Church—the communion of angels and saints that has become one with Christ—and all people of faith and good will. As Bride, being wedded to Christ, the Bridegroom, through the sign of the cross, consummates the salvation of humankind on a cosmic scale. This salvation is manifest externally to greatest proportion, yet its source is in the quiet depths of the human soul and in the Sacred Heart of Christ that is the wellspring of all redemptive activity of the Spirit.[19]

II. The Dark Night of Solitude

Prayer is not only the source of greatest consolation and communion with God, but it is also an activity of severe trial and anguish. As the Carmelite spiritual masters reveal, authentic union with God is accomplished through much solitude and suffering. The primary metaphors used to describe this experience are desert, night, and nakedness. Several divestments take place that refine the soul as in a furnace. Without this process of purification, the soul would not be made capable of receiving the fullness of divine grace and glory. The heart/soul must be expanded according to the measure of the One who is to fill it. By the end of her life, Edith tasted fully the bitterness of the cross as she came to love the cross. For the way of the cross is not bitterness alone but the footpath to the heights of contemplation and blissful union with the Most Holy Trinity.[20]

---

18. Stein, *Self-Portrait in Letters*, 295 (letter to Mother Petra Brüning, December 9, 1938).

19. See Stein, *Science of the Cross*, 176: "Love's highest fulfillment is 'being-one' in free mutual surrender: this is the inter-trinitarian divine life."

20. It is striking to note the symbolic meaning of Edith's love for hiking in the mountains during her youth as it relates to her eventual Carmelite profession—recall Mount Carmel, the site upon which the Carmelite Order was founded in the late twelfth century AD. For instance, she recalls a time at age nineteen when she, Hans Biberstein, and her sisters, Erna and Rosa, "proceeded to Reinerz where the four of us packed ourselves and our luggage into a wagon for the ascent to our destination in the heights"

Even as a child, Edith was called "a book with seven seals" by her older sisters, Else, Elfriede, and Rosa.[21] She was the precocious "baby" of the family and exhibited a hidden interiority where she would often withdraw in deep thought and study.[22] Upon completing her examinations at the *Oberprima* level of secondary school, the principal, playing off the word *Stein* (which literally means "stone" in German), wrote of Edith, "Strike the stone [*Stein*] and treasures will gush forth."[23] Indeed, Edith's interior world was replete with sapiential gems that would gradually pour out into her life and writings. However, even as she aged, Edith maintained a love for childhood, recalling a time (at age twenty) when she "joined in the games the children played on the lawn more than in anything else."[24] Reminiscent of Thérèse of the Child Jesus, Edith wrote to her good friend Fritz Kaufmann, in 1927, "Become like a child and lay your life *with* all the searching and ruminating into the Father's hand. If that cannot yet be achieved, then plead; plead with the unknown and doubted God for help in reaching it. Now you look at me in amazement that I do not hesitate to come to you with wisdom as simple as that of a child. It *is* wisdom *because* it is simple, and all mysteries are concealed in it. And it is a way that most certainly leads to the goal."[25] It is clear in this passage that by this point in her life Edith had become accustomed to living with the ripe faith of the child to which Christ refers in the Gospels.[26] She encourages her friend to do the same—to regard God as the loving Father who cares for us as his children. She also recognizes that this risk of faith is shrouded in intellectual opacity and assaulted by doubts. Nevertheless she insists that divine wisdom is childlike in character

---

(*Life in a Jewish Family*, 133). Little did she know at the time the spiritual heights to which she would ascend later in her life. Cf. Stein, *Self-Portrait in Letters*, 19 (letter to Roman Ingarden, August [7], 1917): "I have been up here since yesterday; it is just beautiful, 1400 meters altitude, very quiet, solitary; and there is a gorgeous view toward the Belchen [Mountain]."

21. Stein, *Life in a Jewish Family*, 63.

22. See ibid., 74, 79: "Within me, however, there was a hidden world. Whatever I saw or heard throughout my days was pondered there ... In fact, when not in school, I became so quiet and taciturn that the whole family noticed it. This was probably due to my being so cocooned in my interior world." Cf. ibid., 278, where Stein speaks of her "solitary battle" in dealing with depression and a lack of self-esteem. Though one must be careful not to equate the mental illness of depression with solitude, it is nevertheless important to show both experiences at work in Edith's interior world.

23. Ibid., 179.

24. Ibid., 209. Cf. ibid., 240: "From childhood on I had loved to make discoveries. When Erna and I were sent out for walks on our own in Breslau or in Hamburg, I used to say, 'Today, we'll go somewhere we have never seen before.'"

25. Stein, *Self-Portrait in Letters*, 51 (letter to Fritz Kaufmann, January 6, 1927).

26. See Matt 18:3; 19:14; Mark 10:15; Luke 18:17.

in its simple lucidity that the arrogant mind cannot fathom. This childlike wisdom is the storehouse of divine mysteries and is the unmatchable path that leads to the spiritual ascent of contemplation. One must admit that one knows nothing before one is welcomed into the contemplation of divine knowledge. Clarity is achieved through concealment. For the spiritual life, the paradox of the cross shines with "the brilliant darkness of a hidden silence."[27] The itinerary of the cross must pass through the dark night of solitude to break through into the unspeakable communion of the blessed in heaven.

It has been said, "Everybody wants to go to heaven but nobody wants to die." This observation implies with irony that one indeed must die to enter heaven. The first thing to die in the life of the redeemed person is sin. Edith echoes the constant demand of the Christian Gospel in recognizing the necessity of the cross to arrive at divine glory: "Thus, when someone desires to suffer, it is not merely a pious reminder of the suffering of the Lord. Voluntary expiatory suffering is what truly and really unites one to the Lord intimately. When it arises, it comes from an already existing relationship with Christ. For, by nature, a person flees from suffering. And the mania for suffering caused by a perverse lust for pain differs completely from the desire to suffer in expiation."[28] Since Christ suffered, we also must suffer with Christ to eradicate sin and to be united with him completely. If we are truly the Body of Christ, then we can say with Paul, "Now I rejoice in my sufferings for your sake, and in my flesh I am filling up what is lacking in the afflictions of Christ on behalf of his body, which is the church."[29] This is to say that willful suffering on behalf of another—whether through acts of prayer, sacrifice, fasting, almsgiving, etc.—participates in the redemption

---

27. Pseudo-Dionysius, "Mystical Hierarchy," in *Complete Works*, 135. Cf. Stein, "Ways to Know God: The 'Symbolic Theology' of Dionysius the Areopagite and Its Objective Presuppositions," in Stein, *Knowledge and Faith*, 83–134; and Stein, *Science of the Cross*, 47: "But we must learn to see and hear, and so on, as though we neither saw nor heard."

28. Stein, *Hidden Life*, 92. Cf. Stein, *Science of the Cross*, 21–22: "He who has decided for Christ is dead to the world and the world to him. He carries in his body the marks of the Lord's wounds, is weak and despised by the people but is precisely therefore strong because the power of God is mighty in the weak. Knowing this, Jesus' disciple not only takes up the cross that is laid upon him, but also crucifies himself: 'Those who belong to Christ Jesus have crucified the flesh with its passions and desires.' They have waged an unrelenting battle against their nature, that the life of sin might die in them and room be made for the life of the spirit." Cf. Gal 5:4.

29. Col 1:24 (NAB). Cf. Stein, *Science of the Cross*, 65: "Our goal is union with God, our way that of the crucified Christ, our becoming one with him takes place when we are crucified."

of the world wrought through the paschal mystery of Christ.[30] We suffer in Christ to the degree that we are united with Christ and to the extent that we love those for whom we suffer. This is a supernatural occurrence and cannot be explained by laws of physics or the instinctive behaviors of animal beings. It is a defining characteristic of what it is to be human: to suffer voluntarily on behalf of the other. The inspiration to act in such an unnatural (that is, supernatural) way cannot be attributed to self-interest, for the genuine act of voluntary expiatory suffering necessarily involves self-abnegation and disinterestedness.[31] As Edith points out, this kind of heroic suffering is worlds apart from the sadomasochistic practices of vice and destruction. Suffering according to the cross signifies a redemptive and life-giving suffering, paradoxically bringing life to the other and to the self inasmuch as the appetites of the flesh are abrogated in order to awaken the vital impetus of the divine Spirit in the soul. Unless the flesh be spiritualized and transfigured, it cannot partake of life eternal.[32]

The spiritual metamorphosis of body and soul—and of the world—takes place according to the paradoxical logic of the cross by moving in two complementary directions: inward and outward, that is, toward contemplative life and toward ethical responsibility and action. Edith insists, in a 1928 letter to her Dominican friend Callista Kopf, that "even in the contemplative life, one may not sever the connection with the world. I even believe that the

---

30. See Stein, *Hidden Life*, 58 (speaking of St. Teresa of Jesus): "The saint also had no other desire than to live in this separation from the world with her little family, to lead them ever more deeply into the spirit of prayer, into the heroic exercise of virtues—humility, obedience, complete giving of oneself, poverty, the most heartfelt love for God and for people—and to consecrate with them this whole life of prayer, sacrifice, voluntary penance (on which, however, she set a wise limit and so obviated an unhealthy enthusiasm) to the glory of God and his church, for the salvation of souls and as a support for priests who were doing battle with the great errors of the time."

31. In addition to sensory goods (let alone lustful appetites), the soul "must divest herself, as well, of all supernatural goods when God grants her any of these" (Stein, *Science of the Cross*, 59); cf. ibid., 81, 115, 119.

32. See 1 Cor 15:36, 42–44, 50, 53: "You fool! What you sow is not brought to life unless it dies... So also is the resurrection of the dead. It is sown corruptible; it is raised incorruptible. It is sown dishonorable; it is raised glorious. It is sown weak; it is raised powerful. It is sown a natural body; it is raised a spiritual body. If there is a natural body, there is also a spiritual one... This I declare, brothers: flesh and blood cannot inherit the kingdom of God, nor does corruption inherit incorruption... For that which is corruptible must clothe itself with incorruptibility, and that which is mortal must clothe itself with immortality"; and John 6:53–54, 63: "Jesus said to them, 'Amen, amen, I say to you, unless you eat the flesh of the Son of Man and drink his blood, you do not have life within you. Whoever eats my flesh and drinks my blood has eternal life, and I will raise him on the last day... It is the spirit that gives life, while the flesh is of no avail. The words I have spoken to you are spirit and life'" (NAB).

deeper one is drawn into God, the more one must 'go out of oneself'; that is, one must go to the world in order to carry the divine life into it."[33] In other words, the further one withdraws into the hidden enclosures of the soul, the more one is compelled to serve others in love.[34] The gift of divine life is uncontainable. Rather it spills over into all interpersonal relationships, yearning to complete and to renew its generative circuits of love.

To become a vessel of divine life is to enter into the impossible mission of the God who makes all things possible: to gather together the People of God from the ends of the earth.[35] While "tarrying in the darkness," "the work of salvation takes place in obscurity and stillness. In the heart's quiet dialogue with God the living building blocks out of which the kingdom of God grows are prepared, the chosen instruments for the construction forged."[36] Just as the shape of the cross is manifested by an intersection of lines running in two different directions, the Christ-life is lived in a simultaneous movement inward and outward—directed toward the other within the self, namely, God, and to the other without, namely, the personal human other. Jesus's twofold commandment of love is signified by the intersection of the cross. Upon the cross, the crucified Christ—Rabbi par excellence and eternal Word of the Father—is brought to silence and stillness. His dead body is then laid in stillness in the dark and dank tomb. Then from this breath-taking stillness eventuates resurrected life. Just so, the soul must quiet itself in great stillness and silence in order to form a more perfect spiritual kiln for the divine Fire that blazes within. Living stones are made pure and strong through the silent operations of the Holy Spirit.[37]

As a final step for gaining a preliminary understanding of the logic of the cross, we now will attempt to ascertain the integral components of such

---

33. Stein, *Self-Portrait in Letters*, 54 (letter to Sr. Callista Kopf, February 12, 1928).

34. See Stein, *Hidden Life*, 6: "Carmelites can repay God's love by their everyday lives in no other way than by carrying out their daily duties faithfully in every respect—all the little sacrifices that a regimen structured day after day in all its details demands of an active spirit; all the self-control that living in close proximity with different kinds of people continually requires and that is achieved with a loving smile; letting no opportunity go by for serving others in love."

35. See Matt 19:26.

36. Stein, *Self-Portrait in Letters*, 307 (letter to Walter Warnach, April 14, 1939), and Stein, *Hidden Life*, 15, respectively. Cf. Stein, *Science of the Cross*, 278: "The darkest path is the most secure."

37. See 1 Pet 2:4–5: "Come to him, a living stone, rejected by human beings but chosen and precious in the sight of God, and, like living stones, let yourselves be built into a spiritual house to be a holy priesthood to offer spiritual sacrifices acceptable to God through Jesus Christ" (NAB). Cf. Thérèse of Lisieux, *Story of a Soul*, 188: "Jesus deigned to show me the road that leads to this Divine Furnace, and this road is the *surrender* of the little child who sleeps without fear in its Father's arms."

logic. What comprises the fundamental traits of a human life that adheres to the logic of the cross?

III. The Cruciform Pattern of the Cross

All of creation—the entire cosmos—adheres to the logic of the cross: the lambent pattern in which life springs forth from death, in which exaltation is conceived in humility, in which hope eternal arises from meaningful suffering. Cosmic order itself is determined according to the logic of the cross. Revealed in Christ is a God who empties Godself out of immeasurable love for humanity.[38] Joseph Ratzinger treasures the epigram of Hölderlin that reflects this very idea:

> "Non coerceri maximo, contineri tamen a minimo, divinum est" (Not to be encompassed by the greatest, but to let oneself be encompassed by the smallest—that is divine). The boundless spirit who bears in himself the totality of Being reaches beyond the "greatest," so that to him it is small, and he reaches into the smallest, because to him nothing is too small. Precisely this overstepping of the greatest and reaching down into the smallest is the true nature of absolute spirit. At the same time we see here a reversal in value of maximum and minimum, greatest and smallest, that is typical of the Christian understanding of reality. To him who as spirit upholds and encompasses the universe, a spirit, a man's heart with its ability to love, is greater than all the milky ways in the universe.[39]

Greatness is revealed in highest resolution through humility, suffering, and servantship. Jesus reveals this both in the witness of his life and in the subversiveness of his teaching. He insists that the greatest is the least and the least is the greatest, that the master is the one who serves, and that those who humble themselves will be exalted. Does not Hölderlin's text encapsulate the paradigmatic essence of divinity if there be one at all? Further, does not this paradoxical idea defy human expectation and the tidy reasoning of worldly commerce? The Gospel of John relates Jesus saying, "Do you realize what I have done for you? You call me 'teacher' and 'master,' and rightly so, for indeed I am. If I, therefore, the master and teacher, have washed your feet, you ought to wash one another's feet. I have given you a model to follow, so that as I have done for you, you should also do."[40] The symbolic gesture of

---

38. See Phil 2:5–11.
39. Ratzinger, *Introduction to Christianity*, 146.
40. John 13:12–15 (NAB).

Jesus washing his disciples' feet sealed the constancy of his life and teaching in which he, without hesitation, stoops to serve his Beloved. As Ratzinger suggests, the Christian understanding of reality is a subversive one, turning the common-sense logic of the world on its head.[41] The holy reversal whereby that which is esteemed most highly is shown to be void of worth in comparison with this God of humility is central to the Christian kerygma. While appearing to be a "sign of contradiction," the cross in fact opens the human soul to its greatest potential through the actualizing power of divine Spirit.[42] God's Spirit is communicated through the channel of the cross. It is the cross that abolishes enmity between God and humanity by bursting the "wall of hostility" built by calloused accretions of sin throughout history.[43] In Christ it is revealed irrevocably that God delights to dwell in the hiddenness, littleness, and fragility of the human soul.

In her final literary work, *The Science of the Cross*, Edith presents a synthesis of the mystical theology of John of the Cross. Masterfully weaving together select passages from the mystical Doctor, Edith aims at detecting the precise pattern of the cross on display in the lives of the saints. She speaks of this pattern as a "science of the saints" wherein obtains a *"holy realism*: the original inner receptivity of the soul reborn in the Holy Spirit . . . *Holy realism* has a certain affinity with the realism of the child who receives and responds to impressions with unimpaired vigor and vitality, and with uninhibited simplicity."[44] A comparative examination of the lives of saints reveals a consistent pattern of living. Just as the scientific method yields similar results through repetitive experimentation, the lives of saints demonstrate a consonant ethos and action that suggests a common genealogy of being infected with the passion of the cross.[45] To live a life of heroic

41. Cf. 1 Cor 1:18—2:16.

42. See Luke 2:34 and 1 Cor 1:18-25; 2:14-15. Cf. Stein, *Hidden Life*, 94: "The Crucified One looks down on us and asks us whether we are still willing to honor what we promised in an hour of grace. And he certainly has reason to ask. More than ever the cross is a sign of contradiction"; and Stein, *Science of the Cross*, 19: ". . . the relation of the prophet himself to his Lord and God . . . [which] demands of him complete dedication and unlimited readiness and removes him from the community of people who think only in natural terms and makes him a sign of contradiction."

43. See Eph 2:14.

44. Stein, *Science of the Cross*, 10–11.

45. See Stein, *Letters to Roman Ingarden*, 266: "If you are really serious with the search for truth in religious things, that is, with the search for God, not for the proof of religious experience, then without a doubt you will find a way. I can only advise you with what I wrote earlier, that you should consider the writings of the great saints and mystics because they are the best source material: the autobiography of St. Teresa (I would recommend that you begin with *Seelenburg*, although this is the main mystical work) and the writings of St. John of the Cross" (letter of January 1, 1928).

virtue cannot be explained by so-called natural causes. Proclaimed by the logic of the cross is a supernatural and divine power that surges through a human person consciously open to the influx of divine will.[46] Accompanying the soul who yearns for God is a radical passivity in relation to divine providence. The saint opens herself without inhibition to the God who gives and takes away—but above all the God who gives. A radical receptivity is exhibited by the soul who, as a child, waits with innocent expectation and wonder before the love of the divine Majesty. Greatest maturity is shown through the most sublime simplicity. The childlike soul then responds with love, adoration, and thanksgiving to this God addressed as *Abba*, Father.

When Jesus, the eternal Son of God, said of the cross, "'whoever does not take up his cross and follow me, is not worthy of me,' or 'if anyone wishes to follow me, let him deny himself, take up his cross and follow me,' then is the cross the symbol (*Sinnbild*) of all that is difficult and oppressive and so against human nature that taking it upon oneself is like a journey to death. And the disciple of Jesus is to take up this burden daily."[47] It is quite intriguing how Jesus speaks of taking up one's cross even before he meets his execution historically. Jesus makes it clear that following him will necessitate the bearing of a cross—a symbolically charged term that indicates the unnatural vocation of suffering for the sake of redemption, suffering for the sake of the other. This is, as Edith recognizes, none other than a courageous journey to death that is to take place on a daily basis. Yet Christ reassures his followers, "Blessed are the poor in spirit, for theirs is the kingdom of heaven."[48] Such a puzzling paradox accessible only to faith! What is so blessed about the cross and poverty of spirit? The manifestation and proclamation of love and the fruit of redemption are the blessed effects of the cross. In enduring the dark night of solitude and great deprivation, the soul enters fully into the redemptive mystery of the cross. Signifying "extreme abandonment," the symbols of "cross and night are the way to heavenly light: that is the joyful

---

46. See Stein, *Science of the Cross*, 122, 166: "This dark, loving knowledge is the surrender of the soul through the will (as her mouth) to the loving approach of the still-concealed God: love, which is not a feeling, but rather a readiness for action and sacrifice, an insertion of one's own will into the divine will in order to be led by it alone . . . Whoever truly wants, in blind faith, nothing more but what God wills, has, with God's grace, reached the highest state a human being can reach. His will is totally purified and free of all constraint through earthly desires; he is united to the divine will through free surrender." Cf. Stein, *Philosophy of Psychology and the Humanities*, 84: "There is a state of resting in God, of complete relaxation of all mental activity, in which you make no plans at all, reach no decision, much less take action, but rather leave everything that's future to the divine will, 'consigning yourself entirely to fate.'"

47. Stein, *Science of the Cross*, 17.

48. Matt 5:3 (NAB).

message of the cross."⁴⁹ When Jesus cries from the cross the opening verse of the Twenty-second Psalm, "My God, my God, why have you abandoned me?" he recapitulates in himself the human being who is horrifically abused and who suffers in excruciating agony unjustly. He appears and speaks in total solidarity with humanity and, at the same time, exposes the redemptive meaning of his suffering proleptically announced at the Last Supper: "Take and eat; this is my body . . . Drink from it, all of you, for this is my blood of the covenant, which will be shed on behalf of many for the forgiveness of sins."⁵⁰ To give oneself in complete abandonment for the sake of the other is the highest expression of love. In the abandonment of the Son of God nailed to the cross is simultaneously the self-abandonment of God the Father and God the Spirit. A Trinitarian abandonment transpires through Jesus's crucifixion—an abandonment that began with the original act of God creating the universe from nothing, loving the entire cosmos into existence. The Trinitarian self-abandonment of God continued through the incarnation of Jesus in the womb of the Blessed Virgin Mary. It reached its climax in the hour of Jesus's passion when he handed himself over, "becoming obedient to death, even death on a cross."⁵¹ In other words, God has nothing left to give to his Bride, the Church. All has been given her without remainder. This is the definitive meaning of the cross.

Deeply informed by the Carmelite spiritual tradition she embraced and in which she found a lasting home, Edith transmits the Teresian and Sanjuanist heritage with great precision and clarity. It is clear that she ruminated on their texts with immense devotion and diligence. Through her astute iterations of their unified message, Edith offers us a succinct summation of Carmelite spirituality in her own texts. In surveying Edith's texts, we are able to explicate the logic of the cross according to three primary characters: alterity, humility, and love. Let us treat each of these components of the science of the cross successively in order to arrive at a more substantial apprehension.

a. Alterity

First, the cruciform life is other-centered rather than self-centered. As evinced above, and as attested throughout the entire tradition of Christian spirituality, "the way of suffering is the surest road to union with the Lord";

---

49. Stein, *Science of the Cross*, 30–31.
50. Matt 26:26–28 (NAB).
51. Phil 2:8 (NAB).

further, "it is God's will that one person should carry another's burden."[52] Suffering can be due to either an obtrusive presence (such as a puncture wound) or an absence of a desired presence (such as a lack of food or water). One thing is clear, suffering occurs in relation to that which is other. As argued above, however, suffering finds its greatest meaning when it is a suffering of voluntary expiation for the sake of the other person. To suffer the other is to love the other. Let it be clear that I am not suggesting any sort of merit tied to suffering inhuman abusive treatment at the hands of another. Such behavior surely must be checked and defended against. Rather, voluntary expiation for the sake of the other can be witnessed in acts such as a mother caring for her sick child, a father forsaking his leisurely retirement in order to care for his son who recently became paralyzed from an accident, a child giving up his turn on the swing so that another child can take his place. The *après vous* ("after you") of which Emmanuel Levinas speaks is relevant as well. Holding the door open for someone or letting another have the right of way in traffic proves a practical application of inner virtue. To concede first place to the other is an act of love. Edith recognized this later in life when she "saw in the others something better and higher than [her]self."[53] In order to esteem the other higher than one's own self demands, first of all, an accurate self-knowledge that leads to a disposition of humility. Being on the lookout to affirm the other requires an inversion of the naturally egocentric attitude. The symbol of the cross is the actualizing agent of such a radical and unnatural (that is, supernatural) inversion. This is nothing less than cardiological conversion caused by divine Gift emptied out, one for the other.

The cross is something other than the self. In fact, it is the cross to which the self is bound. Voluntary expiation means a willful binding of one's body to the duty of the cross, to the vocation of serving the other in love. The cross conducts the exigency of obedience and one cannot love truly without constantly being obedient to the call of the other, both in the form of conscience and in the form of the personal other outside the self. To give up one's body to the harsh edges of the cross is to relinquish the comfort and ease of elegant furniture and fine upholstery. It is only by allowing oneself to be fastened to the cross that one procures the route to

---

52. Stein, *Self-Portrait in Letters*, 151 (letter to Anneliese Lichtenberger, July 26, 1933), and ibid., 155 (letter to Sr. Agnella Stadtmüller, August 27, 1933), respectively.

53. Stein, *Life in a Jewish Family*, 308. Cf. Phil 2:3–4: "Do nothing out of selfishness or out of vainglory; rather, humbly regard others as more important than yourselves, each looking out not for his own interests, but [also] everyone for those of others" (NAB); 1 Cor 10:24: "No one should seek his own advantage, but that of his neighbor" (NAB); Rom 15.

heavenly glory—for others as well as for oneself.[54] The saint is the one who forfeits sensual and spiritual comfort in the name of the other's bodily and spiritual necessities. Without serious sacrifice, the cross remains a complacent chimera of the self-insulated bourgeoisie. Jesus emerged from the proletariat of his time, and anyone who dares to follow him must live in solidarity with the so-called untouchables, renouncing all for the sake of the other and for the sake of his exaltation. When one man gives all that he can, the other suddenly has enough.

b. Humility

"While we are on this earth nothing is more important to us than humility," says Teresa of Jesus.[55] Humility, a term derived from the Latin words *humilis* (meaning "low") and *humus* (meaning "earth, ground, soil, dirt"), is the virtue that tills the earth of the soul in order to prepare it to yield a bountiful crop of love. Next to the term *love*, humility is the premier virtue in the Christian life and for Carmelite spirituality in particular. The works of the Carmelite matriarchs and patriarchs are laced with exhortations on humility. Under the category of humility a host of other terms unpack its meaning, such as kenosis ("self-emptying"), divestment, self-denial, poverty of spirit, self-forgetfulness, nakedness, denudation, self-abasement, littleness, surrender, hiddenness, silence, humiliation, selflessness, dryness, desert, dark night, mortification, and self-renunciation. To be humble is to die a thousand deaths. In humility, one rises in the morning to die, one retires at night to die, one works and plays as an act of death and self-immolation before the urgent needs of the other. This death is accomplished mostly in small, and oftentimes unnoticeable, acts of loving service. In becoming attuned to the saturating call of the other, the humble soul dies to self-sufficiency and to the empty promises of honors, riches, and the tempting projects of self-interested ambition. All becomes empty out of love for the other: time is turned into prayer, money transfigures into almsgiving, and food and drink are displaced by fasting and, in turn, given over to the other who has none.[56]

---

54. See Stein, *Hidden Life*, 99: "The three vows are the nails [that is, poverty, chastity, and obedience]. The more willingly she stretches herself out on the cross and endures the blows of the hammer, the more deeply will she experience the reality of her union with the Crucified. Then being crucified itself becomes for her the marriage feast."

55. Teresa of Avila, *Interior Castle*, 50.

56. See Stein, *Self-Portrait in Letters*, 318 (letter to Sr. Agnella Stadtmüller, March 30, 1940): "Should we strive for perfect love, you ask? Absolutely. For this we were created. [Perfect love] will be our eternal life, and here we have to seek to come as close to it as possible. Jesus became incarnate in order to be our way. What can we do? Try with

Growing in humility is a painful process since its goal is to purify and to sanctify the soul, and to discipline the flesh and its wandering passions. Edith insists that "no spiritual work comes into the world without severe labor pains" and that "a *scientia crucis* <knowledge of the Cross> can be gained only when one comes to feel the Cross radically. I have been convinced of that from the first moment and have said, from my heart: *Ave, Crux, spes unica!* <Hail, Cross, our only hope!>"[57] The path of life is narrow because it enforces the practice of detachment from all sensual, and even spiritual, appetites. All forms of lust are to be banished from the soul that yearns for nuptial union with her Bridegroom. The paradigm of the cross does not function according to the power of its idea alone, but it must be felt directly and experienced connaturally in one's life. Through empathy I can serve to help bear the cross of another. Becoming like Simon of Cyrene, I am able to come to the assistance of my neighbors by exercising loving empathy and constant prayer. Not only this, acute empathy and prayer spill over into concrete actions to make sure that all of my neighbor's needs are met. I become "totally self-forgetful . . . steeped in the life and suffering of Christ."[58] The self is forgotten out of total preoccupation for the welfare of the other. I must forget myself in suffering in order to endure great suffering. Suffering itself acts as an agent of self-forgetfulness. In loving Christ above all things I, too, forget myself. When Christ commands, "love your neighbor as yourself," the point is not to love myself more but to love my neighbor more and myself less. It is paradoxical that in loving my neighbor more and myself less, I reach my highest potential. My self is actualized according to the measure that I give myself away.[59]

In his *Spiritual Exercises*, Ignatius of Loyola writes that "in order to imitate Christ our Lord better and to be more like him here and now, I desire and choose poverty with Christ poor rather than wealth; contempt with Christ laden with it rather than honors. Even further, I desire to be regarded as a useless fool for Christ, who before me was regarded as such, rather than as a wise or prudent person in this world."[60] In the same vein, Edith writes

---

all our might to be empty: the senses mortified; the memory as free as possible from all images of this world and, through hope, directed toward heaven; the understanding stripped of natural seeking and ruminating, directed to God in the straightforward gaze of faith; the will (as I have already said) surrendered to God in love."

57. Ibid., 341 (letter to Mother Ambrosia Antonia Engelmann, <presumably December 1941>). In this section the angle brackets indicate the elucidations of the German editors of Stein's letters.

58. Stein, *Hidden Life*, 13.

59. See ibid., 102: ". . . only one who possesses nothing possesses everything."

60. Ignatius of Loyola, *Spiritual Exercises and Collected Works*, 160.

that "the bride of the humble Savior learns to bear all kinds of humiliation" in searching for "the buried and forgotten wood of humiliation."[61] To follow Christ means to be humiliated as Christ was humiliated. This is an experience that the saint does not seek to evade but one that the saint anticipates with joy. The saint longs to live in complete solidarity with Christ as he emptied himself to the point of abandonment in coming to live in total solidarity with us. Saints regard humiliation as a welcome aid for maturing in holiness and spiritual perfection. They have become "fools on Christ's account" because the world would not accept the strange and subversive testimony of their lives.[62] The logic of the cross is certainly not the logic of this world. Whereas the world prescribes self-assertion and heartless competition, Christ urges his followers to live "daily and hourly crucifying [their] self-will and self-love."[63] What a contrast of values in comparison with the rat race of the world! The reward of the saint is the well-being and exaltation of the other. This is what Jesus means when he says that "your reward will be great in heaven": the other is my reward and responsibility for him is my contest. Heaven is no more than a symbolic term for the terrain in which I am my brother's keeper and in which the Lord is my Shepherd and, therefore, there is nothing I shall want. Was not this the makeup of the original paradise of Eden? Perhaps the reward of heaven is granted paradoxically only to those who forego self-interest and instead exercise disinterested love for the other, and this disinterested love and relationship with the other is itself their reward.[64] What, after all, are castles, riches, and honors in comparison with the incomparable and invaluable other? Christ reveals the true divine nature as one of humility. Is there not something of the cross in God from eternity?

---

61. Stein, *Hidden Life*, 78, 102, respectively.
62. 1 Cor 4:10 (NAB). Cf. 1 Cor 1:18; 3:18; 2 Cor 11:19.
63. Stein, *Hidden Life*, 95.
64. Cf. Levinas, *Alterity and Transcendence*, 109: "The other as face, extraordinary testimony to my freedom, who commands me alterity in the infinite, who elects me to its service and who represents the ethical disturbance of being and is going to lead it [being] along the pathway of ethical dis-interestedness. The coming of the human to ethics passes through this ethical suffering, the disturbance brought by every face, even in an ordered world. This saintliness of the human cannot be expressed on the basis of any category. Are we entering a moment in history in which the good must be loved without promises? Perhaps it is the end of all preaching. May we not be on the eve of a new form of faith, a faith without triumph, as if the only irrefutable value were saintliness, a time when the only right to a reward would be not to expect one? The first and last manifestation of God would be to be without promises."

c. Love

Paul writes in his First Epistle to the Church in Corinth, "So faith, hope, love remain, these three; but the greatest of these is love."[65] It would be inappropriate to speak of the magnitude of the cross without considering love as its very raison d'être. Among what have come to be known as the theological virtues, Paul rightly ranks love as the greatest. Anything other than love is beside the point, for anything outside of love would have no existence at all. Edith defines love as "goodness giving itself away."[66] This, in fact, is a precise way to understand the act of creation philosophically. If it is good to be and if the good determines all ensuing ethical structures of meaning and value, then it follows that the greatest ethical act is to share goodness with another. To love is to share the gift of goodness with another. Gift is the essence of love and of grace. The Eucharist—gift par excellence—is the "happy/blessed gift" (εὐ-χαρισ-τία) that embodies love in the most fitting way: God become Human, bread and wine become Body, Blood, Soul, and Divinity of the God-Man. This is the most extraordinary expression of humility imaginable. Who could have imagined this to come about? The Eucharist, directly tied to the cross, manifests and proclaims God's Gift of Love to humanity: Son and Spirit, Word and Breath, Meaning and Power, given to the point of abandonment, without remainder.

In *Philosophy of Psychology and the Humanities*, a work written even before her conversion to the Catholic faith, Edith indicates the real possibility of loving another to a higher state of being: "The love with which I embrace a human being may be sufficient to fill him with new lifepower if his own breaks down. Indeed, the mere contact with human beings of more intense aliveness may exert an enlivening effect upon those who are jaded or exhausted, who have no activeness as a presupposition on their side."[67] This passage demonstrates the conviction and testimony that human beings can enliven one another through love. Metaphysically speaking, love is the preeminent actuality that gives rise to all potency and to the transition of becoming where potencies are actualized.[68] If you exude a radiant degree of

---

65. 1 Cor 13:13 (NAB).
66. Stein, *Hidden Life*, 38.
67. Stein, *Philosophy of Psychology and the Humanities*, 85. Cf. Lebech, *On the Problem of Human Dignity*, 274: "Hence, love is the only attitude which comprehends the value of the human person fully."
68. Cf. Benedict XVI, *Deus caritas est*, 17: "It is characteristic of mature love that it calls into play all man's potentialities; it engages the whole man, so to speak. Contact with the visible manifestations of God's love can awaken within us a feeling of joy born of the experience of being loved."

love, you very well may lift my spirit according to that same love. This is a tremendous realization and responsibility. We each have the potential—and responsibility—to channel divine Love to one another. In fact, this is the cardinal commandment of Christ: to love. One might oppose such a commandment with the objection, "How can love be commanded? Is not love by definition a free and unconstrained act?" Benedict XVI answers, "Love can be 'commanded' because it has first been given."[69] Therefore we have a responsibility to love, but a responsibility that accompanies the supernatural desire to love the other as I love myself. This desire is supernatural because it is a gift from God and it constantly must overcome the natural urge to look out for oneself only. Authentic love exacts the virtue of self-mastery as a condition for the possibility of becoming a disinterested gift of self, both in an erotic and an agapic sense. If one does not have mastery over oneself—over one's spontaneous passions, appetites, etc.—then one cannot give oneself in a complete, total, and meaningful way to another. In other words, the sincere gift of self follows a disciplined exercise of the virtue of self-mastery. Without self-mastery no love is possible as such.

Humanity is essentially the fragile and vulnerable test-bed for love. Divine love hazards itself in the drama of human civilization and in the precariousness of free will and a world of goods. Yet even more, as created in the *imago Dei*, human beings are called to love as God loves in and through our weak, finite, and ambivalent flesh. To carry the analogy further, the test-bed is destined to be transfigured into an eternal engine of love, emulating by participation the eternal wellspring of all actuality, namely, Actuality itself. In Christ we see the immutable and indelible divine Actuality giving itself over to a state of radical passivity all the way to the cross. Through voluntary expiatory suffering, human beings become co-creators with God in the work of redemption and restoration of finite created being:

> There is a vocation to suffer with Christ and thereby to cooperate with him in his work of salvation. When we are united with the Lord, we are members of the mystical body of Christ: Christ lives on in his members and continues to suffer in them. And the suffering borne in union with the Lord is his suffering, incorporated in the great work of salvation and fruitful therein. That is a fundamental premise of all religious life, above all of the life of Carmel, to stand proxy for sinners through voluntary and joyous suffering, and to cooperate in the salvation of humankind.[70]

69. Ibid., 16.

70. Stein, *Self-Portrait in Letters*, 128 (letter to Anneliese Lichtenberger, the second day of Christmas, 1932).

And this is the point of the cross: salvation of humankind. Voluntary expiatory suffering contributes to the net effect of the salvation of human beings—salvation that takes root in this earthly life and grows into the next. This is the greatest human work. It involves establishing just interhuman (as well as interspecies) relationships and even going beyond these in sacrificial love, in mercy, and in forgiveness. Christ invites us to band together with him in his Church to catalyze the kingdom of God. At the intersection of the material and spiritual realms of being—as neither angel nor animal—human beings serve as the lynchpin of the redemption of the created universe. The Church, as the mystical Body of Christ, is the elixir and sacrament of redemption in the world insofar as She is united as Bride to Christ, the King and Bridegroom. The eternal Son of God became human in order to redeem the world since "human nature, capable of and actually suffering, is a tool for the redemption."[71] Human beings have the cosmic privilege of consciously and meaningfully suffering like no other creature—distinct from animals because of their rational nature, distinct from angels because of their radically vulnerable nature in the playing field of material being. What wondrous creatures in whom God saw fit to bring about the regeneration of the universe, created by the power of divine Love and the uncreated Light of Mount Tabor![72]

The cross, as a chief symbol of love, signifies the intersection of human and divine. It is the seal of God's undying love for humanity, stooping to the lowest possible degree to lift us up into the highest heights of divine glory. As the principal hermeneutic key to love, the cross paradoxically defeats death through the logic of the double negative. The imposture-hero—the antichrist—is overturned by the "Wonder-Counselor, God-Hero, Father-Forever, Prince of Peace," and this One is ridiculed, abused, taunted, harassed, tortured, mocked, beaten, insulted, stripped of his clothes, spat upon, derided, crowned with needle-sharp thorns, nailed to coarse wood, offered bitter drink, and pierced in the side with a lance.[73]

> What wondrous love is this, O my soul, O my soul?
> What wondrous love is this, O my soul?
> What wondrous love is this that caused the Lord of bliss
> To bear the dreadful curse for my soul, for my soul,

---

71. Stein, *Science of the Cross*, 260.

72. See the narrative of the transfiguration of Christ in Matt 17:1–8; Mark 9:2–8; and Luke 9:28–36.

73. Isa 9:5 (NABRE).

> To bear the dreadful curse for my soul?[74]

The cross paradoxically speaks the language of love in a cold and bleeding setting of hate. Only a lover inflamed with the holy passion of love for his beloved could have withstood the cruelty and rejection of this same beloved putting him to death. Yet this he does to convince her, to persuade her, to woo her, to win her back to the covenant relationship they had formed in the beginning. Edith, like the great company of saints, said yes to this divine marriage proposal with the word she inherited from her celestial Mother, *fiat*.

IV. Conclusion

In sum, we have attempted to reiterate the meaning and coherent logic of the cross in order to crown this project in theological anthropology. We first recalled the role the science of the cross played in Edith Stein's personal life. This was a helpful step that served to give palpable flesh to the polyvalent concept of the cross by gathering up a few narrative fragments of Edith's life. Second, we focused on the particular Carmelite charism of the dark night of solitude and showed how solitude figures into the logic of the cross. Finally, we unearthed the primary traits of the cruciform pattern of the cross, namely, alterity, humility, and love. By taking these careful and convicting steps, we have brought the paradigm of the cross into the light of comprehension, if only by attempting to peer momentarily into its dark luminosity and to heed its saturating meaning and power. It must be said that one cannot help trembling in approaching the topic of the cross. Yet it is the cross that reveals both what it is to be fully human and what it is to be less than human.

This book has traversed a variety of avenues into the thought-world of Edith Stein: universal human vocation (chapter 1), spiritual being (chapter 2), the human soul (chapters 3–5), material being (chapter 6), empathy and the other (chapter 7), and the logic of the cross (chapter 8). Altogether, a holistic theological anthropology was developed, but my hope at the book's close is to leave this project open-ended. What we have certified throughout this study is that the human being, created in the image and likeness of God, is utterly wonderful and mysterious (Ps 139). Neither an individual monad nor a nameless part of a collective whole, the human being has been presented as a unique member of the human family, destined to be inducted into the communion of angels and saints within the eternal life that is the Most Holy

---

74. From an early nineteenth-century Christian folk hymn of the American South.

Trinity. As the book began, so it ends: with the vocation to love—to become a total gift of self for the other, enacted through resolute responsibility for the other. Teresa of Avila makes it clear: self-knowledge, detachment, and humility are necessary for one to enter the silent chambers of contemplative prayer, and contemplation is a necessary precursor to ethical living. Theological anthropology implies that human being cannot be understood apart from divine being; finite being cannot be understood apart from eternal being. Building on the work of Stein, I have hoped to extend her work even further, all the while attempting to be faithful to the meanings and spirit of her writings. By approaching the human being from the inside out (the soul), and from the outside in (vocation, empathy, and the other), we have begun to encounter anew the mystery that is human, the mystery of mystery that is divine.

May we close this chapter with the following words of Edith Stein concerning personal decision for or against God. May these words be recalled with no commentary:

> It is not necessary that we come to a correct proof of religious experience before the end of our lives. However, it is necessary that we come to a decision for or against God. That is demanded of us: to decide without a guarantee. That is the great wager of faith. The way leads from faith to understanding, not the other way around. Whoever is too proud to go through this narrow gate does not enter. Whoever does enter acquires in this life a brighter clarity and experiences the legitimacy of "*credo ut intelligam.*" I also believe that it gains us little to begin with construed or fantasized experiences. Where the actual experience is missing, we have to get it from the testimonies of the religious—and there is no lack of them. According to my experience the most impressive come from the Spanish mystics, Teresa and John of the Cross.[75]

Ave, Crux, spes unica!

---

75. Stein, *Letters to Roman Ingarden*, 263 (letter of November 20, 1927).

Epilogue: An Addendum to Suffering

While I was growing up, a very close family friend, Jim Muldoon, expressed to me his adamant opposition against opening to the end of a book without first reading it all the way through. Today we call this procedure a "spoiler." It is difficult to sum up a book that is impossible to sum up. And that is precisely the point. Human being and divine being are mysterious. Indeed, there is much to be said about human and divine being that this book and others like it suggest. However, the point is to enter into a never-ending contemplation about human and divine being as a way to pursue relentlessly the human vocation to become responsible for the other in love.

Instead of offering extended prosaic discourse on human and divine being, I would like to tell a story about another good friend of mine and close with an original poem. These two words, a story and a poem, more than anything else, may capture the essence of human and divine being, even for someone who opened right up to the end of this book to read from end to beginning!

My father, Dr. John Wallenfang, earned his PhD in political science from Purdue University in December 1974. He landed a position at Lake Michigan Community College in Benton Harbor, Michigan, the following year—a position he would hold to the time of his death in December 2003. One of his colleagues, Dr. K. Sundaram, studied philosophy with Dr. Marvin Farber at the University of Buffalo and taught alongside my father during his tenure in Benton Harbor. Sundaram had two sons, Sathyan and Sathish, with his wife, Susan. My parents, John and Linda, adopted me at six weeks after birth and would conceive my brother, Michael, two years later. The Sundaram and Wallenfang families would get together on occasion to share meals, music, and good conversation. I recall putting on mock music recitals for our parents (to our chagrin), watching Indiana Jones movies, and playing chess with Sathish. I also remember having to take off our shoes whenever we entered the Sundaram's home. It was truly holy ground—something I would come to realize much later in life.

Sathish is the main protagonist in my story because he is its hero. Throughout his life, Sathish suffered from macular degeneration, an eye disease that causes loss of vision. On one occasion, his mother invited me to put on a pair of glasses that simulated the way Sathish saw the world. It was like looking through the most cloudy and opaque glass possible. Then I understood: Sathish was virtually blind. Nevertheless, Sathish excelled in many areas: academics, music, intellectual life and culture. He was a real cosmopolitan. He was involved in numerous music ensembles—jazz, classical, concert bands, etc.—and played many different instruments. The amazing thing was that he played by ear primarily. Every ensemble, every piece of music. His intelligence was always stunning. Not only would he beat me in almost every chess match, he seemed to know everything about everything. Sathish's talent took him to Harvard University in 1998 where he earned his bachelor's degree in physics. He continued to play in several music ensembles there and even developed an interest in Italian literature. Upon graduating from Harvard, he earned a master's degree in Italian literature from the University of Toronto. Sathish became engaged to a woman with whom he fell in love, but the engagement later fell through.

While working as an engineer at Whirlpool Corporation in St. Joseph, Michigan, Sathish went to visit a friend whom he had come to know over the past few years. They planned to go horseback riding together during his stay. After mounting his horse, Sathish fell off and hit his head on a fence. He instantly became paralyzed from the neck down. Tragedy had entered the front door of his life and things would never be the same. Instead of living in his own home, he would move into the home in which he was raised, to be cared for by his parents, Sundaram and Susan. They would feed him, bathe him, trim his hair and nails, and empty his urine container with great love. And that is the point of sharing a bit of Sathish's life narrative: love. In the midst of tragedy, hope; in the face of despair, patience; when confronted with the greatest of adversities, courage. This is the essence of human and divine being writ large. Sundaram and Susan continue to exist as a constant gift of self for Sathish and for one another. Sundaram just had retired from teaching for more than thirty years in a field he loved, only to shift to a new (yet old) vocation of caring for his beloved son. Susan would continue to lift up her prayers at daily Mass, prayers new and old, that they would all be able to get through yet another day as trial and as gift.

Sathish's accident occurred while I was finishing up my PhD in constructive theology from Loyola University Chicago in spring of 2010. As circumstances turned out, my family and I were planning to move in with my mother, Linda, while I took a year to write my dissertation, do some student teaching, and (God willing) find a tenure-track teaching position at a university. One of the great beauties of this move was that I could visit Sathish every week, as he lived just up the road. That year I received a tutorial in the meaning of serving the other in love. Countless touching moments I would witness in the ways Sundaram and Susan cared for Sathish with such joy and determination. He would continue to be victorious over me in our chess matches (most of the time), and our intellectual conversations on music, phenomenology, religion, and fate never ceased to stimulate.

Today Sathish is studying for his doctorate in rehabilitation therapy at the University of Pittsburgh. Sundaram and Susan moved into a lovely apartment there with him, and Sathish continues to thrive. His life is a testament to nothing short of perseverance and the power of hope and love. He inspires me in proximity and from afar. I can think of no better way to end a book on the relationship between human and divine being than telling the story—at least in fragments—of Sathish and his family. Though his body has been beset with temporary limits in movement, the soul of Sathish dances to the rhythms of friendship and solicitude. He pursues further graduate studies for the sake of helping others in similar situations by developing technologies that empower. He radiates the zest of life exactly in and through disability. Paradox of paradoxes, eternal being is manifest and proclaimed through the redoubled finitude of finite being. In the shuddering milieu of the limitation of limitation is revealed the transcendence of infinite possibility bearing the sacred and profane name of love.

Suffering, derived from the Latin word *sufferre* ("to bear up, to persevere, to endure"), is the home field of love. It includes those experiences in which love not only is put to the test, but summoned to rise in its "power made perfect in weakness."[1] Only in the shadow of the cross shines the

---

1. 2 Cor 12:9 (NAB). Cf. ibid., 4:7–11, 16–18: "But we hold this treasure in earthen vessels, that the surpassing power may be of God and not from us. We are afflicted in every way, but not constrained; perplexed, but not driven to despair; persecuted, but not abandoned; struck down, but not destroyed; always carrying about in the body the dying of Jesus, so that the life of Jesus may also be manifested in our body. For we who live are constantly being given up to death for the sake of Jesus, so that the life of Jesus may be manifested in our mortal flesh . . . Therefore, we are not discouraged; rather, although our outer self is wasting away, our inner self is being renewed day by day. For this momentary light affliction is producing for us an eternal weight of glory beyond

radiant sun of resurrection. Yet why suffering? What is its purpose, if it has one at all? Two important fruits are borne in suffering. The first is that suffering disorients the self-sufficiency of the self, not only for the one suffering but also for those who witness the suffering of the other. Suffering causes those involved to turn outside of the self for relief, for comfort, for consolation. The one who suffers cannot control the fact that s/he suffers. Vertigo sets in and requires one to transcend the manageable according to the ubiquitous character of suffering's elusive origin and end. Suffering, in essence, is an occasion of self-divestment and transcendence, both for the one who suffers and for the one who comes to the assistance of the sufferer.

In addition to displacement of the self, suffering bears the fruit of recognizing one's human existence as radically dependent on others. When I suffer, I desperately need the help of others. I rely on others to take care of me and to help me through my suffering, even (and especially) at the point of death. Compassion (*com-passio*, that is, "to suffer with" another) enters center stage inasmuch as the suffering of the other is relieved to the extent that I share in the other's suffering. Compassion and empathy distribute the weight of suffering among the bodies and souls of those who dare to suffer alongside the other, to suffer the other in love. Without the drama of suffering, love is left unmanifest and unannounced. Suffering is revealed as the sine qua non for love and genuine solidarity with the other. If there is no plight, there is no need for teamwork and collaboration. Interpersonal communion is fashioned through the shared experience of suffering. Family and friendship are made to the degree that people voluntarily enter into covenant relationship with one another, come what may. Covenant relationships crystallize in the kiln of compassion and empathy.

May this reflection not be interpreted as a final word on the mystery of human suffering. Rather, let these thoughts contribute to ongoing rumination on the experience of compassionate suffering. Suffering is not a bad word. It is not something to be eliminated from the human experience at all costs. It bears the potential to be redemptive. It is something into which to lean instead of fleeing far away. Granted, there are certain kinds of suffering to be stifled: all those experiences that fall under the category of abuse. Likewise, the phenomenon of pain as such is not identical to the meaning of suffering suggested here. Pain relief and palliative care are good measures indeed. However, in the context of twenty-first-century cultural sensibilities of convenience, expedience, and self-gratification, suffering and compassion are concepts in need of recuperation. Because pain, suffering, and abuse

---

all comparison, as we look not to what is seen but to what is unseen; for what is seen is transitory, but what is unseen is eternal" (NAB).

are terms that tend to be conflated, suffering tends to register a pejorative meaning. It has become something to be avoided absolutely. In contrast, John Paul II argues that "true 'compassion' leads to sharing another's pain; it does not kill the person whose suffering we cannot bear."[2] Again, the very meaning of compassion is to suffer with the other, to suffer the other in love. Compassion seeks to alleviate suffering if possible, respecting the exigencies of human dignity. When all suffering cannot be relieved, compassion continues to suffer alongside the other, whether holding his hand, moistening her parched lips with a cold washcloth, or bathing the face of his wounds with gentle and steady hands.

Linda Means Beautiful

There she lies in black and white, without doubt a Carmelite
Blood-stained lips and bald head shine, sunshine morning love divine
Brothers two escort her there, with and without underwear
Like a bride bedecked in jewels, broken breath and bedside drools
Sonnets not in silence speak, save for morphine vigil keep

Nurses nurse the nurse that nursed, nearby comes the hearseless hearse
Latin prayers like incense rise, hidden from the world's disguise
Incubate the soul that lives, passover to throne room His
Speak a word, is this the last? Upward climbs the sailor's mast
Hand held tight, I'm here with you, nothing more can you to do

Midnight falls with shifting shifts, now your turn the veil He lifts
Sleepers wake and sinners soar, far near heights for pleading whore
Take this cup will you to drink, time is up you're on the brink
Secret garden fear takes leave, death not bitter but reprieve
Bliss eternal life you give, wondrous love delight and sieve

---

2. John Paul II, *Evangelium vitae*, 66. Cf. ibid., 15, 19.

Bibliography

Ales Bello, Angela. *Edith Stein: La passione per la verità*. Padova: Messaggero di sant'Antonio, 2003.

———. "Edmund Husserl and Edith Stein: The Question of the Human Subject." Translated by Antonio Calcagno. *American Catholic Philosophical Quarterly* 82 (2008) 143–59.

———. *Fenomenologia dell'essere umano: lineamenti di una filosofia al femminile*. Roma: Città nuova, 1992.

Alfieri, Francesco. *Die Rezeption Edith Steins: Internationale Edith-Stein-Bibliographie 1942–2012*. Würzburg: Echter, 2012.

Allen, Prudence. "Mary and the Vocation of Philosophers." *New Blackfriars* 90:1025 (2009) 50–71.

Andrews, Michael F. "Edith Stein and Max Scheler: Ethics, Empathy, and the Constitution of the Acting Person." *Quaestiones Disputatae* 3 (2012) 33–47.

Apostolic Penitentiary. *Manual of Indulgences: Norms and Grants*. Washington, DC: USCCB, 2006.

Aristotle. *The Complete Works of Aristotle: The Revised Oxford Translation*. Edited by Jonathan Barnes. 2 vols. Princeton: Princeton University Press, 1984.

Augustine of Hippo. *The City of God against the Pagans*. Translated by R. W. Dyson. New York: Cambridge University Press, 2005.

———. *Confessions*. Translated by Henry Chadwick. New York: Oxford University Press, 1998.

Austriaco, Nicanor Pier Giorgio. *Biomedicine and Beatitude: An Introduction to Catholic Bioethics*. Washington, DC: Catholic University of America Press, 2011.

———. "A Theological Fittingness Argument for the Historicity of the Fall of *Homo Sapiens*." *Nova et Vetera* 13 (2015) 651–67.

Baker, Anthony D. *Diagonal Advance: Perfection in Christian Theology*. Eugene, OR: Cascade, 2011.

Balthasar, Hans Urs von. *Theo-logic: Theological Logical Theory*. Vol. 2, *Truth of God*. Translated by Adrian J. Walker. San Francisco: Ignatius, 2004.

Barr, Stephen M. *Modern Physics and Ancient Faith*. Notre Dame: University of Notre Dame Press, 2003.

Baseheart, Mary Catharine. *Person in the World: Introduction to the Philosophy of Edith Stein*. Dordrecht: Kluwer Academic, 1997.

Beckmann-Zöller, Beate. "Edith Stein's Theory of the Person in Her Münster Years (1932–1933)." Translated by Amalie Enns. *American Catholic Philosophical Quarterly* 82 (2008) 47–70.

Behr, John, and Conor Cunningham, eds. *The Role of Death in Life: A Multidisciplinary Examination of the Relationship between Life and Death*. Eugene, OR: Cascade, 2015.

Benedict XVI, Pope. *Deus caritas est*. 2005. http://w2.vatican.va/content/benedict-xvi/en/encyclicals/documents/hf_ben-xvi_enc_20051225_deus-caritas-est.html.

Berkman, Joyce Avrech. "Edith Stein: A Life Unveiled and Veiled." *American Catholic Philosophical Quarterly* 82 (2008) 5–29.

Betschart, Christof. *Unwiederholbares Gottessiegel: Personale Individualität nach Edith Stein*. Tübingen: Institut für Ökumenische Studien der Universität Freiburg Schweiz, 2013.

Boeve, Lieven, Yves de Maeseneer, and Ellen Van Stichel, eds. *Questioning the Human: Toward a Theological Anthropology of the Twenty-First Century*. New York: Fordham University Press, 2014.

Bonino, Serge-Thomas. *Angels and Demons: A Catholic Introduction*. Translated by Michael J. Miller. Washington, DC: Catholic University of America Press, 2016.

Borden, Sarah. *Edith Stein*. New York: Continuum, 2003.

Borden Sharkey, Sarah. *Thine Own Self: Individuality in Edith Stein's Later Writings*. Washington, DC: Catholic University of America Press, 2010.

Bransfield, J. Brian. *The Human Person: According to John Paul II*. Boston: Pauline Books & Media, 2010.

Calcagno, Antonio. "Edith Stein: Is the State Responsible for the Immortal Soul of the Person?" *Logos: A Journal of Catholic Thought and Culture* 5 (2002) 62–75.

———, ed. *Edith Stein: Women, Social-Political Philosophy, Theology, Metaphysics and Public History*. Cham: Springer, 2016.

———. *Lived Experience from the Inside Out: Social and Political Philosophy in Edith Stein*. Pittsburgh: Duquesne University Press, 2014.

———. *The Philosophy of Edith Stein*. Pittsburgh: Duquesne University Press, 2007.

———. "Thinking Community and the State from Within." *American Catholic Philosophical Quarterly* 82 (2008) 31–45.

Cassirer, Ernst. *The Philosophy of the Enlightenment*. Translated by Fritz C. A. Koelln and James P. Pettegrove. Princeton: Princeton University Press, 1951.

Cavadini, John C. "The Anatomy of Wonder: An Augustinian Taxonomy." *Augustinian Studies* 42 (2011) 153–72.

Chauvet, Louis-Marie. *The Sacraments: The Word of God at the Mercy of the Body*. Translated by Madeleine Beaumont. Collegeville, MN: Liturgical Press, 2001.

———. *Les sacrements: Parole de Dieu au risque du corps*. Paris: L'Atelier, 1997.

———. *Symbol and Sacrament: A Sacramental Reinterpretation of Christian Existence*. Translated by Patrick Madigan and Madeleine Beaumont. Collegeville, MN: Liturgical Press, 1995.

Condic, Maureen. "When Does Human Life Begin? The Scientific Evidence and Terminology Revisited." *University of St. Thomas Journal of Law & Public Policy* 8 (2014) 44–81.

Copland, Aaron. *What to Listen for in Music*. New York: New American Library, 2011.

Cunningham, Conor. *Darwin's Pious Idea: Why the Ultra-Darwinists and Creationists Both Get It Wrong*. Grand Rapids: Eerdmans, 2010.

———. "The Difference of Theology and Some Philosophies of Nothing." *Modern Theology* 17 (2001) 289–312.

———. *A Genealogy of Nihilism: Philosophies of Nothing and the Difference of Theology*. London: Routledge, 2002.

———. "*Natura Pura*, the Invention of the Anti-Christ: A Week with No Sabbath." *Communio* 37 (2010) 243–54.

Cunningham, Lawrence S. *An Introduction to Catholicism*. New York: Cambridge University Press, 2009.

Cunningham, Lawrence S., and Keith J. Egan. *Christian Spirituality: Themes from the Tradition*. New York: Paulist, 1996.

Denzinger, Heinrich, and Adolf Schönmetzer. *Enchiridion symbolorum: Definitionum et declarationum de rebus fidei et morum*. 32nd ed. Freiburg: Herder, 1963.

Driessche, Thibault van den. "Le sens du renoncement... Quand Edith Stein commente Jean de la Croix." *Ephemerides Theologicae Lovanienses* 82 (2006) 317–32.

Feser, Edward. *Aquinas: A Beginner's Guide*. Oxford: Oneworld, 2009.

———. *The Last Superstition: A Refutation of the New Atheism*. South Bend, IN: St. Augustine's Press, 2010.

———. *Scholastic Metaphysics: A Contemporary Introduction*. Piscataway, NJ: Editiones Scholasticae, 2014.

Flannery, Austin, ed. *Vatican Council II: The Basic Sixteen Documents*. Northport, NY: Costello, 1996.

Francis, Pope. *Evangelii gaudium*. 2013. https://w2.vatican.va/content/francesco/en/apost_exhortations/documents/papa-francesco_esortazione-ap_20131124_evangelii-gaudium.html.

———. *Laudato si'*. 2015. http://w2.vatican.va/content/francesco/en/encyclicals/documents/papa-francesco_20150524_enciclica-laudato-si.html.

———. *Lumen fidei*. 2013. http://w2.vatican.va/content/francesco/en/encyclicals/documents/papa-francesco_20130629_enciclica-lumen-fidei.html.

Gerl-Falkovitz, Hanna-Barbara. *Unerbittliches Licht: Edith Stein: Philosophie, Mystik, Leben*. Mainz: Grünewald, 1991.

Girard, René. *The Scapegoat*. Translated by Yvonne Freccero. Baltimore: Johns Hopkins University Press, 1986.

Grondin, Jean. *Introduction to Metaphysics: From Parmenides to Levinas*. Translated by Lukas Soderstrom. New York: Columbia University Press, 2012.

Harvey, Timothy. "God as a Field of Force: Personhood and Science in Wolfhart Pannenberg's Pneumatology." *The Heythrop Journal* 52 (2011) 250–59.

Herbstrith, Waltraud. *Edith Stein: A Biography*. Translated by Bernard Bonowitz. San Francisco: Ignatius, 1992.

Houselander, Caryll. *Wood of the Cradle, Wood of the Cross: The Little Way of the Infant Jesus*. Manchester, NH: Sophia Institute, 1995.

Husserl, Edmund. *Analyses Concerning Passive and Active Synthesis: Lectures on Transcendental Logic*. Translated by A. J. Steinbock. Boston: Kluwer Academic, 2001.

———. *The Basic Problems of Phenomenology: From the Lectures, Winter Semester, 1910–1911*. Translated by Ingo Farin and James Hart. Dordrecht: Springer, 2006.

———. *Cartesian Meditations: An Introduction to Phenomenology*. Translated by Dorion Cairns. The Hague: Martinus Nijhoff, 1960.

———. *The Crisis of European Sciences and Transcendental Phenomenology: An Introduction to Phenomenological Philosophy*. Translated by David Carr. Evanston: Northwestern University Press, 1970.

———. *Experience and Judgment: Investigations in a Genealogy of Logic*. Revised and edited by Ludwig Landgrebe. Translated by James Spencer Churchill and Karl Ameriks. Evanston: Northwestern University Press, 1973.

———. *Formal and Transcendental Logic*. Translated by Dorion Cairns. The Hague: M. Nijhoff, 1978.

———. *The Idea of Phenomenology*. Translated by Lee Hardy. Boston: Kluwer Academic, 1999.

———. *Ideas Pertaining to a Pure Phenomenology and to a Phenomenological Philosophy*. First Book. Translated by F. Kersten. The Hague: M. Nijhoff, 1982.

———. *Ideen yu einer reinen Phänomenologie und phänomenologischen Philosophie*. Tübingen: M. Niemeyer, 2002.

———. *Introduction to the Logical Investigations*. Translated by Philip Bossert and C. H. Peters. The Hague: M. Nijhoff, 1975.

———. *Logical Investigations*. Translated by J. N. Findlay. 2 vols. New York: Routledge, 2001.

———. *The Paris Lectures*. Translated by P. Koestenbaum and Steven James Bartlett. The Hague: M. Nijhoff, 1970.

———. *Phenomenological Psychology: Lectures, Summer Semester, 1925*. Translated by John Scanlon. The Hague: M. Nijhoff, 1977.

Ignatius of Loyola. *Ignatius of Loyola: The Spiritual Exercises and Selected Works*. Edited by George E. Ganss. New York: Paulist, 1991.

Janicaud, Dominique, ed. *Phenomenology and the "Theological Turn": The French Debate*. New York: Fordham University Press, 2000.

John of the Cross. *The Collected Works of Saint John of the Cross*. Translated by Kieran Kavanaugh and Otilio Rodriguez. Rev. ed. Washington, DC: ICS, 1991.

John Paul II, Pope. *Dies Domini*. 1998. https://w2.vatican.va/content/john-paul-ii/en/apost_letters/1998/documents/hf_jp-ii_apl_05071998_dies-domini.html.

———. *Evangelium vitae*. 1995. http://w2.vatican.va/content/john-paul-ii/en/encyclicals/documents/hf_jp-ii_enc_25031995_evangelium-vitae.html.

———. *Fides et ratio*. 1998. http://w2.vatican.va/content/john-paul-ii/en/encyclicals/documents/hf_jp-ii_enc_14091998_fides-et-ratio.html.

———. *Man and Woman He Created Them: A Theology of the Body*. Translated by Michael Waldstein. Boston: Pauline Books & Media, 2006.

———. *Mulieris dignitatem*. In *The Theology of the Body: Human Love in the Divine Plan*. Boston: Pauline Books & Media, 1997.

———. *Pope John Paul II on the Genius of Women*. Washington, DC: U. S. Catholic Conference, 2001.

———. *Veritatis splendor*. 1993. http://w2.vatican.va/content/john-paul-ii/en/encyclicals/documents/hf_jp-ii_enc_06081993_veritatis-splendor.html.

Kirchhoffer, David G., Robyn Horner, and Patrick McArdle, eds. *Being Human: Groundwork for a Theological Anthropology for the 21st Century*. Eugene, OR: Wipf & Stock, 2013.

Kovacs, George. "The Way to Ultimate Meaning in Edith Stein's Phenomenology." *Ultimate Reality and Meaning* 26 (2003) 263–82.

Lebech, Mette. *On the Problem of Human Dignity: A Hermeneutical and Phenomenological Investigation*. Würzburg: Königshausen & Neumann, 2009.

Lebech, Mette, and John Haydn Gurmin, eds. *Intersubjectivity, Humanity, Being: Edith Stein's Phenomenology and Christian Philosophy*. Bern: P. Lang, 2015.

Lee, Eric Austin, and Samuel Kimbriel, eds. *The Resounding Soul: Reflections on the Metaphysics and Vivacity of the Human Person*. Eugene, OR: Cascade, 2015.

Levinas, Emmanuel. *Alterity and Transcendence*. Translated by Michael B. Smith. New York: Columbia University Press, 1999.

———. *Beyond the Verse: Talmudic Readings and Lectures*. Translated by Gary D. Mole. Bloomington: Indiana University Press, 1994.

———. *Collected Philosophical Papers*. Translated by Alphonso Lingis. Dordrecht: M. Nijhoff, 1987.

———. *Difficult Freedom: Essays on Judaism*. Translated by Seán Hand. Baltimore: Johns Hopkins University Press, 1990.

———. *Discovering Existence with Husserl*. Translated by Richard A. Cohen and Michael B. Smith. Evanston: Northwestern University Press, 1998.

———. *Emmanuel Levinas: Basic Philosophical Writings*. Edited by Adriaan T. Peperzak, Simon Critchley, and Robert Bernasconi. Bloomington: Indiana University Press, 1996.

———. *Entre Nous: On Thinking-of-the-Other*. Translated by Michael B. Smith and Barbara Harshav. New York: Columbia University Press, 1998.

———. *Ethics and Infinity: Conversations with Philippe Nemo*. Translated by Richard A. Cohen. Pittsburgh: Duquesne University Press, 1985.

———. *Existence and Existents*. Translated by Alphonso Lingis. Pittsburgh: Dusquesne University Press, 2001.

———. *God, Death, and Time*. Translated by Bettina Bergo. Stanford: Stanford University Press, 2000.

———. *Humanism of the Other*. Translated by Nidra Poller. Urbana: University of Illinois Press, 2003.

———. *In the Time of the Nations*. Translated by Michael B. Smith. Bloomington: Indiana University Press, 1994.

———. *The Levinas Reader*. Edited by Seán Hand. Cambridge, MA: Blackwell, 1989.

———. *New Talmudic Readings*. Translated by Richard A. Cohen. Pittsburgh: Duquesne University Press, 1999.

———. *Nine Talmudic Readings*. Translated by Annette Aronowicz. Bloomington: Indiana University Press, 1990.

———. *Of God Who Comes to Mind*. Translated by Bettina Bergo. Stanford: Stanford University Press, 1998.

———. *On Escape*. Translated by Bettina Bergo. Stanford: Stanford University Press, 2003.

———. *Otherwise than Being: or, Beyond Essence.* Translated by Alphonso Lingis. Pittsburgh: Dusquesne University Press, 1981.
———. *Outside the Subject.* Translated by Michael B. Smith. London: Athlone, 1993.
———. *Positivité et transcendance.* Paris: Presses universitaires de France, 2000.
———. *Proper Names.* Translated by Michael B. Smith. Stanford: Stanford University Press, 1996.
———. *The Theory of Intuition in Husserl's Phenomenology.* Translated by André Orianne. 2nd ed. Evanston: Northwestern University Press, 1995.
———. *Time and the Other.* Translated by Richard A. Cohen. Pittsburgh: Dusquesne University Press, 1987.
———. *Totality and Infinity: An Essay on Exteriority.* Translated by Alphonso Lingis. Pittsburgh: Duquesne University Press, 1969.
———. *Unforeseen History.* Translated by Nidra Poller. Urbana: University of Illinois Press, 2004.
Lonergan, Bernard. *Method in Theology.* Toronto: University of Toronto Press, 1971.
López, Antonio. *Gift and the Unity of Being.* Eugene, OR: Cascade, 2014.
MacIntyre, Alasdair C. *Edith Stein: A Philosophical Prologue.* London: Continuum, 2007.
Marion, Jean-Luc. *Being Given: Toward a Phenomenology of Givenness.* Translated by Jeffrey L. Kosky. Stanford: Stanford University Press, 2002.
———. *Cartesian Questions: Method and Metaphysics.* Translated by Jeffrey L. Kosky et al. Chicago: University of Chicago Press, 1999.
———. *Certitudes négatives.* Paris: Grasset, 2010.
———. *Le croire pour le voir: réflections diverses sur la rationalité de la révélation et l'irrationalité de quelques croyants.* Paris: Parole et Silence, 2010.
———. *The Crossing of the Visible.* Translated by James K. A. Smith. Stanford: Stanford University Press, 2004.
———. *Dieu sans l'être.* Paris: Quadrige, 2002.
———. *The Erotic Phenomenon.* Translated by Stephen E. Lewis. Chicago: University of Chicago Press, 2007.
———. *The Essential Writings.* Edited by Kevin Hart. New York: Fordham University Press, 2013.
———. *Givenness and Hermeneutics.* Translated by Jean-Pierre Lafouge. Milwaukee: Marquette University Press, 2013.
———. *Givenness and Revelation.* Translated by Stephen E. Lewis. New York: Oxford University Press, 2016.
———. *God without Being: Hors-Texte.* Translated by Thomas A. Carlson. Chicago: University of Chicago Press, 1991.
———. *The Idol and Distance: Five Studies.* Translated by Thomas A. Carlson. New York: Fordham University Press, 2001.
———. *L'idole et la distance: Cinq études.* Paris: Grasset, 1977.
———. *In Excess: Studies of Saturated Phenomena.* Translated by Robyn Horner and Vincent Berraud. New York: Fordham University Press, 2002.
———. *In the Self's Place: The Approach of Saint Augustine.* Translated by Jeffrey L. Kosky. Stanford: Stanford University Press, 2012.
———. "The Invisibility of the Saint." Translated by Christina M. Gschwandtner. *Critical Inquiry* 35 (2009) 703–10.

———. *Negative Certainties*. Translated by Stephen E. Lewis. Chicago: University of Chicago Press, 2015.

———. *On Descartes' Metaphysical Prism: The Constitution and the Limits of Ontotheology in Cartesian Thought*. Translated by Jeffrey L. Kosky. Chicago: University of Chicago Press, 1999.

———. *On the Ego and on God: Further Cartesian Questions*. Translated by Christina M. Gschwandtner. New York: Fordham University Press, 2007.

———. "La phénoménalité du sacrement: Être et donation." *Communio* 26 (2001) 59–75.

———. *Prolegomena to Charity*. Translated by Stephen E. Lewis. New York: Fordham University Press, 2002.

———. "The Question of the Unconditioned." Translated by Christina M. Gschwandtner. *The Journal of Religion* 93 (2013) 1–24.

———. *The Reason of the Gift*. Translated by Stephen E. Lewis. Charlottesville: University of Virginia Press, 2011.

———. *Reduction and Givenness: Investigations of Husserl, Heidegger, and Phenomenology*. Translated by Thomas A. Carlson. Evanston: Northwestern University Press, 1998.

———. *Réduction et donation: recherches sur Husserl, Heidegger et la phenomenologie*. Paris: Presses universitaires de France, 1989.

———. *The Visible and the Revealed*. Translated by Christina M. Gschwandtner et al. New York: Fordham University Press, 2008.

Maritain, Jacques. *The Degrees of Knowledge*. Translated by Bernard Wall. London: G. Bles, The Centenary Press, 1937.

Martínez, Luis M. *The Sanctifier*. Translated by M. Aquinas. Paterson, NJ: St. Anthony Guild Press, 1957.

Maskulak, Marian. *Edith Stein and the Body-Soul-Spirit at the Center of Holistic Formation*. New York: P. Lang, 2007.

———. "Edith Stein: A Proponent of Human Community and a Voice for Social Change." *Logos: A Journal of Catholic Thought and Culture* 15 (2012) 64–83.

McGinn, Colin. *Basic Structures of Reality: Essays in Metaphysics*. New York: Oxford University Press, 2011.

McGrath, Alister. *Dawkins' God: From "The Selfish Gene" to "The God Delusion"*. 2nd ed. Malden, MA: Wiley Blackwell, 2015.

———. *The Passionate Intellect: Christian Faith and the Discipleship of the Mind*. Downers Grove, IL: InterVarsity, 2010.

———. *Surprised by Meaning: Science, Faith, and How We Make Sense of Things*. Louisville: Westminster John Knox, 2011.

———. *The Twilight of Atheism: The Rise and Fall of Disbelief in the Modern World*. New York: Doubleday, 2006.

———. *Why God Won't Go Away: Is the New Atheism Running on Empty?* Nashville: Thomas Nelson, 2011.

Meis, Anneliese. "El espíritu finio, anticipado por el Espíritu Infinito en la obra *Potenz und Akt* de Edith Stein." *Scripta Theologica* 47 (2015) 9–40.

Milbank, John, and Catherine Pickstock. *Truth in Aquinas*. London: Routledge, 2001.

Mitchell, Jason A. "From Aristotle's Four Causes to Aquinas' Ultimate Causes of Being: Modern Interpretations." *Alpha Omega* 16 (2013) 399–414.

Nabert, Jean. *Elements for an Ethic.* Translated by William J. Petrek. Evanston: Northwestern University Press, 1969.

———. *Le désir de Dieu.* Paris: Cerf, 1996.

Nancy, Jean-Luc. *Listening.* Translated by Charlotte Mandell. New York: Fordham University Press, 2007.

———. *Noli me tangere: On the Raising of the Body.* Translated by Sarah Clift, Pascale-Anne Brault, and Michael Naas. New York: Fordham University Press, 2008.

O'Collins, Gerald. *Christology: A Biblical, Historical, and Systematic Study of Jesus.* 2nd ed. Oxford: Oxford University Press, 2009.

Oderberg, David S. *Real Essentialism.* New York: Routledge, 2007.

Orr, James. "Edith Stein's Critique of Sociality in the Early Heidegger." *Neue Zeitschrift für Systematische Theologie und Religionsphilosophie* 55 (2013) 379–96.

Palade, Tereza-Brindusa. "Why Thinking in Faith? A Reappraisal of Edith Stein's View of Reason." *Forum Philosophicum: International Journal for Philosophy* 15 (2010) 401–12.

Patt, Stephan. *El concepto teológico-místico de "fondo de alma" en la obra de Edith Stein.* Pamplona: Ediciones Universidad de Navarra, 2009.

Paul VI, Pope. *The Liturgy of the Hours According to the Roman Rite.* Translated by the International Commission on English in the Liturgy. New York: Catholic Book, 1975.

Pius XII, Pope. *Humani generis.* 1950. http://w2.vatican.va/content/pius-xii/en/encyclicals/documents/hf_p-xii_enc_12081950_humani-generis.html.

Rabins, Peter V. *The Why of Things: Causality in Science, Medicine, and Life.* New York: Columbia University Press, 2013.

Plato. *Plato: Complete Works.* Edited by John M. Cooper. Indianapolis: Hackett, 1997.

Posselt, Teresia Renata. *Edith Stein: Eine Grosse Frau unseres Jahrhunderts.* 9th ed. Freiburg: Herder, 1963.

———. *Edith Stein: The Life of a Philosopher and Carmelite.* Edited by Susanne M. Batzdorff, Josephine Koeppel, and John Sullivan. Washington, DC: ICS, 2005.

Pseudo-Dionysius. *Pseudo-Dionysius: The Complete Works.* Translated by Colm Luibheid. New York: Paulist, 1987.

Ratzinger, Joseph. *Introduction to Christianity.* Translated by J. R. Foster. San Francisco: Ignatius, 2004.

———. *Truth and Tolerance: Christian Belief and World Religions.* Translated by Henry Taylor. San Francisco: Ignatius, 2004.

Redmond, Walter. "Edith Stein on Evolution." *Logos: A Journal of Catholic Thought and Culture* 13 (2010) 153–76.

———. "A Nothing That Is: Edith Stein on Being Without Essence." *American Catholic Philosophical Quarterly* 82 (2008) 71–86.

Ricoeur, Paul. "Biblical Hermeneutics." *Semeia* 4 (1975) 29–148.

———. *The Conflict of Interpretations: Essays in Hermeneutics.* Edited by Don Ihde. Evanston: Northwestern University Press, 1974.

———. *The Course of Recognition.* Translated by David Pellauer. Cambridge, MA: Harvard University Press, 2005.

———. *Essays on Biblical Interpretation.* Edited by Lewis S. Mudge. Philadelphia: Fortress, 1980.

———. *Fallible Man.* Revised translation by Charles A. Kelbley. Rev. ed. New York: Fordham University Press, 1986.

———. *Figuring the Sacred: Religion, Narrative, and Imagination.* Edited by Mark I. Wallace. Minneapolis: Fortress, 1995.

———. *Freedom and Nature: The Voluntary and the Involuntary.* Translated by Erazim V. Kohák. Evanston: Northwestern University Press, 2007.

———. *Freud and Philosophy: An Essay on Interpretation.* Translated by Denis Savage. New Haven: Yale University Press, 1970.

———. *From Text to Action.* Translated by Kathleen Blamey and John B. Thompson. Essays in Hermeneutics 2. Evanston: Northwestern University Press, 1991.

———. *Hermeneutics and the Human Sciences: Essays on Language, Action and Interpretation.* Translated by John B. Thompson. New York: Cambridge University Press, 1993.

———. *History and Truth.* Translated by Charles A. Kelbley. Evanston: Northwestern University Press, 1965.

———. *Husserl: An Analysis of His Phenomenology.* Translated by Edward G. Ballard and Lester E. Embree. Evanston: Northwestern University Press, 1967.

———. *Interpretation Theory: Discourse and the Surplus of Meaning.* Fort Worth: Texas Christian University Press, 1976.

———. *The Just.* Translated by David Pellauer. Chicago: University of Chicago Press, 2000.

———. *A Key to Husserl's "Ideas I".* Translated by Bond Harris and Jacqueline Bouchard Spurlock. Edited and translation revised by Pol Vandevelde. Milwaukee: Marquette University Press, 1996.

———. *Main Trends in Philosophy.* New York: Holmes & Meier, 1979.

———. "Manifestation and Proclamation." *The Journal of the Blaisdell Institute* 12 (1978) 13–35.

———. *Memory, History, Forgetting.* Translated by David Pellauer and Kathleen Blamey. Chicago: University of Chicago Press, 2004.

———. *Oneself as Another.* Translated by Kathleen Blamey. Chicago: University of Chicago Press, 1994.

———. "Philosophy and Religious Language." *The Journal of Religion* 54 (1974) 71–85.

———. *Reflections on the Just.* Translated by David Pellauer. Chicago: University of Chicago Press, 2007.

———. *The Rule of Metaphor: The Creation of Meaning in Language.* Translated by Robert Czerny, Kathleen McLaughlin, and John Costello. New York: Routledge, 2003.

———. *The Symbolism of Evil.* Translated by Emerson Buchanan. New York: Harper & Row, 1967.

———. *Thinking Biblically: Exegetical and Hermeneutical Studies.* Translated by David Pellauer. Chicago: University of Chicago Press, 1998.

———. *Time and Narrative.* Translated by Kathleen McLaughlin and David Pellauer. 3 vols. Chicago: University of Chicago Press, 1984.

Ross, Susan. *Anthropology: Seeking Light and Beauty.* Collegeville, MN: Liturgical Press, 2012.

Sawicki, Marianne. *Body, Text, and Science: The Literacy of Investigative Practices and the Phenomenology of Edith Stein.* Dordrecht: Kluwer Academic, 1997.

Scheler, Max. *Formalism in Ethics and Non-formal Ethics of Values.* Translated by Manfred S. Frings and Roger L. Funk. 5th rev. ed. Evanston: Northwestern University Press, 1973.

Schindler, D. C. *The Perfection of Freedom: Schiller, Schelling, and Hegel between the Ancients and the Moderns*. Eugene, OR: Cascade, 2012.

Schmitz-Perrin, Rudolf. "Phänomenologie und Scientia Crucis im Denken von Edith Stein: Von der Einfülung zur Mit-Fühlung?" *Freiburger Zeitschrift für Philosophie und Theologie* 42 (1995) 346–66.

Schwartz, Hans. *The Human Being: A Theological Anthropology*. Grand Rapids: Eerdmans, 2013.

Sesé, F. Javier. "La 'Ciencia de la Cruz': La enseñanza de San Juan de la Cruz, a la luz del pensamiento de la Beata Edith Stein." *Scripta Theologica* 24 (1991–92) 643–65.

Shults, F. LeRon. "Spirit and Spirituality: Philosophical Trends in Late Modern Pneumatology." *Pneuma* 30 (2008) 271–87.

Siniscalchi, Glenn B. *Retrieving Apologetics*. Eugene, OR: Pickwick, 2016.

Spaemann, Robert. *Essays in Anthropology: Variations on a Theme*. Translated by Guido de Graaf and James Mumford. Eugene, OR: Cascade, 2010.

———. *Persons: The Difference between "Someone" and "Something"*. New York: Oxford University Press, 2006.

Spitzer, Robert J. *New Proofs for the Existence of God: Contributions of Contemporary Physics and Philosophy*. Grand Rapids: Eerdmans, 2010.

Stein, Edith. *Der Aufbau der menschlichen Person*. Freiburg: Herder, 1994.

———. *Edith Stein: Letters to Roman Ingarden*. Translated by Hugh Candler Hunt. Edited by Maria Amata Neyer. Washington, DC: ICS, 2014.

———. *Essays on Woman*. Translated by Freda Mary Oben. Washington, DC: ICS, 1996.

———. *La estructura de la persona humana*. Translated by José Mardomingo. Madrid: Biblioteca de Autores Cristianos, 1998.

———. *Finite and Eternal Being: An Attempt at an Ascent to the Meaning of Being*. Translated by Kurt F. Reinhardt. Washington, DC: ICS, 2002.

———. *The Hidden Life: Hagiographic Essays, Meditations, Spiritual Texts*. Edited by L. Gelber and Michael Linssen. Translated by Waltraut Stein. Washington, DC: ICS, 1992.

———. *An Investigation Concerning the State*. Edited and translated by Marianne Sawicki. Washington, DC: ICS, 2006.

———. *Knowledge and Faith*. Translated by Walter Redmond. Washington, DC: ICS, 2000.

———. *Life in a Jewish Family: An Autobiography, 1891–1916*. Translated by Josephine Koeppel. Washington, DC: ICS, 1986.

———. *On the Problem of Empathy*. Translated by Waltraut Stein. Washington, DC: ICS, 1989.

———. *Philosophy of Psychology and the Humanities*. Translated by Mary Catherine Baseheart and Marianne Sawicki. Washington, DC: ICS, 2000.

———. *Potency and Act: Studies Toward a Philosophy of Being*. Translated by Walter Redmond. Washington, DC: ICS, 2009.

———. *The Science of the Cross*. Translated by Josephine Koeppel. Washington, DC: ICS, 2002.

———. *The Science of the Cross: A Study of St. John of the Cross*. Edited by L. Gelber and Romaeus Leuven. Translated by Hilda Graef. London: Burns & Oates, 1960.

———. *Self-Portrait in Letters: 1916–1942*. Edited by L. Gelber and Romaeus Leuven. Translated by Josephine Koeppel. Washington, DC: ICS, 1993.

———. *Was ist der Mensch? Theologische Anthropologie*. Freiburg: Herder, 2005.

———. *Welt und Person: Beitrag zum Christlichen Wahrheitsstreben*. Freiburg: Herder, 1962.

Stenger, Victor J. *Quantum Gods: Creation, Chaos, and the Search for Cosmic Consciousness*. Amherst, NY: Prometheus, 2009.

Szanto, Thomas, and Dermot Moran, eds. *Empathy and Collective Intentionality: The Social Philosophy of Edith Stein*. Special issue of *Human Studies* 38:4 (2015).

Tandy, Charles, ed. *Death and Anti-Death*. Vol. 13, *Sixty Years after Albert Einstein (1879–1955)*. Ann Arbor: Ria University Press, 2016.

Tanner, Norman P., ed. *Decrees of the Ecumenical Councils*. Vol. 1, *Nicaea I to Lateran V*. Washington, DC: Georgetown University Press, 1990.

Teilhard de Chardin, Pierre. *Activation of Energy*. Translated by René Hague. London: W. Collins, 1970.

———. *Human Energy*. Translated by J. M. Cohen. London: W. Collins, 1969.

———. *Hymn of the Universe*. Translated by Simon Bartholomew. New York: Harper & Row, 1965.

Teresa of Avila. *The Collected Works of Saint Teresa of Avila*. Translated by Kieran Kananaugh and Otilio Rodriguez. 3 vols. Washington, DC: ICS, 1980.

———. *The Interior Castle: Study Edition*. Translated by Kieran Kavanaugh and Otilio Rodriguez. Washington, DC: ICS, 2010.

Thérèse of Lisieux. *Story of a Soul: The Autobiography of St. Thérèse of Lisieux*. Translated by John Clarke. 3rd ed. Washington, DC: ICS, 1996.

Thomas Aquinas. *Aquinas's Shorter Summa: St. Thomas Aquinas's Own Concise Version of His Summa Theologica*. Translated by Cyril Vollert. Manchester, NH: Sophia Institute, 2002.

———. *Sententia libri Metaphysicae*. http://www.corpusthomisticum.org/cmp03.html#81904.

———. *Summa contra gentiles*. http://www.corpusthomisticum.org/scg1001.html.

———. *Summa theologiae*. http://www.corpusthomisticum.org/sth0000.html.

———. *Summa Theologiae: Questions on God*. Edited by Brian Davies and Brian Leftow. Cambridge: Cambridge University Press, 2006.

———. *Summa Theologica*. Translated by the Fathers of the English Dominican Province. 5 vols. Notre Dame: Ave Maria Press, 1981.

Tillich, Paul. *Systematic Theology*. Vol. 3, *Life and the Spirit; History and the Kingdom of God*. Chicago: University of Chicago Press, 1963.

Tilliette, Xavier. "Edith Stein et la philosophie chrétienne: A propos d'Être fini et Être eternal." *Gregorianum* 71 (1990) 97–113.

Tracy, David. *The Analogical Imagination: Christian Theology and the Culture of Pluralism*. New York: Crossroad, 1981.

Tyler, Peter. "'The Return of the Soul': Psychology, Theology and Soul-Making." *New Blackfriars* 97:1068 (2016) 187–201.

Wallenfang, Donald. "Awaken, O Spirit: The Vocation of Becoming in the Work of Edith Stein." *Logos: A Journal of Catholic Thought and Culture* 15 (2012) 57–74.

———. *Dialectical Anatomy of the Eucharist: An Étude in Phenomenology*. Eugene, OR: Cascade, 2017.

———. "Figures and Forms of Ultimacy: Manifestation and Proclamation as Paradigms of the Sacred." *The International Journal of Religion in Spirituality and Society* 1 (2011) 109–14.

———. "From Albert Einstein to Edith Stein: Understanding the Resurrection of the Body vis-à-vis Natural Science." In *Death and Anti-Death*, edited by Charles Tandy, 13:209–44. Ann Arbor: Ria University Press, 2016.

———. "*Geisteswissenschaft*: Edith Stein's Phenomenological Sketch of the Essence of Spirit." In *Intersubjectivity, Humanity, Being*, edited by Mette Lebech and John Haydn Gurmin, 499–524. Oxford: P. Lang, 2015.

———. "The Heart of the Matter: Edith Stein on the Substance of the Soul." *Logos: A Journal of Catholic Thought and Culture* 17 (2014) 118–42.

———. "Soul Power: Edith Stein's Meta-phenomenological Construction of the Human Soul." In *Edith Stein: Women, Social-Political Philosophy, Theology, Metaphysics and Public History*, edited by Antonio Calcagno, 167–80. Cham: Springer, 2016.

———. "Trilectic of Testimony: A Phenomenological Construal of the Eucharist as Manifestation-Proclamation-Attestation." PhD diss., Loyola University Chicago, 2011.

Webb, Stephen H. *Jesus Christ, Eternal God: Heavenly Flesh and the Metaphysics of Matter*. New York: Oxford University Press, 2012.

Index

a priori, xxiv, 41, 92, 102–3, 135, 150
a posteriori, 61n16, 102
Absolute, xii, 5, 6n14, 8n22, 11n31, 17n49, 31–33, 46, 103n20, 124, 143, 153, 157n18, 158–61, 166, 174, 176, 194, 194n67, 201, 207
actuality, 4–7, 9, 12, 14–15, 17–19, 32, 42, 48–52, 62–66, 70, 73–115, 121–28, 132–44, 153–72, 215–16
Albert of Cologne, 113
angels, 23, 36, 39–48, 70, 76, 83–84, 88–89, 93, 98, 108n36, 115n54, 122, 127, 131, 136, 139, 153, 158n21, 160–63, 202, 217–18
Aquinas, Thomas. *See* Thomas Aquinas.
Aristotle, 3–6, 12, 32n30, 43, 52, 57–59, 63, 65, 70–77, 80–81, 105, 153n5
Augustine of Hippo, xxvii, 49n70, 50, 52n77, 76, 127, 146

Balthasar, Hans Urs von, 15n42, 33n36
beauty, xiv, 5, 112, 190
becoming, 4–19, 29, 35, 50, 52, 57, 59, 61–62, 66n26, 72–75, 81, 90n82, 91–92, 107n34, 109, 113, 134n43, 137–40, 143, 145, 151, 153–54, 159–60, 165–67, 171, 190, 204n29, 210, 212–16
Benedict XVI, 121n10, 171, 215n68, 216
body, xxv, xxviin15, 8, 17n48, 18n52, 19n54, 20, 25, 27–30, 34, 37, 41–51, 54–117, 122n13, 125, 127n26, 128–65, 169n50, 170–79, 183–87, 191, 204–6, 211, 215–17, 222
Bonaventure, xxvii, 193

Carmelite, xv, xviii, xxin2, xxix, xxxi, 54, 118, 120, 136, 198, 200, 202, 206n34, 210, 212, 218, 224
Catholic, xxi, xxviin12, xxvii, xxix, 8, 56–57, 92–93, 144, 150, 162n32, 193, 215
causality, xxiv, 5, 14n39, 57–77, 82, 91, 93, 105, 109, 111n46, 130, 133–34, 137, 153, 157n17, 161, 167, 188n44
 as efficient, 58–63, 70–71, 73, 75–77, 82, 91, 134
 as final, 14, 63, 65, 71–77, 82, 91, 93, 109, 111n46, 115, 130, 133, 137, 153–54, 167
 as formal, 63–81, 130, 137
 as material, 58–62, 70, 75, 82

Chauvet, Louis-Marie, 20, 30n24, 41, 45n60, 49n72, 129n33
Church, xiv, xvii, xxvii, 9n24, 20, 26, 28, 30n20, 30n24, 41, 42n54, 56–57, 113, 124, 137, 140, 145, 162n32, 178n9, 179n10, 199, 202, 204, 205n30, 210, 215, 217
Conrad-Martius, Hedwig, 10, 44–45, 88, 97n6, 108n38
consciousness, xxiii–xxiv, 8n22, 19, 25–26, 33, 37–38, 46, 74, 82, 95–99, 102–9, 118, 129, 134n43, 143, 157n17, 162–64, 174, 178–79, 181, 183–85, 188, 193
contemplation, xxvii, xxix, 2, 31, 49, 68, 71, 86, 101, 121n9, 133, 135, 194, 202, 204, 219–20

dialectic (or dialectical), xxiii–xxiv, 3–4, 6, 38, 55, 92, 98, 104, 134n43, 150–51, 158n21, 180
Dionysius the Areopagite, 39n47, 40n49, 42, 121n10, 160n25, 204n27
Duns Scotus, John, xxvii, 52n77

Einstein, Albert, 91n86, 134, 155, 158n19
elements, 7, 10, 35–39, 43, 45n60, 49n70, 59, 62, 64, 69–70, 73, 75, 83, 98n9, 105, 110n43, 134n43, 143, 156n15, 156n16, 162–70, 178, 181, 183, 191
empathy, xi, xxiv, xxxii, 13, 25, 82–83, 174–95, 200, 213, 218–19, 223
epistemology, 12, 26, 36
ethics, xxiv, xxxii, 1, 12, 58, 101–2, 175–76, 188n43, 192, 194n67, 198, 214n64
evil, 18n51, 51n76, 138n50, 144, 160, 199
evolution, xiii, 7n18, 7n19, 8–12, 19, 24, 29, 32n30, 35, 42n53, 43, 64–66, 70–73, 81–83, 91–92, 106n30, 111n46, 134n43, 153, 155, 162n32, 168–69

freedom, xxxiii, 16–17, 20, 23n4, 27, 32n31, 42n53, 59n13, 71, 87, 93, 96n4, 101, 111n46, 118, 120n8, 125, 128–29, 136, 138–39, 147, 175, 188, 214n64

gift, xiv, 15, 19–20, 31n27, 32–33, 42, 44, 49n71, 51, 90, 111n46, 120, 122, 124–25, 129–31, 136–37, 141, 147, 171, 178–79, 197, 206, 211, 215–16, 219, 221–22
glory, 2, 28, 29n18, 42n55, 47n65, 84n65, 114n52, 122, 125, 128, 139n53, 140–43, 202–5, 211n53, 212, 217, 222n1
goodness, 5, 42n55, 49–50, 112, 120n8, 126–27, 215
grace, xiv, 3, 12, 16–19, 31–32, 40–42, 47n64, 97n7, 118, 120n8, 128, 138, 143–44, 147, 171, 197, 201n15, 202, 208n42, 209n46, 215

Heidegger, Martin, xxiv, xxviii–xxix, xxxii, 9, 150, 169n49
Holy Spirit, 15, 21–22, 93, 105, 112–15, 119–20, 131, 144n67, 158n21, 171, 178n9, 206, 208
Houselander, Caryll, 147n75
Husserl, Edmund, xxiin5, xxiii–iv, xxviii–ix, 2, 8n22, 9, 19, 36, 55, 78n45, 98, 102–3, 174, 180–81

Ignatius of Loyola, 213
infinite, xxi–iv, 3, 12–15, 39–41, 48, 60–61, 91, 100n3, 103, 113, 116, 120n8, 124, 127, 129n31, 134n43, 137n48, 138n50, 143, 145, 165, 214n64, 222
Ingarden, Roman, xxi, xxiin3, xxiin5, xxiin6, xxivn10, xxviin12, xxviiin17, xxix, xxxin24, 66, 100n13, 177n7, 199n8, 201n15, 203n20, 208n45, 219n75
intellect, xxx, 20–22, 25, 31, 37, 40n49, 46n64, 48, 56–58, 60–61, 71, 73, 84, 87–88, 93, 95, 99, 127, 132n42, 133, 135, 143–44, 147, 152n4, 185, 188, 190–91, 203, 221
intellectual object, 44, 67, 119
intentionality, 36, 41, 97, 114
intuition, 26, 46, 98, 180
Irenaeus of Lyons, 137n48

Jerome, 193
Jewish, xxxii, 40, 150, 197n2, 198–99
John of the Cross, 18, 96n3, 120, 122n13, 197, 208, 219
John Paul II, 15n43, 122n13, 178–79, 224

Kant, Immanuel, xxiiin8, 86, 104, 180

language, xii–xiv, 3n4, 14, 32, 41n52, 44, 46n63, 57, 85, 87, 89, 107, 128, 130, 150, 169n50, 179, 193, 218
Levinas, Emmanuel, xxiv, xxix, xxxii, 1, 49n71, 51n75, 150, 154n8, 169n49, 174n1, 175–76, 189–90, 197n2, 200n12, 211, 214n64
Lombard, Peter, 193
Lonergan, Bernard, 30n22

Marion, Jean-Luc, xxiiin8, xxiv, xxix, 29, 112n48, 150, 180n13, 189n46
Maritain, Jacques, 76
mathematics, 30, 66–69
metaphysics, xii, xviii, xxii–viii, 3–6, 11–12, 14, 20, 22, 32, 34, 38, 41, 55, 58–59, 63, 66–68, 71n34, 77, 81, 85, 98, 102–4, 112–13, 116, 118, 131, 133–35, 143, 150–52, 157, 159, 172, 180, 189n46

Nancy, Jean-Luc, 40, 123n17
Nietzsche, Friedrich, xii
nothingness, 32, 91, 106n33

ontology, xxiv, xxxii, 4n5, 12, 26, 28, 50, 52, 57, 64, 82, 92, 151, 157–58, 166, 168
organism, 4, 8n22, 11, 15n42, 43, 59, 71–72, 79n50, 80–88, 92, 100, 106, 108–11, 132, 135, 154–55, 162–66, 177n7

Paul VI, 113n50
perception, xxiii, 38, 48, 67–68, 95–98, 100, 102, 118–19, 132n42, 152n4, 183, 185–88, 192
phenomenology, xii, xvii–xviii, xxii–xxix, 2, 5, 8n22, 11, 19, 22, 25–26, 34, 38, 55, 98, 102–4, 112, 116, 118, 130, 143, 150–51, 170, 174, 180–81, 222
philosophy, xiv, xxii, xxiv, xxvn12, xxvi, xxviii–xxxii, 1, 3–4, 11n31, 19, 33, 50, 54–55, 57–58, 60–61, 66, 78n45, 96n4, 149–50, 159, 166, 173, 200n12, 220
plant, 4, 7n19, 9n26, 17, 79n50, 86, 88, 169n50, 201n15
Plato, xxvii, 15n42, 52, 66, 68, 78, 136
potentiality, 4–7, 9, 12, 32, 35, 37, 48n68, 50, 52, 70, 77, 80–81, 88n76, 91–92, 109–10, 123, 126–28, 134–35, 142, 144, 153, 155, 157, 159–60
prime matter, 35, 70, 108–10, 155, 157n16, 158

Ratzinger, Joseph, 111n46, 115, 192n63, 207–8
Reinach, Adolf, 199
revelation, xiv, xxiin4, xxviii, 9, 19–20, 28–29, 40n49, 41, 46, 48–49, 53, 76, 80, 98, 105, 112, 131, 139n53, 141
Ricoeur, Paul, xxix, 8n23, 151n2, 175–76, 194n67

Scheler, Max, 188n43
scholasticism, xxivn10, 133, 180
spacetime, 70, 81, 96, 126–27, 135, 137, 142, 145, 155, 157, 162
suffering, xv, 30–31, 51, 61n19, 120n8, 131, 139n53, 145, 196–99, 202, 204–5, 207, 209–11, 213–17, 220–24
supernatural, xxx, 11, 14n37, 30n20, 46–47, 61, 88, 91n84, 98, 101–2, 119, 144, 150, 179n10, 193, 197, 205, 209, 211, 216

Teresa of Avila, 49n70, 94, 117, 120–21, 176n6, 212n55, 219
theology, xi, xxii, xxv, xxvii–ix, 11, 21–23, 26, 28, 30n22, 49n71, 55, 57, 60, 61n16, 90n82, 92n87, 93, 104n25, 118n2, 122n13, 123, 150, 158n21, 162n32, 173, 178, 198, 204n27, 208, 222

Thérèse of Lisieux, 145, 176n6, 206n37
Thomas Aquinas, xxiv–xxv, xxvii, 3–6, 8n22, 12n34, 32n30, 43, 52, 55, 58n7, 60, 62, 66n27, 71n35, 74, 77, 80, 98, 104, 105n26, 113, 132, 135n45, 154, 193
Tillich, Paul, 49n71
Tracy, David, 151n2
transcendence, xxx, 7, 28, 38, 49n71, 101, 103n20, 135, 171, 214n64, 222–23
truth, xxii–iii, xxv, xxvii, xxx, 3, 5, 8n23, 9n24, 19, 26–27, 33, 42n54, 45n60, 48, 56, 66–67, 69, 77, 89n80, 91, 112–13, 116, 127–28, 143–44, 147, 189, 192, 208n45

universal, xxvn12, xxxi, 2, 5, 9, 13–14, 19, 62, 66, 77, 83–84, 88, 103, 129n31, 133, 141–42, 146–47, 149, 163, 170n50, 218

values, 179n10, 187–88, 191, 214
virtues, 51, 58, 72, 88–89, 180, 194, 200, 205n30, 215, 216
vocation, xxiii, xxvii, xxxi, xxxii, 1–3, 9, 13–15, 19–20, 29, 31, 40, 44, 45n60, 46, 77, 88, 91–93, 101, 119, 124–25, 127, 130, 141–42, 147, 149, 169, 177, 179, 193–94, 197, 200, 209, 211, 216, 218–21

Wallenfang, Donald, xi–iv, xxxiii, 91n86, 151n2, 220–21
whatness, xxxii

www.ingramcontent.com/pod-product-compliance
Lightning Source LLC
Chambersburg PA
CBHW030614230426
43661CB00053B/1981